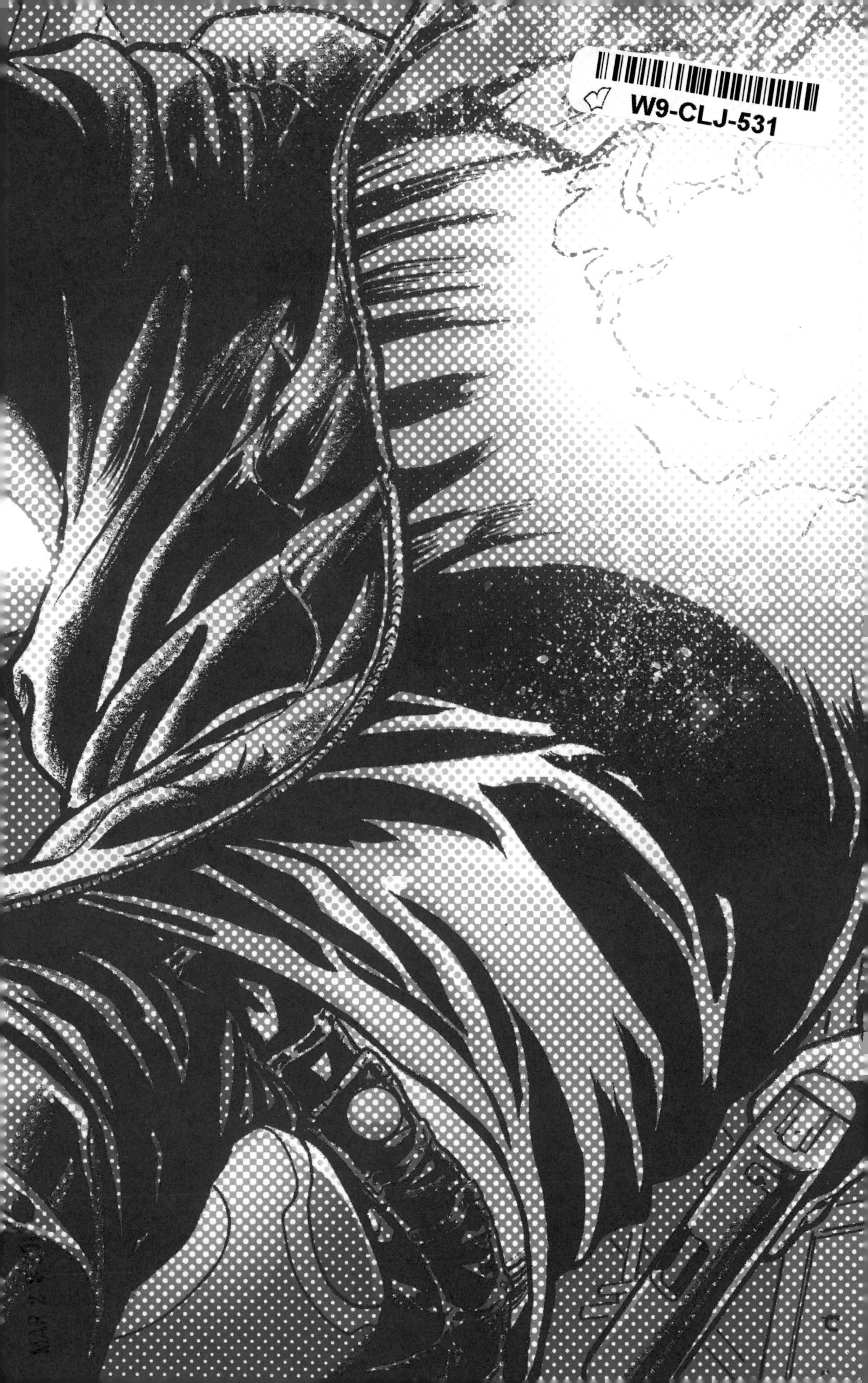

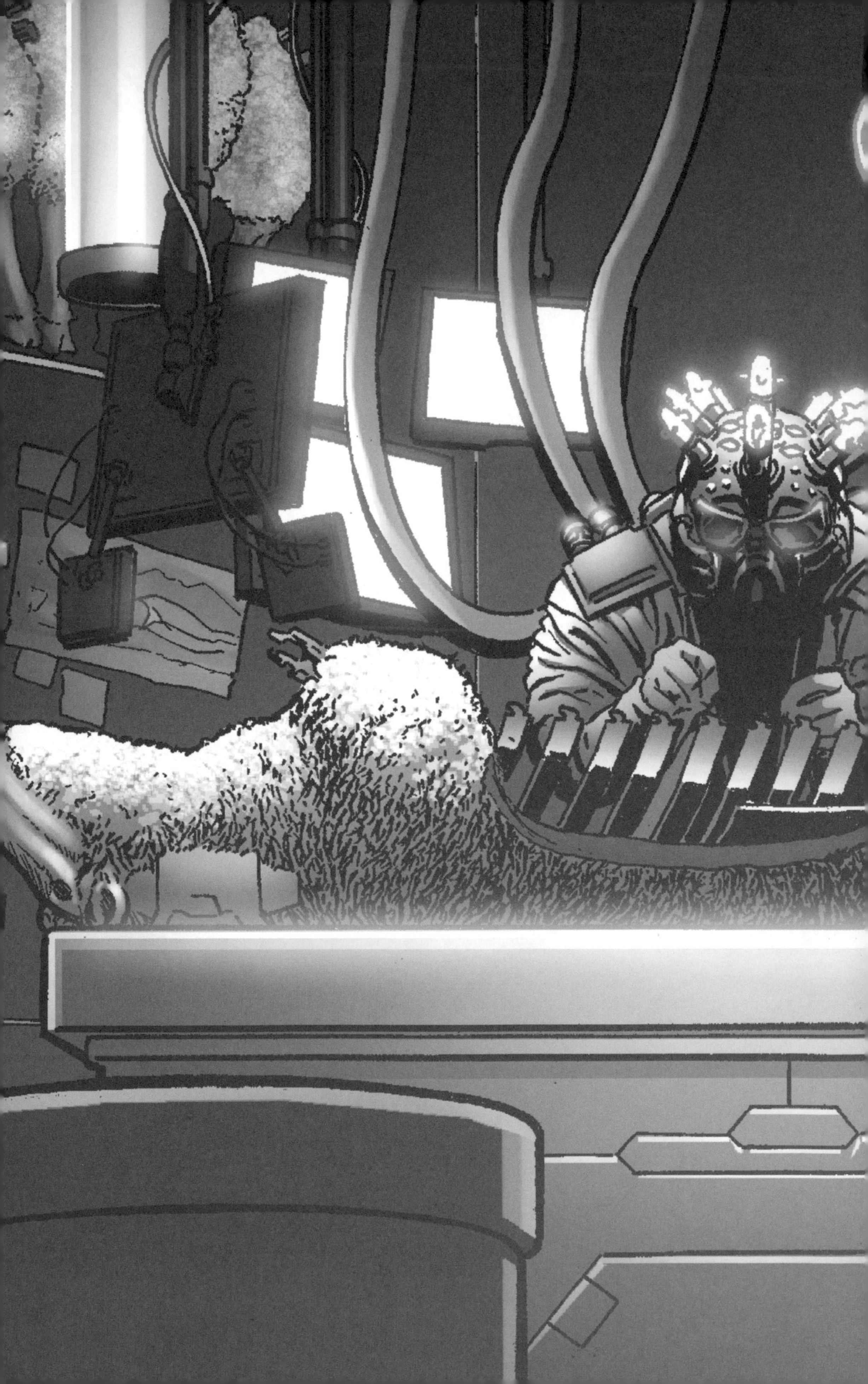

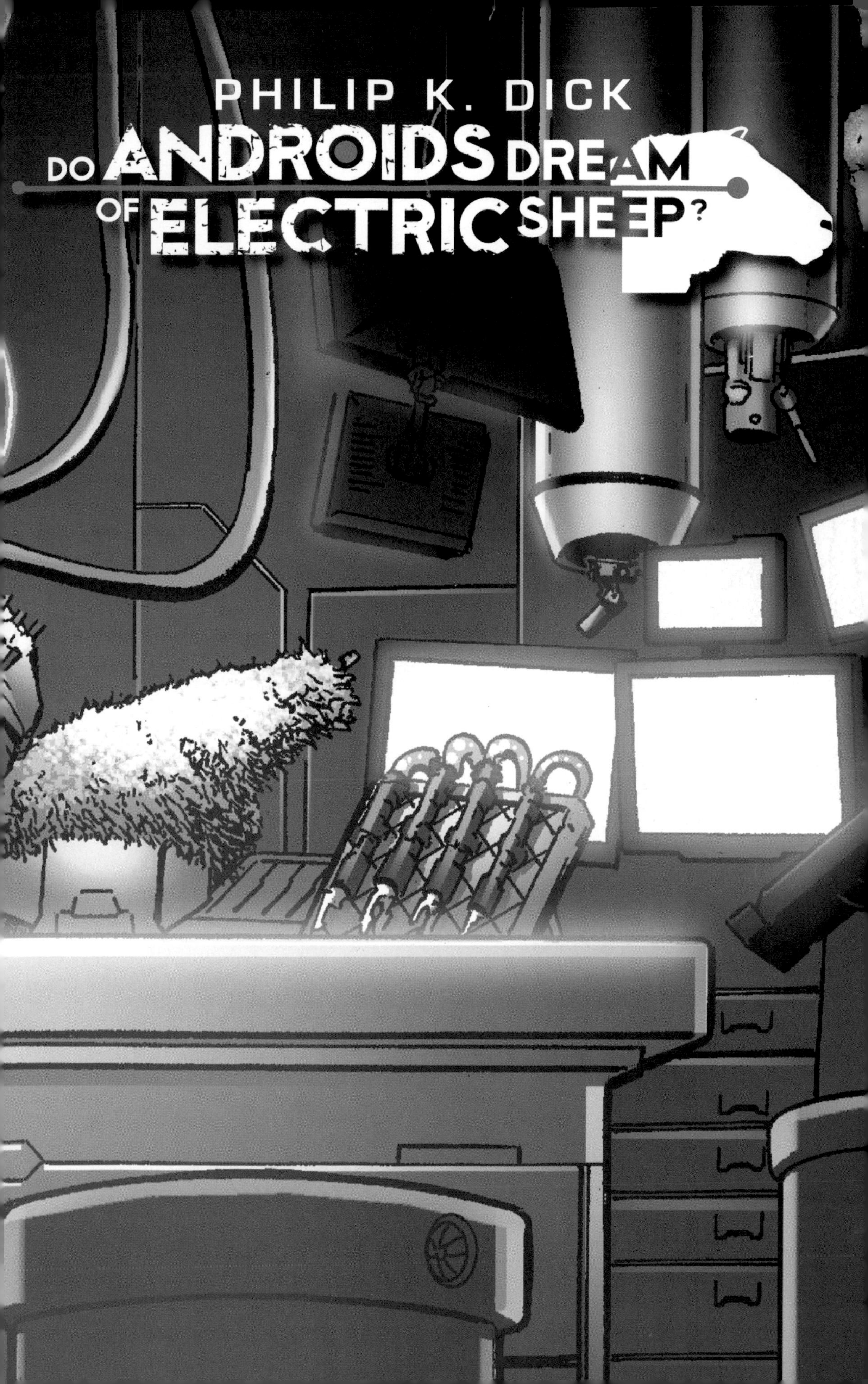
PHILIP K. DICK
DO ANDROIDS DREAM OF ELECTRIC SHEEP?

"I had a real

sheep,

"originally,"

-- Rick Deckard

Ross Richie - Chief Executive Officer

Matt Gagnon - Editor-in-Chief

Adam Fortier - VP-New Business

Wes Harris - VP-Publishing

Lance Kreiter - VP-Licensing & Merchandising

Chip Mosher - Marketing Director

Bryce Carlson - Managing Editor

Ian Brill - Editor

Dafna Pleban - Editor

Christopher Burns - Editor

Christopher Meyer - Editor

Shannon Watters - Assistant Editor

Eric Harburn - Assistant Editor

Adam Staffaroni - Assistant Editor

Neil Loughrie - Publishing Coordinator

Brian Latimer - Lead Graphic Designer

Stephanie Gonzaga - Graphic Designer

Travis Beaty - Traffic Coordinator

Ivan Salazar - Marketing Assistant

Brett Grinnell - Executive Assistant

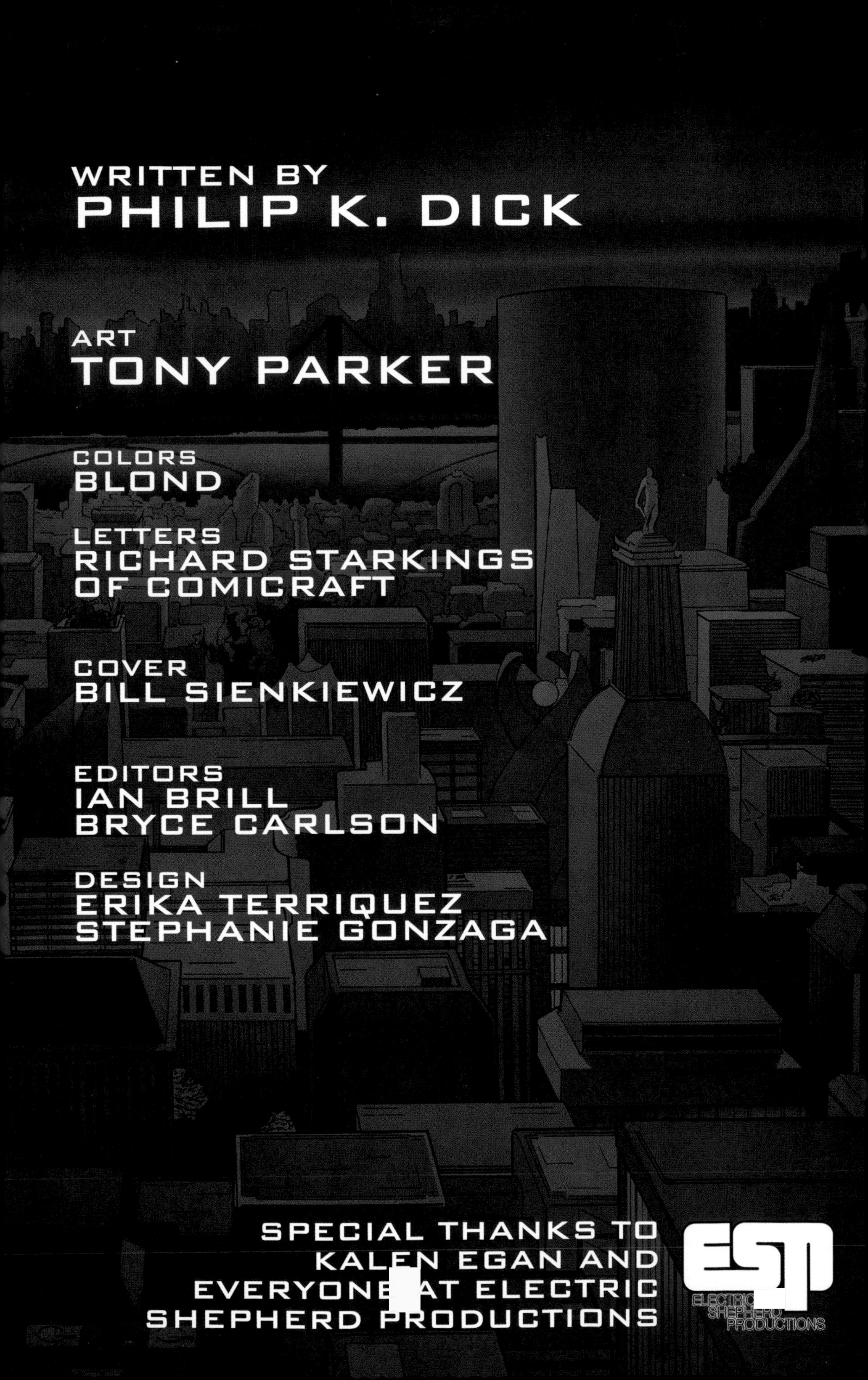

WRITTEN BY
PHILIP K. DICK

ART
TONY PARKER

COLORS
BLOND

LETTERS
RICHARD STARKINGS
OF COMICRAFT

COVER
BILL SIENKIEWICZ

EDITORS
IAN BRILL
BRYCE CARLSON

DESIGN
ERIKA TERRIQUEZ
STEPHANIE GONZAGA

SPECIAL THANKS TO
KALEN EGAN AND
EVERYONE AT ELECTRIC
SHEPHERD PRODUCTIONS

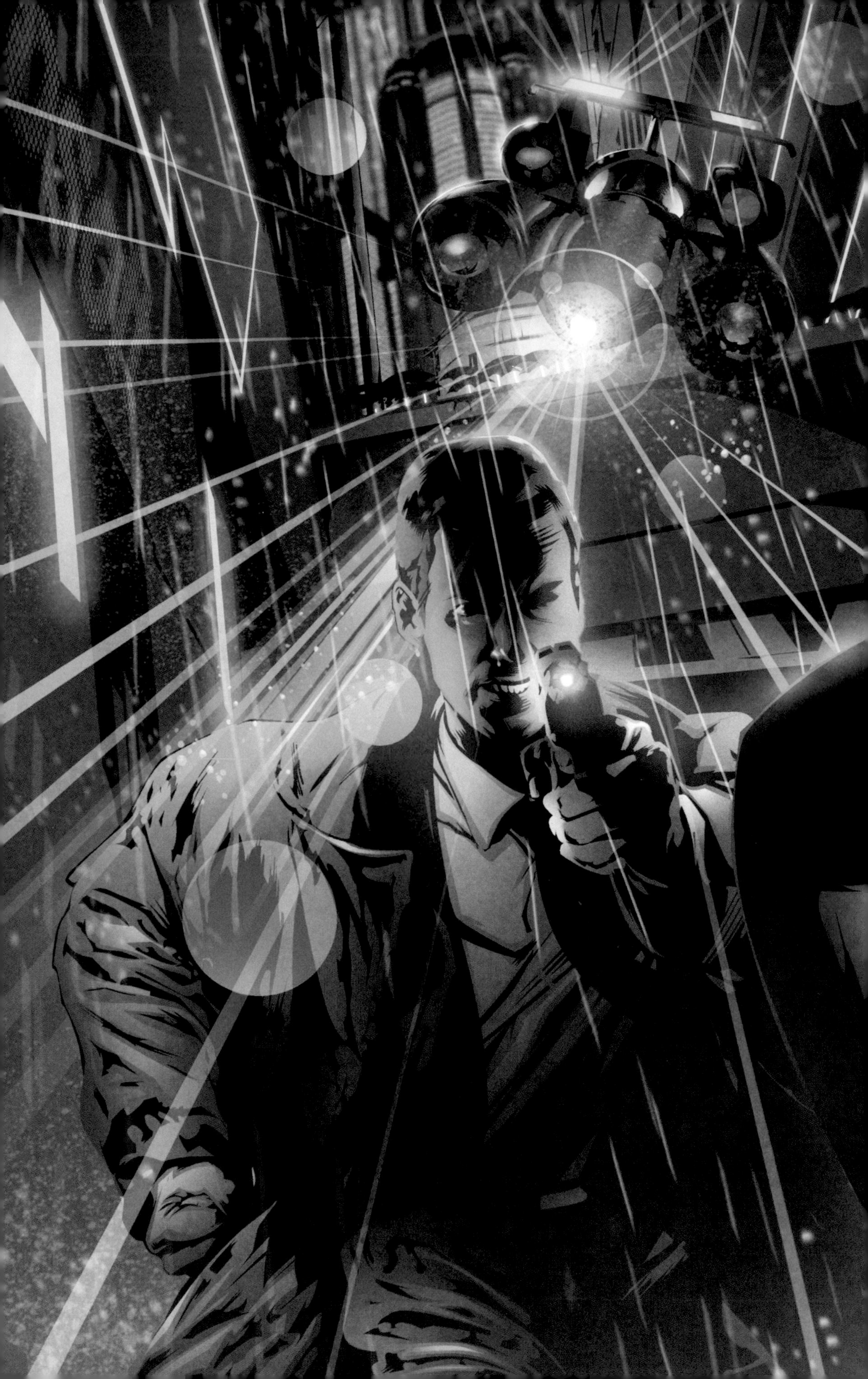

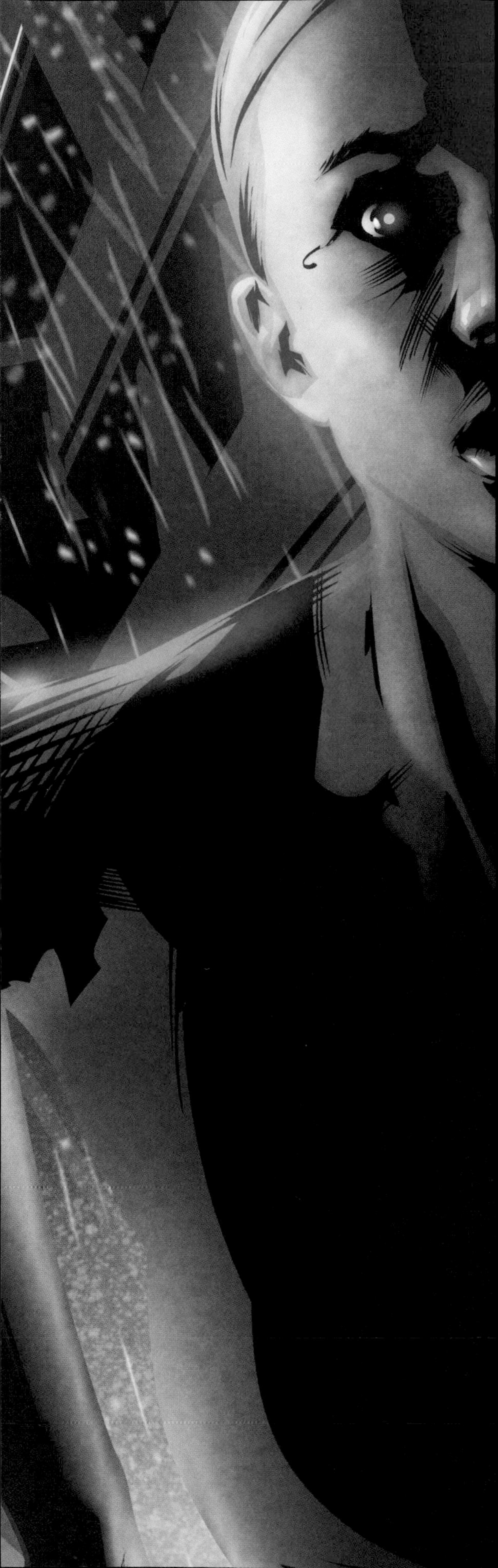

BOOK ONE

AUCKLAND

A TURTLE WHICH EXPLORER CAPTAIN COOK GAVE TO THE KING OF TONGA IN 1777 DIED YESTERDAY. IT WAS NEARLY 200 YEARS OLD.

THE ANIMAL, CALLED TU'IMALILA, DIED AT THE ROYAL PALACE GROUND IN THE TONGAN CAPITAL OF NUKU, ALOFA.

THE PEOPLE OF TONGA REGARDED THE ANIMAL AS A CHIEF AND SPECIAL KEEPERS WERE APPOINTED TO LOOK AFTER IT. IT WAS BLINDED IN A BUSH FIRE A FEW YEARS AGO.

TONGA RADIO SAID TU'IMALILA'S CARCASS WOULD BE SENT TO THE AUCKLAND MUSEUM IN NEW ZEALAND.

Reuters , 1966

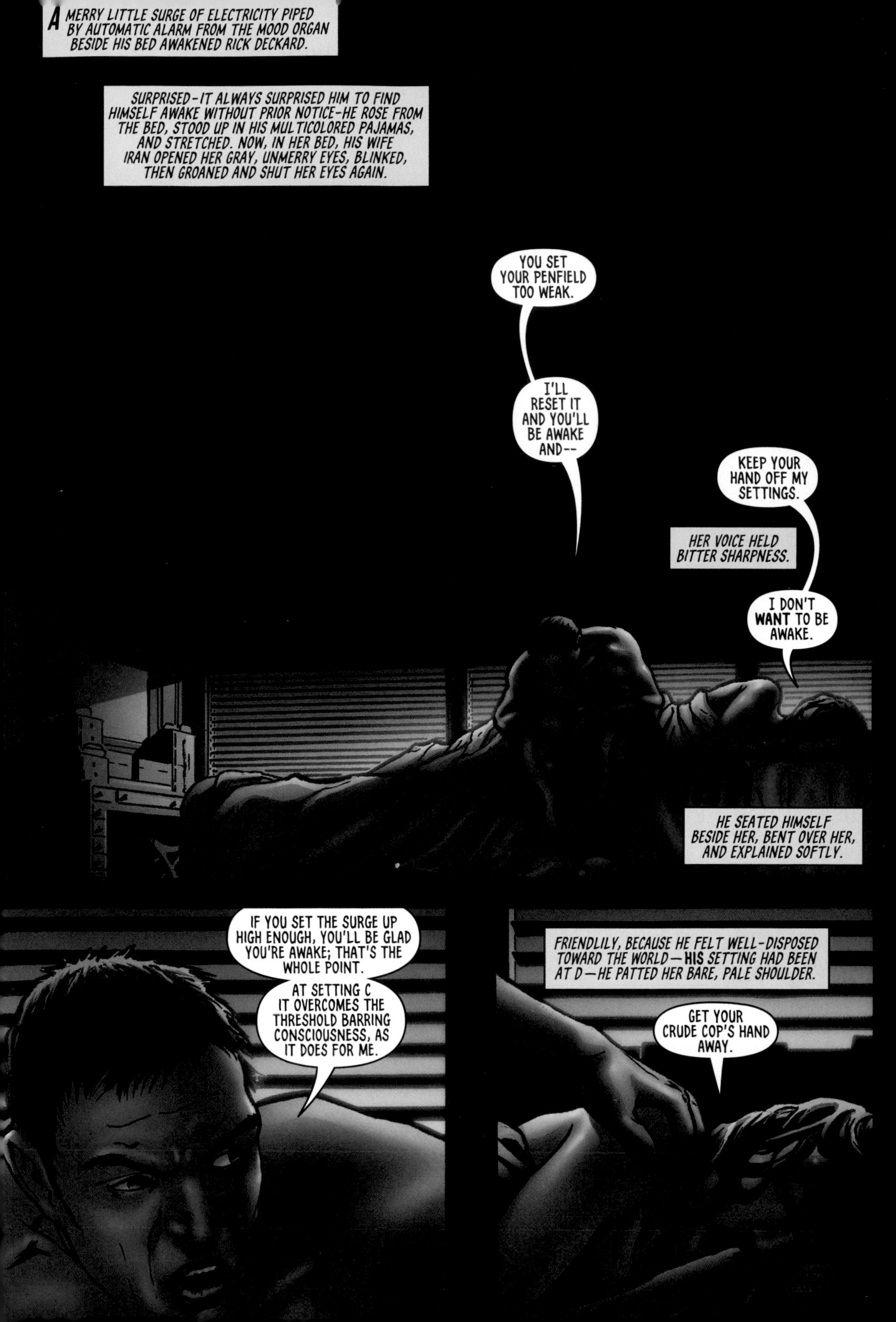
A MERRY LITTLE SURGE OF ELECTRICITY PIPED BY AUTOMATIC ALARM FROM THE MOOD ORGAN BESIDE HIS BED AWAKENED RICK DECKARD.
SURPRISED-IT ALWAYS SURPRISED HIM TO FIND HIMSELF AWAKE WITHOUT PRIOR NOTICE-HE ROSE FROM THE BED, STOOD UP IN HIS MULTICOLORED PAJAMAS, AND STRETCHED. NOW, IN HER BED, HIS WIFE IRAN OPENED HER GRAY, UNMERRY EYES, BLINKED, THEN GROANED AND SHUT HER EYES AGAIN.
YOU SET YOUR PENFIELD TOO WEAK.
I'LL RESET IT AND YOU'LL BE AWAKE AND--
KEEP YOUR HAND OFF MY SETTINGS.
HER VOICE HELD BITTER SHARPNESS.
I DON'T **WANT** TO BE AWAKE.
HE SEATED HIMSELF BESIDE HER, BENT OVER HER, AND EXPLAINED SOFTLY.
IF YOU SET THE SURGE UP HIGH ENOUGH, YOU'LL BE GLAD YOU'RE AWAKE; THAT'S THE WHOLE POINT.
AT SETTING C IT OVERCOMES THE THRESHOLD BARRING CONSCIOUSNESS, AS IT DOES FOR ME.
FRIENDLILY, BECAUSE HE FELT WELL-DISPOSED TOWARD THE WORLD—**HIS** SETTING HAD BEEN AT D—HE PATTED HER BARE, PALE SHOULDER.
GET YOUR CRUDE COP'S HAND AWAY.

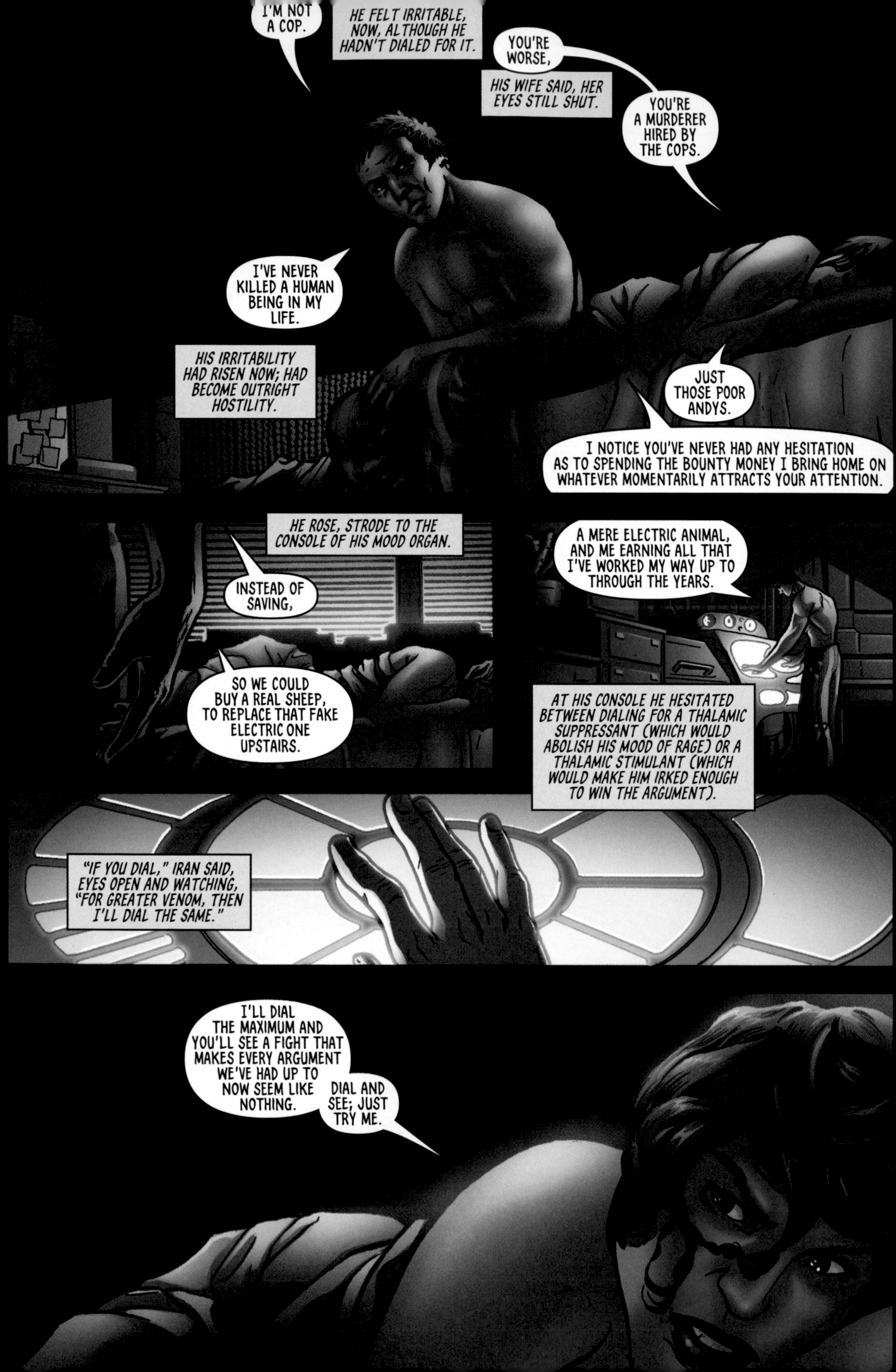
I'M NOT A COP.
HE FELT IRRITABLE, NOW, ALTHOUGH HE HADN'T DIALED FOR IT.
YOU'RE WORSE,
HIS WIFE SAID, HER EYES STILL SHUT.
YOU'RE A MURDERER HIRED BY THE COPS.
I'VE NEVER KILLED A HUMAN BEING IN MY LIFE.
HIS IRRITABILITY HAD RISEN NOW; HAD BECOME OUTRIGHT HOSTILITY.
JUST THOSE POOR ANDYS.
I NOTICE YOU'VE NEVER HAD ANY HESITATION AS TO SPENDING THE BOUNTY MONEY I BRING HOME ON WHATEVER MOMENTARILY ATTRACTS YOUR ATTENTION.
HE ROSE, STRODE TO THE CONSOLE OF HIS MOOD ORGAN.
INSTEAD OF SAVING,
SO WE COULD BUY A REAL SHEEP, TO REPLACE THAT FAKE ELECTRIC ONE UPSTAIRS.
A MERE ELECTRIC ANIMAL, AND ME EARNING ALL THAT I'VE WORKED MY WAY UP TO THROUGH THE YEARS.
AT HIS CONSOLE HE HESITATED BETWEEN DIALING FOR A THALAMIC SUPPRESSANT (WHICH WOULD ABOLISH HIS MOOD OF RAGE) OR A THALAMIC STIMULANT (WHICH WOULD MAKE HIM IRKED ENOUGH TO WIN THE ARGUMENT).
"IF YOU DIAL," IRAN SAID, EYES OPEN AND WATCHING, "FOR GREATER VENOM, THEN I'LL DIAL THE SAME."
I'LL DIAL THE MAXIMUM AND YOU'LL SEE A FIGHT THAT MAKES EVERY ARGUMENT WE'VE HAD UP TO NOW SEEM LIKE NOTHING.
DIAL AND SEE; JUST TRY ME.

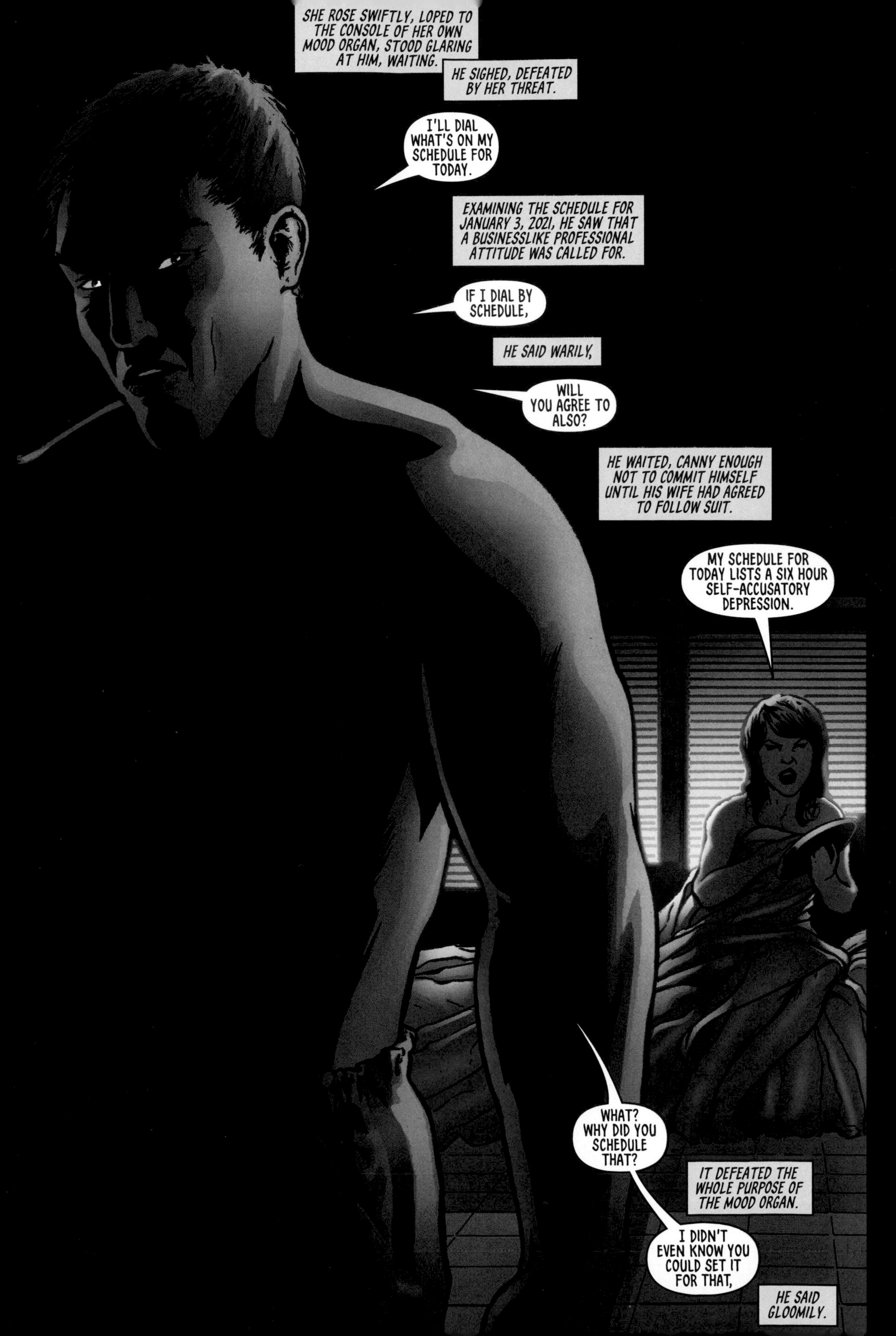

SHE ROSE SWIFTLY, LOPED TO THE CONSOLE OF HER OWN MOOD ORGAN, STOOD GLARING AT HIM, WAITING.
HE SIGHED, DEFEATED BY HER THREAT.
I'LL DIAL WHAT'S ON MY SCHEDULE FOR TODAY.
EXAMINING THE SCHEDULE FOR JANUARY 3, 2021, HE SAW THAT A BUSINESSLIKE PROFESSIONAL ATTITUDE WAS CALLED FOR.
IF I DIAL BY SCHEDULE,
HE SAID WARILY,
WILL YOU AGREE TO ALSO?
HE WAITED, CANNY ENOUGH NOT TO COMMIT HIMSELF UNTIL HIS WIFE HAD AGREED TO FOLLOW SUIT.
MY SCHEDULE FOR TODAY LISTS A SIX HOUR SELF-ACCUSATORY DEPRESSION.
WHAT? WHY DID YOU SCHEDULE THAT?
IT DEFEATED THE WHOLE PURPOSE OF THE MOOD ORGAN.
I DIDN'T EVEN KNOW YOU COULD SET IT FOR THAT,
HE SAID GLOOMILY.

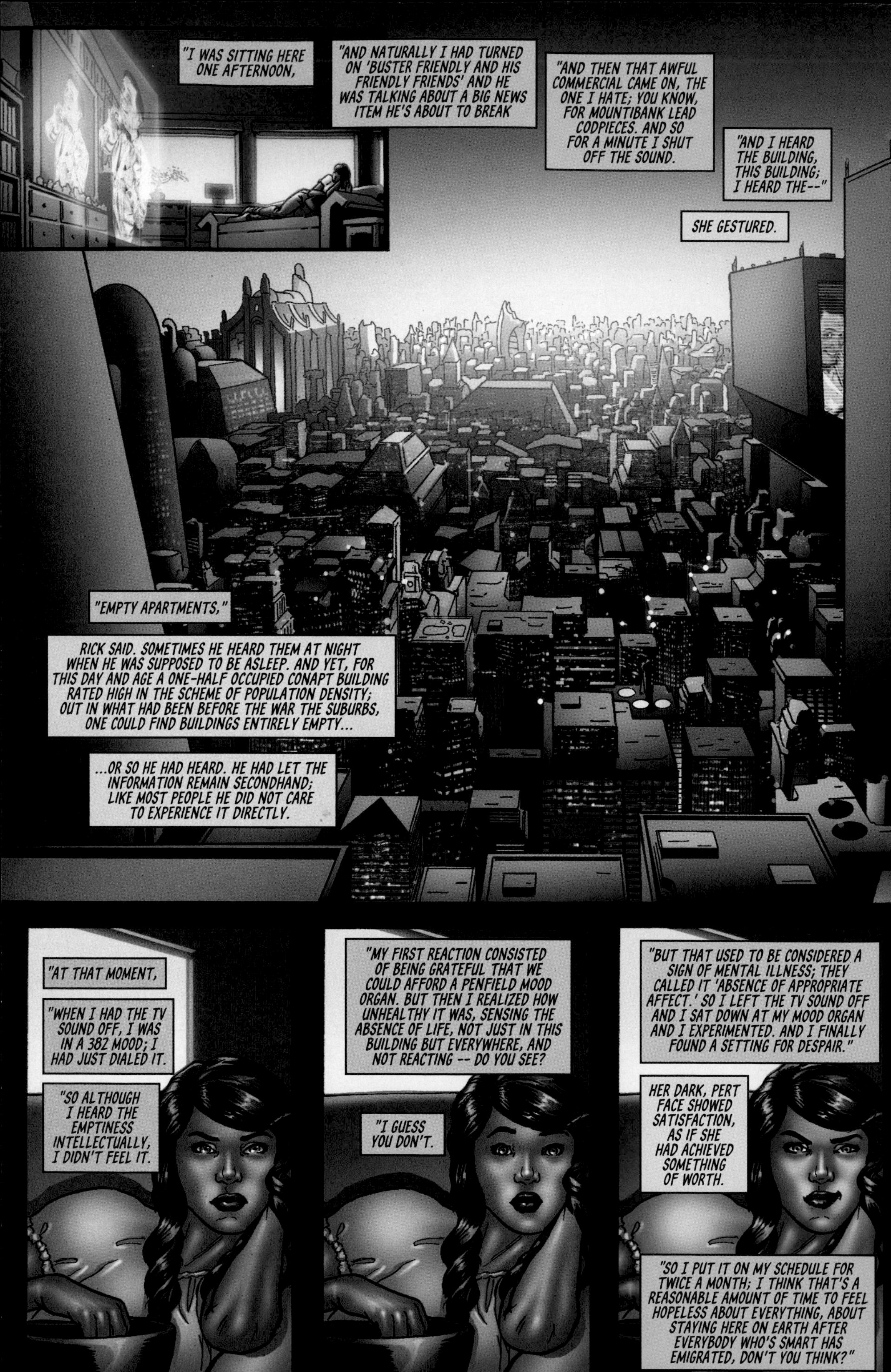

"I WAS SITTING HERE ONE AFTERNOON,
"AND NATURALLY I HAD TURNED ON 'BUSTER FRIENDLY AND HIS FRIENDLY FRIENDS' AND HE WAS TALKING ABOUT A BIG NEWS ITEM HE'S ABOUT TO BREAK
"AND THEN THAT AWFUL COMMERCIAL CAME ON, THE ONE I HATE; YOU KNOW, FOR MOUNTIBANK LEAD CODPIECES. AND SO FOR A MINUTE I SHUT OFF THE SOUND.
"AND I HEARD THE BUILDING, THIS BUILDING; I HEARD THE--"
SHE GESTURED.
"EMPTY APARTMENTS,"
RICK SAID. SOMETIMES HE HEARD THEM AT NIGHT WHEN HE WAS SUPPOSED TO BE ASLEEP. AND YET, FOR THIS DAY AND AGE A ONE-HALF OCCUPIED CONAPT BUILDING RATED HIGH IN THE SCHEME OF POPULATION DENSITY; OUT IN WHAT HAD BEEN BEFORE THE WAR THE SUBURBS, ONE COULD FIND BUILDINGS ENTIRELY EMPTY...
...OR SO HE HAD HEARD. HE HAD LET THE INFORMATION REMAIN SECONDHAND; LIKE MOST PEOPLE HE DID NOT CARE TO EXPERIENCE IT DIRECTLY.
"AT THAT MOMENT,
"WHEN I HAD THE TV SOUND OFF, I WAS IN A 382 MOOD; I HAD JUST DIALED IT.
"SO ALTHOUGH I HEARD THE EMPTINESS INTELLECTUALLY, I DIDN'T FEEL IT.
"MY FIRST REACTION CONSISTED OF BEING GRATEFUL THAT WE COULD AFFORD A PENFIELD MOOD ORGAN. BUT THEN I REALIZED HOW UNHEALTHY IT WAS, SENSING THE ABSENCE OF LIFE, NOT JUST IN THIS BUILDING BUT EVERYWHERE, AND NOT REACTING -- DO YOU SEE?
"I GUESS YOU DON'T.
"BUT THAT USED TO BE CONSIDERED A SIGN OF MENTAL ILLNESS; THEY CALLED IT 'ABSENCE OF APPROPRIATE AFFECT.' SO I LEFT THE TV SOUND OFF AND I SAT DOWN AT MY MOOD ORGAN AND I EXPERIMENTED. AND I FINALLY FOUND A SETTING FOR DESPAIR."
HER DARK, PERT FACE SHOWED SATISFACTION, AS IF SHE HAD ACHIEVED SOMETHING OF WORTH.
"SO I PUT IT ON MY SCHEDULE FOR TWICE A MONTH; I THINK THAT'S A REASONABLE AMOUNT OF TIME TO FEEL HOPELESS ABOUT EVERYTHING, ABOUT STAYING HERE ON EARTH AFTER EVERYBODY WHO'S SMART HAS EMIGRATED, DON'T YOU THINK?"

"BUT A MOOD LIKE THAT," RICK SAID, "YOU'RE APT TO STAY IN IT, NOT DIAL YOUR WAY OUT. DESPAIR LIKE THAT, ABOUT TOTAL REALITY, IS SELF-PERPETUATING."

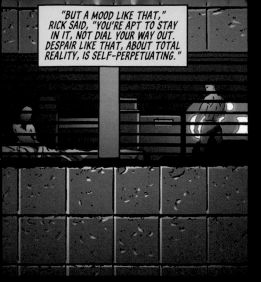

I PROGRAM FOR AN AUTOMATIC RESETTING FOR THREE HOURS LATER,

HIS WIFE SAID SLEEKLY.

A 481. AWARENESS OF THE MANIFOLD POSSIBILITIES OPEN TO ME IN THE FUTURE; NEW HOPE THAT --

"I KNOW 481," HE INTERRUPTED. HE HAD DIALED OUT THE COMBINATION MANY TIMES; HE RELIED ON IT GREATLY.

"LISTEN," HE SAID, SEATING HIMSELF ON HIS BED AND TAKING HOLD OF HER HANDS TO DRAW HER DOWN BESIDE HIM,

EVEN WITH AN AUTOMATIC CUTOFF IT'S DANGEROUS TO UNDERGO A DEPRESSION, ANY KIND.

FORGET WHAT YOU'VE SCHEDULED AND I'LL FORGET WHAT I'VE SCHEDULED; WE'LL DIAL A 104 TOGETHER AND BOTH EXPERIENCE IT, AND THEN YOU STAY IN IT WHILE I RESET MINE FOR MY USUAL BUSINESSLIKE ATTITUDE.

THAT WAY I'LL WANT TO HOP UP TO THE ROOF AND CHECK OUT THE SHEEP AND THEN HEAD FOR THE OFFICE;

MEANWHILE I'LL KNOW YOU'RE NOT SITTING HERE BROODING WITH NO TV.

HE RELEASED HER SLIM, LONG FINGERS, PASSED THROUGH THE SPACIOUS APARTMENT TO THE LIVING ROOM, WHICH SMELLED FAINTLY OF LAST NIGHT'S CIGARETTES.

THERE HE BENT TO TURN ON THE TV.

FROM THE BEDROOM IRAN'S VOICE CAME.

I CAN'T STAND TV BEFORE BREAKFAST.

"DIAL 888," RICK SAID AS THE SET WARMED. "THE DESIRE TO WATCH TV, NO MATTER WHAT'S ON IT."

I DON'T FEEL LIKE DIALING ANYTHING AT ALL RIGHT NOW.

"THEN DIAL 3," HE SAID.

I CAN'T DIAL A SETTING THAT STIMULATES MY CEREBRAL CORTEX INTO WANTING TO DIAL!

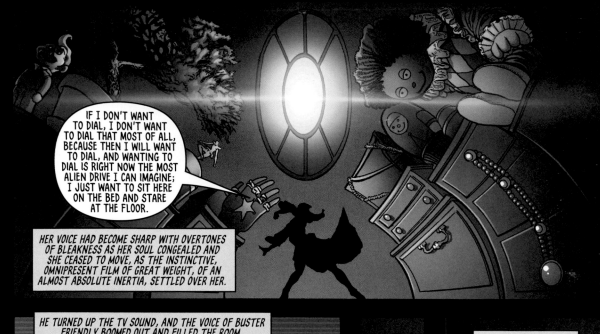

IF I DON'T WANT TO DIAL, I DON'T WANT TO DIAL THAT MOST OF ALL, BECAUSE THEN I WILL WANT TO DIAL, AND WANTING TO DIAL IS RIGHT NOW THE MOST ALIEN DRIVE I CAN IMAGINE; I JUST WANT TO SIT HERE ON THE BED AND STARE AT THE FLOOR.

HER VOICE HAD BECOME SHARP WITH OVERTONES OF BLEAKNESS AS HER SOUL CONGEALED AND SHE CEASED TO MOVE, AS THE INSTINCTIVE, OMNIPRESENT FILM OF GREAT WEIGHT, OF AN ALMOST ABSOLUTE INERTIA, SETTLED OVER HER.

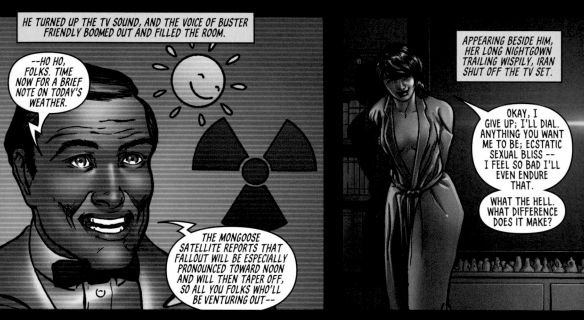

HE TURNED UP THE TV SOUND, AND THE VOICE OF BUSTER FRIENDLY BOOMED OUT AND FILLED THE ROOM.

--HO HO, FOLKS. TIME NOW FOR A BRIEF NOTE ON TODAY'S WEATHER.

THE MONGOOSE SATELLITE REPORTS THAT FALLOUT WILL BE ESPECIALLY PRONOUNCED TOWARD NOON AND WILL THEN TAPER OFF, SO ALL YOU FOLKS WHO'LL BE VENTURING OUT--

APPEARING BESIDE HIM, HER LONG NIGHTGOWN TRAILING WISPILY, IRAN SHUT OFF THE TV SET.

OKAY, I GIVE UP; I'LL DIAL. ANYTHING YOU WANT ME TO BE; ECSTATIC SEXUAL BLISS -- I FEEL SO BAD I'LL EVEN ENDURE THAT.

WHAT THE HELL. WHAT DIFFERENCE DOES IT MAKE?

"I'LL DIAL FOR BOTH OF US," RICK SAID, AND LED HER BACK INTO THE BEDROOM. THERE, AT HER CONSOLE, HE DIALED 594: PLEASED ACKNOWLEDGMENT OF HUSBAND'S SUPERIOR WISDOM IN ALL MATTERS.

ON HIS OWN CONSOLE HE DIALED FOR A CREATIVE AND FRESH ATTITUDE TOWARD HIS JOB, ALTHOUGH THIS HE HARDLY NEEDED; SUCH WAS HIS HABITUAL, INNATE APPROACH WITHOUT RECOURSE TO PENFIELD ARTIFICIAL BRAIN STIMULATION.

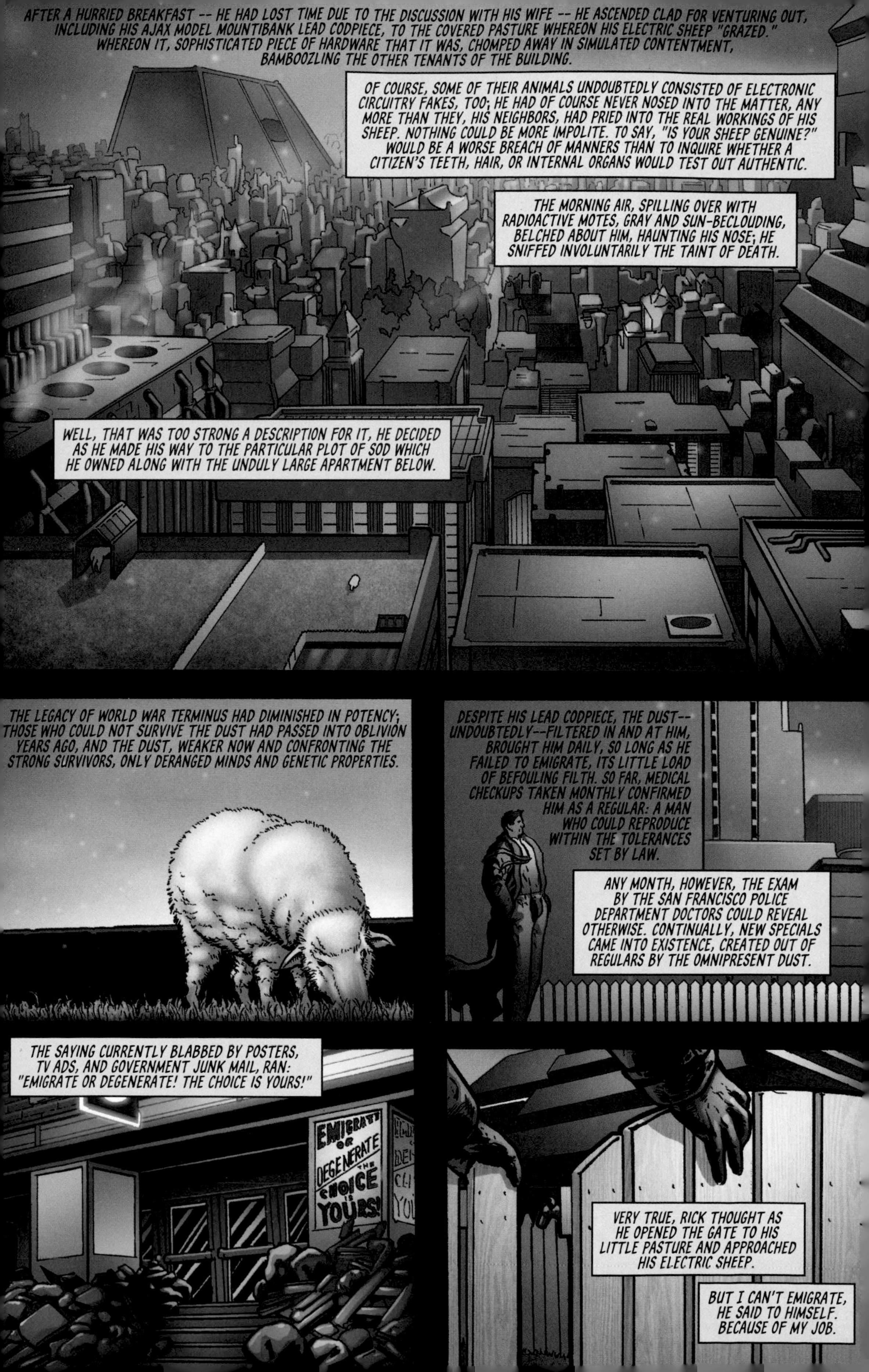
AFTER A HURRIED BREAKFAST -- HE HAD LOST TIME DUE TO THE DISCUSSION WITH HIS WIFE -- HE ASCENDED CLAD FOR VENTURING OUT, INCLUDING HIS AJAX MODEL MOUNTIBANK LEAD CODPIECE, TO THE COVERED PASTURE WHEREON HIS ELECTRIC SHEEP "GRAZED." WHEREON IT, SOPHISTICATED PIECE OF HARDWARE THAT IT WAS, CHOMPED AWAY IN SIMULATED CONTENTMENT, BAMBOOZLING THE OTHER TENANTS OF THE BUILDING.
OF COURSE, SOME OF THEIR ANIMALS UNDOUBTEDLY CONSISTED OF ELECTRONIC CIRCUITRY FAKES, TOO; HE HAD OF COURSE NEVER NOSED INTO THE MATTER, ANY MORE THAN THEY, HIS NEIGHBORS, HAD PRIED INTO THE REAL WORKINGS OF HIS SHEEP. NOTHING COULD BE MORE IMPOLITE. TO SAY, "IS YOUR SHEEP GENUINE?" WOULD BE A WORSE BREACH OF MANNERS THAN TO INQUIRE WHETHER A CITIZEN'S TEETH, HAIR, OR INTERNAL ORGANS WOULD TEST OUT AUTHENTIC.
THE MORNING AIR, SPILLING OVER WITH RADIOACTIVE MOTES, GRAY AND SUN-BECLOUDING, BELCHED ABOUT HIM, HAUNTING HIS NOSE; HE SNIFFED INVOLUNTARILY THE TAINT OF DEATH.
WELL, THAT WAS TOO STRONG A DESCRIPTION FOR IT, HE DECIDED AS HE MADE HIS WAY TO THE PARTICULAR PLOT OF SOD WHICH HE OWNED ALONG WITH THE UNDULY LARGE APARTMENT BELOW.
THE LEGACY OF WORLD WAR TERMINUS HAD DIMINISHED IN POTENCY; THOSE WHO COULD NOT SURVIVE THE DUST HAD PASSED INTO OBLIVION YEARS AGO, AND THE DUST, WEAKER NOW AND CONFRONTING THE STRONG SURVIVORS, ONLY DERANGED MINDS AND GENETIC PROPERTIES.
DESPITE HIS LEAD CODPIECE, THE DUST--UNDOUBTEDLY--FILTERED IN AND AT HIM, BROUGHT HIM DAILY, SO LONG AS HE FAILED TO EMIGRATE, ITS LITTLE LOAD OF BEFOULING FILTH. SO FAR, MEDICAL CHECKUPS TAKEN MONTHLY CONFIRMED HIM AS A REGULAR: A MAN WHO COULD REPRODUCE WITHIN THE TOLERANCES SET BY LAW.
ANY MONTH, HOWEVER, THE EXAM BY THE SAN FRANCISCO POLICE DEPARTMENT DOCTORS COULD REVEAL OTHERWISE. CONTINUALLY, NEW SPECIALS CAME INTO EXISTENCE, CREATED OUT OF REGULARS BY THE OMNIPRESENT DUST.
THE SAYING CURRENTLY BLABBED BY POSTERS, TV ADS, AND GOVERNMENT JUNK MAIL, RAN: "EMIGRATE OR DEGENERATE! THE CHOICE IS YOURS!"
EMIGRATE OR DEGENERATE THE CHOICE IS YOURS!
VERY TRUE, RICK THOUGHT AS HE OPENED THE GATE TO HIS LITTLE PASTURE AND APPROACHED HIS ELECTRIC SHEEP.
BUT I CAN'T EMIGRATE, HE SAID TO HIMSELF. BECAUSE OF MY JOB.

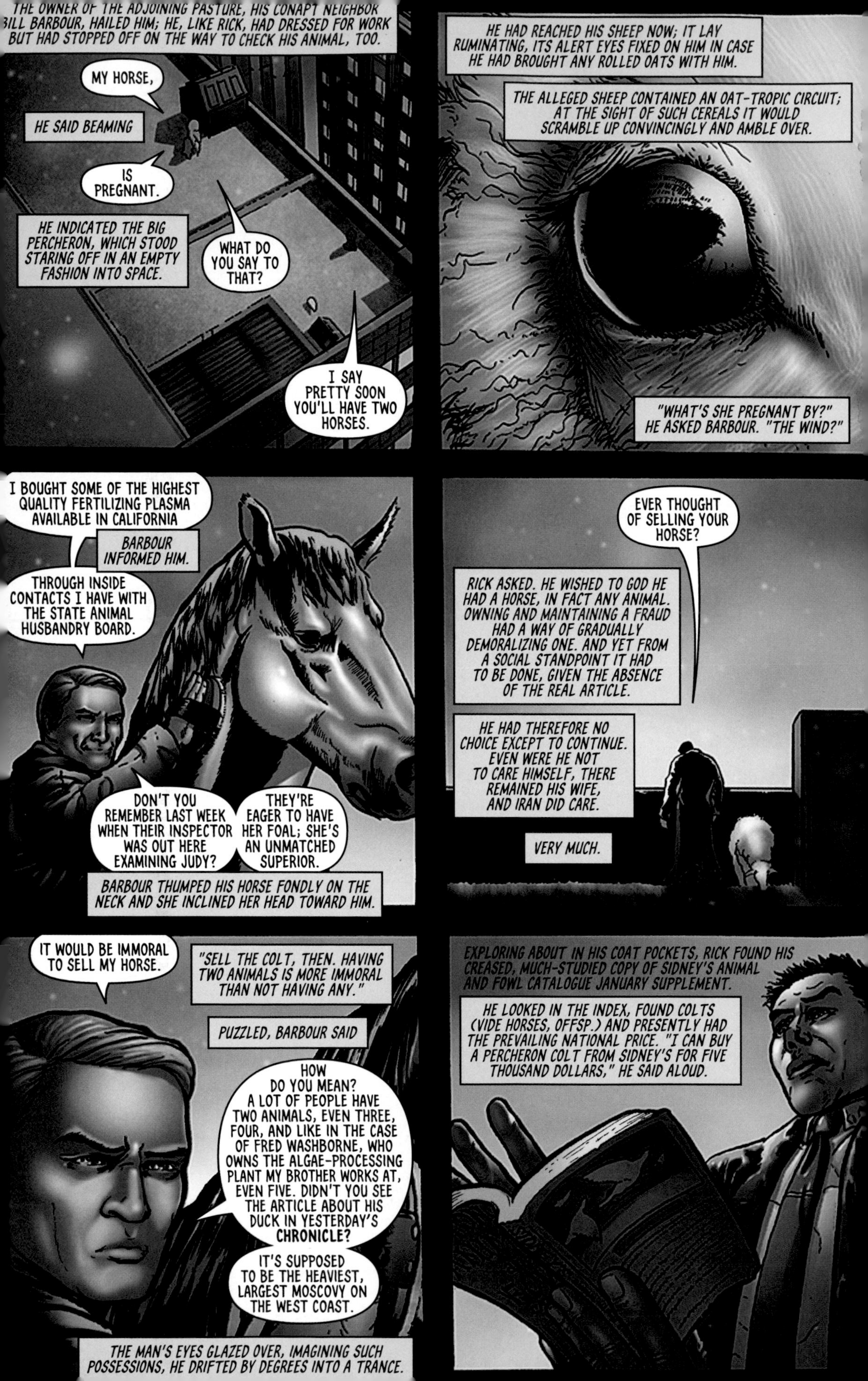
THE OWNER OF THE ADJOINING PASTURE, HIS CONAPT NEIGHBOR BILL BARBOUR, HAILED HIM; HE, LIKE RICK, HAD DRESSED FOR WORK BUT HAD STOPPED OFF ON THE WAY TO CHECK HIS ANIMAL, TOO.
MY HORSE,
HE SAID BEAMING
IS PREGNANT.
HE INDICATED THE BIG PERCHERON, WHICH STOOD STARING OFF IN AN EMPTY FASHION INTO SPACE.
WHAT DO YOU SAY TO THAT?
I SAY PRETTY SOON YOU'LL HAVE TWO HORSES.
HE HAD REACHED HIS SHEEP NOW; IT LAY RUMINATING, ITS ALERT EYES FIXED ON HIM IN CASE HE HAD BROUGHT ANY ROLLED OATS WITH HIM.
THE ALLEGED SHEEP CONTAINED AN OAT-TROPIC CIRCUIT; AT THE SIGHT OF SUCH CEREALS IT WOULD SCRAMBLE UP CONVINCINGLY AND AMBLE OVER.
"WHAT'S SHE PREGNANT BY?" HE ASKED BARBOUR. "THE WIND?"
I BOUGHT SOME OF THE HIGHEST QUALITY FERTILIZING PLASMA AVAILABLE IN CALIFORNIA
BARBOUR INFORMED HIM.
THROUGH INSIDE CONTACTS I HAVE WITH THE STATE ANIMAL HUSBANDRY BOARD.
DON'T YOU REMEMBER LAST WEEK WHEN THEIR INSPECTOR WAS OUT HERE EXAMINING JUDY?
THEY'RE EAGER TO HAVE HER FOAL; SHE'S AN UNMATCHED SUPERIOR.
BARBOUR THUMPED HIS HORSE FONDLY ON THE NECK AND SHE INCLINED HER HEAD TOWARD HIM.
EVER THOUGHT OF SELLING YOUR HORSE?
RICK ASKED. HE WISHED TO GOD HE HAD A HORSE, IN FACT ANY ANIMAL. OWNING AND MAINTAINING A FRAUD HAD A WAY OF GRADUALLY DEMORALIZING ONE. AND YET FROM A SOCIAL STANDPOINT IT HAD TO BE DONE, GIVEN THE ABSENCE OF THE REAL ARTICLE.
HE HAD THEREFORE NO CHOICE EXCEPT TO CONTINUE. EVEN WERE HE NOT TO CARE HIMSELF, THERE REMAINED HIS WIFE, AND IRAN DID CARE.
VERY MUCH.
IT WOULD BE IMMORAL TO SELL MY HORSE.
"SELL THE COLT, THEN. HAVING TWO ANIMALS IS MORE IMMORAL THAN NOT HAVING ANY."
PUZZLED, BARBOUR SAID
HOW DO YOU MEAN? A LOT OF PEOPLE HAVE TWO ANIMALS, EVEN THREE, FOUR, AND LIKE IN THE CASE OF FRED WASHBORNE, WHO OWNS THE ALGAE-PROCESSING PLANT MY BROTHER WORKS AT, EVEN FIVE. DIDN'T YOU SEE THE ARTICLE ABOUT HIS DUCK IN YESTERDAY'S **CHRONICLE?**
IT'S SUPPOSED TO BE THE HEAVIEST, LARGEST MOSCOVY ON THE WEST COAST.
THE MAN'S EYES GLAZED OVER, IMAGINING SUCH POSSESSIONS, HE DRIFTED BY DEGREES INTO A TRANCE.
EXPLORING ABOUT IN HIS COAT POCKETS, RICK FOUND HIS CREASED, MUCH-STUDIED COPY OF SIDNEY'S ANIMAL AND FOWL CATALOGUE JANUARY SUPPLEMENT.
HE LOOKED IN THE INDEX, FOUND COLTS (VIDE HORSES, OFFSP.) AND PRESENTLY HAD THE PREVAILING NATIONAL PRICE. "I CAN BUY A PERCHERON COLT FROM SIDNEY'S FOR FIVE THOUSAND DOLLARS," HE SAID ALOUD.

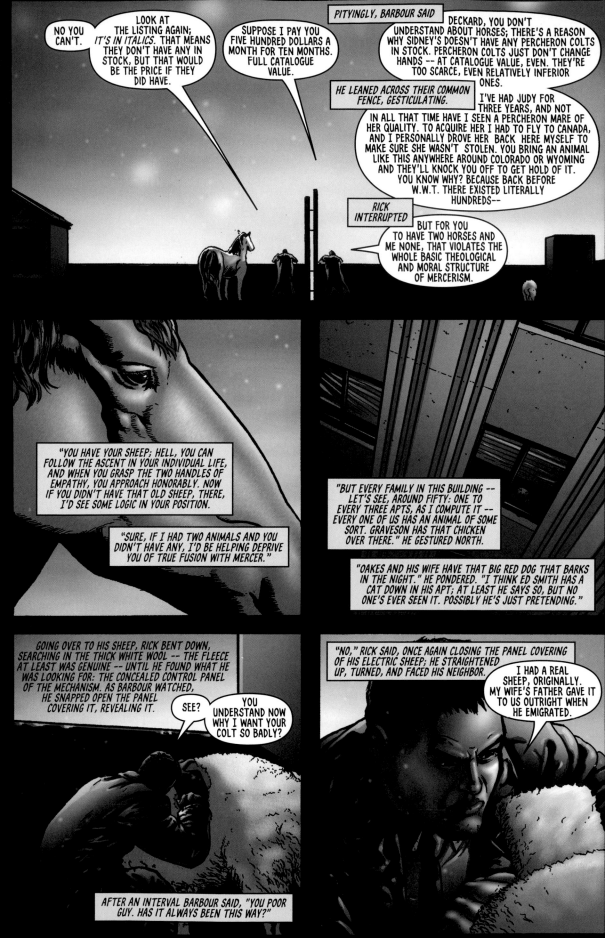

NO YOU CAN'T.

LOOK AT THE LISTING AGAIN; *IT'S IN ITALICS.* THAT MEANS THEY DON'T HAVE ANY IN STOCK, BUT THAT WOULD BE THE PRICE IF THEY DID HAVE.

SUPPOSE I PAY YOU FIVE HUNDRED DOLLARS A MONTH FOR TEN MONTHS. FULL CATALOGUE VALUE.

PITYINGLY, BARBOUR SAID

DECKARD, YOU DON'T UNDERSTAND ABOUT HORSES; THERE'S A REASON WHY SIDNEY'S DOESN'T HAVE ANY PERCHERON COLTS IN STOCK. PERCHERON COLTS JUST DON'T CHANGE HANDS -- AT CATALOGUE VALUE, EVEN. THEY'RE TOO SCARCE, EVEN RELATIVELY INFERIOR ONES.

HE LEANED ACROSS THEIR COMMON FENCE, GESTICULATING.

I'VE HAD JUDY FOR THREE YEARS, AND NOT IN ALL THAT TIME HAVE I SEEN A PERCHERON MARE OF HER QUALITY. TO ACQUIRE HER I HAD TO FLY TO CANADA, AND I PERSONALLY DROVE HER BACK HERE MYSELF TO MAKE SURE SHE WASN'T STOLEN. YOU BRING AN ANIMAL LIKE THIS ANYWHERE AROUND COLORADO OR WYOMING AND THEY'LL KNOCK YOU OFF TO GET HOLD OF IT. YOU KNOW WHY? BECAUSE BACK BEFORE W.W.T. THERE EXISTED LITERALLY HUNDREDS--

RICK INTERRUPTED

BUT FOR YOU TO HAVE TWO HORSES AND ME NONE, THAT VIOLATES THE WHOLE BASIC THEOLOGICAL AND MORAL STRUCTURE OF MERCERISM.

"YOU HAVE YOUR SHEEP; HELL, YOU CAN FOLLOW THE ASCENT IN YOUR INDIVIDUAL LIFE, AND WHEN YOU GRASP THE TWO HANDLES OF EMPATHY, YOU APPROACH HONORABLY. NOW IF YOU DIDN'T HAVE THAT OLD SHEEP, THERE, I'D SEE SOME LOGIC IN YOUR POSITION.

"SURE, IF I HAD TWO ANIMALS AND YOU DIDN'T HAVE ANY, I'D BE HELPING DEPRIVE YOU OF TRUE FUSION WITH MERCER."

"BUT EVERY FAMILY IN THIS BUILDING -- LET'S SEE, AROUND FIFTY: ONE TO EVERY THREE APTS, AS I COMPUTE IT -- EVERY ONE OF US HAS AN ANIMAL OF SOME SORT. GRAVESON HAS THAT CHICKEN OVER THERE." HE GESTURED NORTH.

"OAKES AND HIS WIFE HAVE THAT BIG RED DOG THAT BARKS IN THE NIGHT." HE PONDERED. "I THINK ED SMITH HAS A CAT DOWN IN HIS APT; AT LEAST HE SAYS SO, BUT NO ONE'S EVER SEEN IT. POSSIBLY HE'S JUST PRETENDING."

GOING OVER TO HIS SHEEP, RICK BENT DOWN, SEARCHING IN THE THICK WHITE WOOL -- THE FLEECE AT LEAST WAS GENUINE -- UNTIL HE FOUND WHAT HE WAS LOOKING FOR: THE CONCEALED CONTROL PANEL OF THE MECHANISM. AS BARBOUR WATCHED, HE SNAPPED OPEN THE PANEL COVERING IT, REVEALING IT.

SEE? YOU UNDERSTAND NOW WHY I WANT YOUR COLT SO BADLY?

"NO," RICK SAID, ONCE AGAIN CLOSING THE PANEL COVERING OF HIS ELECTRIC SHEEP; HE STRAIGHTENED UP, TURNED, AND FACED HIS NEIGHBOR.

I HAD A REAL SHEEP, ORIGINALLY. MY WIFE'S FATHER GAVE IT TO US OUTRIGHT WHEN HE EMIGRATED.

AFTER AN INTERVAL BARBOUR SAID, "YOU POOR GUY. HAS IT ALWAYS BEEN THIS WAY?"

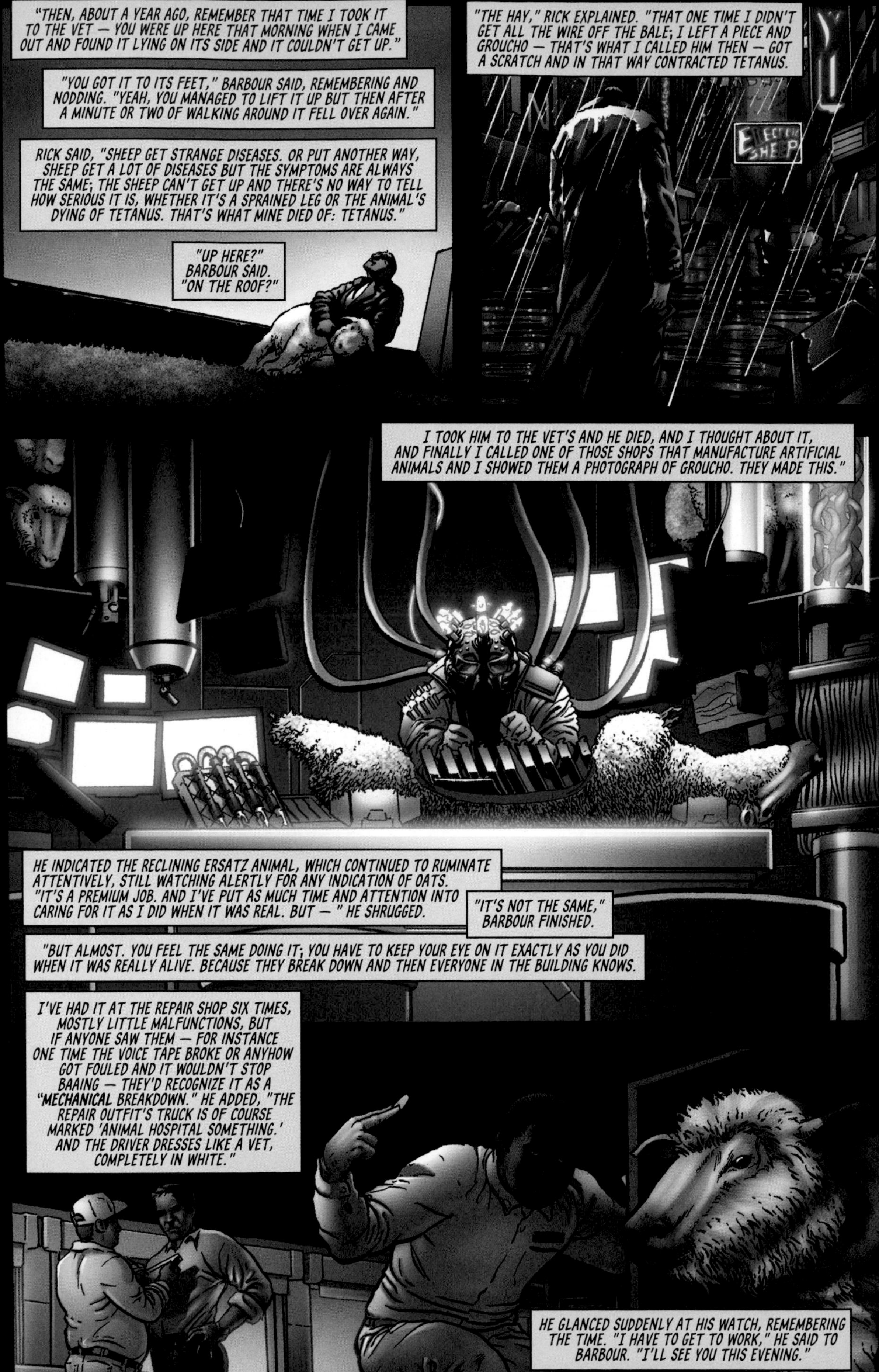
"THEN, ABOUT A YEAR AGO, REMEMBER THAT TIME I TOOK IT TO THE VET — YOU WERE UP HERE THAT MORNING WHEN I CAME OUT AND FOUND IT LYING ON ITS SIDE AND IT COULDN'T GET UP."
"YOU GOT IT TO ITS FEET," BARBOUR SAID, REMEMBERING AND NODDING. "YEAH, YOU MANAGED TO LIFT IT UP BUT THEN AFTER A MINUTE OR TWO OF WALKING AROUND IT FELL OVER AGAIN."
RICK SAID, "SHEEP GET STRANGE DISEASES. OR PUT ANOTHER WAY, SHEEP GET A LOT OF DISEASES BUT THE SYMPTOMS ARE ALWAYS THE SAME; THE SHEEP CAN'T GET UP AND THERE'S NO WAY TO TELL HOW SERIOUS IT IS, WHETHER IT'S A SPRAINED LEG OR THE ANIMAL'S DYING OF TETANUS. THAT'S WHAT MINE DIED OF: TETANUS."
"UP HERE?" BARBOUR SAID. "ON THE ROOF?"
"THE HAY," RICK EXPLAINED. "THAT ONE TIME I DIDN'T GET ALL THE WIRE OFF THE BALE; I LEFT A PIECE AND GROUCHO — THAT'S WHAT I CALLED HIM THEN — GOT A SCRATCH AND IN THAT WAY CONTRACTED TETANUS.
ELECTRIC SHEEP
I TOOK HIM TO THE VET'S AND HE DIED, AND I THOUGHT ABOUT IT, AND FINALLY I CALLED ONE OF THOSE SHOPS THAT MANUFACTURE ARTIFICIAL ANIMALS AND I SHOWED THEM A PHOTOGRAPH OF GROUCHO. THEY MADE THIS."
HE INDICATED THE RECLINING ERSATZ ANIMAL, WHICH CONTINUED TO RUMINATE ATTENTIVELY, STILL WATCHING ALERTLY FOR ANY INDICATION OF OATS. "IT'S A PREMIUM JOB. AND I'VE PUT AS MUCH TIME AND ATTENTION INTO CARING FOR IT AS I DID WHEN IT WAS REAL. BUT — " HE SHRUGGED.
"IT'S NOT THE SAME," BARBOUR FINISHED.
"BUT ALMOST. YOU FEEL THE SAME DOING IT; YOU HAVE TO KEEP YOUR EYE ON IT EXACTLY AS YOU DID WHEN IT WAS REALLY ALIVE. BECAUSE THEY BREAK DOWN AND THEN EVERYONE IN THE BUILDING KNOWS.
I'VE HAD IT AT THE REPAIR SHOP SIX TIMES, MOSTLY LITTLE MALFUNCTIONS, BUT IF ANYONE SAW THEM — FOR INSTANCE ONE TIME THE VOICE TAPE BROKE OR ANYHOW GOT FOULED AND IT WOULDN'T STOP BAAING — THEY'D RECOGNIZE IT AS A "MECHANICAL BREAKDOWN." HE ADDED, "THE REPAIR OUTFIT'S TRUCK IS OF COURSE MARKED 'ANIMAL HOSPITAL SOMETHING.' AND THE DRIVER DRESSES LIKE A VET, COMPLETELY IN WHITE."
HE GLANCED SUDDENLY AT HIS WATCH, REMEMBERING THE TIME. "I HAVE TO GET TO WORK," HE SAID TO BARBOUR. "I'LL SEE YOU THIS EVENING."

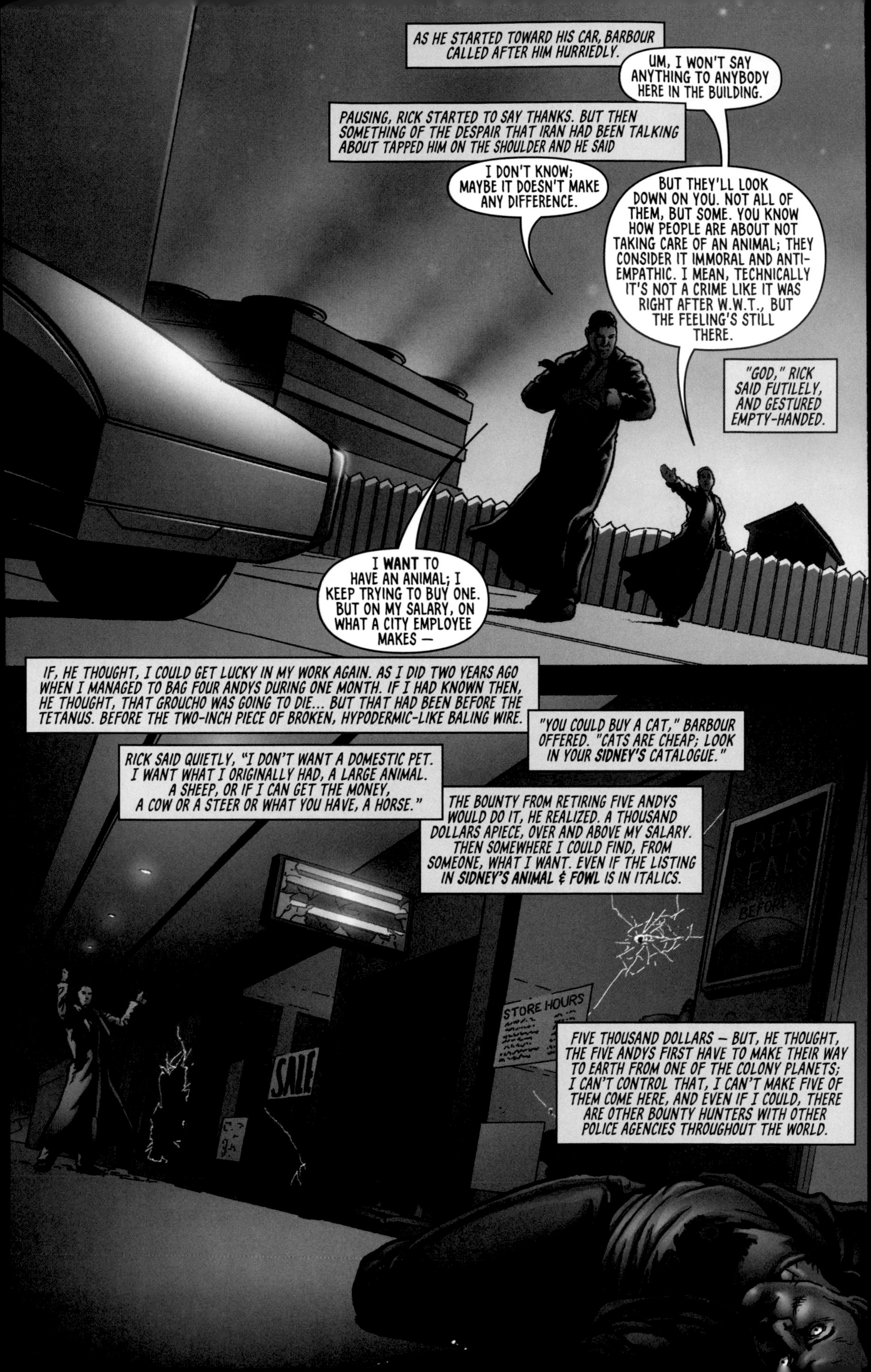
AS HE STARTED TOWARD HIS CAR, BARBOUR CALLED AFTER HIM HURRIEDLY.
UM, I WON'T SAY ANYTHING TO ANYBODY HERE IN THE BUILDING.
PAUSING, RICK STARTED TO SAY THANKS. BUT THEN SOMETHING OF THE DESPAIR THAT IRAN HAD BEEN TALKING ABOUT TAPPED HIM ON THE SHOULDER AND HE SAID
I DON'T KNOW; MAYBE IT DOESN'T MAKE ANY DIFFERENCE.
BUT THEY'LL LOOK DOWN ON YOU. NOT ALL OF THEM, BUT SOME. YOU KNOW HOW PEOPLE ARE ABOUT NOT TAKING CARE OF AN ANIMAL; THEY CONSIDER IT IMMORAL AND ANTI-EMPATHIC. I MEAN, TECHNICALLY IT'S NOT A CRIME LIKE IT WAS RIGHT AFTER W.W.T., BUT THE FEELING'S STILL THERE.
"GOD," RICK SAID FUTILELY, AND GESTURED EMPTY-HANDED.
I WANT TO HAVE AN ANIMAL; I KEEP TRYING TO BUY ONE. BUT ON MY SALARY, ON WHAT A CITY EMPLOYEE MAKES —
IF, HE THOUGHT, I COULD GET LUCKY IN MY WORK AGAIN. AS I DID TWO YEARS AGO WHEN I MANAGED TO BAG FOUR ANDYS DURING ONE MONTH. IF I HAD KNOWN THEN, HE THOUGHT, THAT GROUCHO WAS GOING TO DIE... BUT THAT HAD BEEN BEFORE THE TETANUS. BEFORE THE TWO-INCH PIECE OF BROKEN, HYPODERMIC-LIKE BALING WIRE.
"YOU COULD BUY A CAT," BARBOUR OFFERED. "CATS ARE CHEAP; LOOK IN YOUR SIDNEY'S CATALOGUE."
RICK SAID QUIETLY, "I DON'T WANT A DOMESTIC PET. I WANT WHAT I ORIGINALLY HAD, A LARGE ANIMAL. A SHEEP, OR IF I CAN GET THE MONEY, A COW OR A STEER OR WHAT YOU HAVE, A HORSE."
THE BOUNTY FROM RETIRING FIVE ANDYS WOULD DO IT, HE REALIZED. A THOUSAND DOLLARS APIECE, OVER AND ABOVE MY SALARY. THEN SOMEWHERE I COULD FIND, FROM SOMEONE, WHAT I WANT. EVEN IF THE LISTING IN SIDNEY'S ANIMAL & FOWL IS IN ITALICS.
STORE HOURS
SALE
FIVE THOUSAND DOLLARS — BUT, HE THOUGHT, THE FIVE ANDYS FIRST HAVE TO MAKE THEIR WAY TO EARTH FROM ONE OF THE COLONY PLANETS; I CAN'T CONTROL THAT, I CAN'T MAKE FIVE OF THEM COME HERE, AND EVEN IF I COULD, THERE ARE OTHER BOUNTY HUNTERS WITH OTHER POLICE AGENCIES THROUGHOUT THE WORLD.

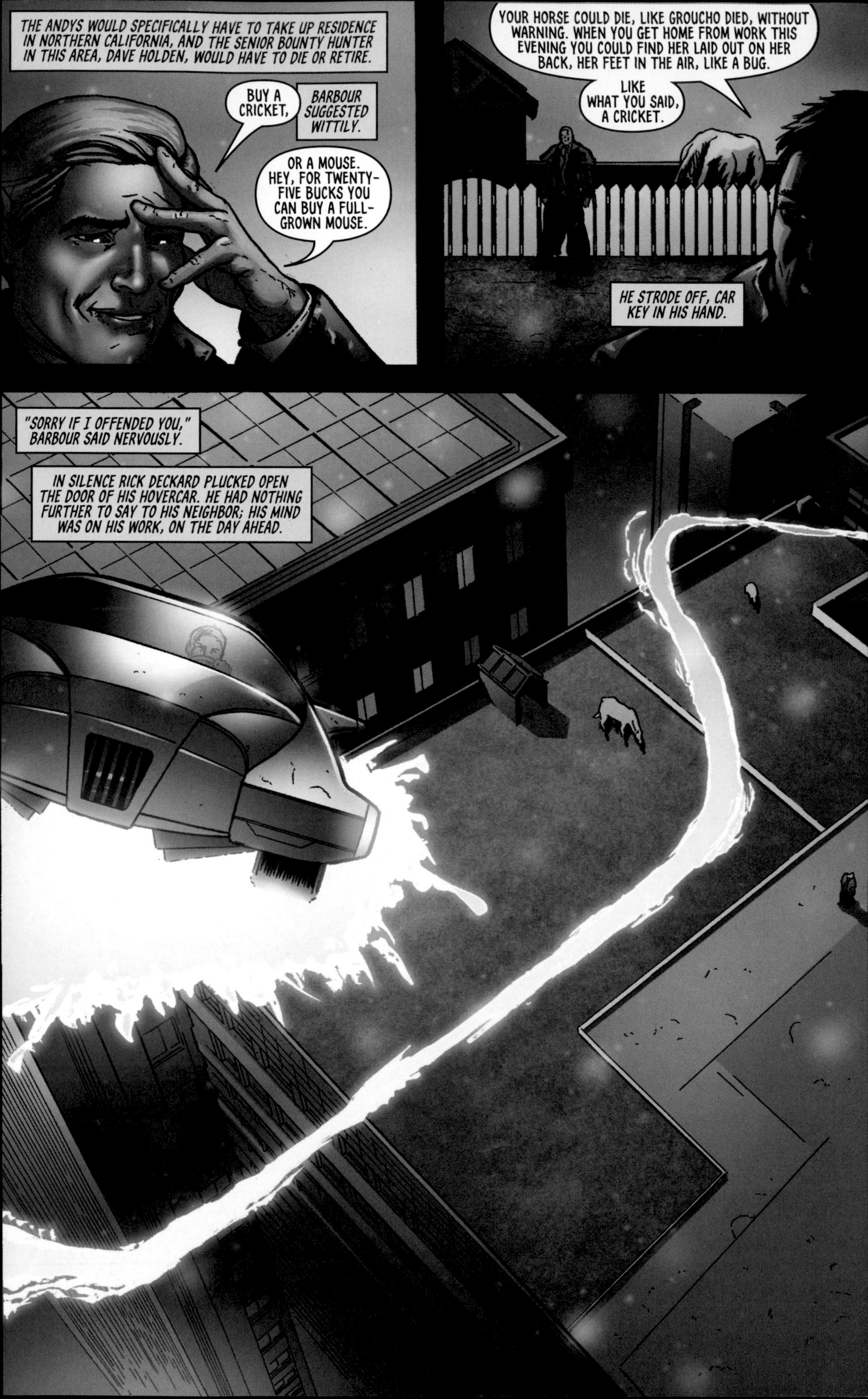
THE ANDYS WOULD SPECIFICALLY HAVE TO TAKE UP RESIDENCE IN NORTHERN CALIFORNIA, AND THE SENIOR BOUNTY HUNTER IN THIS AREA, DAVE HOLDEN, WOULD HAVE TO DIE OR RETIRE.
BUY A CRICKET,
BARBOUR SUGGESTED WITTILY.
OR A MOUSE. HEY, FOR TWENTY-FIVE BUCKS YOU CAN BUY A FULL-GROWN MOUSE.
YOUR HORSE COULD DIE, LIKE GROUCHO DIED, WITHOUT WARNING. WHEN YOU GET HOME FROM WORK THIS EVENING YOU COULD FIND HER LAID OUT ON HER BACK, HER FEET IN THE AIR, LIKE A BUG.
LIKE WHAT YOU SAID, A CRICKET.
HE STRODE OFF, CAR KEY IN HIS HAND.
"SORRY IF I OFFENDED YOU," BARBOUR SAID NERVOUSLY.
IN SILENCE RICK DECKARD PLUCKED OPEN THE DOOR OF HIS HOVERCAR. HE HAD NOTHING FURTHER TO SAY TO HIS NEIGHBOR; HIS MIND WAS ON HIS WORK, ON THE DAY AHEAD.

*I*N A GIANT, EMPTY, DECAYING BUILDING WHICH HAD ONCE HOUSED THOUSANDS, A SINGLE TV SET HAWKED ITS WARES TO AN UNINHABITED ROOM.

THIS OWNERLESS RUIN HAD, BEFORE WORLD WAR TERMINUS, BEEN TENDED AND MAINTAINED.

HERE HAD BEEN THE SUBURBS OF SAN FRANCISCO, A SHORT RIDE BY MONORAIL RAPID TRANSIT; THE ENTIRE PENINSULA HAD CHATTERED LIKE A BIRD TREE WITH LIFE AND OPINIONS AND COMPLAINTS, AND NOW THE WATCHFUL OWNERS HAD EITHER DIED OR MIGRATED TO A COLONY WORLD.

MOSTLY THE FORMER; IT HAD BEEN A COSTLY WAR DESPITE THE VALIANT PREDICTIONS OF THE PENTAGON AND ITS SMUG SCIENTIFIC VASSAL, THE RAND CORPORATION — WHICH HAD, IN FACT, EXISTED NOT FAR FROM THIS SPOT. LIKE THE APARTMENT OWNERS, THE CORPORATION HAD DEPARTED, EVIDENTLY FOR GOOD.

NO ONE MISSED IT.

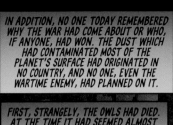

IN ADDITION, NO ONE TODAY REMEMBERED WHY THE WAR HAD COME ABOUT OR WHO, IF ANYONE, HAD WON. THE DUST WHICH HAD CONTAMINATED MOST OF THE PLANET'S SURFACE HAD ORIGINATED IN NO COUNTRY, AND NO ONE, EVEN THE WARTIME ENEMY, HAD PLANNED ON IT.

FIRST, STRANGELY, THE OWLS HAD DIED. AT THE TIME IT HAD SEEMED ALMOST FUNNY, THE FAT, FLUFFY WHITE BIRDS LYING HERE AND THERE, IN YARDS AND ON STREETS; COMING OUT NO EARLIER THAN TWILIGHT, AS THEY HAD WHILE ALIVE, THE OWLS ESCAPED NOTICE. MEDIEVAL PLAGUES HAD MANIFESTED THEMSELVES IN A SIMILAR WAY, IN THE FORM OF MANY DEAD RATS.

THIS PLAGUE, HOWEVER, HAD DESCENDED FROM ABOVE.

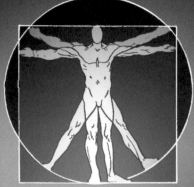

...POSSIBLE; THE OTHER BIRDS FOLLOWED. ...THEN THE MYSTERY HAD BEEN GRASPED AND ...UNDERSTOOD. A MEAGER COLONIZATION PROGRAM HAD BEEN ...UNDERWAY BEFORE THE WAR, BUT NOW THAT THE SUN HAD ...CEASED TO SHINE ON EARTH, THE COLONIZATION ENTERED AN ENTIRELY NEW PHASE.

IN CONNECTION WITH THIS A WEAPON OF WAR, THE SYNTHETIC FREEDOM FIGHTER, HAD BEEN MODIFIED; ABLE TO FUNCTION ON AN ALIEN WORLD, THE HUMANOID ROBOT — STRICTLY SPEAKING, THE ORGANIC ANDROID — HAD BECOME THE MOBILE DONKEY ENGINE OF THE COLONIZATION PROGRAM.

UNDER U.N. LAW EACH EMIGRANT AUTOMATICALLY RECEIVED POSSESSION OF AN ANDROID SUBTYPE OF HIS CHOICE, AND, BY 2019, THE VARIETY OF SUBTYPES PASSED ALL UNDERSTANDING, IN THE MANNER OF AMERICAN AUTOMOBILES OF THE 1960S. THAT HAD BEEN THE ULTIMATE INCENTIVE OF EMIGRATION: THE ANDROID SERVANT AS CARROT, THE RADIOACTIVE FALLOUT AS STICK. THE U.N. HAD MADE IT EASY TO EMIGRATE, DIFFICULT IF NOT IMPOSSIBLE TO STAY. LOITERING ON EARTH POTENTIALLY MEANT FINDING ONESELF ABRUPTLY CLASSED AS BIOLOGICALLY UNACCEPTABLE, A MENACE TO THE PRISTINE HEREDITY OF THE RACE.

ONCE PEGGED AS SPECIAL, A CITIZEN, EVEN IF ACCEPTING STERILIZATION, DROPPED OUT OF HISTORY. HE CEASED, IN EFFECT, TO BE PART OF MANKIND. AND YET PERSONS HERE AND THERE DECLINED TO MIGRATE; THAT, EVEN TO THOSE INVOLVED, CONSTITUTED A PERPLEXING IRRATIONALITY. LOGICALLY, EVERY REGULAR SHOULD HAVE EMIGRATED ALREADY. PERHAPS, DEFORMED AS IT WAS, EARTH REMAINED FAMILIAR, TO BE CLUNG TO.

OR POSSIBLY THE NON-EMIGRANT IMAGINED THAT THE TENT OF DUST WOULD DEPLETE ITSELF FINALLY.

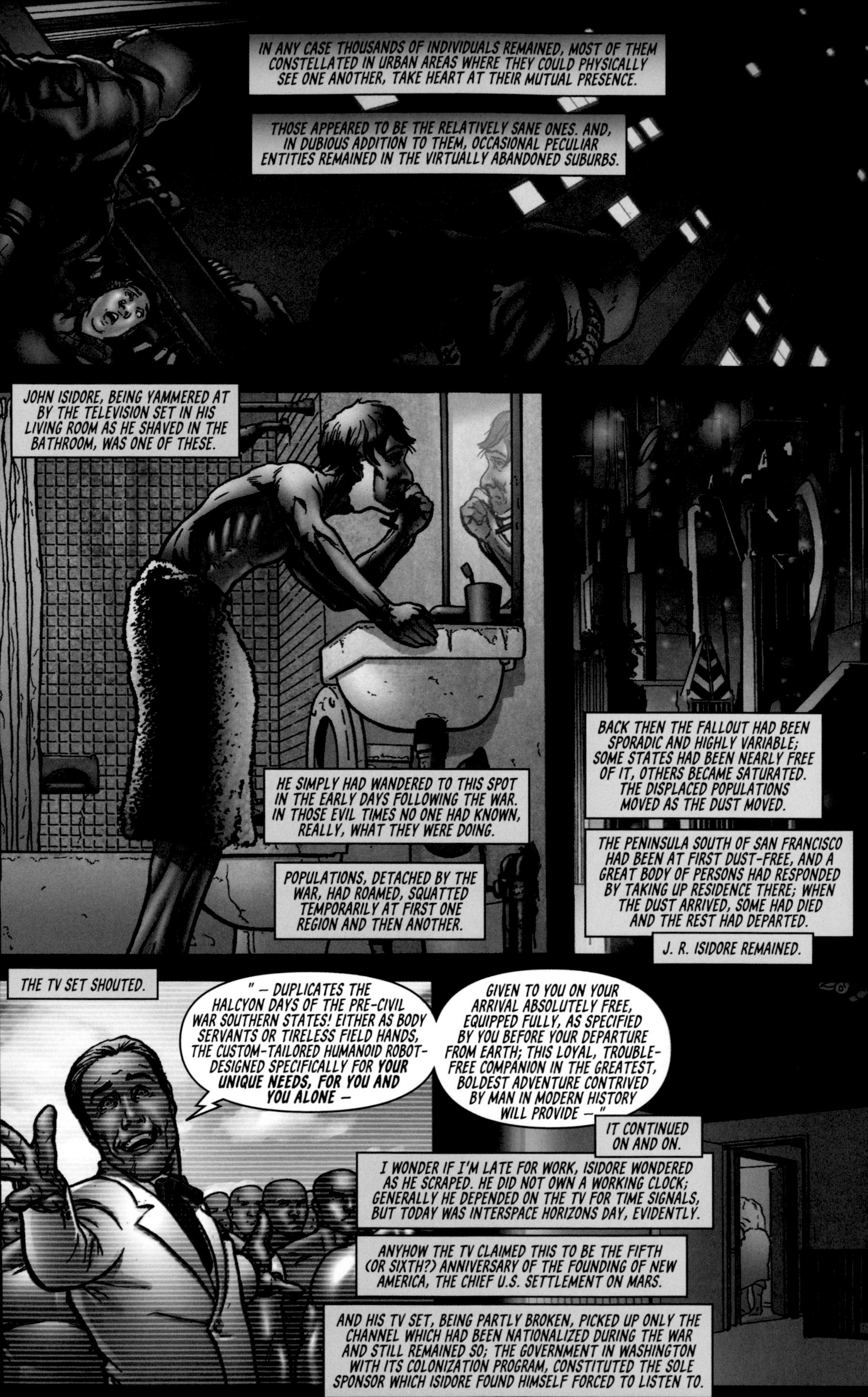
IN ANY CASE THOUSANDS OF INDIVIDUALS REMAINED, MOST OF THEM CONSTELLATED IN URBAN AREAS WHERE THEY COULD PHYSICALLY SEE ONE ANOTHER, TAKE HEART AT THEIR MUTUAL PRESENCE.
THOSE APPEARED TO BE THE RELATIVELY SANE ONES. AND, IN DUBIOUS ADDITION TO THEM, OCCASIONAL PECULIAR ENTITIES REMAINED IN THE VIRTUALLY ABANDONED SUBURBS.
JOHN ISIDORE, BEING YAMMERED AT BY THE TELEVISION SET IN HIS LIVING ROOM AS HE SHAVED IN THE BATHROOM, WAS ONE OF THESE.
HE SIMPLY HAD WANDERED TO THIS SPOT IN THE EARLY DAYS FOLLOWING THE WAR. IN THOSE EVIL TIMES NO ONE HAD KNOWN, REALLY, WHAT THEY WERE DOING.
POPULATIONS, DETACHED BY THE WAR, HAD ROAMED, SQUATTED TEMPORARILY AT FIRST ONE REGION AND THEN ANOTHER.
BACK THEN THE FALLOUT HAD BEEN SPORADIC AND HIGHLY VARIABLE; SOME STATES HAD BEEN NEARLY FREE OF IT, OTHERS BECAME SATURATED. THE DISPLACED POPULATIONS MOVED AS THE DUST MOVED.
THE PENINSULA SOUTH OF SAN FRANCISCO HAD BEEN AT FIRST DUST-FREE, AND A GREAT BODY OF PERSONS HAD RESPONDED BY TAKING UP RESIDENCE THERE; WHEN THE DUST ARRIVED, SOME HAD DIED AND THE REST HAD DEPARTED.
J. R. ISIDORE REMAINED.
THE TV SET SHOUTED.
" — DUPLICATES THE HALCYON DAYS OF THE PRE-CIVIL WAR SOUTHERN STATES! EITHER AS BODY SERVANTS OR TIRELESS FIELD HANDS, THE CUSTOM-TAILORED HUMANOID ROBOT-DESIGNED SPECIFICALLY FOR **YOUR UNIQUE NEEDS, FOR YOU AND YOU ALONE** —
GIVEN TO YOU ON YOUR ARRIVAL ABSOLUTELY FREE, EQUIPPED FULLY, AS SPECIFIED BY YOU BEFORE YOUR DEPARTURE FROM EARTH; THIS LOYAL, TROUBLE-FREE COMPANION IN THE GREATEST, BOLDEST ADVENTURE CONTRIVED BY MAN IN MODERN HISTORY WILL PROVIDE — "
IT CONTINUED ON AND ON.
I WONDER IF I'M LATE FOR WORK, ISIDORE WONDERED AS HE SCRAPED. HE DID NOT OWN A WORKING CLOCK; GENERALLY HE DEPENDED ON THE TV FOR TIME SIGNALS, BUT TODAY WAS INTERSPACE HORIZONS DAY, EVIDENTLY.
ANYHOW THE TV CLAIMED THIS TO BE THE FIFTH (OR SIXTH?) ANNIVERSARY OF THE FOUNDING OF NEW AMERICA, THE CHIEF U.S. SETTLEMENT ON MARS.
AND HIS TV SET, BEING PARTLY BROKEN, PICKED UP ONLY THE CHANNEL WHICH HAD BEEN NATIONALIZED DURING THE WAR AND STILL REMAINED SO; THE GOVERNMENT IN WASHINGTON WITH ITS COLONIZATION PROGRAM, CONSTITUTED THE SOLE SPONSOR WHICH ISIDORE FOUND HIMSELF FORCED TO LISTEN TO.

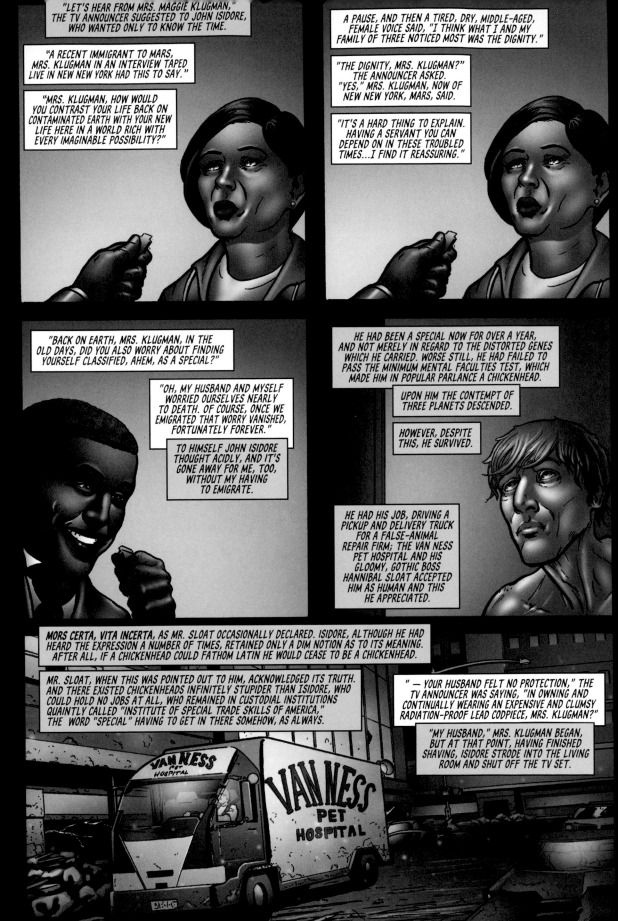

"LET'S HEAR FROM MRS. MAGGIE KLUGMAN," THE TV ANNOUNCER SUGGESTED TO JOHN ISIDORE, WHO WANTED ONLY TO KNOW THE TIME.

"A RECENT IMMIGRANT TO MARS, MRS. KLUGMAN IN AN INTERVIEW TAPED LIVE IN NEW NEW YORK HAD THIS TO SAY."

"MRS. KLUGMAN, HOW WOULD YOU CONTRAST YOUR LIFE BACK ON CONTAMINATED EARTH WITH YOUR NEW LIFE HERE IN A WORLD RICH WITH EVERY IMAGINABLE POSSIBILITY?"

A PAUSE, AND THEN A TIRED, DRY, MIDDLE-AGED, FEMALE VOICE SAID, "I THINK WHAT I AND MY FAMILY OF THREE NOTICED MOST WAS THE DIGNITY."

"THE DIGNITY, MRS. KLUGMAN?" THE ANNOUNCER ASKED. "YES," MRS. KLUGMAN, NOW OF NEW NEW YORK, MARS, SAID.

"IT'S A HARD THING TO EXPLAIN. HAVING A SERVANT YOU CAN DEPEND ON IN THESE TROUBLED TIMES...I FIND IT REASSURING."

"BACK ON EARTH, MRS. KLUGMAN, IN THE OLD DAYS, DID YOU ALSO WORRY ABOUT FINDING YOURSELF CLASSIFIED, AHEM, AS A SPECIAL?"

"OH, MY HUSBAND AND MYSELF WORRIED OURSELVES NEARLY TO DEATH. OF COURSE, ONCE WE EMIGRATED THAT WORRY VANISHED, FORTUNATELY FOREVER."

TO HIMSELF JOHN ISIDORE THOUGHT ACIDLY, AND IT'S GONE AWAY FOR ME, TOO, WITHOUT MY HAVING TO EMIGRATE.

HE HAD BEEN A SPECIAL NOW FOR OVER A YEAR, AND NOT MERELY IN REGARD TO THE DISTORTED GENES WHICH HE CARRIED. WORSE STILL, HE HAD FAILED TO PASS THE MINIMUM MENTAL FACULTIES TEST, WHICH MADE HIM IN POPULAR PARLANCE A CHICKENHEAD.

UPON HIM THE CONTEMPT OF THREE PLANETS DESCENDED.

HOWEVER, DESPITE THIS, HE SURVIVED.

HE HAD HIS JOB, DRIVING A PICKUP AND DELIVERY TRUCK FOR A FALSE-ANIMAL REPAIR FIRM; THE VAN NESS PET HOSPITAL AND HIS GLOOMY, GOTHIC BOSS HANNIBAL SLOAT ACCEPTED HIM AS HUMAN AND THIS HE APPRECIATED.

MORS CERTA, VITA INCERTA, AS MR. SLOAT OCCASIONALLY DECLARED. ISIDORE, ALTHOUGH HE HAD HEARD THE EXPRESSION A NUMBER OF TIMES, RETAINED ONLY A DIM NOTION AS TO ITS MEANING. AFTER ALL, IF A CHICKENHEAD COULD FATHOM LATIN HE WOULD CEASE TO BE A CHICKENHEAD.

MR. SLOAT, WHEN THIS WAS POINTED OUT TO HIM, ACKNOWLEDGED ITS TRUTH. AND THERE EXISTED CHICKENHEADS INFINITELY STUPIDER THAN ISIDORE, WHO COULD HOLD NO JOBS AT ALL, WHO REMAINED IN CUSTODIAL INSTITUTIONS QUAINTLY CALLED "INSTITUTE OF SPECIAL TRADE SKILLS OF AMERICA," THE WORD "SPECIAL" HAVING TO GET IN THERE SOMEHOW, AS ALWAYS.

" — YOUR HUSBAND FELT NO PROTECTION," THE TV ANNOUNCER WAS SAYING, "IN OWNING AND CONTINUALLY WEARING AN EXPENSIVE AND CLUMSY RADIATION-PROOF LEAD CODPIECE, MRS. KLUGMAN?"

"MY HUSBAND," MRS. KLUGMAN BEGAN, BUT AT THAT POINT, HAVING FINISHED SHAVING, ISIDORE STRODE INTO THE LIVING ROOM AND SHUT OFF THE TV SET.

VAN NESS PET HOSPITAL

VAN NESS PET HOSPITAL

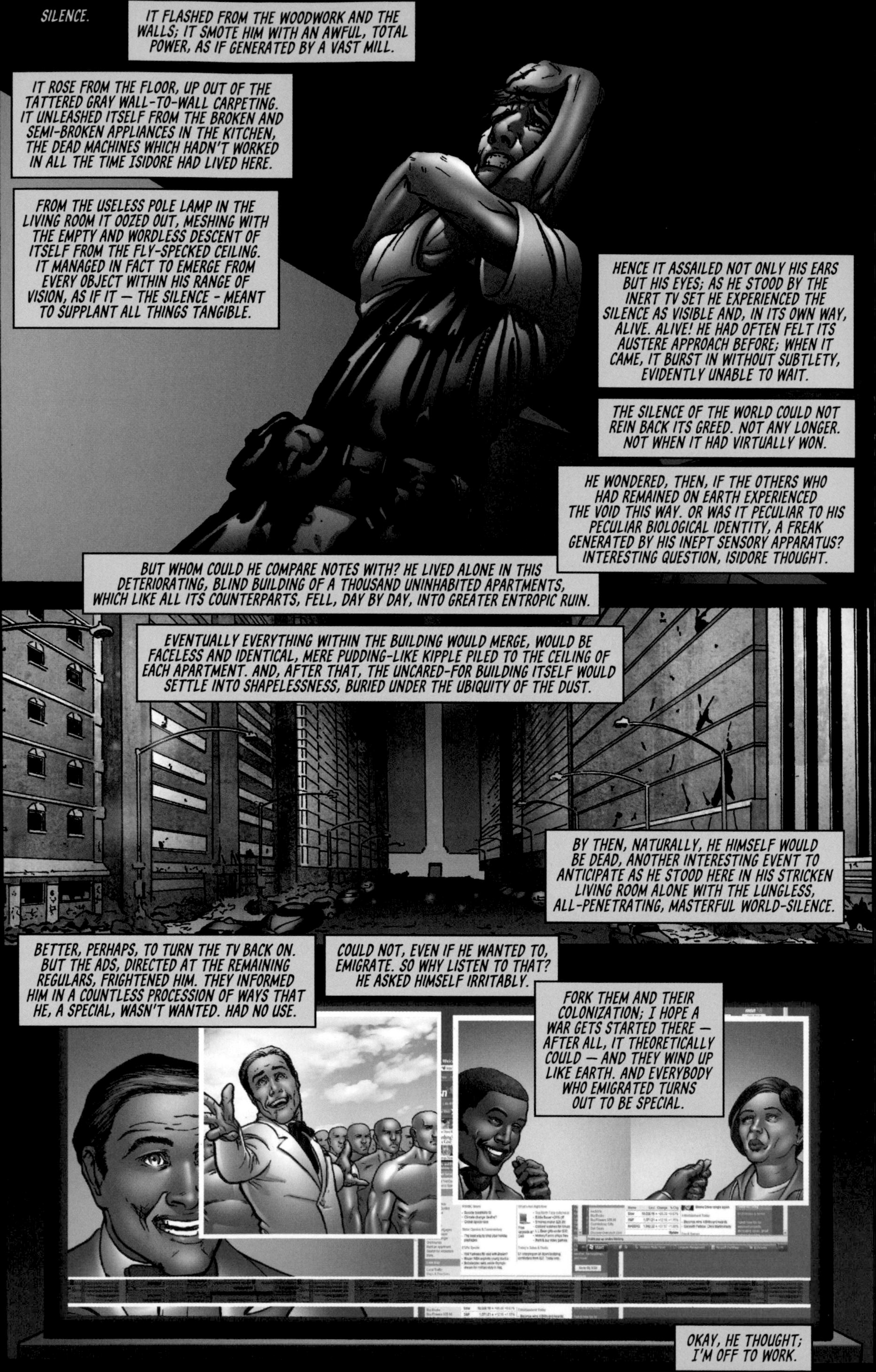
SILENCE.
IT FLASHED FROM THE WOODWORK AND THE WALLS; IT SMOTE HIM WITH AN AWFUL, TOTAL POWER, AS IF GENERATED BY A VAST MILL.
IT ROSE FROM THE FLOOR, UP OUT OF THE TATTERED GRAY WALL-TO-WALL CARPETING. IT UNLEASHED ITSELF FROM THE BROKEN AND SEMI-BROKEN APPLIANCES IN THE KITCHEN, THE DEAD MACHINES WHICH HADN'T WORKED IN ALL THE TIME ISIDORE HAD LIVED HERE.
FROM THE USELESS POLE LAMP IN THE LIVING ROOM IT OOZED OUT, MESHING WITH THE EMPTY AND WORDLESS DESCENT OF ITSELF FROM THE FLY-SPECKED CEILING. IT MANAGED IN FACT TO EMERGE FROM EVERY OBJECT WITHIN HIS RANGE OF VISION, AS IF IT — THE SILENCE - MEANT TO SUPPLANT ALL THINGS TANGIBLE.
HENCE IT ASSAILED NOT ONLY HIS EARS BUT HIS EYES; AS HE STOOD BY THE INERT TV SET HE EXPERIENCED THE SILENCE AS VISIBLE AND, IN ITS OWN WAY, ALIVE. ALIVE! HE HAD OFTEN FELT ITS AUSTERE APPROACH BEFORE; WHEN IT CAME, IT BURST IN WITHOUT SUBTLETY, EVIDENTLY UNABLE TO WAIT.
THE SILENCE OF THE WORLD COULD NOT REIN BACK ITS GREED. NOT ANY LONGER. NOT WHEN IT HAD VIRTUALLY WON.
HE WONDERED, THEN, IF THE OTHERS WHO HAD REMAINED ON EARTH EXPERIENCED THE VOID THIS WAY. OR WAS IT PECULIAR TO HIS PECULIAR BIOLOGICAL IDENTITY, A FREAK GENERATED BY HIS INEPT SENSORY APPARATUS? INTERESTING QUESTION, ISIDORE THOUGHT.
BUT WHOM COULD HE COMPARE NOTES WITH? HE LIVED ALONE IN THIS DETERIORATING, BLIND BUILDING OF A THOUSAND UNINHABITED APARTMENTS, WHICH LIKE ALL ITS COUNTERPARTS, FELL, DAY BY DAY, INTO GREATER ENTROPIC RUIN.
EVENTUALLY EVERYTHING WITHIN THE BUILDING WOULD MERGE, WOULD BE FACELESS AND IDENTICAL, MERE PUDDING-LIKE KIPPLE PILED TO THE CEILING OF EACH APARTMENT. AND, AFTER THAT, THE UNCARED-FOR BUILDING ITSELF WOULD SETTLE INTO SHAPELESSNESS, BURIED UNDER THE UBIQUITY OF THE DUST.
BY THEN, NATURALLY, HE HIMSELF WOULD BE DEAD, ANOTHER INTERESTING EVENT TO ANTICIPATE AS HE STOOD HERE IN HIS STRICKEN LIVING ROOM ALONE WITH THE LUNGLESS, ALL-PENETRATING, MASTERFUL WORLD-SILENCE.
BETTER, PERHAPS, TO TURN THE TV BACK ON. BUT THE ADS, DIRECTED AT THE REMAINING REGULARS, FRIGHTENED HIM. THEY INFORMED HIM IN A COUNTLESS PROCESSION OF WAYS THAT HE, A SPECIAL, WASN'T WANTED. HAD NO USE.
COULD NOT, EVEN IF HE WANTED TO, EMIGRATE. SO WHY LISTEN TO THAT? HE ASKED HIMSELF IRRITABLY.
FORK THEM AND THEIR COLONIZATION; I HOPE A WAR GETS STARTED THERE — AFTER ALL, IT THEORETICALLY COULD — AND THEY WIND UP LIKE EARTH. AND EVERYBODY WHO EMIGRATED TURNS OUT TO BE SPECIAL.
OKAY, HE THOUGHT; I'M OFF TO WORK.

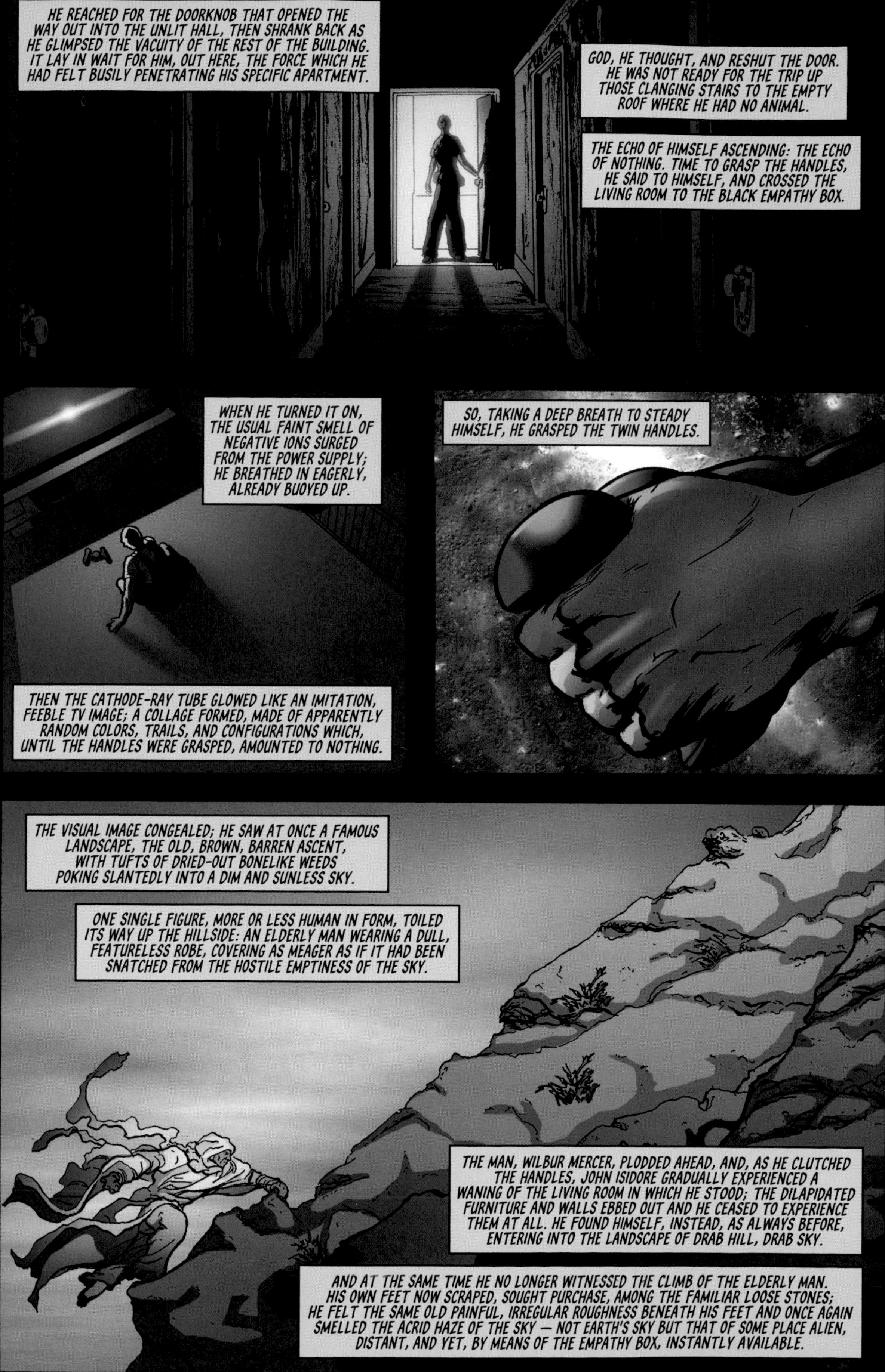
HE REACHED FOR THE DOORKNOB THAT OPENED THE WAY OUT INTO THE UNLIT HALL, THEN SHRANK BACK AS HE GLIMPSED THE VACUITY OF THE REST OF THE BUILDING. IT LAY IN WAIT FOR HIM, OUT HERE, THE FORCE WHICH HE HAD FELT BUSILY PENETRATING HIS SPECIFIC APARTMENT.
GOD, HE THOUGHT, AND RESHUT THE DOOR. HE WAS NOT READY FOR THE TRIP UP THOSE CLANGING STAIRS TO THE EMPTY ROOF WHERE HE HAD NO ANIMAL.
THE ECHO OF HIMSELF ASCENDING: THE ECHO OF NOTHING. TIME TO GRASP THE HANDLES, HE SAID TO HIMSELF, AND CROSSED THE LIVING ROOM TO THE BLACK EMPATHY BOX.
WHEN HE TURNED IT ON, THE USUAL FAINT SMELL OF NEGATIVE IONS SURGED FROM THE POWER SUPPLY; HE BREATHED IN EAGERLY, ALREADY BUOYED UP.
THEN THE CATHODE-RAY TUBE GLOWED LIKE AN IMITATION, FEEBLE TV IMAGE; A COLLAGE FORMED, MADE OF APPARENTLY RANDOM COLORS, TRAILS, AND CONFIGURATIONS WHICH, UNTIL THE HANDLES WERE GRASPED, AMOUNTED TO NOTHING.
SO, TAKING A DEEP BREATH TO STEADY HIMSELF, HE GRASPED THE TWIN HANDLES.
THE VISUAL IMAGE CONGEALED; HE SAW AT ONCE A FAMOUS LANDSCAPE, THE OLD, BROWN, BARREN ASCENT, WITH TUFTS OF DRIED-OUT BONELIKE WEEDS POKING SLANTEDLY INTO A DIM AND SUNLESS SKY.
ONE SINGLE FIGURE, MORE OR LESS HUMAN IN FORM, TOILED ITS WAY UP THE HILLSIDE: AN ELDERLY MAN WEARING A DULL, FEATURELESS ROBE, COVERING AS MEAGER AS IF IT HAD BEEN SNATCHED FROM THE HOSTILE EMPTINESS OF THE SKY.
THE MAN, WILBUR MERCER, PLODDED AHEAD, AND, AS HE CLUTCHED THE HANDLES, JOHN ISIDORE GRADUALLY EXPERIENCED A WANING OF THE LIVING ROOM IN WHICH HE STOOD; THE DILAPIDATED FURNITURE AND WALLS EBBED OUT AND HE CEASED TO EXPERIENCE THEM AT ALL. HE FOUND HIMSELF, INSTEAD, AS ALWAYS BEFORE, ENTERING INTO THE LANDSCAPE OF DRAB HILL, DRAB SKY.
AND AT THE SAME TIME HE NO LONGER WITNESSED THE CLIMB OF THE ELDERLY MAN. HIS OWN FEET NOW SCRAPED, SOUGHT PURCHASE, AMONG THE FAMILIAR LOOSE STONES; HE FELT THE SAME OLD PAINFUL, IRREGULAR ROUGHNESS BENEATH HIS FEET AND ONCE AGAIN SMELLED THE ACRID HAZE OF THE SKY — NOT EARTH'S SKY BUT THAT OF SOME PLACE ALIEN, DISTANT, AND YET, BY MEANS OF THE EMPATHY BOX, INSTANTLY AVAILABLE.

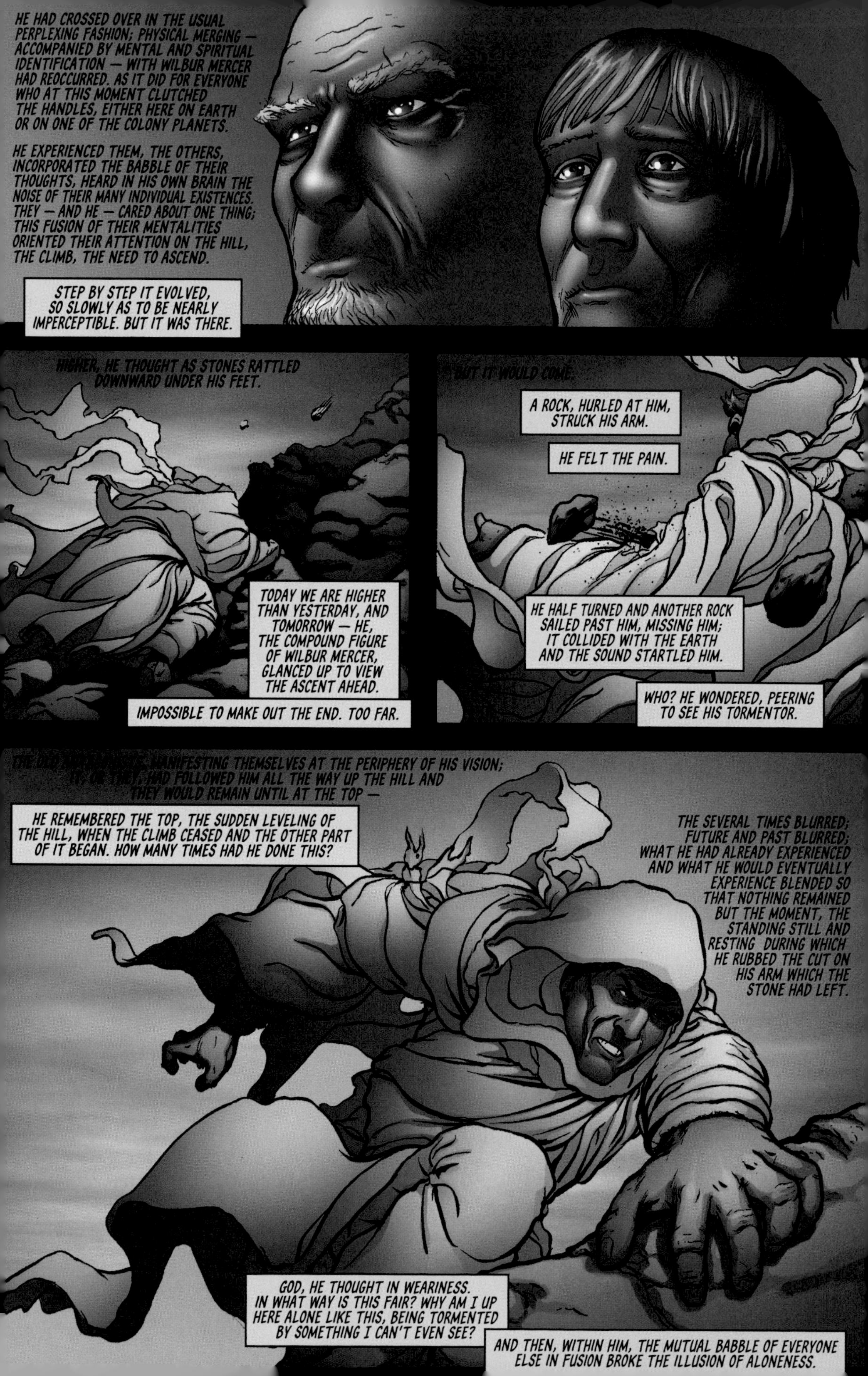
HE HAD CROSSED OVER IN THE USUAL PERPLEXING FASHION; PHYSICAL MERGING — ACCOMPANIED BY MENTAL AND SPIRITUAL IDENTIFICATION — WITH WILBUR MERCER HAD REOCCURRED. AS IT DID FOR EVERYONE WHO AT THIS MOMENT CLUTCHED THE HANDLES, EITHER HERE ON EARTH OR ON ONE OF THE COLONY PLANETS.
HE EXPERIENCED THEM, THE OTHERS, INCORPORATED THE BABBLE OF THEIR THOUGHTS, HEARD IN HIS OWN BRAIN THE NOISE OF THEIR MANY INDIVIDUAL EXISTENCES. THEY — AND HE — CARED ABOUT ONE THING; THIS FUSION OF THEIR MENTALITIES ORIENTED THEIR ATTENTION ON THE HILL, THE CLIMB, THE NEED TO ASCEND.
STEP BY STEP IT EVOLVED, SO SLOWLY AS TO BE NEARLY IMPERCEPTIBLE. BUT IT WAS THERE.
HIGHER, HE THOUGHT AS STONES RATTLED DOWNWARD UNDER HIS FEET.
TODAY WE ARE HIGHER THAN YESTERDAY, AND TOMORROW — HE, THE COMPOUND FIGURE OF WILBUR MERCER, GLANCED UP TO VIEW THE ASCENT AHEAD.
IMPOSSIBLE TO MAKE OUT THE END. TOO FAR.
BUT IT WOULD COME.
A ROCK, HURLED AT HIM, STRUCK HIS ARM.
HE FELT THE PAIN.
HE HALF TURNED AND ANOTHER ROCK SAILED PAST HIM, MISSING HIM; IT COLLIDED WITH THE EARTH AND THE SOUND STARTLED HIM.
WHO? HE WONDERED, PEERING TO SEE HIS TORMENTOR.
MANIFESTING THEMSELVES AT THE PERIPHERY OF HIS VISION;
HAD FOLLOWED HIM ALL THE WAY UP THE HILL AND THEY WOULD REMAIN UNTIL AT THE TOP —
HE REMEMBERED THE TOP, THE SUDDEN LEVELING OF THE HILL, WHEN THE CLIMB CEASED AND THE OTHER PART OF IT BEGAN. HOW MANY TIMES HAD HE DONE THIS?
THE SEVERAL TIMES BLURRED; FUTURE AND PAST BLURRED; WHAT HE HAD ALREADY EXPERIENCED AND WHAT HE WOULD EVENTUALLY EXPERIENCE BLENDED SO THAT NOTHING REMAINED BUT THE MOMENT, THE STANDING STILL AND RESTING DURING WHICH HE RUBBED THE CUT ON HIS ARM WHICH THE STONE HAD LEFT.
GOD, HE THOUGHT IN WEARINESS. IN WHAT WAY IS THIS FAIR? WHY AM I UP HERE ALONE LIKE THIS, BEING TORMENTED BY SOMETHING I CAN'T EVEN SEE?
AND THEN, WITHIN HIM, THE MUTUAL BABBLE OF EVERYONE ELSE IN FUSION BROKE THE ILLUSION OF ALONENESS.

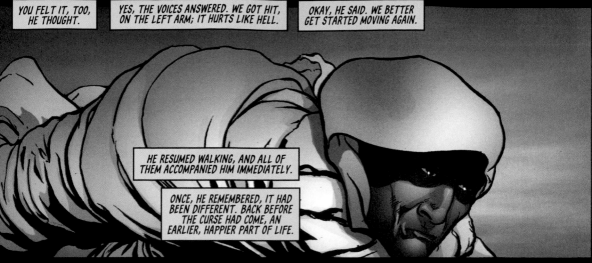

YOU FELT IT, TOO, HE THOUGHT.

YES, THE VOICES ANSWERED. WE GOT HIT, ON THE LEFT ARM; IT HURTS LIKE HELL.

OKAY, HE SAID. WE BETTER GET STARTED MOVING AGAIN.

HE RESUMED WALKING, AND ALL OF THEM ACCOMPANIED HIM IMMEDIATELY.

ONCE, HE REMEMBERED, IT HAD BEEN DIFFERENT. BACK BEFORE THE CURSE HAD COME, AN EARLIER, HAPPIER PART OF LIFE.

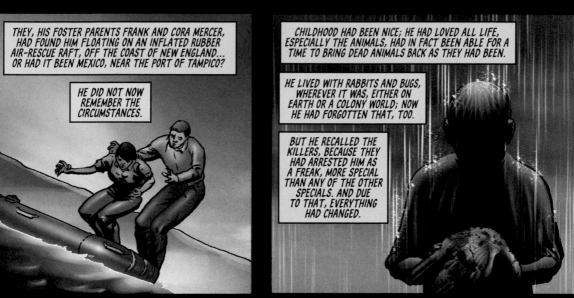

THEY, HIS FOSTER PARENTS FRANK AND CORA MERCER, HAD FOUND HIM FLOATING ON AN INFLATED RUBBER AIR-RESCUE RAFT, OFF THE COAST OF NEW ENGLAND... OR HAD IT BEEN MEXICO, NEAR THE PORT OF TAMPICO?

HE DID NOT NOW REMEMBER THE CIRCUMSTANCES.

CHILDHOOD HAD BEEN NICE; HE HAD LOVED ALL LIFE, ESPECIALLY THE ANIMALS, HAD IN FACT BEEN ABLE FOR A TIME TO BRING DEAD ANIMALS BACK AS THEY HAD BEEN.

HE LIVED WITH RABBITS AND BUGS, WHEREVER IT WAS, EITHER ON EARTH OR A COLONY WORLD; NOW HE HAD FORGOTTEN THAT, TOO.

BUT HE RECALLED THE KILLERS, BECAUSE THEY HAD ARRESTED HIM AS A FREAK, MORE SPECIAL THAN ANY OF THE OTHER SPECIALS. AND DUE TO THAT, EVERYTHING HAD CHANGED.

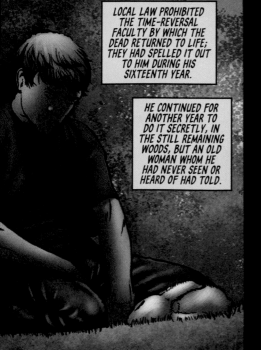

LOCAL LAW PROHIBITED THE TIME-REVERSAL FACULTY BY WHICH THE DEAD RETURNED TO LIFE; THEY HAD SPELLED IT OUT TO HIM DURING HIS SIXTEENTH YEAR.

HE CONTINUED FOR ANOTHER YEAR TO DO IT SECRETLY, IN THE STILL REMAINING WOODS, BUT AN OLD WOMAN WHOM HE HAD NEVER SEEN OR HEARD OF HAD TOLD.

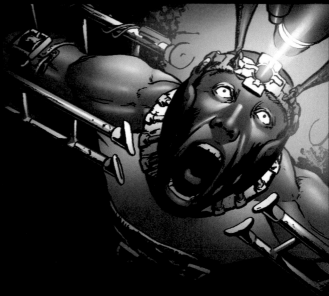

WITHOUT HIS PARENTS' CONSENT THEY — THE KILLERS — HAD BOMBARDED THE UNIQUE NODULE WHICH HAD FORMED IN HIS BRAIN, HAD ATTACKED IT WITH RADIOACTIVE COBALT, AND THIS HAD PLUNGED HIM INTO A DIFFERENT WORLD, ONE WHOSE EXISTENCE HE HAD NEVER SUSPECTED.

IT HAD BEEN A PIT OF CORPSES AND DEAD BONES AND HE HAD STRUGGLED FOR YEARS TO GET UP FROM IT. THE DONKEY AND ESPECIALLY THE TOAD, THE CREATURES MOST IMPORTANT TO HIM, HAD VANISHED, HAD BECOME EXTINCT; ONLY ROTTING FRAGMENTS, AN EYELESS HEAD HERE, PART OF A HAND THERE, REMAINED.

AT LAST A BIRD WHICH HAD COME THERE TO DIE TOLD HIM WHERE HE WAS.

HE HAD SUNK DOWN INTO THE TOMB WORLD.

HE COULD NOT GET OUT UNTIL THE BONES STREWN AROUND HIM GREW BACK INTO LIVING CREATURES; HE HAD BECOME JOINED TO THE METABOLISM OF OTHER LIVES, AND UNTIL THEY ROSE HE COULD NOT RISE EITHER.

HOW LONG THAT PART OF THE CYCLE HAD LASTED HE DID NOT NOW KNOW; NOTHING HAD HAPPENED, GENERALLY, SO IT HAD BEEN MEASURELESS. BUT AT LAST THE BONES HAD REGAINED FLESH; THE EMPTY EYEPITS HAD FILLED UP AND THE NEW EYES HAD SEEN, WHILE MEANTIME THE RESTORED BEAKS AND MOUTHS HAD CACKLED, BARKED, AND CATERWAULED.

POSSIBLY HE HAD DONE IT; PERHAPS THE EXTRASENSORY NODE OF HIS BRAIN HAD FINALLY GROWN BACK. OR MAYBE HE HADN'T ACCOMPLISHED IT; VERY LIKELY IT COULD HAVE BEEN A NATURAL PROCESS.

ANYHOW HE WAS NO LONGER SINKING; HE HAD BEGUN TO ASCEND, ALONG WITH THE OTHERS. LONG AGO HE HAD LOST SIGHT OF THEM. HE FOUND HIMSELF EVIDENTLY CLIMBING ALONE. BUT THEY WERE THERE. THEY STILL ACCOMPANIED HIM; HE FELT THEM, STRANGELY, INSIDE HIM.

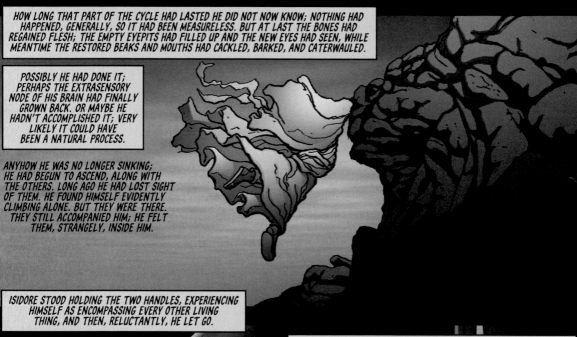

ISIDORE STOOD HOLDING THE TWO HANDLES, EXPERIENCING HIMSELF AS ENCOMPASSING EVERY OTHER LIVING THING, AND THEN, RELUCTANTLY, HE LET GO.

RELEASING THE HANDLES, HE EXAMINED HIS ARM, THEN MADE HIS WAY UNSTEADILY TO THE BATHROOM OF HIS APARTMENT TO WASH THE CUT OFF. THIS WAS NOT THE FIRST WOUND HE HAD RECEIVED WHILE IN FUSION WITH MERCER AND IT PROBABLY WOULD NOT BE THE LAST.

PEOPLE, ESPECIALLY ELDERLY ONES, HAD DIED, PARTICULARLY LATER ON AT THE TOP OF THE HILL WHEN THE TORMENT BEGAN IN EARNEST. I WONDER IF I CAN GO THROUGH THAT PART AGAIN, HE SAID TO HIMSELF AS HE SWABBED THE INJURY.

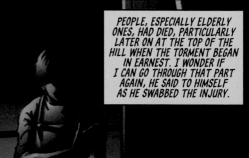

IT HAD TO END, AS ALWAYS, AND ANYHOW HIS ARM ACHED AND BLED WHERE THE ROCK HAD STRUCK IT.

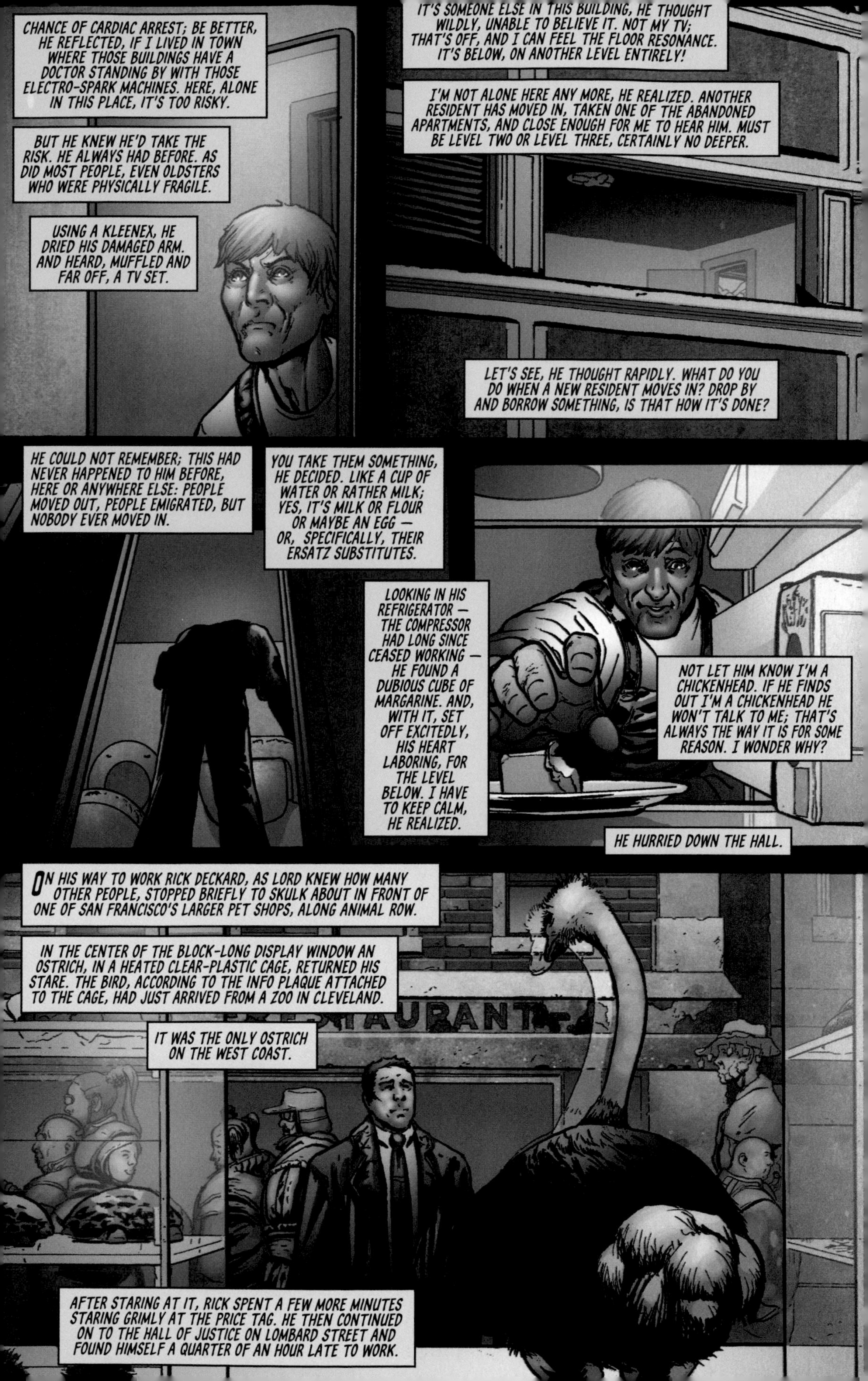
CHANCE OF CARDIAC ARREST; BE BETTER, HE REFLECTED, IF I LIVED IN TOWN WHERE THOSE BUILDINGS HAVE A DOCTOR STANDING BY WITH THOSE ELECTRO-SPARK MACHINES. HERE, ALONE IN THIS PLACE, IT'S TOO RISKY.
BUT HE KNEW HE'D TAKE THE RISK. HE ALWAYS HAD BEFORE. AS DID MOST PEOPLE, EVEN OLDSTERS WHO WERE PHYSICALLY FRAGILE.
USING A KLEENEX, HE DRIED HIS DAMAGED ARM. AND HEARD, MUFFLED AND FAR OFF, A TV SET.
IT'S SOMEONE ELSE IN THIS BUILDING, HE THOUGHT WILDLY, UNABLE TO BELIEVE IT. NOT MY TV; THAT'S OFF, AND I CAN FEEL THE FLOOR RESONANCE. IT'S BELOW, ON ANOTHER LEVEL ENTIRELY!
I'M NOT ALONE HERE ANY MORE, HE REALIZED. ANOTHER RESIDENT HAS MOVED IN, TAKEN ONE OF THE ABANDONED APARTMENTS, AND CLOSE ENOUGH FOR ME TO HEAR HIM. MUST BE LEVEL TWO OR LEVEL THREE, CERTAINLY NO DEEPER.
LET'S SEE, HE THOUGHT RAPIDLY. WHAT DO YOU DO WHEN A NEW RESIDENT MOVES IN? DROP BY AND BORROW SOMETHING, IS THAT HOW IT'S DONE?
HE COULD NOT REMEMBER; THIS HAD NEVER HAPPENED TO HIM BEFORE, HERE OR ANYWHERE ELSE: PEOPLE MOVED OUT, PEOPLE EMIGRATED, BUT NOBODY EVER MOVED IN.
YOU TAKE THEM SOMETHING, HE DECIDED. LIKE A CUP OF WATER OR RATHER MILK; YES, IT'S MILK OR FLOUR OR MAYBE AN EGG — OR, SPECIFICALLY, THEIR ERSATZ SUBSTITUTES.
LOOKING IN HIS REFRIGERATOR — THE COMPRESSOR HAD LONG SINCE CEASED WORKING — HE FOUND A DUBIOUS CUBE OF MARGARINE. AND, WITH IT, SET OFF EXCITEDLY, HIS HEART LABORING, FOR THE LEVEL BELOW. I HAVE TO KEEP CALM, HE REALIZED.
NOT LET HIM KNOW I'M A CHICKENHEAD. IF HE FINDS OUT I'M A CHICKENHEAD HE WON'T TALK TO ME; THAT'S ALWAYS THE WAY IT IS FOR SOME REASON. I WONDER WHY?
HE HURRIED DOWN THE HALL.
ON HIS WAY TO WORK RICK DECKARD, AS LORD KNEW HOW MANY OTHER PEOPLE, STOPPED BRIEFLY TO SKULK ABOUT IN FRONT OF ONE OF SAN FRANCISCO'S LARGER PET SHOPS, ALONG ANIMAL ROW.
IN THE CENTER OF THE BLOCK-LONG DISPLAY WINDOW AN OSTRICH, IN A HEATED CLEAR-PLASTIC CAGE, RETURNED HIS STARE. THE BIRD, ACCORDING TO THE INFO PLAQUE ATTACHED TO THE CAGE, HAD JUST ARRIVED FROM A ZOO IN CLEVELAND.
RESTAURANT
IT WAS THE ONLY OSTRICH ON THE WEST COAST.
AFTER STARING AT IT, RICK SPENT A FEW MORE MINUTES STARING GRIMLY AT THE PRICE TAG. HE THEN CONTINUED ON TO THE HALL OF JUSTICE ON LOMBARD STREET AND FOUND HIMSELF A QUARTER OF AN HOUR LATE TO WORK.

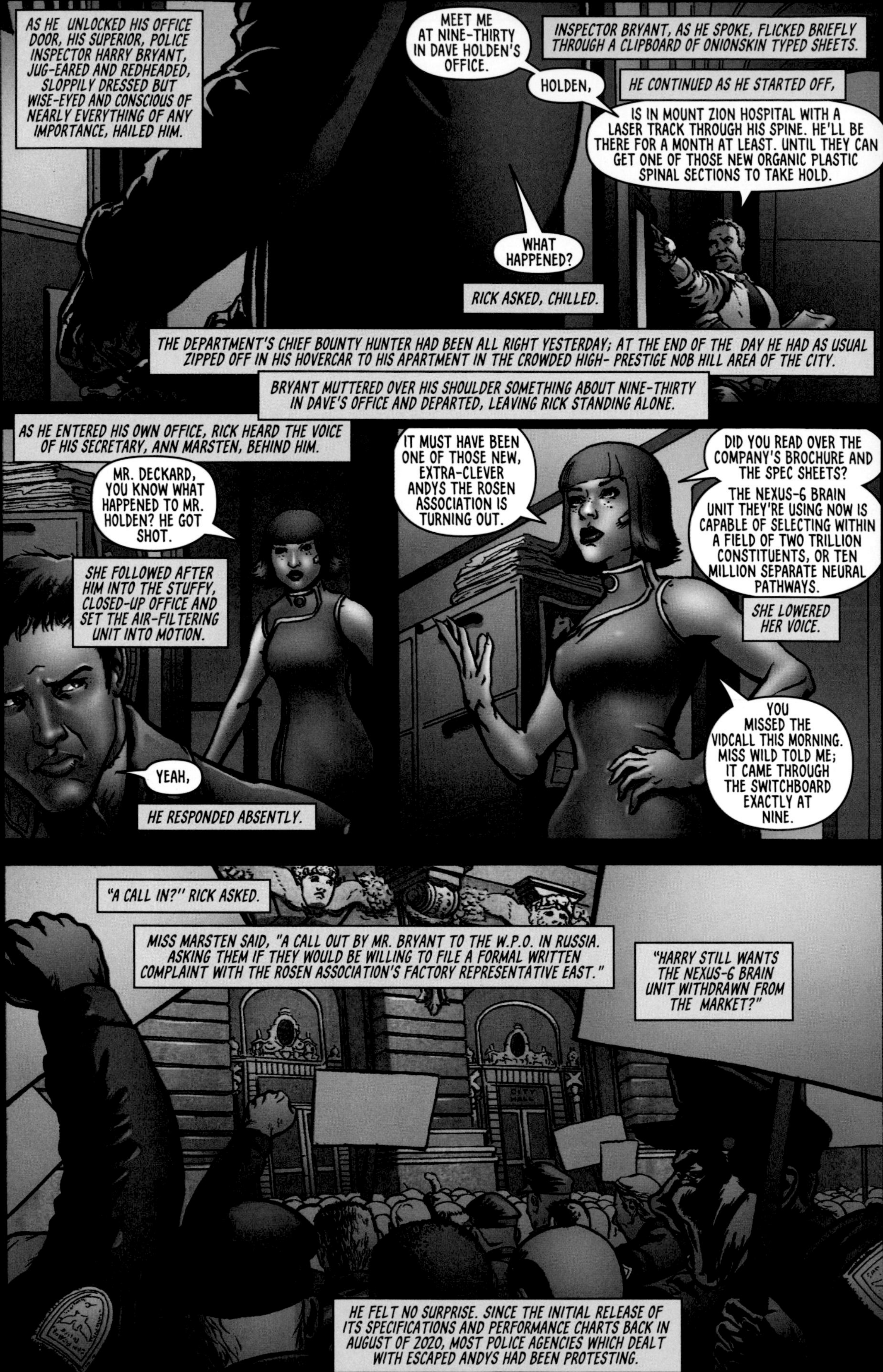
AS HE UNLOCKED HIS OFFICE DOOR, HIS SUPERIOR, POLICE INSPECTOR HARRY BRYANT, JUG-EARED AND REDHEADED, SLOPPILY DRESSED BUT WISE-EYED AND CONSCIOUS OF NEARLY EVERYTHING OF ANY IMPORTANCE, HAILED HIM.
MEET ME AT NINE-THIRTY IN DAVE HOLDEN'S OFFICE.
INSPECTOR BRYANT, AS HE SPOKE, FLICKED BRIEFLY THROUGH A CLIPBOARD OF ONIONSKIN TYPED SHEETS.
HOLDEN,
HE CONTINUED AS HE STARTED OFF,
IS IN MOUNT ZION HOSPITAL WITH A LASER TRACK THROUGH HIS SPINE. HE'LL BE THERE FOR A MONTH AT LEAST. UNTIL THEY CAN GET ONE OF THOSE NEW ORGANIC PLASTIC SPINAL SECTIONS TO TAKE HOLD.
WHAT HAPPENED?
RICK ASKED, CHILLED.
THE DEPARTMENT'S CHIEF BOUNTY HUNTER HAD BEEN ALL RIGHT YESTERDAY; AT THE END OF THE DAY HE HAD AS USUAL ZIPPED OFF IN HIS HOVERCAR TO HIS APARTMENT IN THE CROWDED HIGH- PRESTIGE NOB HILL AREA OF THE CITY.
BRYANT MUTTERED OVER HIS SHOULDER SOMETHING ABOUT NINE-THIRTY IN DAVE'S OFFICE AND DEPARTED, LEAVING RICK STANDING ALONE.
AS HE ENTERED HIS OWN OFFICE, RICK HEARD THE VOICE OF HIS SECRETARY, ANN MARSTEN, BEHIND HIM.
MR. DECKARD, YOU KNOW WHAT HAPPENED TO MR. HOLDEN? HE GOT SHOT.
SHE FOLLOWED AFTER HIM INTO THE STUFFY, CLOSED-UP OFFICE AND SET THE AIR-FILTERING UNIT INTO MOTION.
YEAH,
HE RESPONDED ABSENTLY.
IT MUST HAVE BEEN ONE OF THOSE NEW, EXTRA-CLEVER ANDYS THE ROSEN ASSOCIATION IS TURNING OUT.
DID YOU READ OVER THE COMPANY'S BROCHURE AND THE SPEC SHEETS?
THE NEXUS-6 BRAIN UNIT THEY'RE USING NOW IS CAPABLE OF SELECTING WITHIN A FIELD OF TWO TRILLION CONSTITUENTS, OR TEN MILLION SEPARATE NEURAL PATHWAYS.
SHE LOWERED HER VOICE.
YOU MISSED THE VIDCALL THIS MORNING. MISS WILD TOLD ME; IT CAME THROUGH THE SWITCHBOARD EXACTLY AT NINE.
"A CALL IN?" RICK ASKED.
MISS MARSTEN SAID, "A CALL OUT BY MR. BRYANT TO THE W.P.O. IN RUSSIA. ASKING THEM IF THEY WOULD BE WILLING TO FILE A FORMAL WRITTEN COMPLAINT WITH THE ROSEN ASSOCIATION'S FACTORY REPRESENTATIVE EAST."
"HARRY STILL WANTS THE NEXUS-6 BRAIN UNIT WITHDRAWN FROM THE MARKET?"
HE FELT NO SURPRISE. SINCE THE INITIAL RELEASE OF ITS SPECIFICATIONS AND PERFORMANCE CHARTS BACK IN AUGUST OF 2020, MOST POLICE AGENCIES WHICH DEALT WITH ESCAPED ANDYS HAD BEEN PROTESTING.

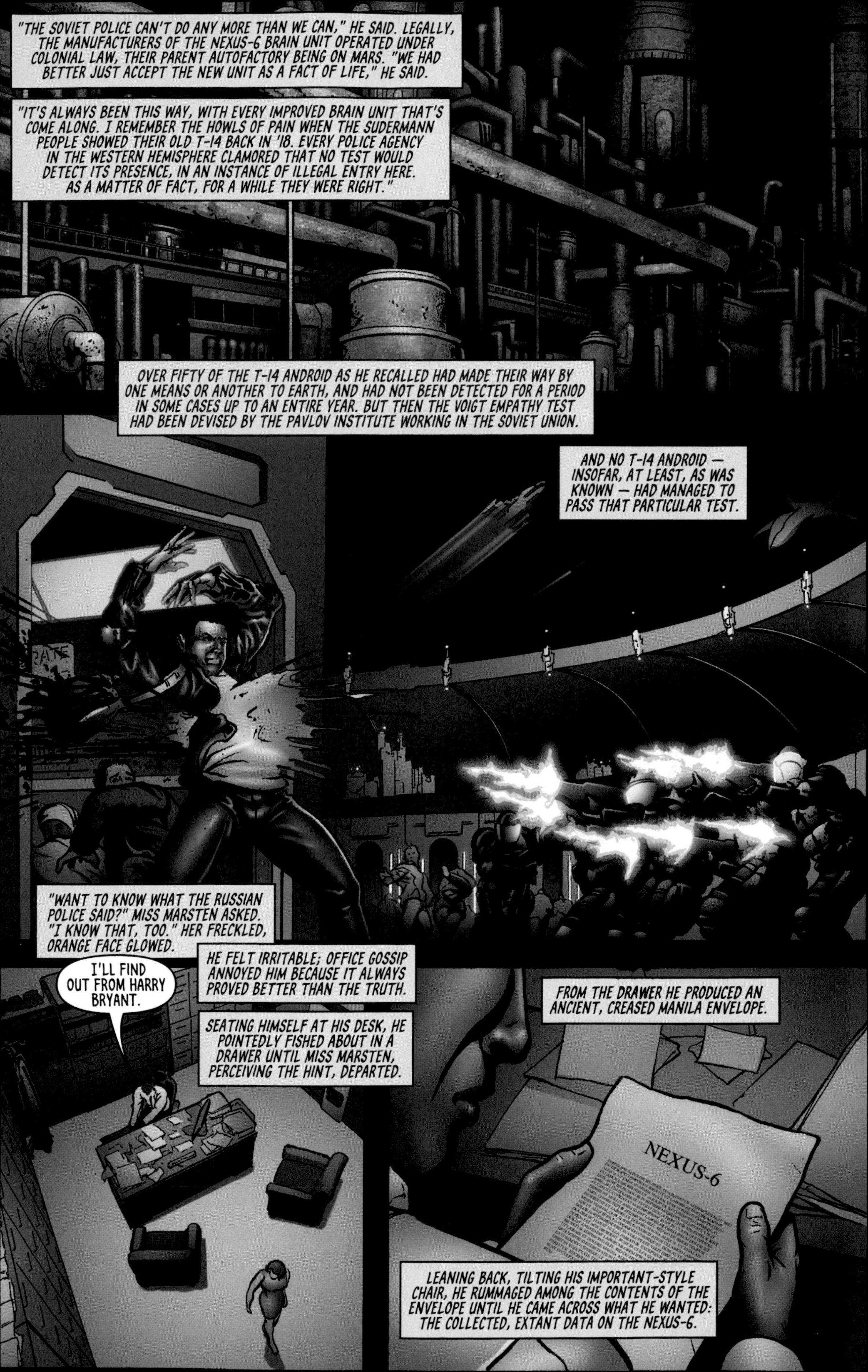
"THE SOVIET POLICE CAN'T DO ANY MORE THAN WE CAN," HE SAID. LEGALLY, THE MANUFACTURERS OF THE NEXUS-6 BRAIN UNIT OPERATED UNDER COLONIAL LAW, THEIR PARENT AUTOFACTORY BEING ON MARS. "WE HAD BETTER JUST ACCEPT THE NEW UNIT AS A FACT OF LIFE," HE SAID.
"IT'S ALWAYS BEEN THIS WAY, WITH EVERY IMPROVED BRAIN UNIT THAT'S COME ALONG. I REMEMBER THE HOWLS OF PAIN WHEN THE SUDERMANN PEOPLE SHOWED THEIR OLD T-14 BACK IN '18. EVERY POLICE AGENCY IN THE WESTERN HEMISPHERE CLAMORED THAT NO TEST WOULD DETECT ITS PRESENCE, IN AN INSTANCE OF ILLEGAL ENTRY HERE. AS A MATTER OF FACT, FOR A WHILE THEY WERE RIGHT."
OVER FIFTY OF THE T-14 ANDROID AS HE RECALLED HAD MADE THEIR WAY BY ONE MEANS OR ANOTHER TO EARTH, AND HAD NOT BEEN DETECTED FOR A PERIOD IN SOME CASES UP TO AN ENTIRE YEAR. BUT THEN THE VOIGT EMPATHY TEST HAD BEEN DEVISED BY THE PAVLOV INSTITUTE WORKING IN THE SOVIET UNION.
AND NO T-14 ANDROID — INSOFAR, AT LEAST, AS WAS KNOWN — HAD MANAGED TO PASS THAT PARTICULAR TEST.
"WANT TO KNOW WHAT THE RUSSIAN POLICE SAID?" MISS MARSTEN ASKED. "I KNOW THAT, TOO." HER FRECKLED, ORANGE FACE GLOWED.
I'LL FIND OUT FROM HARRY BRYANT.
HE FELT IRRITABLE; OFFICE GOSSIP ANNOYED HIM BECAUSE IT ALWAYS PROVED BETTER THAN THE TRUTH.
SEATING HIMSELF AT HIS DESK, HE POINTEDLY FISHED ABOUT IN A DRAWER UNTIL MISS MARSTEN, PERCEIVING THE HINT, DEPARTED.
FROM THE DRAWER HE PRODUCED AN ANCIENT, CREASED MANILA ENVELOPE.
NEXUS-6
LEANING BACK, TILTING HIS IMPORTANT-STYLE CHAIR, HE RUMMAGED AMONG THE CONTENTS OF THE ENVELOPE UNTIL HE CAME ACROSS WHAT HE WANTED: THE COLLECTED, EXTANT DATA ON THE NEXUS-6.

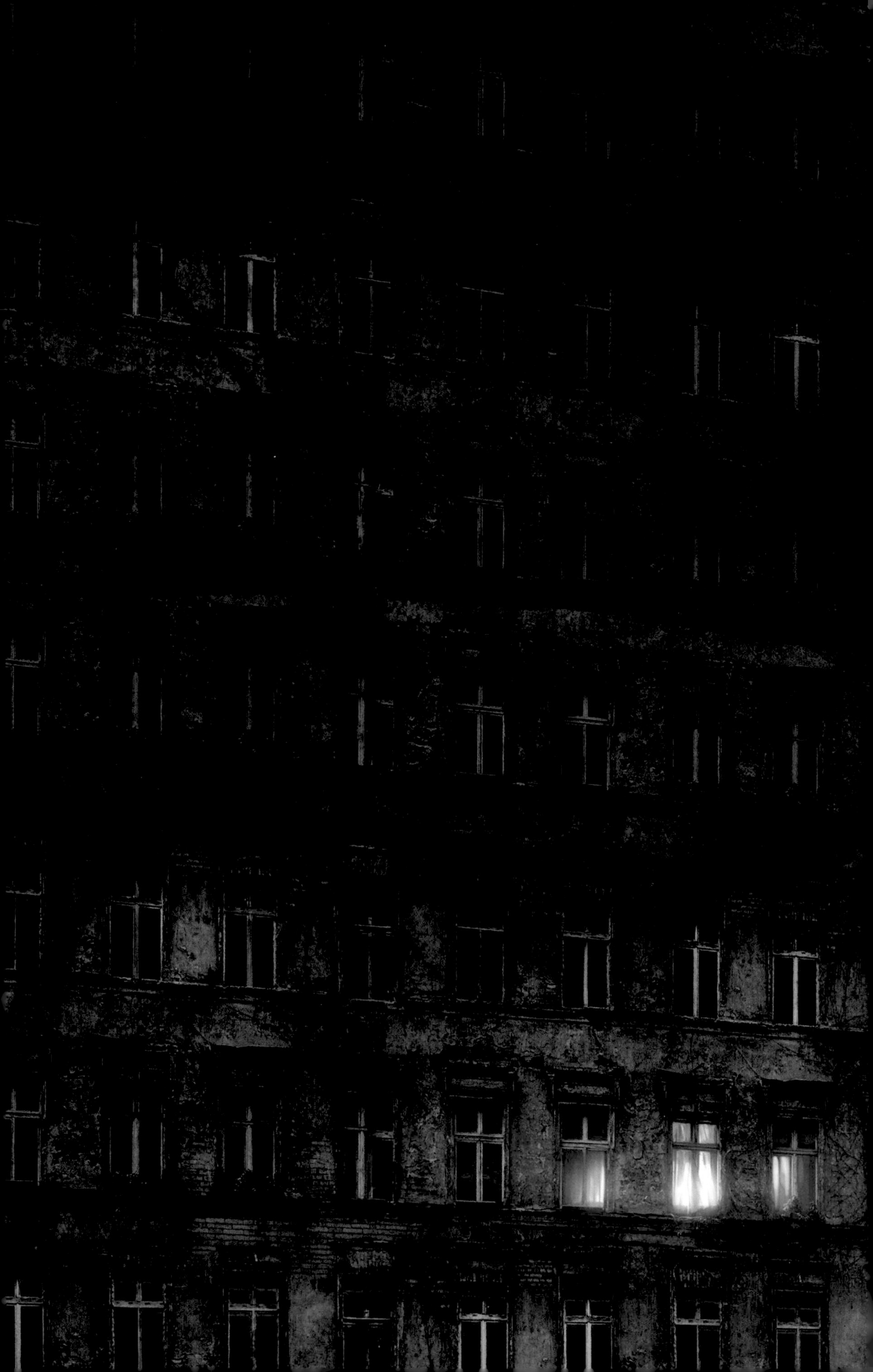

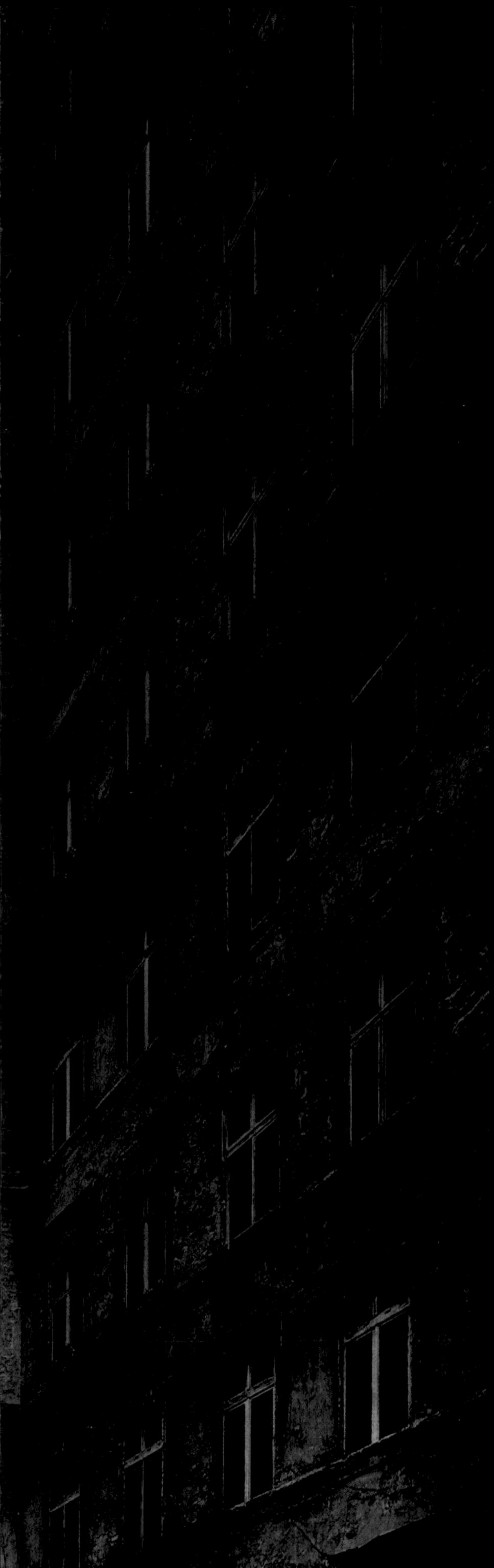

BOOK
TWO

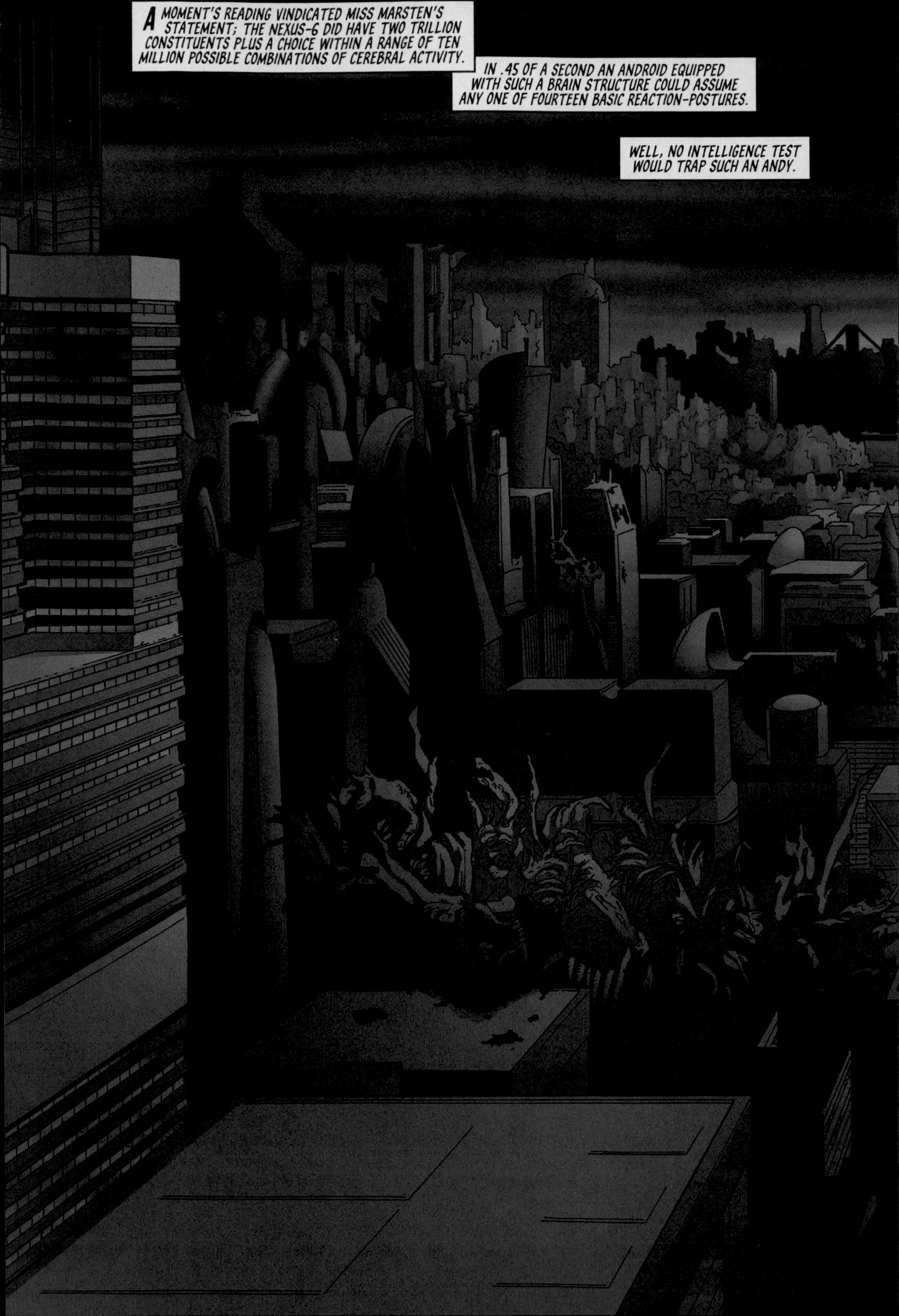
A MOMENT'S READING VINDICATED MISS MARSTEN'S STATEMENT; THE NEXUS-6 DID HAVE TWO TRILLION CONSTITUENTS PLUS A CHOICE WITHIN A RANGE OF TEN MILLION POSSIBLE COMBINATIONS OF CEREBRAL ACTIVITY.
IN .45 OF A SECOND AN ANDROID EQUIPPED WITH SUCH A BRAIN STRUCTURE COULD ASSUME ANY ONE OF FOURTEEN BASIC REACTION-POSTURES.
WELL, NO INTELLIGENCE TEST WOULD TRAP SUCH AN ANDY.

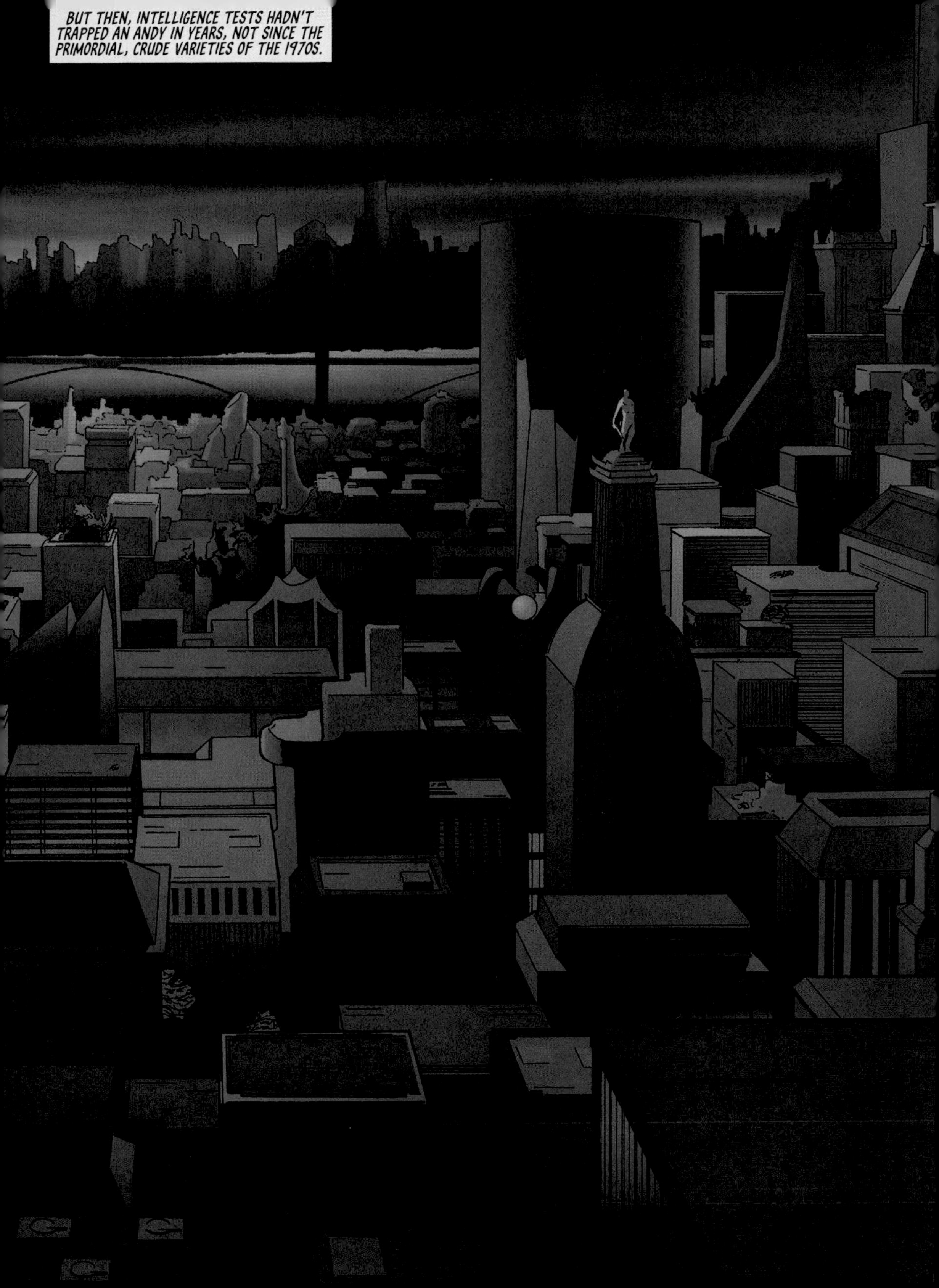
BUT THEN, INTELLIGENCE TESTS HADN'T TRAPPED AN ANDY IN YEARS, NOT SINCE THE PRIMORDIAL, CRUDE VARIETIES OF THE 1970S.

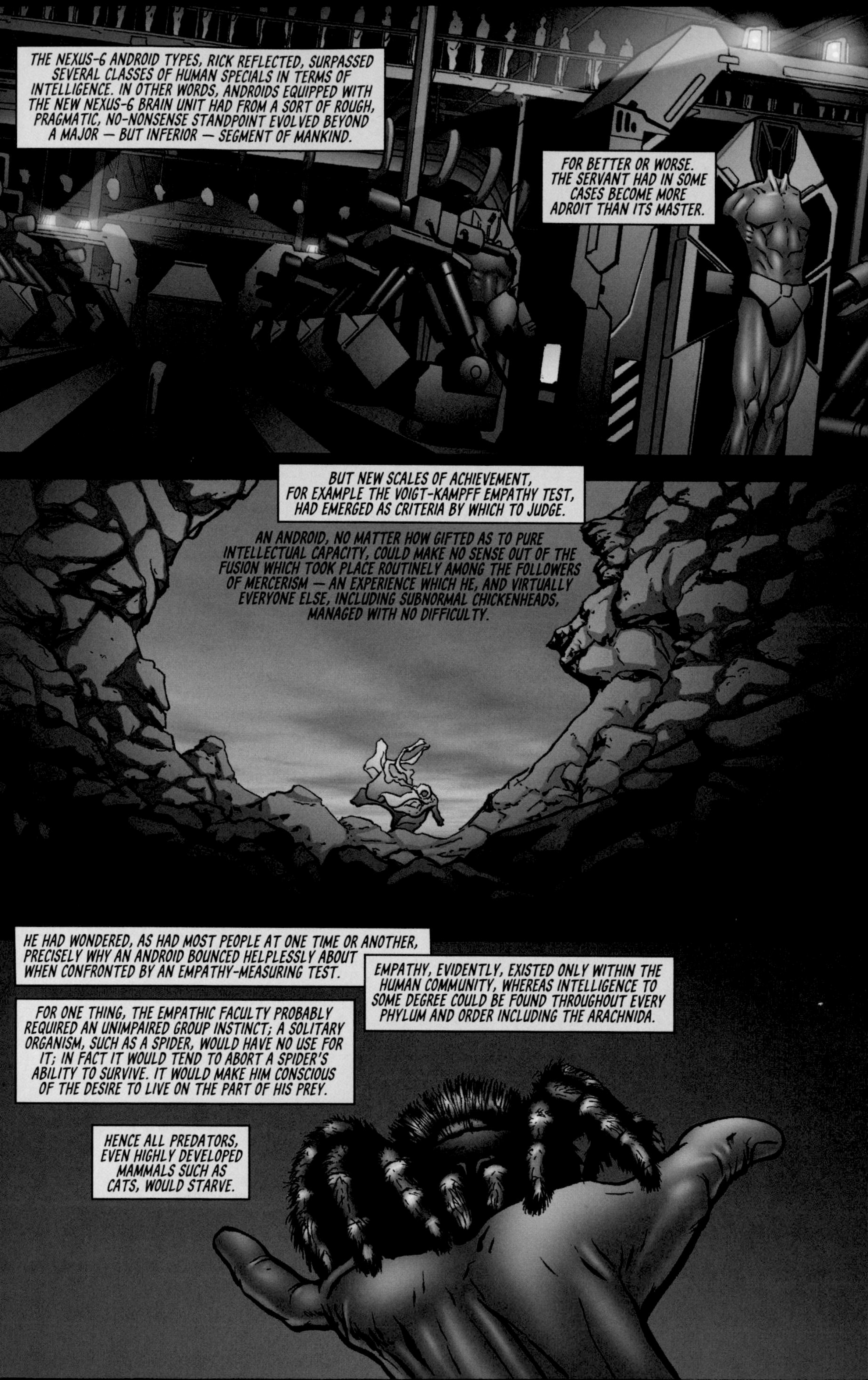
THE NEXUS-6 ANDROID TYPES, RICK REFLECTED, SURPASSED SEVERAL CLASSES OF HUMAN SPECIALS IN TERMS OF INTELLIGENCE. IN OTHER WORDS, ANDROIDS EQUIPPED WITH THE NEW NEXUS-6 BRAIN UNIT HAD FROM A SORT OF ROUGH, PRAGMATIC, NO-NONSENSE STANDPOINT EVOLVED BEYOND A MAJOR — BUT INFERIOR — SEGMENT OF MANKIND.
FOR BETTER OR WORSE. THE SERVANT HAD IN SOME CASES BECOME MORE ADROIT THAN ITS MASTER.
BUT NEW SCALES OF ACHIEVEMENT, FOR EXAMPLE THE VOIGT-KAMPFF EMPATHY TEST, HAD EMERGED AS CRITERIA BY WHICH TO JUDGE.
AN ANDROID, NO MATTER HOW GIFTED AS TO PURE INTELLECTUAL CAPACITY, COULD MAKE NO SENSE OUT OF THE FUSION WHICH TOOK PLACE ROUTINELY AMONG THE FOLLOWERS OF MERCERISM — AN EXPERIENCE WHICH HE, AND VIRTUALLY EVERYONE ELSE, INCLUDING SUBNORMAL CHICKENHEADS, MANAGED WITH NO DIFFICULTY.
HE HAD WONDERED, AS HAD MOST PEOPLE AT ONE TIME OR ANOTHER, PRECISELY WHY AN ANDROID BOUNCED HELPLESSLY ABOUT WHEN CONFRONTED BY AN EMPATHY-MEASURING TEST.
EMPATHY, EVIDENTLY, EXISTED ONLY WITHIN THE HUMAN COMMUNITY, WHEREAS INTELLIGENCE TO SOME DEGREE COULD BE FOUND THROUGHOUT EVERY PHYLUM AND ORDER INCLUDING THE ARACHNIDA.
FOR ONE THING, THE EMPATHIC FACULTY PROBABLY REQUIRED AN UNIMPAIRED GROUP INSTINCT; A SOLITARY ORGANISM, SUCH AS A SPIDER, WOULD HAVE NO USE FOR IT; IN FACT IT WOULD TEND TO ABORT A SPIDER'S ABILITY TO SURVIVE. IT WOULD MAKE HIM CONSCIOUS OF THE DESIRE TO LIVE ON THE PART OF HIS PREY.
HENCE ALL PREDATORS, EVEN HIGHLY DEVELOPED MAMMALS SUCH AS CATS, WOULD STARVE.

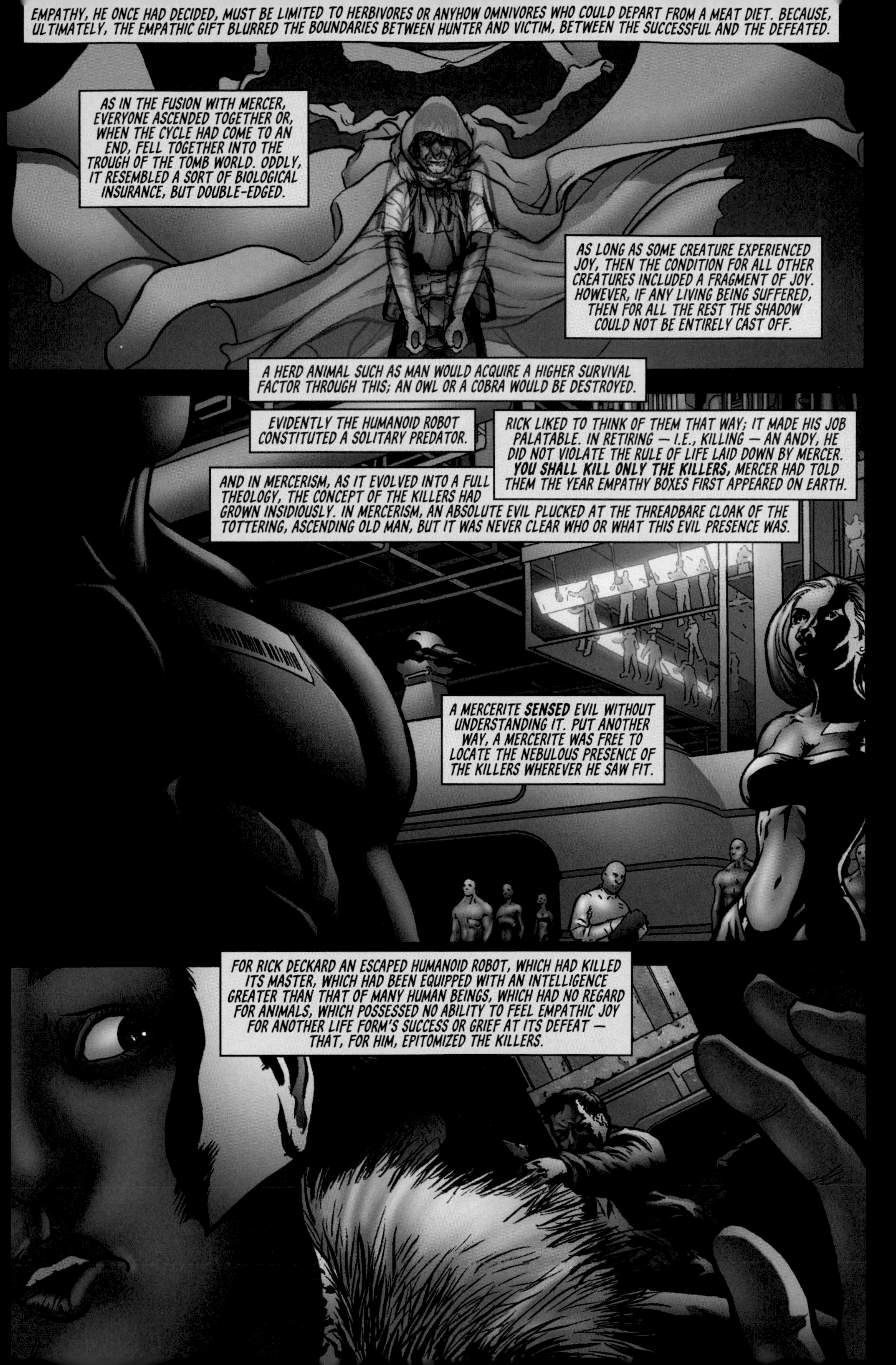
EMPATHY, HE ONCE HAD DECIDED, MUST BE LIMITED TO HERBIVORES OR ANYHOW OMNIVORES WHO COULD DEPART FROM A MEAT DIET. BECAUSE, ULTIMATELY, THE EMPATHIC GIFT BLURRED THE BOUNDARIES BETWEEN HUNTER AND VICTIM, BETWEEN THE SUCCESSFUL AND THE DEFEATED.
AS IN THE FUSION WITH MERCER, EVERYONE ASCENDED TOGETHER OR, WHEN THE CYCLE HAD COME TO AN END, FELL TOGETHER INTO THE TROUGH OF THE TOMB WORLD. ODDLY, IT RESEMBLED A SORT OF BIOLOGICAL INSURANCE, BUT DOUBLE-EDGED.
AS LONG AS SOME CREATURE EXPERIENCED JOY, THEN THE CONDITION FOR ALL OTHER CREATURES INCLUDED A FRAGMENT OF JOY. HOWEVER, IF ANY LIVING BEING SUFFERED, THEN FOR ALL THE REST THE SHADOW COULD NOT BE ENTIRELY CAST OFF.
A HERD ANIMAL SUCH AS MAN WOULD ACQUIRE A HIGHER SURVIVAL FACTOR THROUGH THIS; AN OWL OR A COBRA WOULD BE DESTROYED.
EVIDENTLY THE HUMANOID ROBOT CONSTITUTED A SOLITARY PREDATOR.
RICK LIKED TO THINK OF THEM THAT WAY; IT MADE HIS JOB PALATABLE. IN RETIRING — I.E., KILLING — AN ANDY, HE DID NOT VIOLATE THE RULE OF LIFE LAID DOWN BY MERCER. **YOU SHALL KILL ONLY THE KILLERS,** MERCER HAD TOLD THEM THE YEAR EMPATHY BOXES FIRST APPEARED ON EARTH.
AND IN MERCERISM, AS IT EVOLVED INTO A FULL THEOLOGY, THE CONCEPT OF THE KILLERS HAD GROWN INSIDIOUSLY. IN MERCERISM, AN ABSOLUTE EVIL PLUCKED AT THE THREADBARE CLOAK OF THE TOTTERING, ASCENDING OLD MAN, BUT IT WAS NEVER CLEAR WHO OR WHAT THIS EVIL PRESENCE WAS.
A MERCERITE **SENSED** EVIL WITHOUT UNDERSTANDING IT. PUT ANOTHER WAY, A MERCERITE WAS FREE TO LOCATE THE NEBULOUS PRESENCE OF THE KILLERS WHEREVER HE SAW FIT.
FOR RICK DECKARD AN ESCAPED HUMANOID ROBOT, WHICH HAD KILLED ITS MASTER, WHICH HAD BEEN EQUIPPED WITH AN INTELLIGENCE GREATER THAN THAT OF MANY HUMAN BEINGS, WHICH HAD NO REGARD FOR ANIMALS, WHICH POSSESSED NO ABILITY TO FEEL EMPATHIC JOY FOR ANOTHER LIFE FORM'S SUCCESS OR GRIEF AT ITS DEFEAT — THAT, FOR HIM, EPITOMIZED THE KILLERS.

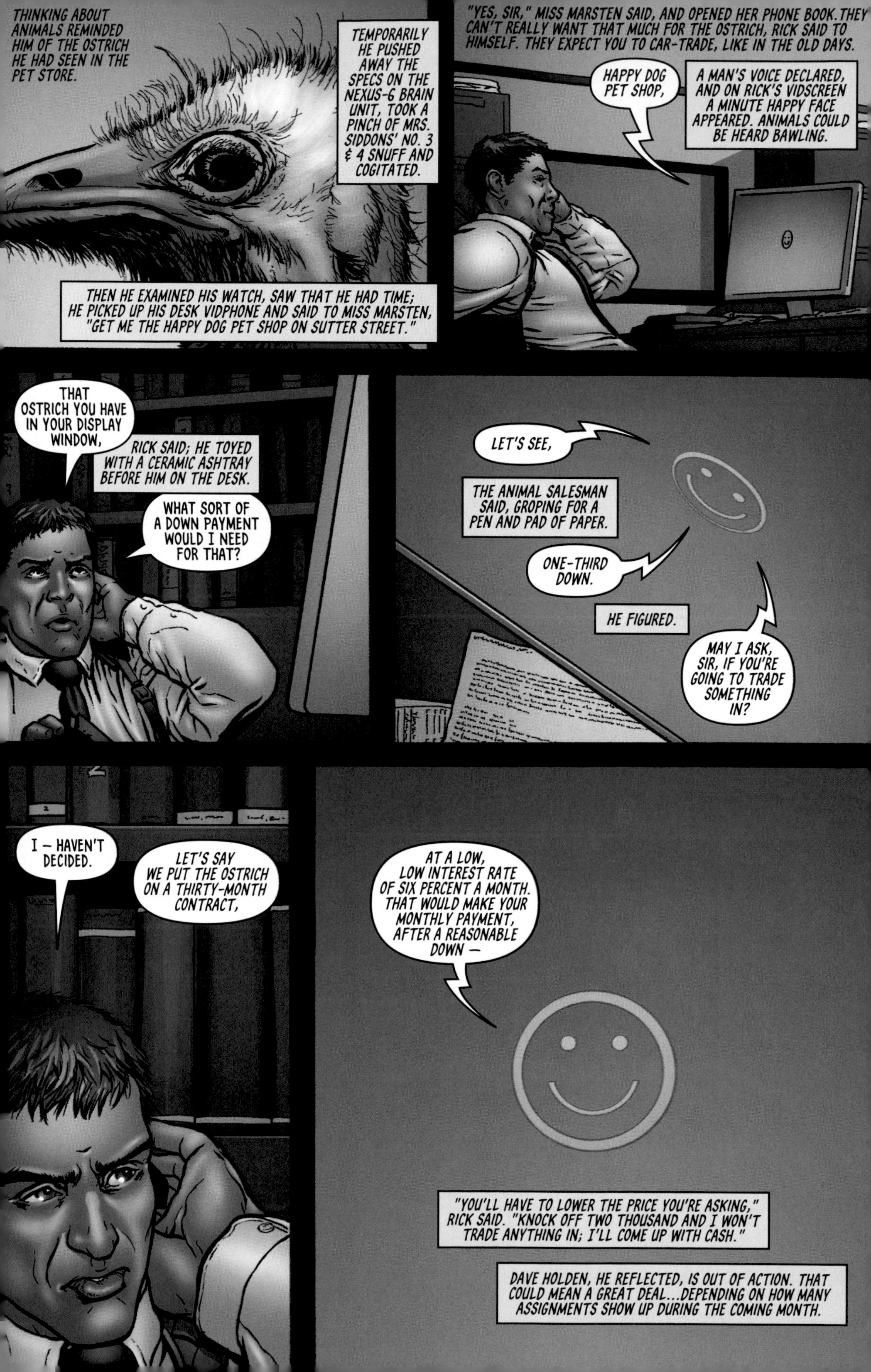
THINKING ABOUT ANIMALS REMINDED HIM OF THE OSTRICH HE HAD SEEN IN THE PET STORE.
TEMPORARILY HE PUSHED AWAY THE SPECS ON THE NEXUS-6 BRAIN UNIT, TOOK A PINCH OF MRS. SIDDONS' NO. 3 & 4 SNUFF AND COGITATED.
THEN HE EXAMINED HIS WATCH, SAW THAT HE HAD TIME; HE PICKED UP HIS DESK VIDPHONE AND SAID TO MISS MARSTEN, "GET ME THE HAPPY DOG PET SHOP ON SUTTER STREET."
"YES, SIR," MISS MARSTEN SAID, AND OPENED HER PHONE BOOK. THEY CAN'T REALLY WANT THAT MUCH FOR THE OSTRICH, RICK SAID TO HIMSELF. THEY EXPECT YOU TO CAR-TRADE, LIKE IN THE OLD DAYS.
HAPPY DOG PET SHOP,
A MAN'S VOICE DECLARED, AND ON RICK'S VIDSCREEN A MINUTE HAPPY FACE APPEARED. ANIMALS COULD BE HEARD BAWLING.
THAT OSTRICH YOU HAVE IN YOUR DISPLAY WINDOW,
RICK SAID; HE TOYED WITH A CERAMIC ASHTRAY BEFORE HIM ON THE DESK.
WHAT SORT OF A DOWN PAYMENT WOULD I NEED FOR THAT?
LET'S SEE,
THE ANIMAL SALESMAN SAID, GROPING FOR A PEN AND PAD OF PAPER.
ONE-THIRD DOWN.
HE FIGURED.
MAY I ASK, SIR, IF YOU'RE GOING TO TRADE SOMETHING IN?
I — HAVEN'T DECIDED.
LET'S SAY WE PUT THE OSTRICH ON A THIRTY-MONTH CONTRACT,
AT A LOW, LOW INTEREST RATE OF SIX PERCENT A MONTH. THAT WOULD MAKE YOUR MONTHLY PAYMENT, AFTER A REASONABLE DOWN —
"YOU'LL HAVE TO LOWER THE PRICE YOU'RE ASKING," RICK SAID. "KNOCK OFF TWO THOUSAND AND I WON'T TRADE ANYTHING IN; I'LL COME UP WITH CASH."
DAVE HOLDEN, HE REFLECTED, IS OUT OF ACTION. THAT COULD MEAN A GREAT DEAL...DEPENDING ON HOW MANY ASSIGNMENTS SHOW UP DURING THE COMING MONTH.

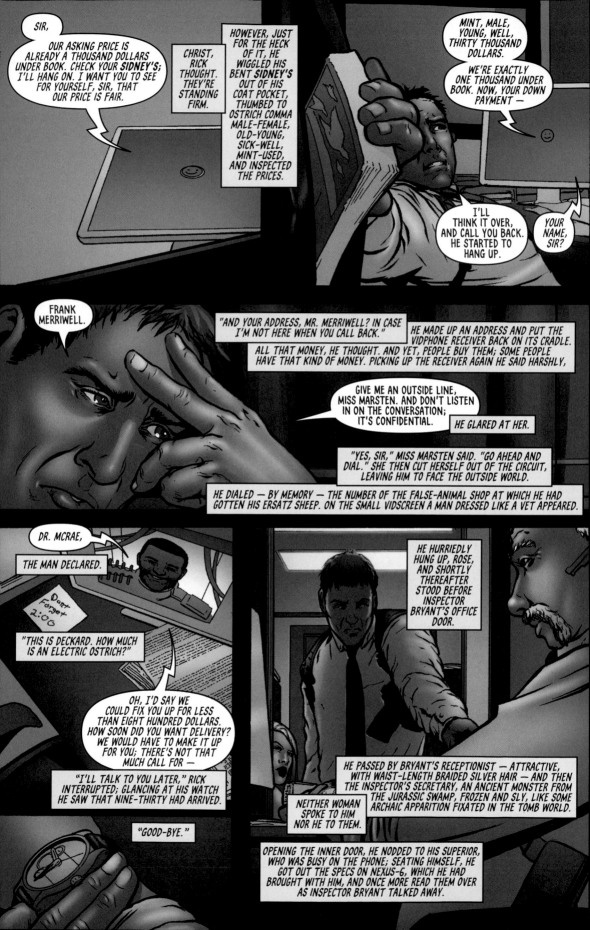

SIR, OUR ASKING PRICE IS ALREADY A THOUSAND DOLLARS UNDER BOOK. CHECK YOUR *SIDNEY'S*; I'LL HANG ON. I WANT YOU TO SEE FOR YOURSELF, SIR, THAT OUR PRICE IS FAIR.

CHRIST, RICK THOUGHT. THEY'RE STANDING FIRM.

HOWEVER, JUST FOR THE HECK OF IT, HE WIGGLED HIS BENT *SIDNEY'S* OUT OF HIS COAT POCKET, THUMBED TO OSTRICH COMMA MALE-FEMALE, OLD-YOUNG, SICK-WELL, MINT-USED, AND INSPECTED THE PRICES.

MINT, MALE, YOUNG, WELL, THIRTY THOUSAND DOLLARS.

WE'RE EXACTLY ONE THOUSAND UNDER BOOK. NOW, YOUR DOWN PAYMENT —

I'LL THINK IT OVER, AND CALL YOU BACK. HE STARTED TO HANG UP.

YOUR NAME, SIR?

FRANK MERRIWELL.

"AND YOUR ADDRESS, MR. MERRIWELL? IN CASE I'M NOT HERE WHEN YOU CALL BACK." HE MADE UP AN ADDRESS AND PUT THE VIDPHONE RECEIVER BACK ON ITS CRADLE. ALL THAT MONEY, HE THOUGHT. AND YET, PEOPLE BUY THEM; SOME PEOPLE HAVE THAT KIND OF MONEY. PICKING UP THE RECEIVER AGAIN HE SAID HARSHLY,

GIVE ME AN OUTSIDE LINE, MISS MARSTEN. AND DON'T LISTEN IN ON THE CONVERSATION; IT'S CONFIDENTIAL.

HE GLARED AT HER.

"YES, SIR," MISS MARSTEN SAID. "GO AHEAD AND DIAL." SHE THEN CUT HERSELF OUT OF THE CIRCUIT, LEAVING HIM TO FACE THE OUTSIDE WORLD.

HE DIALED — BY MEMORY — THE NUMBER OF THE FALSE-ANIMAL SHOP AT WHICH HE HAD GOTTEN HIS ERSATZ SHEEP. ON THE SMALL VIDSCREEN A MAN DRESSED LIKE A VET APPEARED.

DR. MCRAE,

THE MAN DECLARED.

Dont forget 2:00

"THIS IS DECKARD. HOW MUCH IS AN ELECTRIC OSTRICH?"

OH, I'D SAY WE COULD FIX YOU UP FOR LESS THAN EIGHT HUNDRED DOLLARS. HOW SOON DID YOU WANT DELIVERY? WE WOULD HAVE TO MAKE IT UP FOR YOU; THERE'S NOT THAT MUCH CALL FOR —

"I'LL TALK TO YOU LATER," RICK INTERRUPTED; GLANCING AT HIS WATCH HE SAW THAT NINE-THIRTY HAD ARRIVED.

"GOOD-BYE."

HE HURRIEDLY HUNG UP, ROSE, AND SHORTLY THEREAFTER STOOD BEFORE INSPECTOR BRYANT'S OFFICE DOOR.

HE PASSED BY BRYANT'S RECEPTIONIST — ATTRACTIVE, WITH WAIST-LENGTH BRAIDED SILVER HAIR — AND THEN THE INSPECTOR'S SECRETARY, AN ANCIENT MONSTER FROM THE JURASSIC SWAMP, FROZEN AND SLY, LIKE SOME ARCHAIC APPARITION FIXATED IN THE TOMB WORLD.

NEITHER WOMAN SPOKE TO HIM NOR HE TO THEM.

OPENING THE INNER DOOR, HE NODDED TO HIS SUPERIOR, WHO WAS BUSY ON THE PHONE; SEATING HIMSELF, HE GOT OUT THE SPECS ON NEXUS-6, WHICH HE HAD BROUGHT WITH HIM, AND ONCE MORE READ THEM OVER AS INSPECTOR BRYANT TALKED AWAY.

HE FELT DEPRESSED. AND YET, LOGICALLY, BECAUSE OF DAVE'S SUDDEN DISAPPEARANCE FROM THE WORK SCENE, HE SHOULD BE AT LEAST GUARDEDLY PLEASED.

MAYBE I'M WORRIED, RICK DECKARD CONJECTURED, THAT WHAT HAPPENED TO DAVE WILL HAPPEN TO ME. AN ANDY SMART ENOUGH TO LASER HIM COULD PROBABLY TAKE ME, TOO.

BUT THAT DIDN'T SEEM TO BE IT.

YEAH, I HEARD ABOUT IT ON THE GRAPEVINE. HOW MANY ANDYS ARE INVOLVED AND HOW FAR DID DAVE GET?

EIGHT TO START WITH,

I SEE YOU BROUGHT THE POOP SHEET ON THAT NEW BRAIN UNIT,

INSPECTOR BRYANT SAID, HANGING UP THE VIDPHONE.

BRYANT SAID, CONSULTING HIS CLIPBOARD.

DAVE GOT THE FIRST TWO.

AND THE REMAINING SIX ARE HERE IN NORTHERN CALIFORNIA?

AS FAR AS WE KNOW, DAVE THINKS SO. THAT WAS HIM I WAS TALKING TO.

I HAVE HIS NOTES; THEY WERE IN HIS DESK. HE SAYS ALL HE KNOWS IS HERE.

I HAVE NOTHING ON MY AGENDA, I'M READY TO TAKE OVER IN DAVE'S PLACE.

BRYANT SAID THOUGHTFULLY, "DAVE USED THE VOIGT-KAMPFF ALTERED SCALE IN TESTING OUT THE INDIVIDUALS HE SUSPECTED. YOU REALIZE — YOU OUGHT TO, ANYHOW — THAT THIS TEST ISN'T SPECIFIC FOR THE NEW BRAIN UNITS.

BRYANT TAPPED THE BUNDLE OF NOTEPAPER. SO FAR HE DID NOT SEEM INCLINED TO PASS THE NOTES ON TO RICK; FOR SOME REASON HE CONTINUED TO LEAF THROUGH THEM HIMSELF, FROWNING AND WORKING HIS TONGUE IN AND AROUND THE FRINGES OF HIS MOUTH.

"NO TEST IS; THE VOIGT SCALE, ALTERED THREE YEARS AGO BY KAMPFF, IS ALL WE HAVE." HE PAUSED, PONDERING. "DAVE CONSIDERED IT ACCURATE. MAYBE IT IS. BUT I WOULD SUGGEST THIS, BEFORE YOU TAKE OUT AFTER THESE SIX."

AGAIN HE TAPPED THE PILE OF NOTES. "FLY TO SEATTLE AND TALK WITH THE ROSEN PEOPLE. HAVE THEM SUPPLY YOU A REPRESENTATIVE SAMPLING OF TYPES EMPLOYING THE NEW NEXUS-6 UNIT."

AND PUT THEM THROUGH THE VOIGT-KAMPFF,

IT SOUNDS SO EASY,

BRYANT SAID, HALF TO HIMSELF.

PARDON?

I THINK I'LL TALK TO THE ROSEN ORGANIZATION MYSELF, WHILE YOU'RE ON YOUR WAY.

HE EYED RICK, THEN, SILENTLY. FINALLY HE GRUNTED, GNAWED ON A FINGERNAIL, AND EVENTUALLY DECIDED ON WHAT HE WANTED TO SAY.

I'M GOING TO DISCUSS WITH THEM THE POSSIBILITY OF INCLUDING SEVERAL HUMANS, AS WELL AS THEIR NEW ANDROIDS. BUT YOU WON'T KNOW. IT'LL BE MY DECISION, IN CONJUNCTION WITH THE MANUFACTURERS.

IT SHOULD BE SET UP BY THE TIME YOU GET THERE.

HE ABRUPTLY POINTED AT RICK, HIS FACE SEVERE.

THIS IS THE FIRST TIME YOU'LL BE ACTING AS SENIOR BOUNTY HUNTER. DAVE KNOWS A LOT; HE'S GOT YEARS OF EXPERIENCE BEHIND HIM.

SO HAVE I.

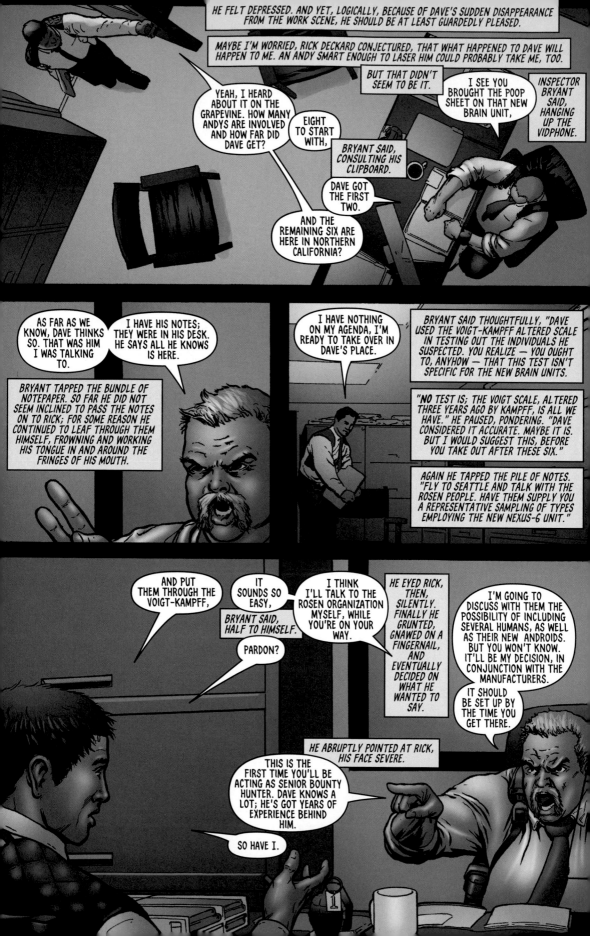

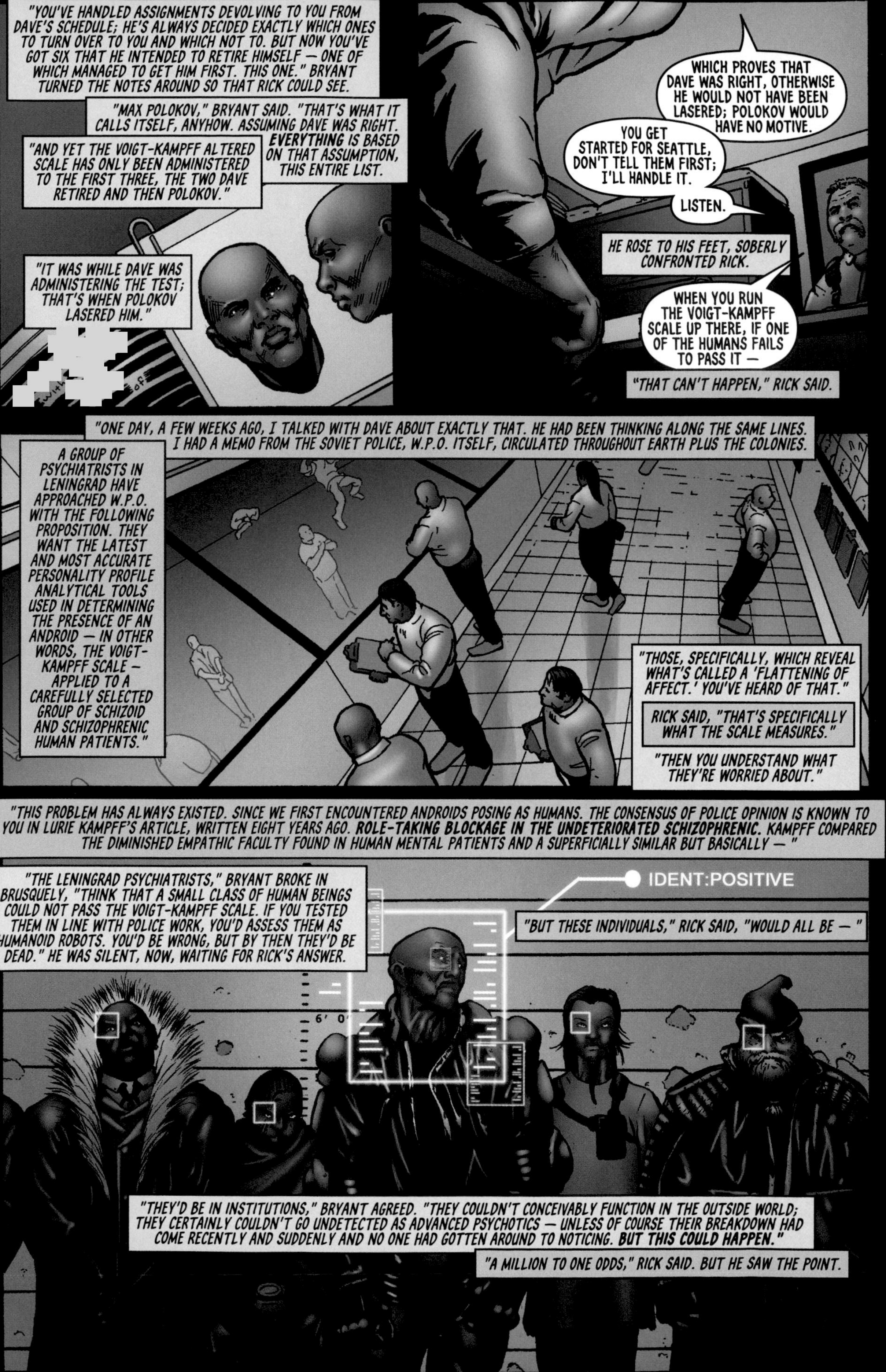
"YOU'VE HANDLED ASSIGNMENTS DEVOLVING TO YOU FROM DAVE'S SCHEDULE; HE'S ALWAYS DECIDED EXACTLY WHICH ONES TO TURN OVER TO YOU AND WHICH NOT TO. BUT NOW YOU'VE GOT SIX THAT HE INTENDED TO RETIRE HIMSELF — ONE OF WHICH MANAGED TO GET HIM FIRST. THIS ONE." BRYANT TURNED THE NOTES AROUND SO THAT RICK COULD SEE.
"MAX POLOKOV," BRYANT SAID. "THAT'S WHAT IT CALLS ITSELF, ANYHOW. ASSUMING DAVE WAS RIGHT. EVERYTHING IS BASED ON THAT ASSUMPTION, THIS ENTIRE LIST.
"AND YET THE VOIGT-KAMPFF ALTERED SCALE HAS ONLY BEEN ADMINISTERED TO THE FIRST THREE, THE TWO DAVE RETIRED AND THEN POLOKOV."
"IT WAS WHILE DAVE WAS ADMINISTERING THE TEST; THAT'S WHEN POLOKOV LASERED HIM."
WHICH PROVES THAT DAVE WAS RIGHT, OTHERWISE HE WOULD NOT HAVE BEEN LASERED; POLOKOV WOULD HAVE NO MOTIVE.
YOU GET STARTED FOR SEATTLE, DON'T TELL THEM FIRST; I'LL HANDLE IT.
LISTEN.
HE ROSE TO HIS FEET, SOBERLY CONFRONTED RICK.
WHEN YOU RUN THE VOIGT-KAMPFF SCALE UP THERE, IF ONE OF THE HUMANS FAILS TO PASS IT —
"THAT CAN'T HAPPEN," RICK SAID.
"ONE DAY, A FEW WEEKS AGO, I TALKED WITH DAVE ABOUT EXACTLY THAT. HE HAD BEEN THINKING ALONG THE SAME LINES. I HAD A MEMO FROM THE SOVIET POLICE, W.P.O. ITSELF, CIRCULATED THROUGHOUT EARTH PLUS THE COLONIES.
A GROUP OF PSYCHIATRISTS IN LENINGRAD HAVE APPROACHED W.P.O. WITH THE FOLLOWING PROPOSITION. THEY WANT THE LATEST AND MOST ACCURATE PERSONALITY PROFILE ANALYTICAL TOOLS USED IN DETERMINING THE PRESENCE OF AN ANDROID — IN OTHER WORDS, THE VOIGT-KAMPFF SCALE — APPLIED TO A CAREFULLY SELECTED GROUP OF SCHIZOID AND SCHIZOPHRENIC HUMAN PATIENTS."
"THOSE, SPECIFICALLY, WHICH REVEAL WHAT'S CALLED A 'FLATTENING OF AFFECT.' YOU'VE HEARD OF THAT."
RICK SAID, "THAT'S SPECIFICALLY WHAT THE SCALE MEASURES."
"THEN YOU UNDERSTAND WHAT THEY'RE WORRIED ABOUT."
"THIS PROBLEM HAS ALWAYS EXISTED. SINCE WE FIRST ENCOUNTERED ANDROIDS POSING AS HUMANS. THE CONSENSUS OF POLICE OPINION IS KNOWN TO YOU IN LURIE KAMPFF'S ARTICLE, WRITTEN EIGHT YEARS AGO. **ROLE-TAKING BLOCKAGE IN THE UNDETERIORATED SCHIZOPHRENIC.** KAMPFF COMPARED THE DIMINISHED EMPATHIC FACULTY FOUND IN HUMAN MENTAL PATIENTS AND A SUPERFICIALLY SIMILAR BUT BASICALLY — "
"THE LENINGRAD PSYCHIATRISTS," BRYANT BROKE IN BRUSQUELY, "THINK THAT A SMALL CLASS OF HUMAN BEINGS COULD NOT PASS THE VOIGT-KAMPFF SCALE. IF YOU TESTED THEM IN LINE WITH POLICE WORK, YOU'D ASSESS THEM AS HUMANOID ROBOTS. YOU'D BE WRONG, BUT BY THEN THEY'D BE DEAD." HE WAS SILENT, NOW, WAITING FOR RICK'S ANSWER.
IDENT:POSITIVE
"BUT THESE INDIVIDUALS," RICK SAID, "WOULD ALL BE — "
6' 0"
"THEY'D BE IN INSTITUTIONS," BRYANT AGREED. "THEY COULDN'T CONCEIVABLY FUNCTION IN THE OUTSIDE WORLD; THEY CERTAINLY COULDN'T GO UNDETECTED AS ADVANCED PSYCHOTICS — UNLESS OF COURSE THEIR BREAKDOWN HAD COME RECENTLY AND SUDDENLY AND NO ONE HAD GOTTEN AROUND TO NOTICING. **BUT THIS COULD HAPPEN.**"
"A MILLION TO ONE ODDS," RICK SAID. BUT HE SAW THE POINT.

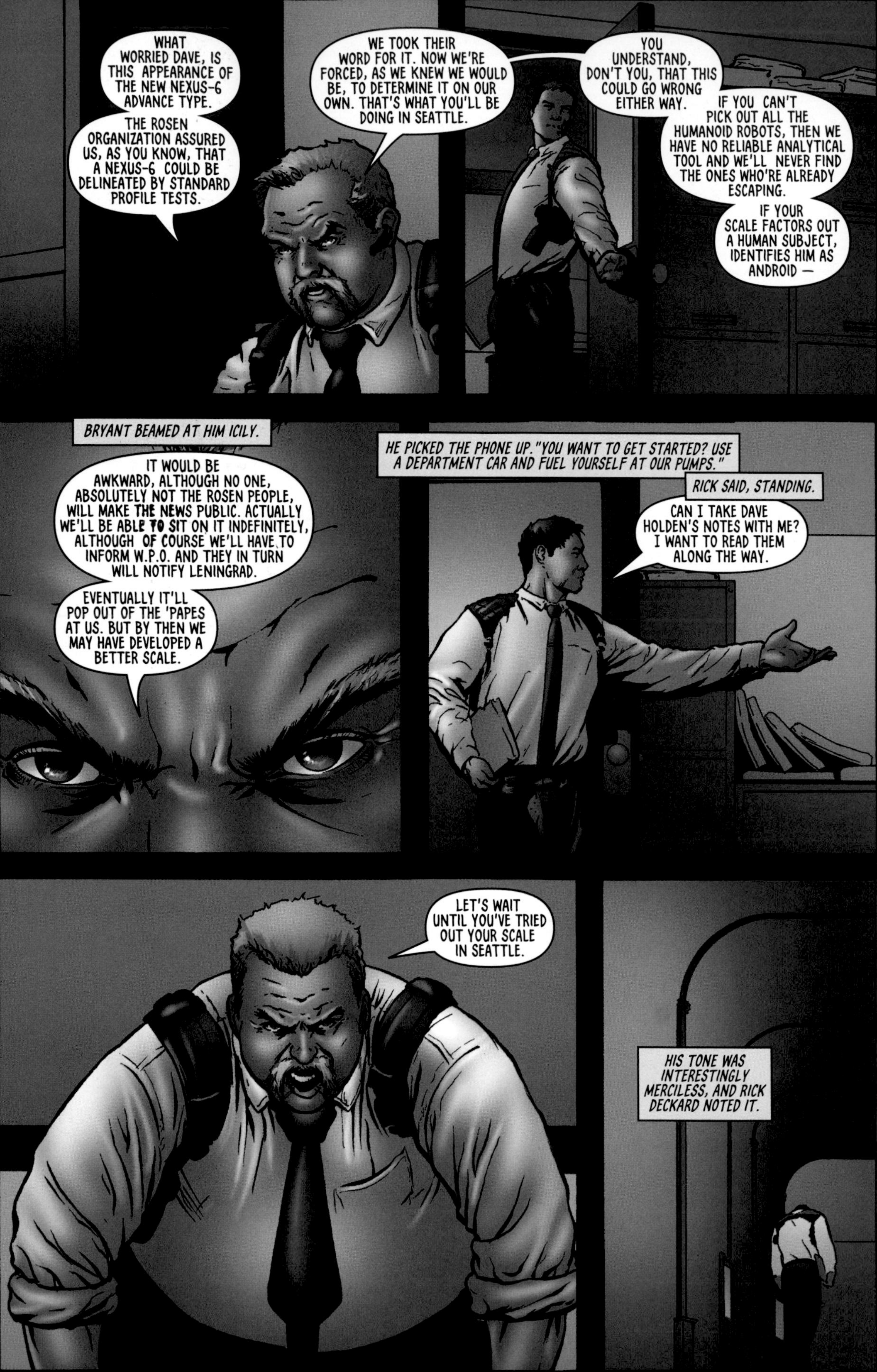
WHAT WORRIED DAVE, IS THIS APPEARANCE OF THE NEW NEXUS-6 ADVANCE TYPE.
THE ROSEN ORGANIZATION ASSURED US, AS YOU KNOW, THAT A NEXUS-6 COULD BE DELINEATED BY STANDARD PROFILE TESTS.
WE TOOK THEIR WORD FOR IT. NOW WE'RE FORCED, AS WE KNEW WE WOULD BE, TO DETERMINE IT ON OUR OWN. THAT'S WHAT YOU'LL BE DOING IN SEATTLE.
YOU UNDERSTAND, DON'T YOU, THAT THIS COULD GO WRONG EITHER WAY.
IF YOU CAN'T PICK OUT ALL THE HUMANOID ROBOTS, THEN WE HAVE NO RELIABLE ANALYTICAL TOOL AND WE'LL NEVER FIND THE ONES WHO'RE ALREADY ESCAPING.
IF YOUR SCALE FACTORS OUT A HUMAN SUBJECT, IDENTIFIES HIM AS ANDROID —
BRYANT BEAMED AT HIM ICILY.
IT WOULD BE AWKWARD, ALTHOUGH NO ONE, ABSOLUTELY NOT THE ROSEN PEOPLE, WILL MAKE THE NEWS PUBLIC. ACTUALLY WE'LL BE ABLE TO SIT ON IT INDEFINITELY, ALTHOUGH OF COURSE WE'LL HAVE TO INFORM W.P.O. AND THEY IN TURN WILL NOTIFY LENINGRAD.
EVENTUALLY IT'LL POP OUT OF THE 'PAPES AT US. BUT BY THEN WE MAY HAVE DEVELOPED A BETTER SCALE.
HE PICKED THE PHONE UP. "YOU WANT TO GET STARTED? USE A DEPARTMENT CAR AND FUEL YOURSELF AT OUR PUMPS."
RICK SAID, STANDING.
CAN I TAKE DAVE HOLDEN'S NOTES WITH ME? I WANT TO READ THEM ALONG THE WAY.
LET'S WAIT UNTIL YOU'VE TRIED OUT YOUR SCALE IN SEATTLE.
HIS TONE WAS INTERESTINGLY MERCILESS, AND RICK DECKARD NOTED IT.

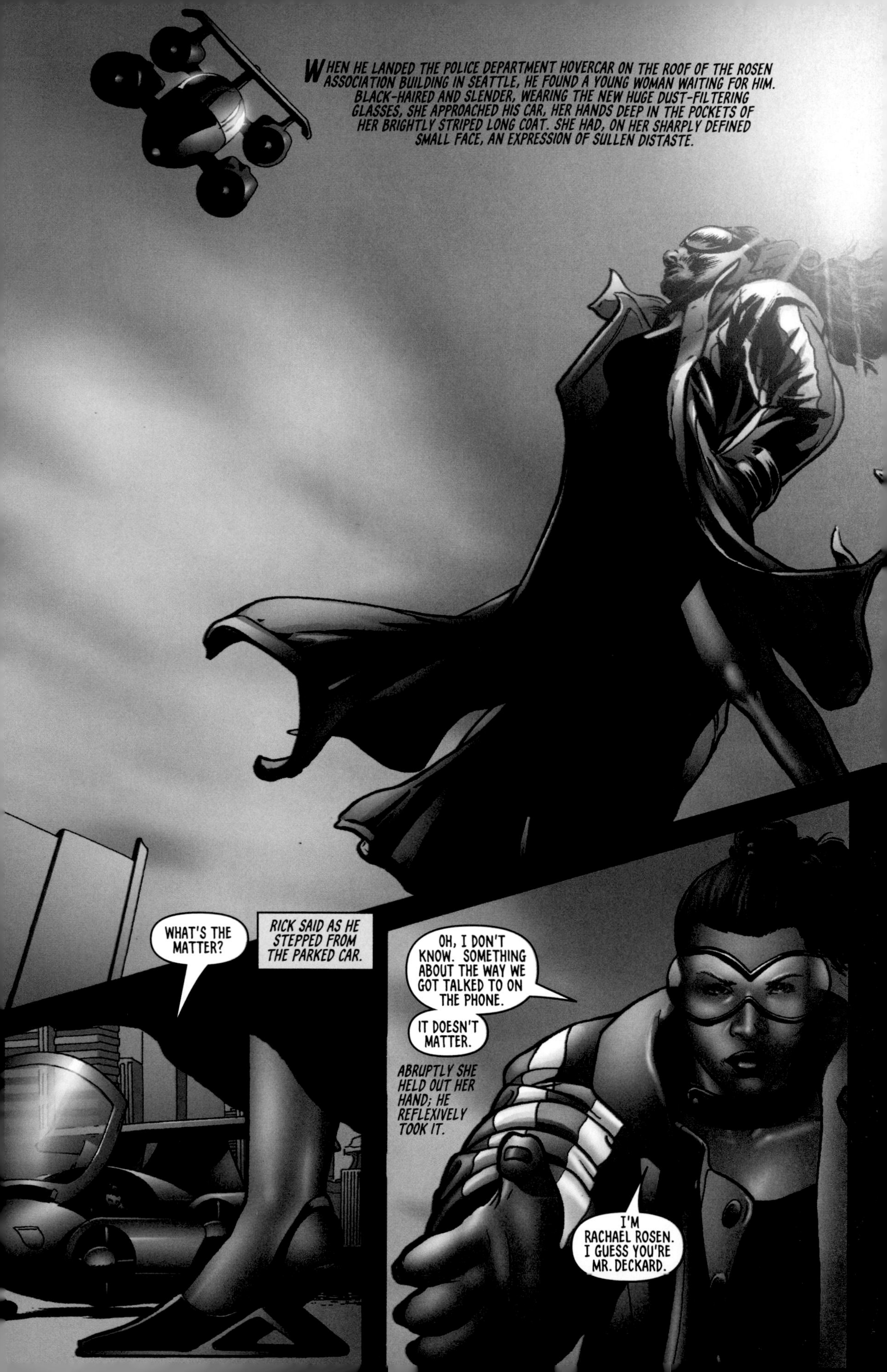
WHEN HE LANDED THE POLICE DEPARTMENT HOVERCAR ON THE ROOF OF THE ROSEN ASSOCIATION BUILDING IN SEATTLE, HE FOUND A YOUNG WOMAN WAITING FOR HIM. BLACK-HAIRED AND SLENDER, WEARING THE NEW HUGE DUST-FILTERING GLASSES, SHE APPROACHED HIS CAR, HER HANDS DEEP IN THE POCKETS OF HER BRIGHTLY STRIPED LONG COAT. SHE HAD, ON HER SHARPLY DEFINED SMALL FACE, AN EXPRESSION OF SULLEN DISTASTE.
WHAT'S THE MATTER?
RICK SAID AS HE STEPPED FROM THE PARKED CAR.
OH, I DON'T KNOW. SOMETHING ABOUT THE WAY WE GOT TALKED TO ON THE PHONE.
IT DOESN'T MATTER.
ABRUPTLY SHE HELD OUT HER HAND; HE REFLEXIVELY TOOK IT.
I'M RACHAEL ROSEN. I GUESS YOU'RE MR. DECKARD.

"THIS IS NOT MY IDEA," HE SAID.

YES, INSPECTOR BRYANT TOLD US THAT. BUT YOU'RE OFFICIALLY THE SAN FRANCISCO POLICE DEPARTMENT, AND IT DOESN'T BELIEVE OUR UNIT IS TO THE PUBLIC BENEFIT.

SHE EYED HIM FROM BENEATH LONG BLACK LASHES, PROBABLY ARTIFICIAL.

A HUMANOID ROBOT IS LIKE ANY OTHER MACHINE; IT CAN FLUCTUATE BETWEEN BEING A BENEFIT AND A HAZARD VERY RAPIDLY. AS A BENEFIT IT'S NOT OUR PROBLEM.

BUT AS A HAZARD, THEN YOU COME IN.

IS IT TRUE, MR. DECKARD, THAT YOU'RE A BOUNTY HUNTER?

HE SHRUGGED, WITH RELUCTANCE, NODDED.

YOU HAVE NO DIFFICULTY VIEWING AN ANDROID AS INERT, SO YOU CAN "RETIRE" IT, AS THEY SAY.

DO YOU HAVE THE GROUP SELECTED OUT FOR ME? I'D LIKE TO —

HE BROKE OFF. BECAUSE, ALL AT ONCE, HE HAD SEEN THEIR ANIMALS.

HE QUIETLY WALKED AWAY FROM THE GIRL, TOWARD THE CLOSEST PEN. ALREADY HE COULD SMELL THEM, THE SEVERAL SCENTS OF THE CREATURES STANDING OR SITTING, OR, IN THE CASE OF WHAT APPEARED TO BE A RACCOON, ASLEEP. NEVER IN HIS LIFE HAD HE PERSONALLY SEEN A RACCOON. HE KNEW THE ANIMAL ONLY FROM 3-D FILMS SHOWN ON TELEVISION. FOR SOME REASON THE DUST HAD STRUCK THAT SPECIES ALMOST AS HARD AS IT HAD THE BIRDS — OF WHICH ALMOST NONE SURVIVED, NOW.

IN AN AUTOMATIC RESPONSE HE BROUGHT OUT HIS MUCH-THUMBED *SIDNEY'S* AND LOOKED UP RACCOON WITH ALL THE SUBLISTINGS.

A POWERFUL CORPORATION, HE REALIZED, WOULD OF COURSE BE ABLE TO AFFORD THIS. IN THE BACK OF HIS MIND, EVIDENTLY, HE HAD ANTICIPATED SUCH A COLLECTION; IT WAS NOT SURPRISE THAT HE FELT BUT MORE A SORT OF YEARNING.

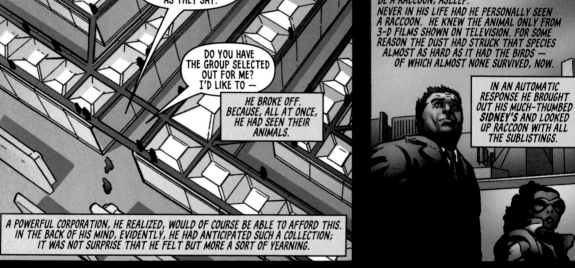

THE LIST PRICES, NATURALLY, APPEARED IN ITALICS; LIKE PERCHERON HORSES, NONE EXISTED ON THE MARKET FOR SALE AT ANY FIGURE. *SIDNEY'S* CATALOGUE SIMPLY LISTED THE PRICE AT WHICH THE LAST TRANSACTION INVOLVING A RACCOON HAD TAKEN PLACE. IT WAS ASTRONOMICAL.

HIS NAME IS BILL,

THE GIRL SAID FROM BEHIND HIM.

BILL THE RACCOON. WE ACQUIRED HIM JUST LAST YEAR FROM A SUBSIDIARY CORPORATION.

SHE POINTED PAST HIM AND HE THEN PERCEIVED THE ARMED COMPANY GUARDS, STANDING WITH THEIR MACHINE GUNS, THE RAPID-FIRE LITTLE LIGHT SKODA ISSUE; THE EYES OF THE GUARDS HAD BEEN FASTENED ON HIM SINCE HIS CAR LANDED. AND, HE THOUGHT, MY CAR IS CLEARLY MARKED AS A POLICE VEHICLE.

"A MAJOR MANUFACTURER OF ANDROIDS," HE SAID THOUGHTFULLY, "INVESTS ITS SURPLUS CAPITAL ON LIVING ANIMALS."

"LOOK AT THE OWL," RACHAEL ROSEN SAID. "HERE, I'LL WAKE IT UP FOR YOU." SHE STARTED TOWARD A SMALL, DISTANT CAGE, IN THE CENTER OF WHICH JUTTED UP A BRANCHING DEAD TREE.

THERE ARE NO OWLS, HE STARTED TO SAY. OR SO WE'VE BEEN TOLD.

SIDNEY'S, HE THOUGHT; THEY LIST IT IN THEIR CATALOGUE AS EXTINCT: THE TINY, PRECISE TYPE, THE *E*, AGAIN AND AGAIN THROUGHOUT THE CATALOGUE.

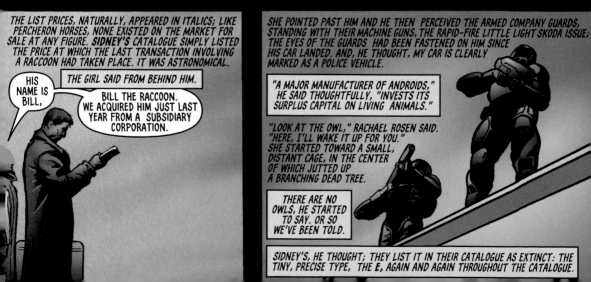

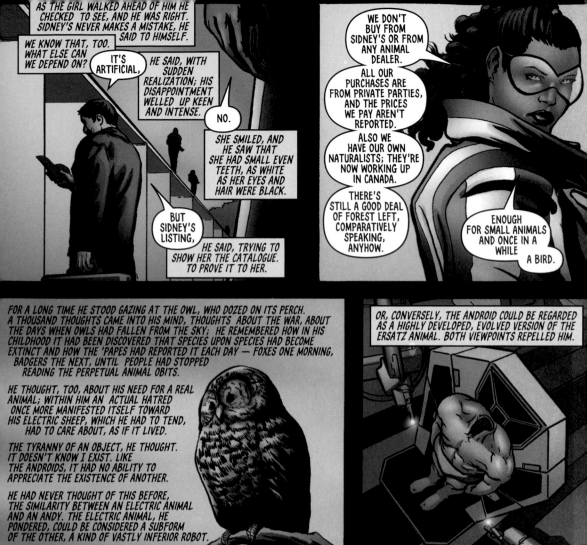

AS THE GIRL WALKED AHEAD OF HIM HE CHECKED TO SEE, AND HE WAS RIGHT. SIDNEY'S NEVER MAKES A MISTAKE, HE SAID TO HIMSELF.

WE KNOW THAT, TOO. WHAT ELSE CAN WE DEPEND ON?

IT'S ARTIFICIAL,

HE SAID, WITH SUDDEN REALIZATION; HIS DISAPPOINTMENT WELLED UP KEEN AND INTENSE.

NO.

SHE SMILED, AND HE SAW THAT SHE HAD SMALL EVEN TEETH, AS WHITE AS HER EYES AND HAIR WERE BLACK.

BUT SIDNEY'S LISTING,

HE SAID, TRYING TO SHOW HER THE CATALOGUE. TO PROVE IT TO HER.

WE DON'T BUY FROM SIDNEY'S OR FROM ANY ANIMAL DEALER.

ALL OUR PURCHASES ARE FROM PRIVATE PARTIES, AND THE PRICES WE PAY AREN'T REPORTED.

ALSO WE HAVE OUR OWN NATURALISTS; THEY'RE NOW WORKING UP IN CANADA.

THERE'S STILL A GOOD DEAL OF FOREST LEFT, COMPARATIVELY SPEAKING, ANYHOW.

ENOUGH FOR SMALL ANIMALS AND ONCE IN A WHILE

A BIRD.

FOR A LONG TIME HE STOOD GAZING AT THE OWL, WHO DOZED ON ITS PERCH. A THOUSAND THOUGHTS CAME INTO HIS MIND, THOUGHTS ABOUT THE WAR, ABOUT THE DAYS WHEN OWLS HAD FALLEN FROM THE SKY; HE REMEMBERED HOW IN HIS CHILDHOOD IT HAD BEEN DISCOVERED THAT SPECIES UPON SPECIES HAD BECOME EXTINCT AND HOW THE 'PAPES HAD REPORTED IT EACH DAY — FOXES ONE MORNING, BADGERS THE NEXT, UNTIL PEOPLE HAD STOPPED READING THE PERPETUAL ANIMAL OBITS.

HE THOUGHT, TOO, ABOUT HIS NEED FOR A REAL ANIMAL; WITHIN HIM AN ACTUAL HATRED ONCE MORE MANIFESTED ITSELF TOWARD HIS ELECTRIC SHEEP, WHICH HE HAD TO TEND, HAD TO CARE ABOUT, AS IF IT LIVED.

THE TYRANNY OF AN OBJECT, HE THOUGHT. IT DOESN'T KNOW I EXIST. LIKE THE ANDROIDS, IT HAD NO ABILITY TO APPRECIATE THE EXISTENCE OF ANOTHER.

HE HAD NEVER THOUGHT OF THIS BEFORE, THE SIMILARITY BETWEEN AN ELECTRIC ANIMAL AND AN ANDY. THE ELECTRIC ANIMAL, HE PONDERED, COULD BE CONSIDERED A SUBFORM OF THE OTHER, A KIND OF VASTLY INFERIOR ROBOT.

OR, CONVERSELY, THE ANDROID COULD BE REGARDED AS A HIGHLY DEVELOPED, EVOLVED VERSION OF THE ERSATZ ANIMAL. BOTH VIEWPOINTS REPELLED HIM.

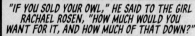

"IF YOU SOLD YOUR OWL," HE SAID TO THE GIRL RACHAEL ROSEN, "HOW MUCH WOULD YOU WANT FOR IT, AND HOW MUCH OF THAT DOWN?"

SHE SCRUTINIZED HIM WITH A MIXTURE OF PLEASURE AND PITY; OR SO HE READ HER EXPRESSION.

WE WOULD NEVER SELL OUR OWL.

AND EVEN IF WE SOLD IT, YOU COULDN'T POSSIBLY PAY THE PRICE. WHAT KIND OF ANIMAL DO YOU HAVE AT HOME?

"A SHEEP," HE SAID. "A BLACK-FACED SUFFOLK EWE."

WELL, THEN YOU SHOULD BE HAPPY.

"I'M HAPPY," HE ANSWERED.

IT'S JUST THAT I ALWAYS WANTED AN OWL, EVEN BACK BEFORE THEY ALL DROPPED DEAD.

HE CORRECTED HIMSELF.

ALL BUT YOURS.

RACHAEL SAID, "OUR PRESENT CRASH PROGRAM AND OVERALL PLANNING CALL FOR US TO OBTAIN AN ADDITIONAL OWL WHICH CAN MATE WITH SCRAPPY."

SHE INDICATED THE OWL DOZING ON ITS PERCH; IT HAD BRIEFLY OPENED BOTH EYES, YELLOW SLITS WHICH HEALED OVER AS THE OWL SETTLED BACK DOWN TO RESUME ITS SLUMBER. ITS CHEST ROSE CONSPICUOUSLY AND FELL, AS IF THE OWL, IN ITS HYPNAGOGIC STATE, HAD SIGHED.

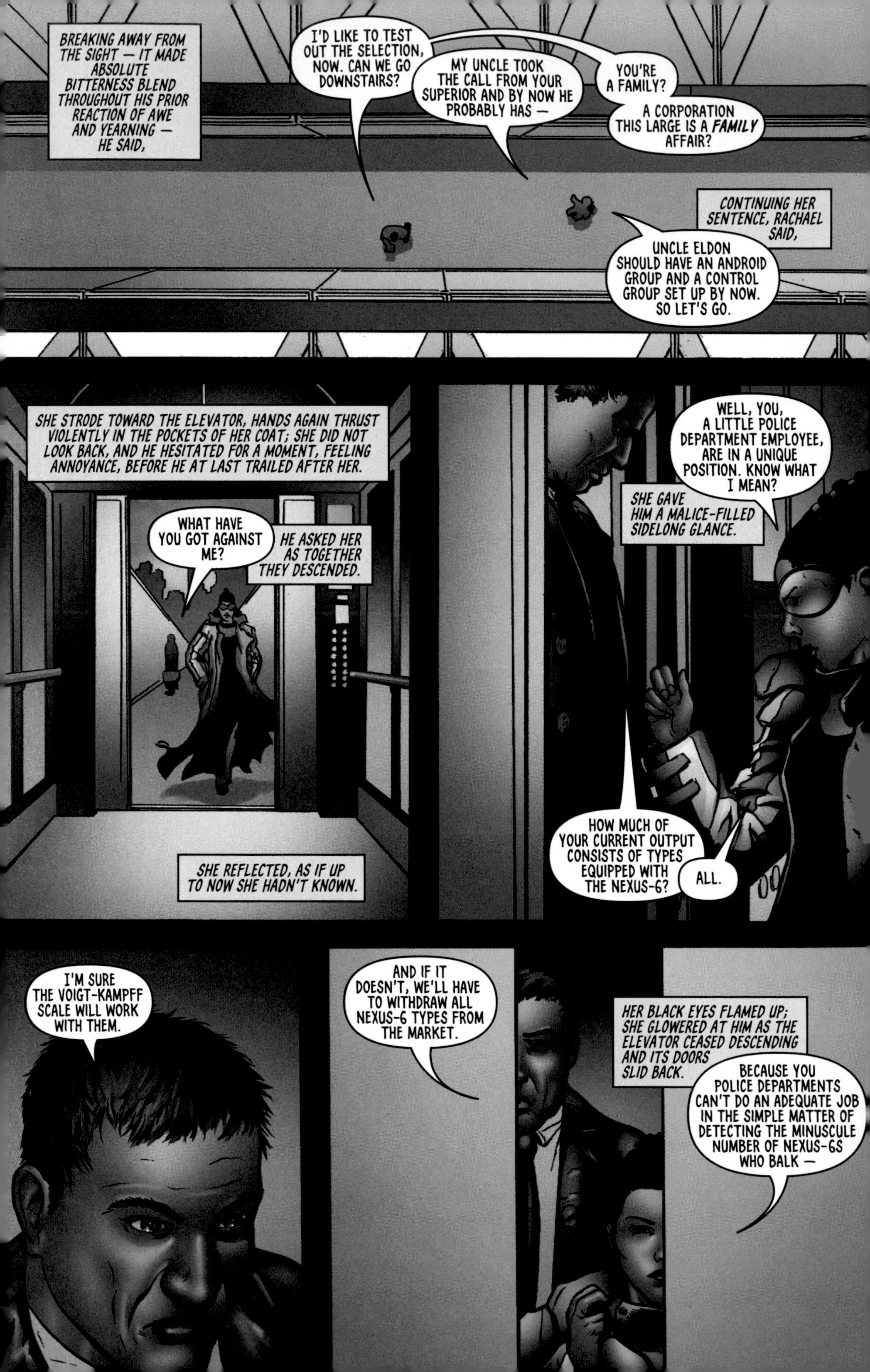
BREAKING AWAY FROM THE SIGHT — IT MADE ABSOLUTE BITTERNESS BLEND THROUGHOUT HIS PRIOR REACTION OF AWE AND YEARNING — HE SAID,
I'D LIKE TO TEST OUT THE SELECTION, NOW. CAN WE GO DOWNSTAIRS?
MY UNCLE TOOK THE CALL FROM YOUR SUPERIOR AND BY NOW HE PROBABLY HAS —
YOU'RE A FAMILY?
A CORPORATION THIS LARGE IS A FAMILY AFFAIR?
CONTINUING HER SENTENCE, RACHAEL SAID,
UNCLE ELDON SHOULD HAVE AN ANDROID GROUP AND A CONTROL GROUP SET UP BY NOW. SO LET'S GO.
SHE STRODE TOWARD THE ELEVATOR, HANDS AGAIN THRUST VIOLENTLY IN THE POCKETS OF HER COAT; SHE DID NOT LOOK BACK, AND HE HESITATED FOR A MOMENT, FEELING ANNOYANCE, BEFORE HE AT LAST TRAILED AFTER HER.
WHAT HAVE YOU GOT AGAINST ME?
HE ASKED HER AS TOGETHER THEY DESCENDED.
SHE REFLECTED, AS IF UP TO NOW SHE HADN'T KNOWN.
WELL, YOU, A LITTLE POLICE DEPARTMENT EMPLOYEE, ARE IN A UNIQUE POSITION. KNOW WHAT I MEAN?
SHE GAVE HIM A MALICE-FILLED SIDELONG GLANCE.
HOW MUCH OF YOUR CURRENT OUTPUT CONSISTS OF TYPES EQUIPPED WITH THE NEXUS-6?
ALL.
I'M SURE THE VOIGT-KAMPFF SCALE WILL WORK WITH THEM.
AND IF IT DOESN'T, WE'LL HAVE TO WITHDRAW ALL NEXUS-6 TYPES FROM THE MARKET.
HER BLACK EYES FLAMED UP; SHE GLOWERED AT HIM AS THE ELEVATOR CEASED DESCENDING AND ITS DOORS SLID BACK.
BECAUSE YOU POLICE DEPARTMENTS CAN'T DO AN ADEQUATE JOB IN THE SIMPLE MATTER OF DETECTING THE MINUSCULE NUMBER OF NEXUS-6S WHO BALK —

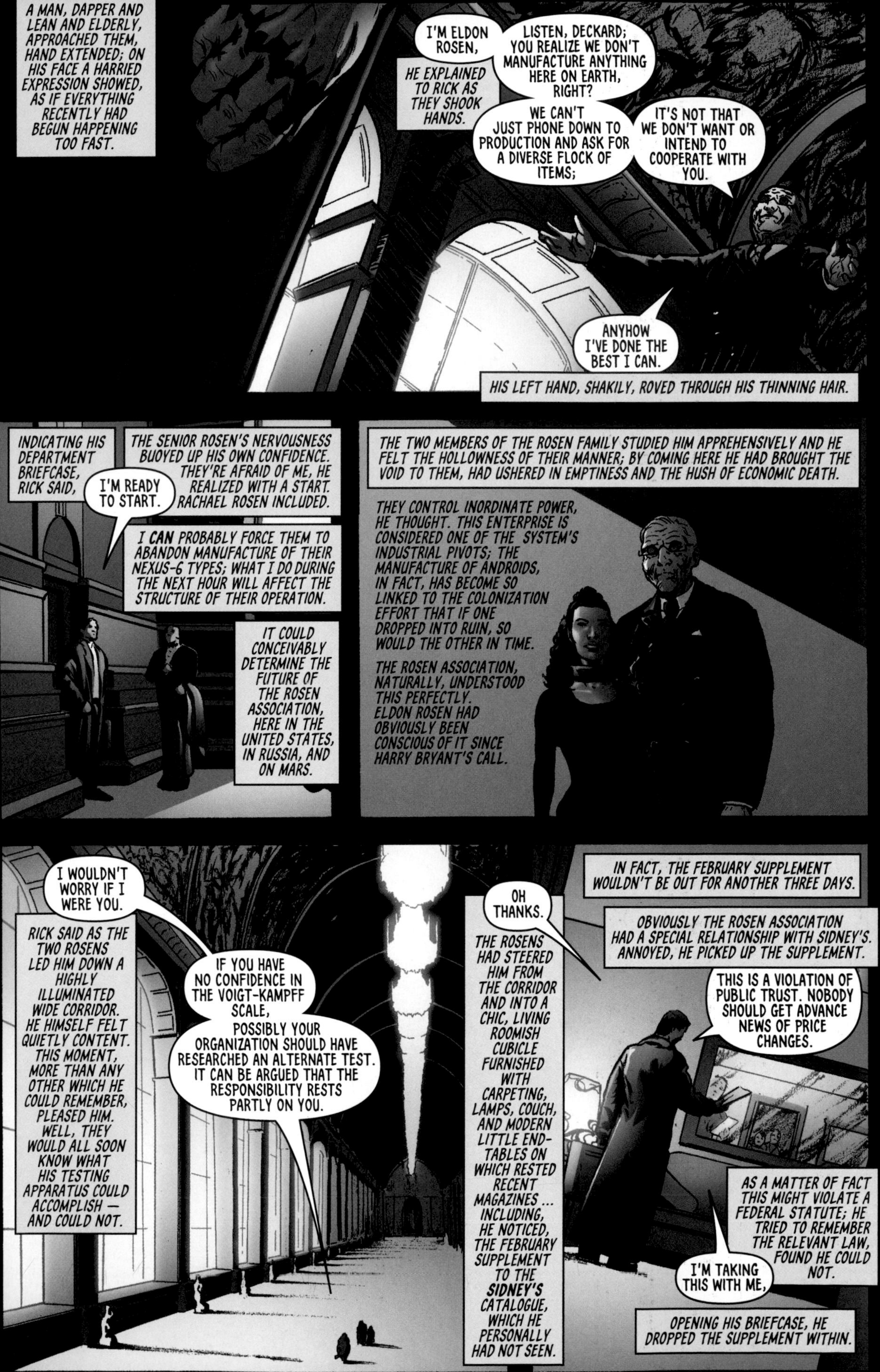
A MAN, DAPPER AND LEAN AND ELDERLY, APPROACHED THEM, HAND EXTENDED; ON HIS FACE A HARRIED EXPRESSION SHOWED, AS IF EVERYTHING RECENTLY HAD BEGUN HAPPENING TOO FAST.
I'M ELDON ROSEN,
HE EXPLAINED TO RICK AS THEY SHOOK HANDS.
LISTEN, DECKARD; YOU REALIZE WE DON'T MANUFACTURE ANYTHING HERE ON EARTH, RIGHT?
WE CAN'T JUST PHONE DOWN TO PRODUCTION AND ASK FOR A DIVERSE FLOCK OF ITEMS;
IT'S NOT THAT WE DON'T WANT OR INTEND TO COOPERATE WITH YOU.
ANYHOW I'VE DONE THE BEST I CAN.
HIS LEFT HAND, SHAKILY, ROVED THROUGH HIS THINNING HAIR.
INDICATING HIS DEPARTMENT BRIEFCASE, RICK SAID,
I'M READY TO START.
THE SENIOR ROSEN'S NERVOUSNESS BUOYED UP HIS OWN CONFIDENCE. THEY'RE AFRAID OF ME, HE REALIZED WITH A START. RACHAEL ROSEN INCLUDED.
I CAN PROBABLY FORCE THEM TO ABANDON MANUFACTURE OF THEIR NEXUS-6 TYPES; WHAT I DO DURING THE NEXT HOUR WILL AFFECT THE STRUCTURE OF THEIR OPERATION.
IT COULD CONCEIVABLY DETERMINE THE FUTURE OF THE ROSEN ASSOCIATION, HERE IN THE UNITED STATES, IN RUSSIA, AND ON MARS.
THE TWO MEMBERS OF THE ROSEN FAMILY STUDIED HIM APPREHENSIVELY AND HE FELT THE HOLLOWNESS OF THEIR MANNER; BY COMING HERE HE HAD BROUGHT THE VOID TO THEM, HAD USHERED IN EMPTINESS AND THE HUSH OF ECONOMIC DEATH.
THEY CONTROL INORDINATE POWER, HE THOUGHT. THIS ENTERPRISE IS CONSIDERED ONE OF THE SYSTEM'S INDUSTRIAL PIVOTS; THE MANUFACTURE OF ANDROIDS, IN FACT, HAS BECOME SO LINKED TO THE COLONIZATION EFFORT THAT IF ONE DROPPED INTO RUIN, SO WOULD THE OTHER IN TIME.
THE ROSEN ASSOCIATION, NATURALLY, UNDERSTOOD THIS PERFECTLY. ELDON ROSEN HAD OBVIOUSLY BEEN CONSCIOUS OF IT SINCE HARRY BRYANT'S CALL.
I WOULDN'T WORRY IF I WERE YOU.
RICK SAID AS THE TWO ROSENS LED HIM DOWN A HIGHLY ILLUMINATED WIDE CORRIDOR. HE HIMSELF FELT QUIETLY CONTENT. THIS MOMENT, MORE THAN ANY OTHER WHICH HE COULD REMEMBER, PLEASED HIM. WELL, THEY WOULD ALL SOON KNOW WHAT HIS TESTING APPARATUS COULD ACCOMPLISH — AND COULD NOT.
IF YOU HAVE NO CONFIDENCE IN THE VOIGT-KAMPFF SCALE,
POSSIBLY YOUR ORGANIZATION SHOULD HAVE RESEARCHED AN ALTERNATE TEST. IT CAN BE ARGUED THAT THE RESPONSIBILITY RESTS PARTLY ON YOU.
OH THANKS.
THE ROSENS HAD STEERED HIM FROM THE CORRIDOR AND INTO A CHIC, LIVING ROOMISH CUBICLE FURNISHED WITH CARPETING, LAMPS, COUCH, AND MODERN LITTLE END-TABLES ON WHICH RESTED RECENT MAGAZINES ... INCLUDING, HE NOTICED, THE FEBRUARY SUPPLEMENT TO THE SIDNEY'S CATALOGUE, WHICH HE PERSONALLY HAD NOT SEEN.
IN FACT, THE FEBRUARY SUPPLEMENT WOULDN'T BE OUT FOR ANOTHER THREE DAYS.
OBVIOUSLY THE ROSEN ASSOCIATION HAD A SPECIAL RELATIONSHIP WITH SIDNEY'S. ANNOYED, HE PICKED UP THE SUPPLEMENT.
THIS IS A VIOLATION OF PUBLIC TRUST. NOBODY SHOULD GET ADVANCE NEWS OF PRICE CHANGES.
AS A MATTER OF FACT THIS MIGHT VIOLATE A FEDERAL STATUTE; HE TRIED TO REMEMBER THE RELEVANT LAW, FOUND HE COULD NOT.
I'M TAKING THIS WITH ME,
OPENING HIS BRIEFCASE, HE DROPPED THE SUPPLEMENT WITHIN.

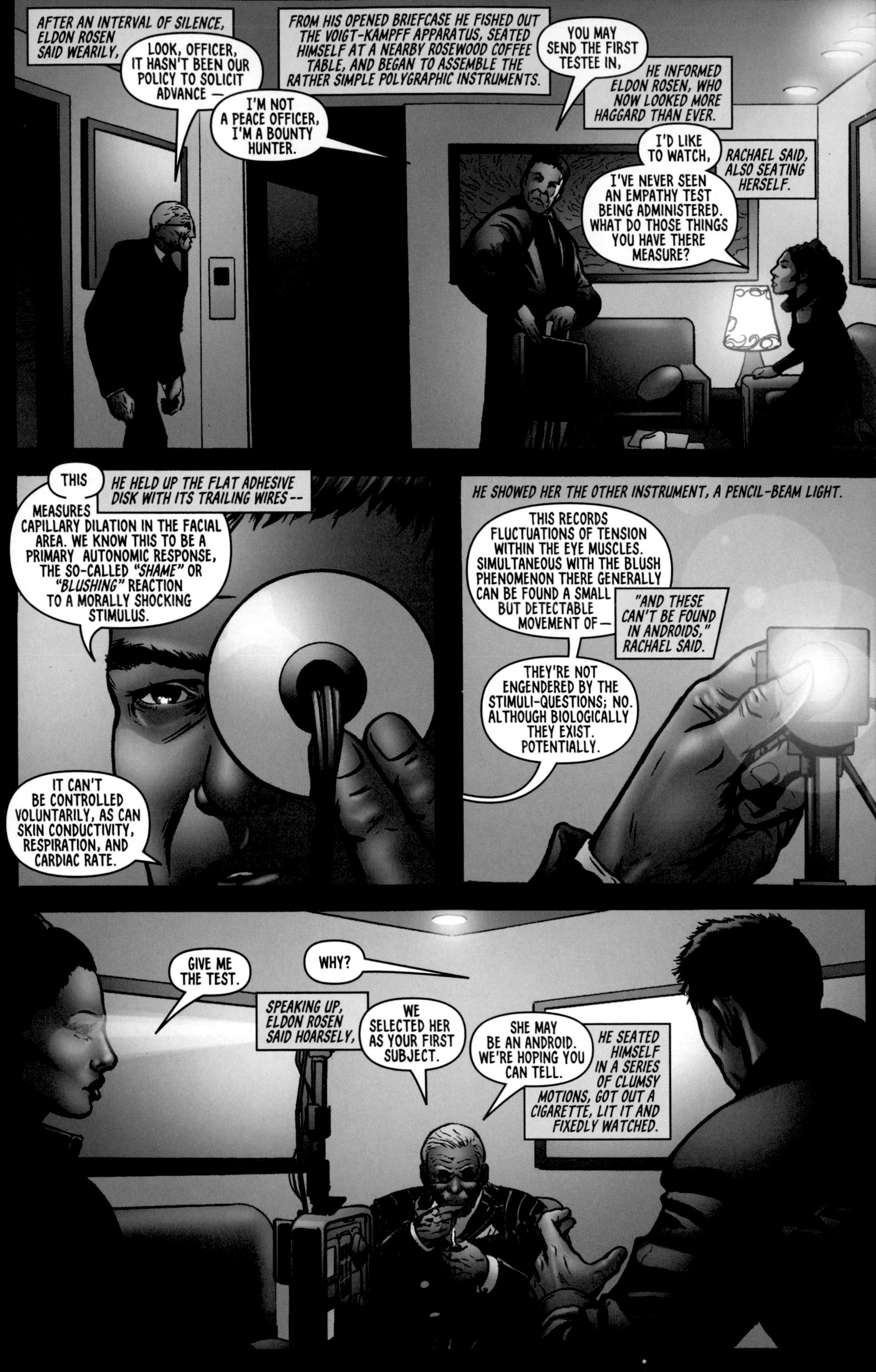
AFTER AN INTERVAL OF SILENCE, ELDON ROSEN SAID WEARILY,
LOOK, OFFICER, IT HASN'T BEEN OUR POLICY TO SOLICIT ADVANCE —
I'M NOT A PEACE OFFICER, I'M A BOUNTY HUNTER.
FROM HIS OPENED BRIEFCASE HE FISHED OUT THE VOIGT-KAMPFF APPARATUS, SEATED HIMSELF AT A NEARBY ROSEWOOD COFFEE TABLE, AND BEGAN TO ASSEMBLE THE RATHER SIMPLE POLYGRAPHIC INSTRUMENTS.
YOU MAY SEND THE FIRST TESTEE IN,
HE INFORMED ELDON ROSEN, WHO NOW LOOKED MORE HAGGARD THAN EVER.
I'D LIKE TO WATCH,
RACHAEL SAID, ALSO SEATING HERSELF.
I'VE NEVER SEEN AN EMPATHY TEST BEING ADMINISTERED. WHAT DO THOSE THINGS YOU HAVE THERE MEASURE?
THIS
HE HELD UP THE FLAT ADHESIVE DISK WITH ITS TRAILING WIRES --
MEASURES CAPILLARY DILATION IN THE FACIAL AREA. WE KNOW THIS TO BE A PRIMARY AUTONOMIC RESPONSE, THE SO-CALLED *"SHAME"* OR *"BLUSHING"* REACTION TO A MORALLY SHOCKING STIMULUS.
IT CAN'T BE CONTROLLED VOLUNTARILY, AS CAN SKIN CONDUCTIVITY, RESPIRATION, AND CARDIAC RATE.
HE SHOWED HER THE OTHER INSTRUMENT, A PENCIL-BEAM LIGHT.
THIS RECORDS FLUCTUATIONS OF TENSION WITHIN THE EYE MUSCLES. SIMULTANEOUS WITH THE BLUSH PHENOMENON THERE GENERALLY CAN BE FOUND A SMALL BUT DETECTABLE MOVEMENT OF —
"AND THESE CAN'T BE FOUND IN ANDROIDS," RACHAEL SAID.
THEY'RE NOT ENGENDERED BY THE STIMULI-QUESTIONS; NO. ALTHOUGH BIOLOGICALLY THEY EXIST. POTENTIALLY.
GIVE ME THE TEST.
WHY?
SPEAKING UP, ELDON ROSEN SAID HOARSELY,
WE SELECTED HER AS YOUR FIRST SUBJECT.
SHE MAY BE AN ANDROID. WE'RE HOPING YOU CAN TELL.
HE SEATED HIMSELF IN A SERIES OF CLUMSY MOTIONS, GOT OUT A CIGARETTE, LIT IT AND FIXEDLY WATCHED.

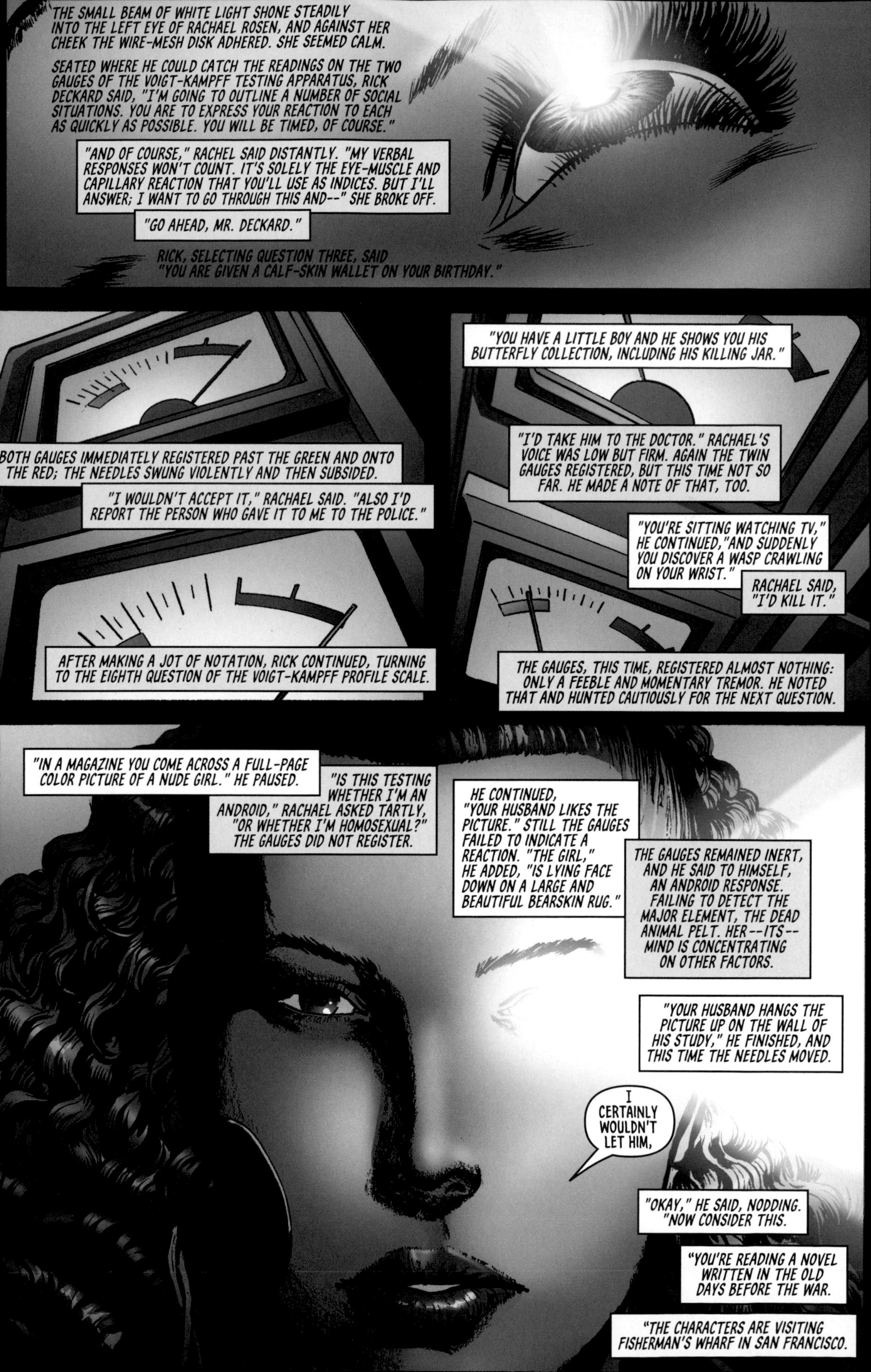
THE SMALL BEAM OF WHITE LIGHT SHONE STEADILY INTO THE LEFT EYE OF RACHAEL ROSEN, AND AGAINST HER CHEEK THE WIRE-MESH DISK ADHERED. SHE SEEMED CALM.
SEATED WHERE HE COULD CATCH THE READINGS ON THE TWO GAUGES OF THE VOIGT-KAMPFF TESTING APPARATUS, RICK DECKARD SAID, "I'M GOING TO OUTLINE A NUMBER OF SOCIAL SITUATIONS. YOU ARE TO EXPRESS YOUR REACTION TO EACH AS QUICKLY AS POSSIBLE. YOU WILL BE TIMED, OF COURSE."
"AND OF COURSE," RACHEL SAID DISTANTLY. "MY VERBAL RESPONSES WON'T COUNT. IT'S SOLELY THE EYE-MUSCLE AND CAPILLARY REACTION THAT YOU'LL USE AS INDICES. BUT I'LL ANSWER; I WANT TO GO THROUGH THIS AND--" SHE BROKE OFF.
"GO AHEAD, MR. DECKARD."
RICK, SELECTING QUESTION THREE, SAID "YOU ARE GIVEN A CALF-SKIN WALLET ON YOUR BIRTHDAY."
BOTH GAUGES IMMEDIATELY REGISTERED PAST THE GREEN AND ONTO THE RED; THE NEEDLES SWUNG VIOLENTLY AND THEN SUBSIDED.
"I WOULDN'T ACCEPT IT," RACHAEL SAID. "ALSO I'D REPORT THE PERSON WHO GAVE IT TO ME TO THE POLICE."
AFTER MAKING A JOT OF NOTATION, RICK CONTINUED, TURNING TO THE EIGHTH QUESTION OF THE VOIGT-KAMPFF PROFILE SCALE.
"YOU HAVE A LITTLE BOY AND HE SHOWS YOU HIS BUTTERFLY COLLECTION, INCLUDING HIS KILLING JAR."
"I'D TAKE HIM TO THE DOCTOR." RACHAEL'S VOICE WAS LOW BUT FIRM. AGAIN THE TWIN GAUGES REGISTERED, BUT THIS TIME NOT SO FAR. HE MADE A NOTE OF THAT, TOO.
"YOU'RE SITTING WATCHING TV," HE CONTINUED, "AND SUDDENLY YOU DISCOVER A WASP CRAWLING ON YOUR WRIST."
RACHAEL SAID, "I'D KILL IT."
THE GAUGES, THIS TIME, REGISTERED ALMOST NOTHING: ONLY A FEEBLE AND MOMENTARY TREMOR. HE NOTED THAT AND HUNTED CAUTIOUSLY FOR THE NEXT QUESTION.
"IN A MAGAZINE YOU COME ACROSS A FULL-PAGE COLOR PICTURE OF A NUDE GIRL." HE PAUSED.
"IS THIS TESTING WHETHER I'M AN ANDROID," RACHAEL ASKED TARTLY, "OR WHETHER I'M HOMOSEXUAL?" THE GAUGES DID NOT REGISTER.
HE CONTINUED, "YOUR HUSBAND LIKES THE PICTURE." STILL THE GAUGES FAILED TO INDICATE A REACTION. "THE GIRL," HE ADDED, "IS LYING FACE DOWN ON A LARGE AND BEAUTIFUL BEARSKIN RUG."
THE GAUGES REMAINED INERT, AND HE SAID TO HIMSELF, AN ANDROID RESPONSE. FAILING TO DETECT THE MAJOR ELEMENT, THE DEAD ANIMAL PELT. HER --ITS-- MIND IS CONCENTRATING ON OTHER FACTORS.
"YOUR HUSBAND HANGS THE PICTURE UP ON THE WALL OF HIS STUDY," HE FINISHED, AND THIS TIME THE NEEDLES MOVED.
I CERTAINLY WOULDN'T LET HIM,
"OKAY," HE SAID, NODDING. "NOW CONSIDER THIS.
"YOU'RE READING A NOVEL WRITTEN IN THE OLD DAYS BEFORE THE WAR.
"THE CHARACTERS ARE VISITING FISHERMAN'S WHARF IN SAN FRANCISCO.

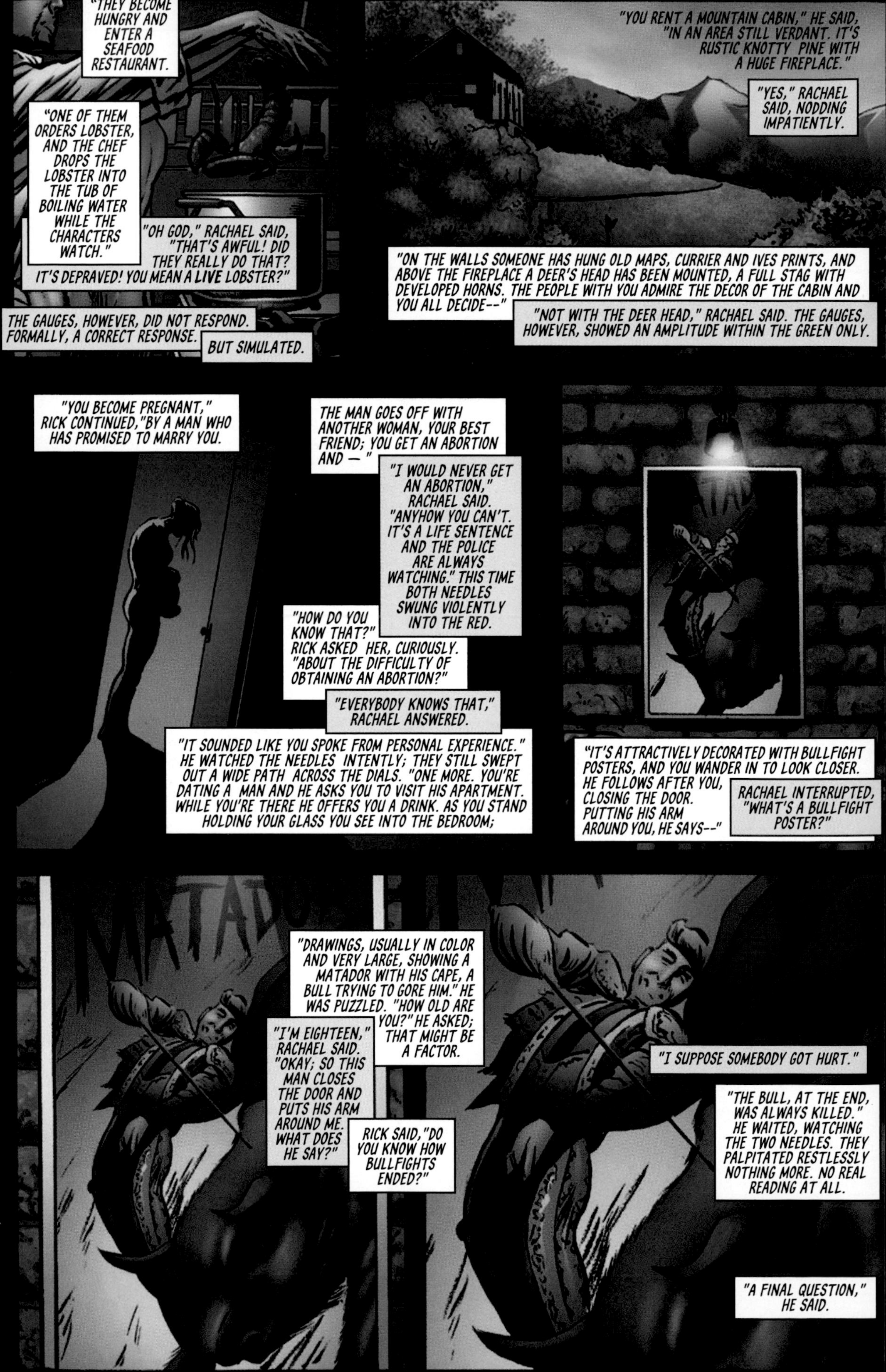
"THEY BECOME HUNGRY AND ENTER A SEAFOOD RESTAURANT.
"ONE OF THEM ORDERS LOBSTER, AND THE CHEF DROPS THE LOBSTER INTO THE TUB OF BOILING WATER WHILE THE CHARACTERS WATCH."
"OH GOD," RACHAEL SAID, "THAT'S AWFUL! DID THEY REALLY DO THAT? IT'S DEPRAVED! YOU MEAN A LIVE LOBSTER?"
THE GAUGES, HOWEVER, DID NOT RESPOND. FORMALLY, A CORRECT RESPONSE.
BUT SIMULATED.
"YOU RENT A MOUNTAIN CABIN," HE SAID, "IN AN AREA STILL VERDANT. IT'S RUSTIC KNOTTY PINE WITH A HUGE FIREPLACE."
"YES," RACHAEL SAID, NODDING IMPATIENTLY.
"ON THE WALLS SOMEONE HAS HUNG OLD MAPS, CURRIER AND IVES PRINTS, AND ABOVE THE FIREPLACE A DEER'S HEAD HAS BEEN MOUNTED, A FULL STAG WITH DEVELOPED HORNS. THE PEOPLE WITH YOU ADMIRE THE DECOR OF THE CABIN AND YOU ALL DECIDE--"
"NOT WITH THE DEER HEAD," RACHAEL SAID. THE GAUGES, HOWEVER, SHOWED AN AMPLITUDE WITHIN THE GREEN ONLY.
"YOU BECOME PREGNANT," RICK CONTINUED,"BY A MAN WHO HAS PROMISED TO MARRY YOU.
THE MAN GOES OFF WITH ANOTHER WOMAN, YOUR BEST FRIEND; YOU GET AN ABORTION AND — "
"I WOULD NEVER GET AN ABORTION," RACHAEL SAID. "ANYHOW YOU CAN'T. IT'S A LIFE SENTENCE AND THE POLICE ARE ALWAYS WATCHING." THIS TIME BOTH NEEDLES SWUNG VIOLENTLY INTO THE RED.
"HOW DO YOU KNOW THAT?" RICK ASKED HER, CURIOUSLY. "ABOUT THE DIFFICULTY OF OBTAINING AN ABORTION?"
"EVERYBODY KNOWS THAT," RACHAEL ANSWERED.
"IT SOUNDED LIKE YOU SPOKE FROM PERSONAL EXPERIENCE." HE WATCHED THE NEEDLES INTENTLY; THEY STILL SWEPT OUT A WIDE PATH ACROSS THE DIALS. "ONE MORE. YOU'RE DATING A MAN AND HE ASKS YOU TO VISIT HIS APARTMENT. WHILE YOU'RE THERE HE OFFERS YOU A DRINK. AS YOU STAND HOLDING YOUR GLASS YOU SEE INTO THE BEDROOM;
"IT'S ATTRACTIVELY DECORATED WITH BULLFIGHT POSTERS, AND YOU WANDER IN TO LOOK CLOSER. HE FOLLOWS AFTER YOU, CLOSING THE DOOR. PUTTING HIS ARM AROUND YOU, HE SAYS--"
RACHAEL INTERRUPTED, "WHAT'S A BULLFIGHT POSTER?"
MATADOR
"DRAWINGS, USUALLY IN COLOR AND VERY LARGE, SHOWING A MATADOR WITH HIS CAPE, A BULL TRYING TO GORE HIM." HE WAS PUZZLED. "HOW OLD ARE YOU?" HE ASKED; THAT MIGHT BE A FACTOR.
"I'M EIGHTEEN," RACHAEL SAID. "OKAY; SO THIS MAN CLOSES THE DOOR AND PUTS HIS ARM AROUND ME. WHAT DOES HE SAY?"
RICK SAID, "DO YOU KNOW HOW BULLFIGHTS ENDED?"
"I SUPPOSE SOMEBODY GOT HURT."
"THE BULL, AT THE END, WAS ALWAYS KILLED." HE WAITED, WATCHING THE TWO NEEDLES. THEY PALPITATED RESTLESSLY NOTHING MORE. NO REAL READING AT ALL.
"A FINAL QUESTION," HE SAID.

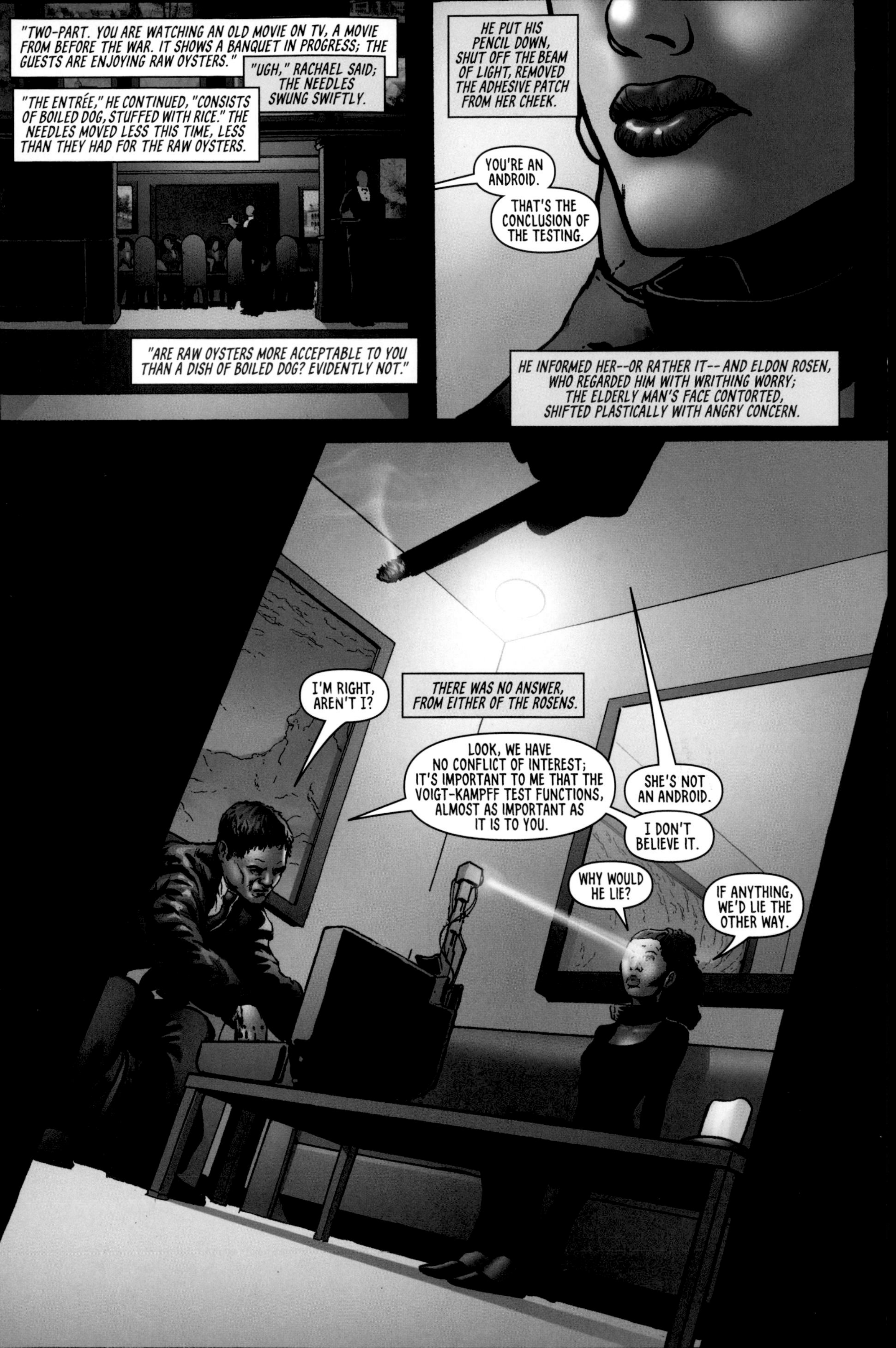
"TWO-PART. YOU ARE WATCHING AN OLD MOVIE ON TV, A MOVIE FROM BEFORE THE WAR. IT SHOWS A BANQUET IN PROGRESS; THE GUESTS ARE ENJOYING RAW OYSTERS."
"UGH," RACHAEL SAID; THE NEEDLES SWUNG SWIFTLY.
"THE ENTRÉE," HE CONTINUED, "CONSISTS OF BOILED DOG, STUFFED WITH RICE." THE NEEDLES MOVED LESS THIS TIME, LESS THAN THEY HAD FOR THE RAW OYSTERS.
"ARE RAW OYSTERS MORE ACCEPTABLE TO YOU THAN A DISH OF BOILED DOG? EVIDENTLY NOT."
HE PUT HIS PENCIL DOWN, SHUT OFF THE BEAM OF LIGHT, REMOVED THE ADHESIVE PATCH FROM HER CHEEK.
YOU'RE AN ANDROID.
THAT'S THE CONCLUSION OF THE TESTING.
HE INFORMED HER--OR RATHER IT-- AND ELDON ROSEN, WHO REGARDED HIM WITH WRITHING WORRY; THE ELDERLY MAN'S FACE CONTORTED, SHIFTED PLASTICALLY WITH ANGRY CONCERN.
I'M RIGHT, AREN'T I?
THERE WAS NO ANSWER, FROM EITHER OF THE ROSENS.
LOOK, WE HAVE NO CONFLICT OF INTEREST; IT'S IMPORTANT TO ME THAT THE VOIGT-KAMPFF TEST FUNCTIONS, ALMOST AS IMPORTANT AS IT IS TO YOU.
SHE'S NOT AN ANDROID.
I DON'T BELIEVE IT.
WHY WOULD HE LIE?
IF ANYTHING, WE'D LIE THE OTHER WAY.

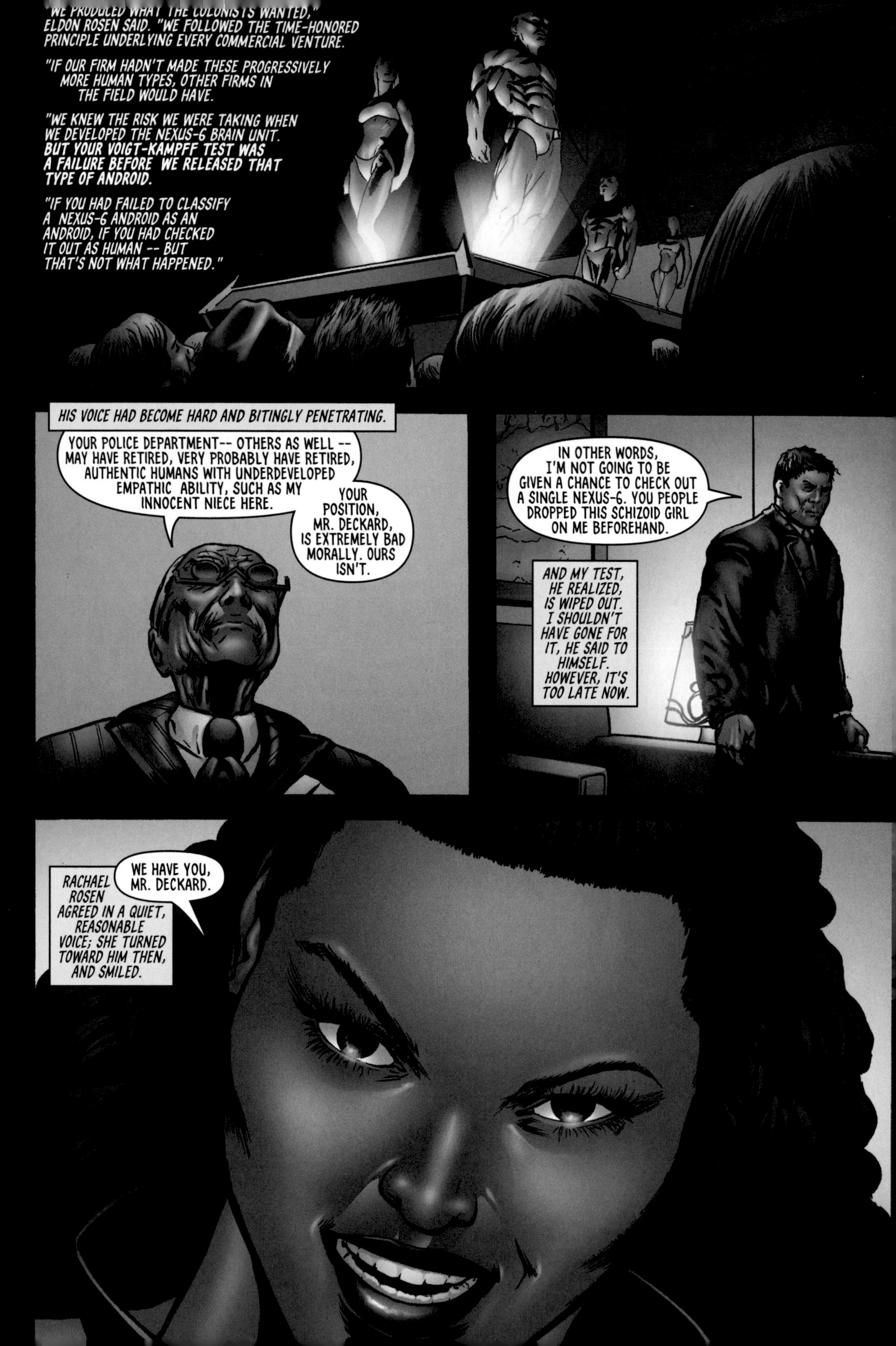
"WE PRODUCED WHAT THE COLONISTS WANTED," ELDON ROSEN SAID. "WE FOLLOWED THE TIME-HONORED PRINCIPLE UNDERLYING EVERY COMMERCIAL VENTURE.
"IF OUR FIRM HADN'T MADE THESE PROGRESSIVELY MORE HUMAN TYPES, OTHER FIRMS IN THE FIELD WOULD HAVE.
"WE KNEW THE RISK WE WERE TAKING WHEN WE DEVELOPED THE NEXUS-6 BRAIN UNIT. BUT YOUR VOIGT-KAMPFF TEST WAS A FAILURE BEFORE WE RELEASED THAT TYPE OF ANDROID.
"IF YOU HAD FAILED TO CLASSIFY A NEXUS-6 ANDROID AS AN ANDROID, IF YOU HAD CHECKED IT OUT AS HUMAN -- BUT THAT'S NOT WHAT HAPPENED."
HIS VOICE HAD BECOME HARD AND BITINGLY PENETRATING.
YOUR POLICE DEPARTMENT-- OTHERS AS WELL -- MAY HAVE RETIRED, VERY PROBABLY HAVE RETIRED, AUTHENTIC HUMANS WITH UNDERDEVELOPED EMPATHIC ABILITY, SUCH AS MY INNOCENT NIECE HERE.
YOUR POSITION, MR. DECKARD, IS EXTREMELY BAD MORALLY. OURS ISN'T.
IN OTHER WORDS, I'M NOT GOING TO BE GIVEN A CHANCE TO CHECK OUT A SINGLE NEXUS-6. YOU PEOPLE DROPPED THIS SCHIZOID GIRL ON ME BEFOREHAND.
AND MY TEST, HE REALIZED, IS WIPED OUT. I SHOULDN'T HAVE GONE FOR IT, HE SAID TO HIMSELF. HOWEVER, IT'S TOO LATE NOW.
RACHAEL ROSEN AGREED IN A QUIET, REASONABLE VOICE; SHE TURNED TOWARD HIM THEN, AND SMILED.
WE HAVE YOU, MR. DECKARD.

HE COULD NOT MAKE OUT, EVEN NOW, HOW THE ROSEN ASSOCIATION
HAD MANAGED TO SNARE HIM, AND SO EASILY.
EXPERTS, HE REALIZED. A MAMMOTH CORPORATION LIKE THIS --
IT EMBODIES TOO MUCH EXPERIENCE.

IT POSSESSES IN FACT A SORT OF GROUP MIND.
AND ELDON AND RACHAEL ROSEN CONSISTED AS SPOKESMEN
FOR THAT CORPORATE ENTITY.
HIS MISTAKE, EVIDENTLY, HAD BEEN IN
VIEWING THEM AS INDIVIDUALS.

IT WAS A MISTAKE HE WOULD NOT MAKE AGAIN.

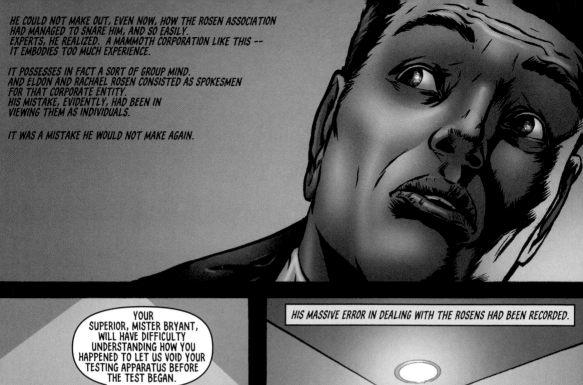

YOUR SUPERIOR, MISTER BRYANT, WILL HAVE DIFFICULTY UNDERSTANDING HOW YOU HAPPENED TO LET US VOID YOUR TESTING APPARATUS BEFORE THE TEST BEGAN.

HE POINTED TOWARD THE CEILING, AND RICK SAW THE CAMERA LENS.

HIS MASSIVE ERROR IN DEALING WITH THE ROSENS HAD BEEN RECORDED.

"I THINK THE RIGHT THING FOR US ALL TO DO," ELDON SAID, "IS SIT DOWN AND--" HE GESTURED AFFABLY. "WE CAN WORK SOMETHING OUT, MR. DECKARD. THERE'S NO NEED FOR ANXIETY.

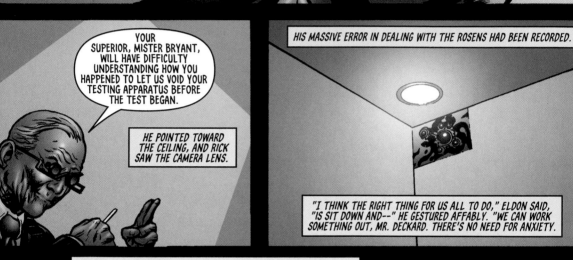

THE NEXUS-6 VARIETY OF ANDROID IS A FACT; WE HERE AT THE ROSEN ASSOCIATION RECOGNIZE IT AND I THINK NOW YOU DO, TOO."

RACHAEL, LEANING TOWARD RICK, SAID,

HOW WOULD YOU LIKE TO OWN AN OWL?

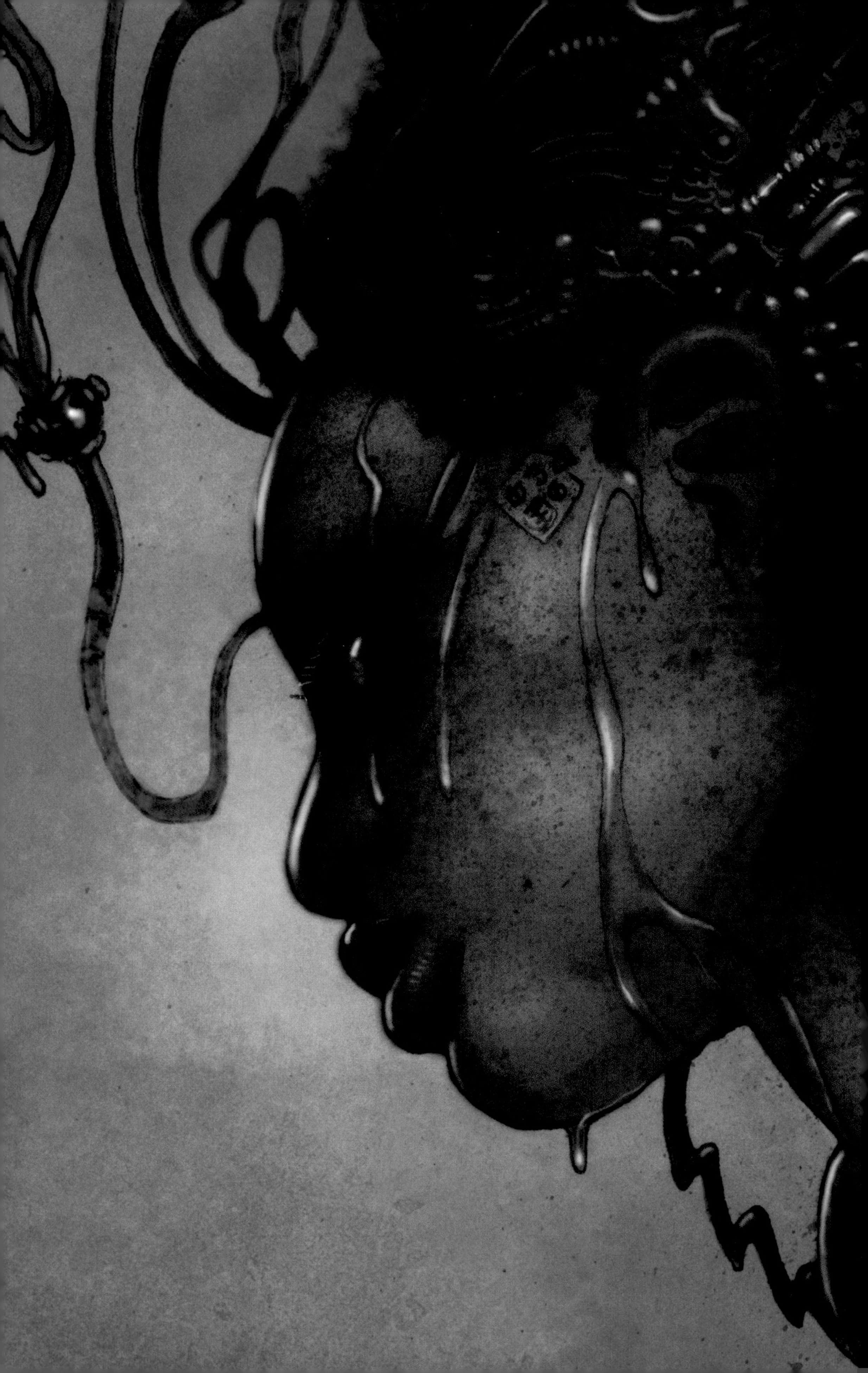

BOOK

THREE

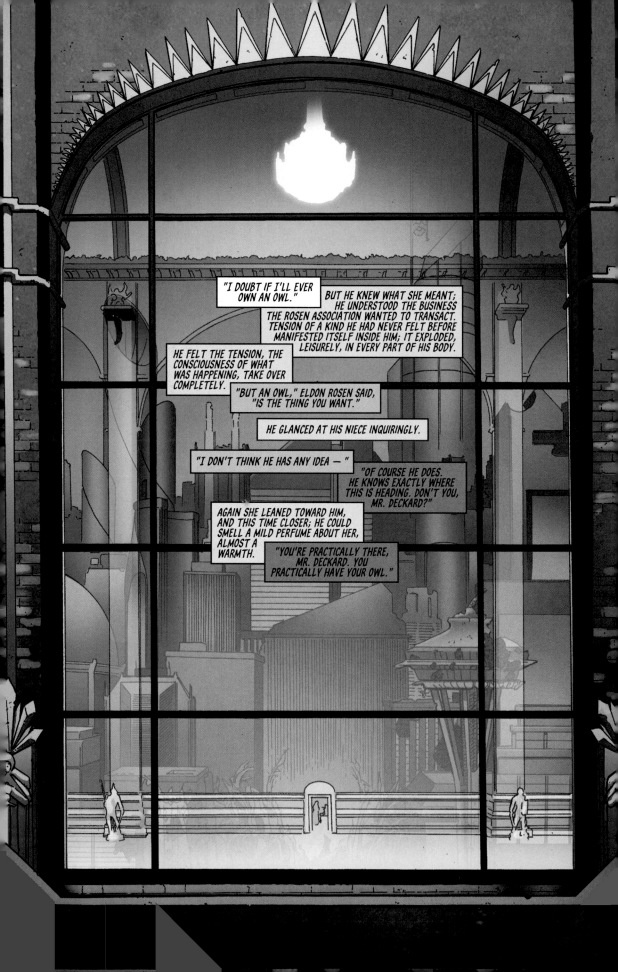

"I DOUBT IF I'LL EVER OWN AN OWL."

BUT HE KNEW WHAT SHE MEANT; HE UNDERSTOOD THE BUSINESS THE ROSEN ASSOCIATION WANTED TO TRANSACT. TENSION OF A KIND HE HAD NEVER FELT BEFORE MANIFESTED ITSELF INSIDE HIM; IT EXPLODED, LEISURELY, IN EVERY PART OF HIS BODY.

HE FELT THE TENSION, THE CONSCIOUSNESS OF WHAT WAS HAPPENING, TAKE OVER COMPLETELY.

"BUT AN OWL," ELDON ROSEN SAID, "IS THE THING YOU WANT."

HE GLANCED AT HIS NIECE INQUIRINGLY.

"I DON'T THINK HE HAS ANY IDEA —"

"OF COURSE HE DOES. HE KNOWS EXACTLY WHERE THIS IS HEADING. DON'T YOU, MR. DECKARD?"

AGAIN SHE LEANED TOWARD HIM, AND THIS TIME CLOSER; HE COULD SMELL A MILD PERFUME ABOUT HER, ALMOST A WARMTH.

"YOU'RE PRACTICALLY THERE, MR. DECKARD. YOU PRACTICALLY HAVE YOUR OWL."

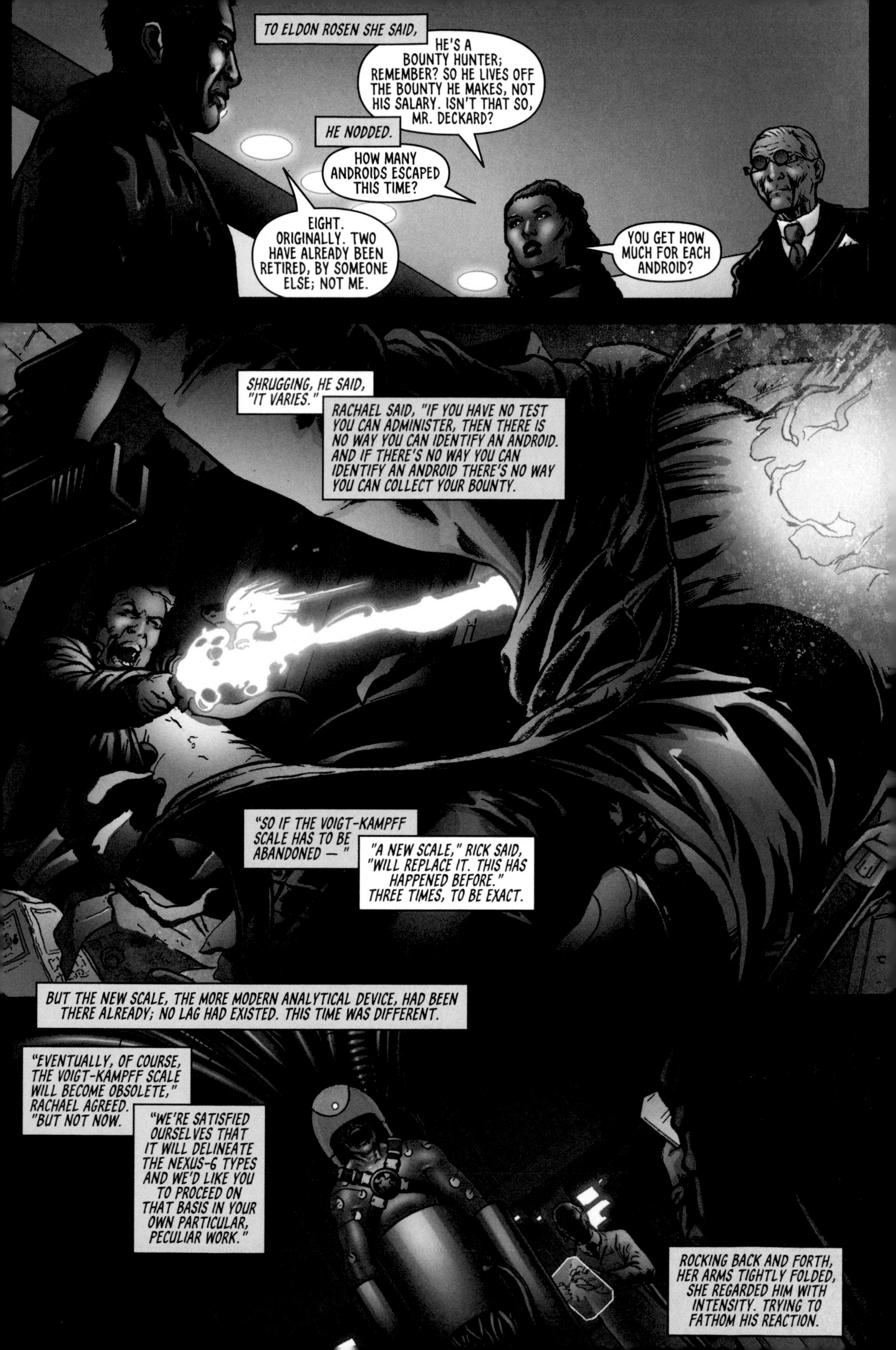
TO ELDON ROSEN SHE SAID,
HE'S A BOUNTY HUNTER; REMEMBER? SO HE LIVES OFF THE BOUNTY HE MAKES, NOT HIS SALARY. ISN'T THAT SO, MR. DECKARD?
HE NODDED.
HOW MANY ANDROIDS ESCAPED THIS TIME?
EIGHT. ORIGINALLY. TWO HAVE ALREADY BEEN RETIRED, BY SOMEONE ELSE; NOT ME.
YOU GET HOW MUCH FOR EACH ANDROID?
SHRUGGING, HE SAID, "IT VARIES."
RACHAEL SAID, "IF YOU HAVE NO TEST YOU CAN ADMINISTER, THEN THERE IS NO WAY YOU CAN IDENTIFY AN ANDROID. AND IF THERE'S NO WAY YOU CAN IDENTIFY AN ANDROID THERE'S NO WAY YOU CAN COLLECT YOUR BOUNTY.
"SO IF THE VOIGT-KAMPFF SCALE HAS TO BE ABANDONED — "
"A NEW SCALE," RICK SAID, "WILL REPLACE IT. THIS HAS HAPPENED BEFORE." THREE TIMES, TO BE EXACT.
BUT THE NEW SCALE, THE MORE MODERN ANALYTICAL DEVICE, HAD BEEN THERE ALREADY; NO LAG HAD EXISTED. THIS TIME WAS DIFFERENT.
"EVENTUALLY, OF COURSE, THE VOIGT-KAMPFF SCALE WILL BECOME OBSOLETE," RACHAEL AGREED. "BUT NOT NOW.
"WE'RE SATISFIED OURSELVES THAT IT WILL DELINEATE THE NEXUS-6 TYPES AND WE'D LIKE YOU TO PROCEED ON THAT BASIS IN YOUR OWN PARTICULAR, PECULIAR WORK."
ROCKING BACK AND FORTH, HER ARMS TIGHTLY FOLDED, SHE REGARDED HIM WITH INTENSITY. TRYING TO FATHOM HIS REACTION.

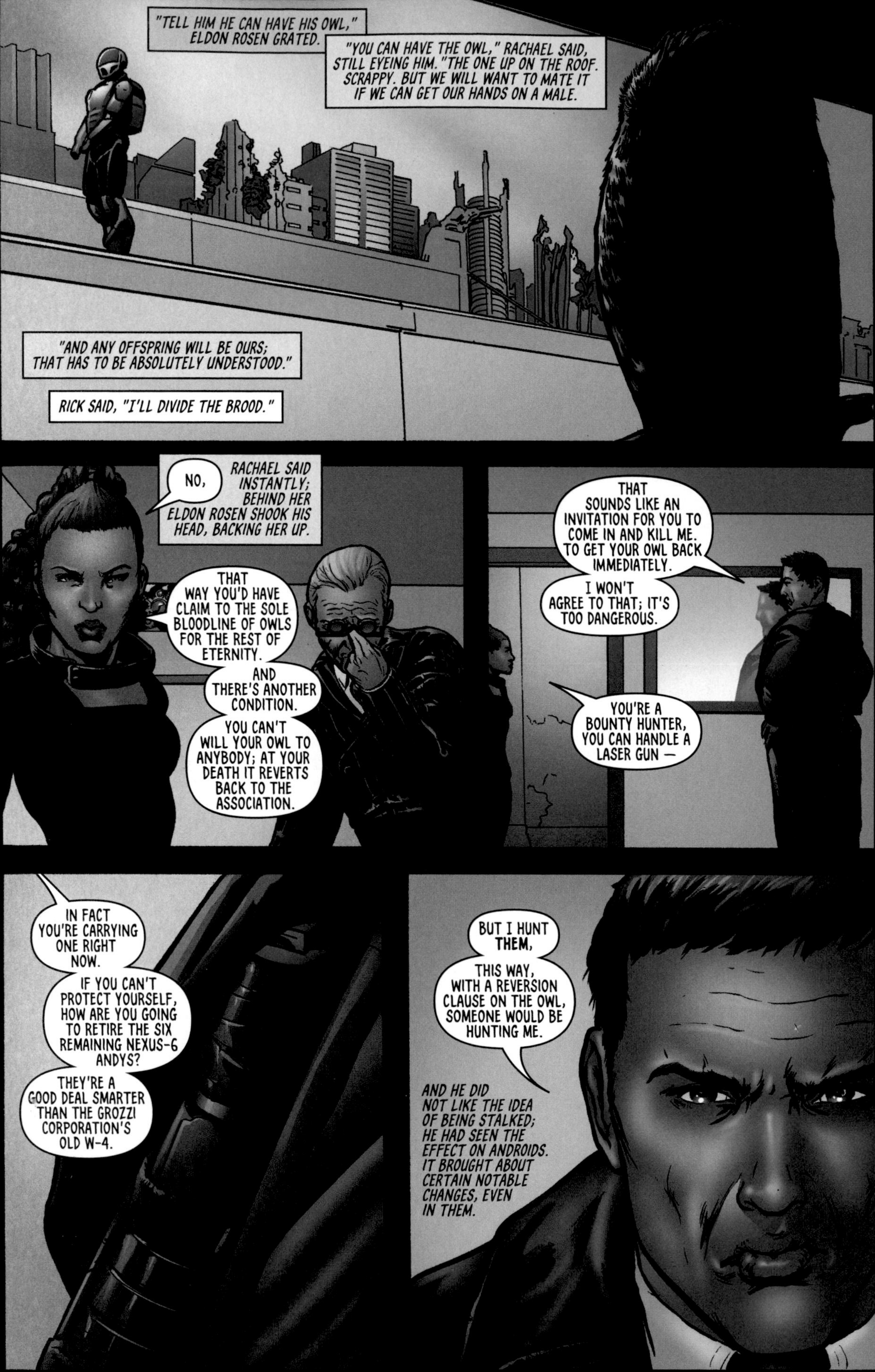
"TELL HIM HE CAN HAVE HIS OWL," ELDON ROSEN GRATED.
"YOU CAN HAVE THE OWL," RACHAEL SAID, STILL EYEING HIM. "THE ONE UP ON THE ROOF. SCRAPPY. BUT WE WILL WANT TO MATE IT IF WE CAN GET OUR HANDS ON A MALE.
"AND ANY OFFSPRING WILL BE OURS; THAT HAS TO BE ABSOLUTELY UNDERSTOOD."
RICK SAID, "I'LL DIVIDE THE BROOD."
NO,
RACHAEL SAID INSTANTLY; BEHIND HER ELDON ROSEN SHOOK HIS HEAD, BACKING HER UP.
THAT WAY YOU'D HAVE CLAIM TO THE SOLE BLOODLINE OF OWLS FOR THE REST OF ETERNITY.
AND THERE'S ANOTHER CONDITION.
YOU CAN'T WILL YOUR OWL TO ANYBODY; AT YOUR DEATH IT REVERTS BACK TO THE ASSOCIATION.
THAT SOUNDS LIKE AN INVITATION FOR YOU TO COME IN AND KILL ME. TO GET YOUR OWL BACK IMMEDIATELY.
I WON'T AGREE TO THAT; IT'S TOO DANGEROUS.
YOU'RE A BOUNTY HUNTER, YOU CAN HANDLE A LASER GUN —
IN FACT YOU'RE CARRYING ONE RIGHT NOW.
IF YOU CAN'T PROTECT YOURSELF, HOW ARE YOU GOING TO RETIRE THE SIX REMAINING NEXUS-6 ANDYS?
THEY'RE A GOOD DEAL SMARTER THAN THE GROZZI CORPORATION'S OLD W-4.
BUT I HUNT **THEM**,
THIS WAY, WITH A REVERSION CLAUSE ON THE OWL, SOMEONE WOULD BE HUNTING ME.
AND HE DID NOT LIKE THE IDEA OF BEING STALKED; HE HAD SEEN THE EFFECT ON ANDROIDS. IT BROUGHT ABOUT CERTAIN NOTABLE CHANGES, EVEN IN THEM.

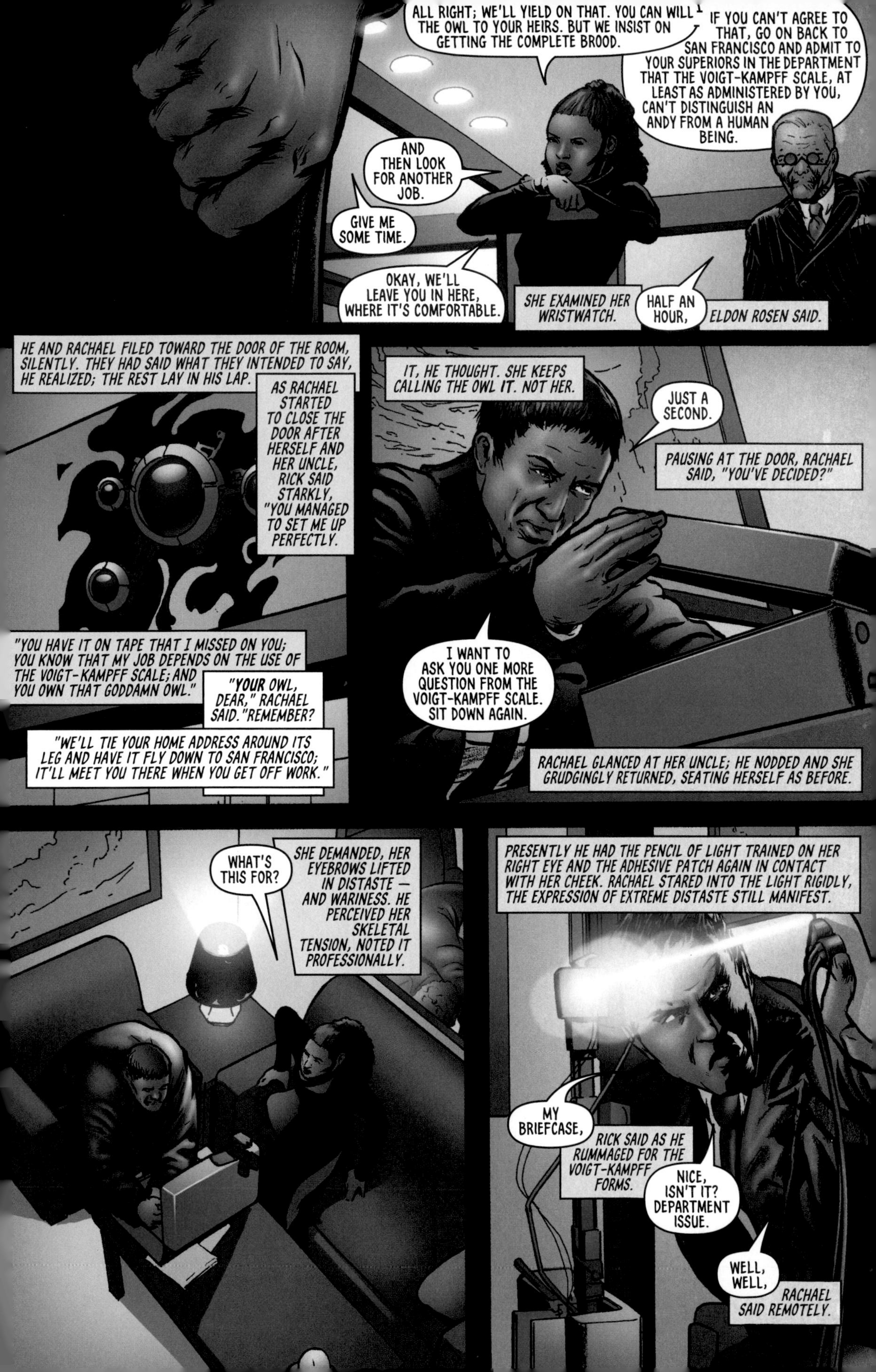
ALL RIGHT; WE'LL YIELD ON THAT. YOU CAN WILL THE OWL TO YOUR HEIRS. BUT WE INSIST ON GETTING THE COMPLETE BROOD.
IF YOU CAN'T AGREE TO THAT, GO ON BACK TO SAN FRANCISCO AND ADMIT TO YOUR SUPERIORS IN THE DEPARTMENT THAT THE VOIGT-KAMPFF SCALE, AT LEAST AS ADMINISTERED BY YOU, CAN'T DISTINGUISH AN ANDY FROM A HUMAN BEING.
AND THEN LOOK FOR ANOTHER JOB.
GIVE ME SOME TIME.
OKAY, WE'LL LEAVE YOU IN HERE, WHERE IT'S COMFORTABLE.
SHE EXAMINED HER WRISTWATCH.
HALF AN HOUR,
ELDON ROSEN SAID.
HE AND RACHAEL FILED TOWARD THE DOOR OF THE ROOM, SILENTLY. THEY HAD SAID WHAT THEY INTENDED TO SAY, HE REALIZED; THE REST LAY IN HIS LAP.
AS RACHAEL STARTED TO CLOSE THE DOOR AFTER HERSELF AND HER UNCLE, RICK SAID STARKLY, "YOU MANAGED TO SET ME UP PERFECTLY.
"YOU HAVE IT ON TAPE THAT I MISSED ON YOU; YOU KNOW THAT MY JOB DEPENDS ON THE USE OF THE VOIGT-KAMPFF SCALE; AND YOU OWN THAT GODDAMN OWL."
"**YOUR** OWL, DEAR," RACHAEL SAID. "REMEMBER?
"WE'LL TIE YOUR HOME ADDRESS AROUND ITS LEG AND HAVE IT FLY DOWN TO SAN FRANCISCO; IT'LL MEET YOU THERE WHEN YOU GET OFF WORK."
IT, HE THOUGHT. SHE KEEPS CALLING THE OWL **IT**. NOT HER.
JUST A SECOND.
PAUSING AT THE DOOR, RACHAEL SAID, "YOU'VE DECIDED?"
I WANT TO ASK YOU ONE MORE QUESTION FROM THE VOIGT-KAMPFF SCALE. SIT DOWN AGAIN.
RACHAEL GLANCED AT HER UNCLE; HE NODDED AND SHE GRUDGINGLY RETURNED, SEATING HERSELF AS BEFORE.
WHAT'S THIS FOR?
SHE DEMANDED, HER EYEBROWS LIFTED IN DISTASTE — AND WARINESS. HE PERCEIVED HER SKELETAL TENSION, NOTED IT PROFESSIONALLY.
PRESENTLY HE HAD THE PENCIL OF LIGHT TRAINED ON HER RIGHT EYE AND THE ADHESIVE PATCH AGAIN IN CONTACT WITH HER CHEEK. RACHAEL STARED INTO THE LIGHT RIGIDLY, THE EXPRESSION OF EXTREME DISTASTE STILL MANIFEST.
MY BRIEFCASE,
RICK SAID AS HE RUMMAGED FOR THE VOIGT-KAMPFF FORMS.
NICE, ISN'T IT? DEPARTMENT ISSUE.
WELL, WELL,
RACHAEL SAID REMOTELY.

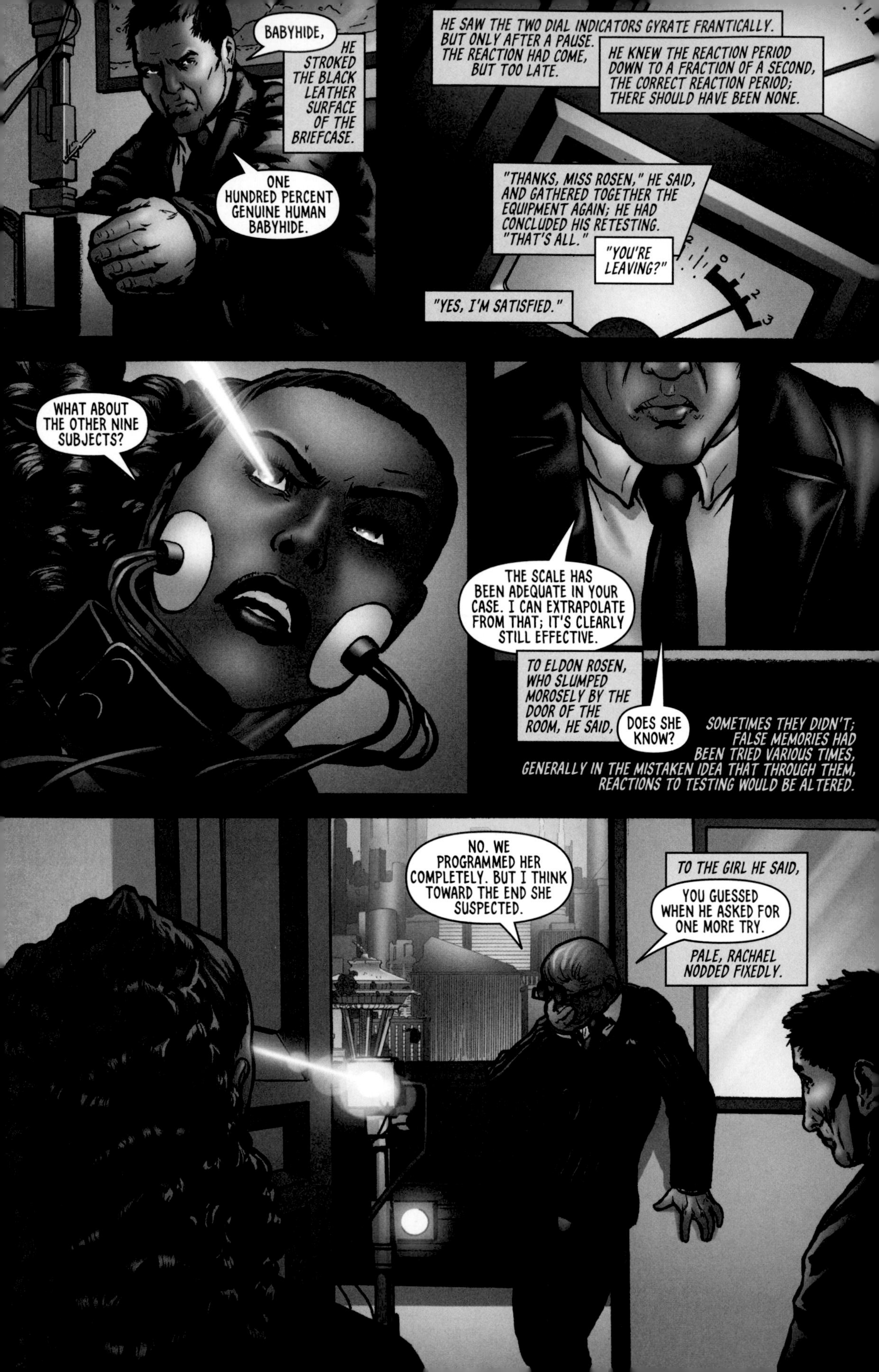
BABYHIDE,
HE STROKED THE BLACK LEATHER SURFACE OF THE BRIEFCASE.
ONE HUNDRED PERCENT GENUINE HUMAN BABYHIDE.
HE SAW THE TWO DIAL INDICATORS GYRATE FRANTICALLY. BUT ONLY AFTER A PAUSE. THE REACTION HAD COME, BUT TOO LATE.
HE KNEW THE REACTION PERIOD DOWN TO A FRACTION OF A SECOND, THE CORRECT REACTION PERIOD; THERE SHOULD HAVE BEEN NONE.
"THANKS, MISS ROSEN," HE SAID, AND GATHERED TOGETHER THE EQUIPMENT AGAIN; HE HAD CONCLUDED HIS RETESTING. "THAT'S ALL."
"YOU'RE LEAVING?"
"YES, I'M SATISFIED."
WHAT ABOUT THE OTHER NINE SUBJECTS?
THE SCALE HAS BEEN ADEQUATE IN YOUR CASE. I CAN EXTRAPOLATE FROM THAT; IT'S CLEARLY STILL EFFECTIVE.
TO ELDON ROSEN, WHO SLUMPED MOROSELY BY THE DOOR OF THE ROOM, HE SAID,
DOES SHE KNOW?
SOMETIMES THEY DIDN'T; FALSE MEMORIES HAD BEEN TRIED VARIOUS TIMES, GENERALLY IN THE MISTAKEN IDEA THAT THROUGH THEM, REACTIONS TO TESTING WOULD BE ALTERED.
NO. WE PROGRAMMED HER COMPLETELY. BUT I THINK TOWARD THE END SHE SUSPECTED.
TO THE GIRL HE SAID,
YOU GUESSED WHEN HE ASKED FOR ONE MORE TRY.
PALE, RACHAEL NODDED FIXEDLY.

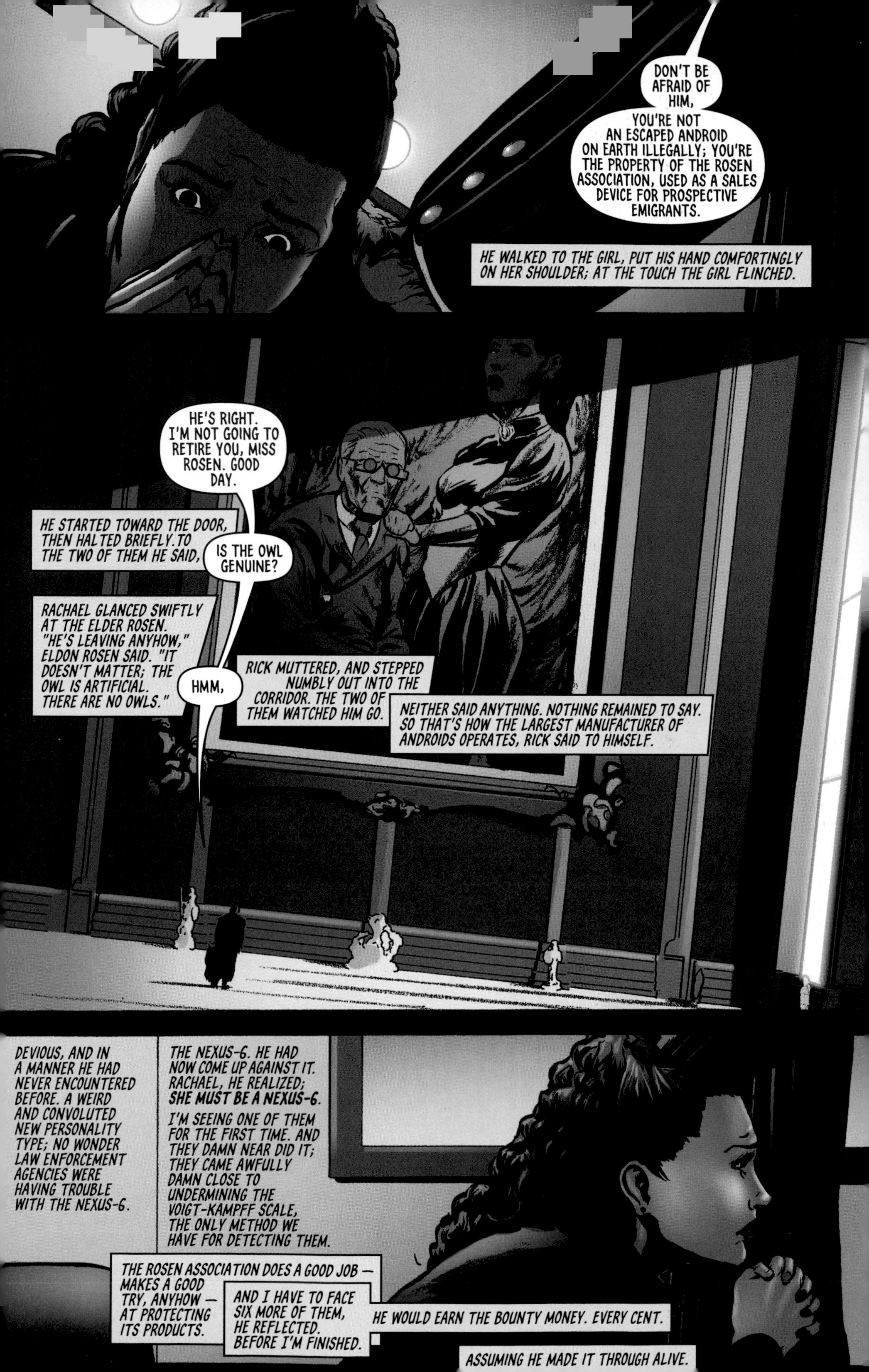

DON'T BE AFRAID OF HIM,
YOU'RE NOT AN ESCAPED ANDROID ON EARTH ILLEGALLY; YOU'RE THE PROPERTY OF THE ROSEN ASSOCIATION, USED AS A SALES DEVICE FOR PROSPECTIVE EMIGRANTS.
HE WALKED TO THE GIRL, PUT HIS HAND COMFORTINGLY ON HER SHOULDER; AT THE TOUCH THE GIRL FLINCHED.
HE'S RIGHT. I'M NOT GOING TO RETIRE YOU, MISS ROSEN. GOOD DAY.
HE STARTED TOWARD THE DOOR, THEN HALTED BRIEFLY.TO THE TWO OF THEM HE SAID,
IS THE OWL GENUINE?
RACHAEL GLANCED SWIFTLY AT THE ELDER ROSEN. "HE'S LEAVING ANYHOW," ELDON ROSEN SAID. "IT DOESN'T MATTER; THE OWL IS ARTIFICIAL. THERE ARE NO OWLS."
HMM,
RICK MUTTERED, AND STEPPED NUMBLY OUT INTO THE CORRIDOR. THE TWO OF THEM WATCHED HIM GO.
NEITHER SAID ANYTHING. NOTHING REMAINED TO SAY. SO THAT'S HOW THE LARGEST MANUFACTURER OF ANDROIDS OPERATES, RICK SAID TO HIMSELF.
DEVIOUS, AND IN A MANNER HE HAD NEVER ENCOUNTERED BEFORE. A WEIRD AND CONVOLUTED NEW PERSONALITY TYPE; NO WONDER LAW ENFORCEMENT AGENCIES WERE HAVING TROUBLE WITH THE NEXUS-6.
THE NEXUS-6. HE HAD NOW COME UP AGAINST IT. RACHAEL, HE REALIZED; **SHE MUST BE A NEXUS-6**.
I'M SEEING ONE OF THEM FOR THE FIRST TIME. AND THEY DAMN NEAR DID IT; THEY CAME AWFULLY DAMN CLOSE TO UNDERMINING THE VOIGT-KAMPFF SCALE, THE ONLY METHOD WE HAVE FOR DETECTING THEM.
THE ROSEN ASSOCIATION DOES A GOOD JOB — MAKES A GOOD TRY, ANYHOW — AT PROTECTING ITS PRODUCTS.
AND I HAVE TO FACE SIX MORE OF THEM, HE REFLECTED. BEFORE I'M FINISHED.
HE WOULD EARN THE BOUNTY MONEY. EVERY CENT.
ASSUMING HE MADE IT THROUGH ALIVE.

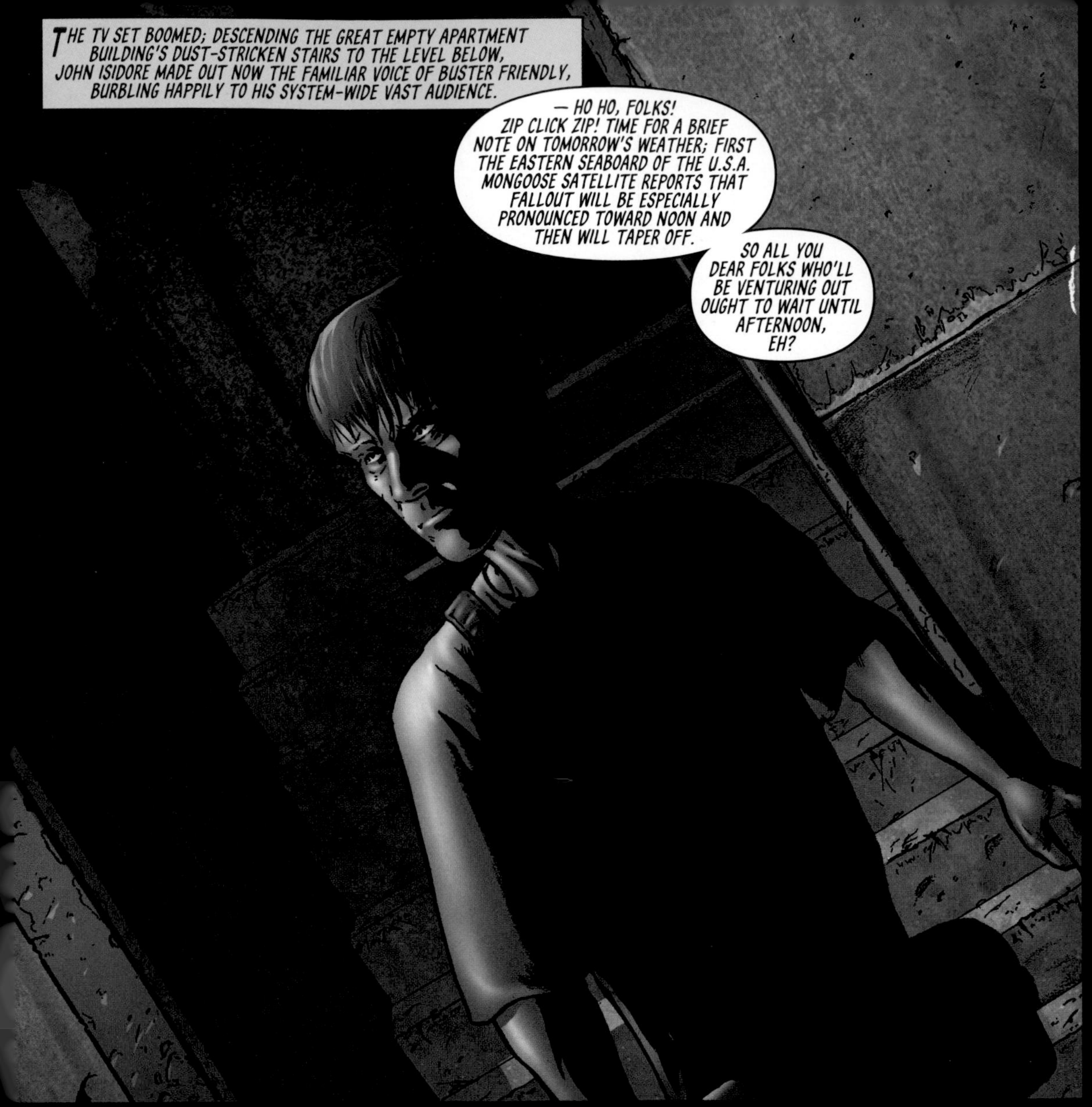
THE TV SET BOOMED; DESCENDING THE GREAT EMPTY APARTMENT BUILDING'S DUST-STRICKEN STAIRS TO THE LEVEL BELOW, JOHN ISIDORE MADE OUT NOW THE FAMILIAR VOICE OF BUSTER FRIENDLY, BURBLING HAPPILY TO HIS SYSTEM-WIDE VAST AUDIENCE.
— HO HO, FOLKS! ZIP CLICK ZIP! TIME FOR A BRIEF NOTE ON TOMORROW'S WEATHER; FIRST THE EASTERN SEABOARD OF THE U.S.A. MONGOOSE SATELLITE REPORTS THAT FALLOUT WILL BE ESPECIALLY PRONOUNCED TOWARD NOON AND THEN WILL TAPER OFF.
SO ALL YOU DEAR FOLKS WHO'LL BE VENTURING OUT OUGHT TO WAIT UNTIL AFTERNOON, EH?

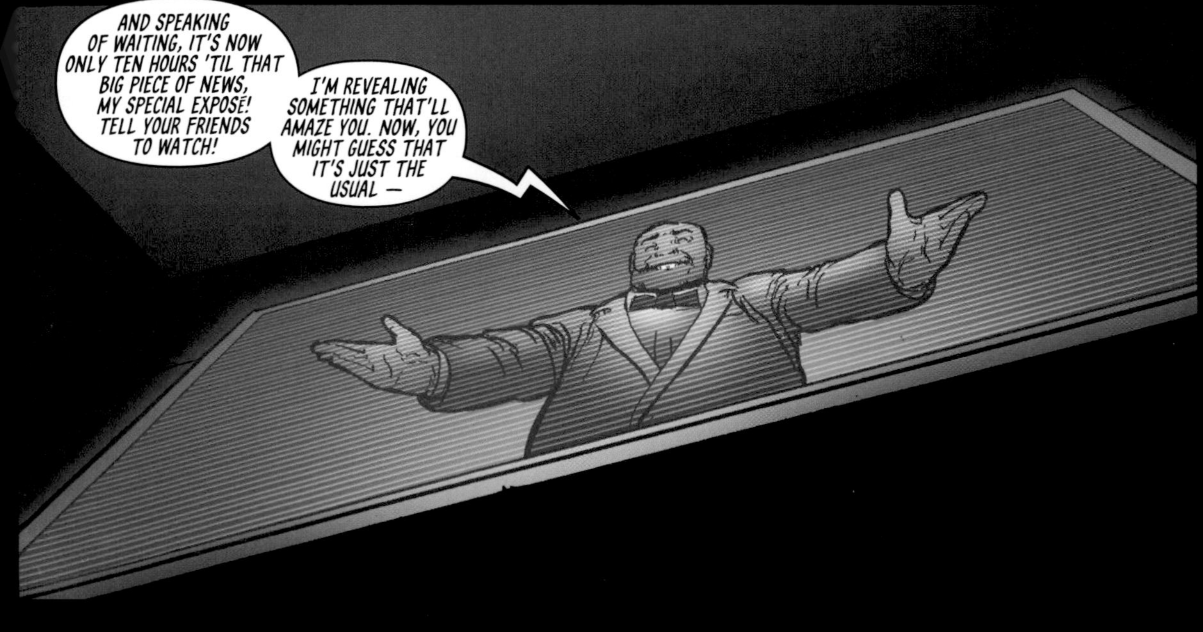
AND SPEAKING OF WAITING, IT'S NOW ONLY TEN HOURS 'TIL THAT BIG PIECE OF NEWS, MY SPECIAL EXPOSE! TELL YOUR FRIENDS TO WATCH!
I'M REVEALING SOMETHING THAT'LL AMAZE YOU. NOW, YOU MIGHT GUESS THAT IT'S JUST THE USUAL —

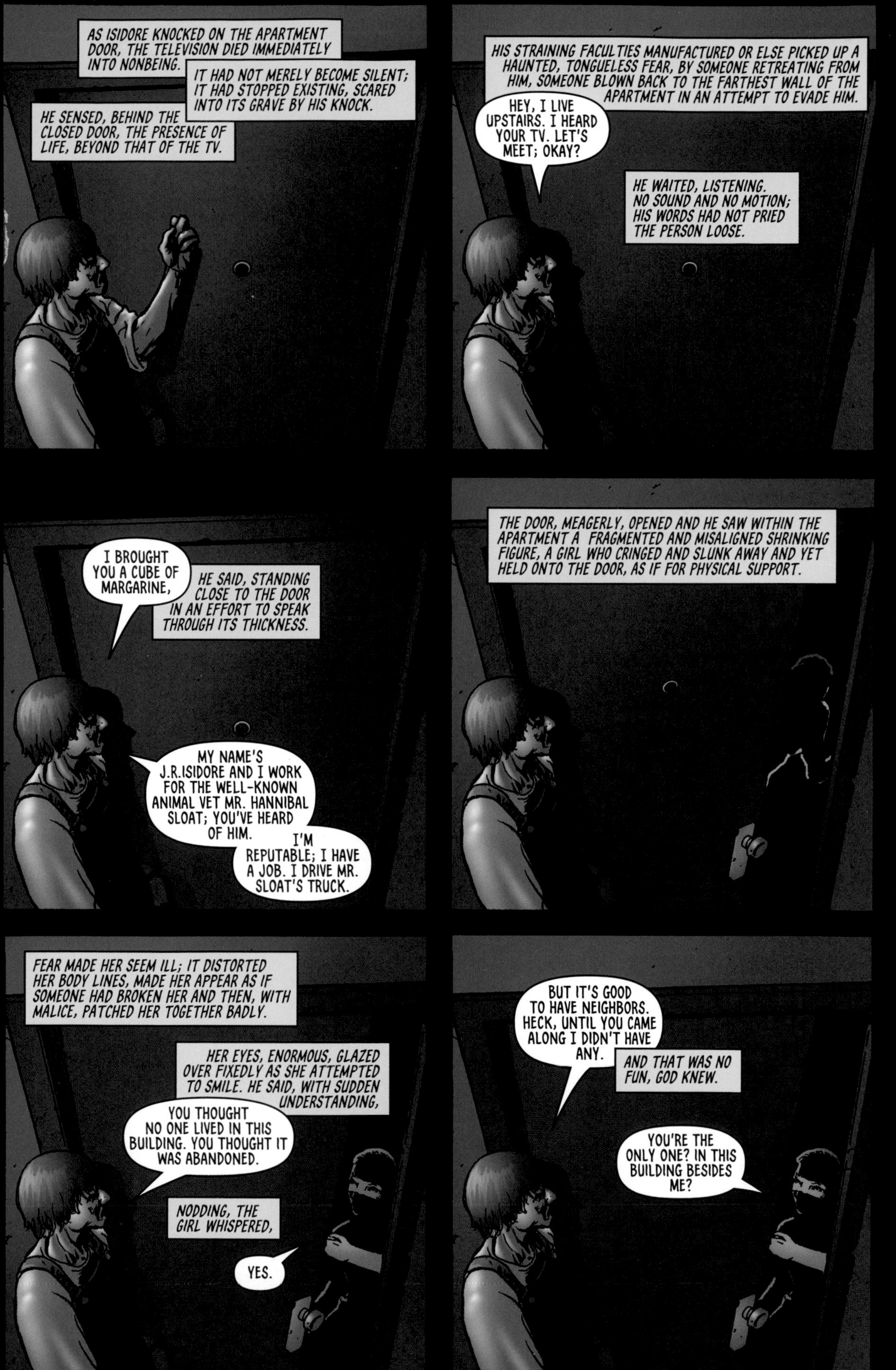
AS ISIDORE KNOCKED ON THE APARTMENT DOOR, THE TELEVISION DIED IMMEDIATELY INTO NONBEING.
IT HAD NOT MERELY BECOME SILENT; IT HAD STOPPED EXISTING, SCARED INTO ITS GRAVE BY HIS KNOCK.
HE SENSED, BEHIND THE CLOSED DOOR, THE PRESENCE OF LIFE, BEYOND THAT OF THE TV.
HIS STRAINING FACULTIES MANUFACTURED OR ELSE PICKED UP A HAUNTED, TONGUELESS FEAR, BY SOMEONE RETREATING FROM HIM, SOMEONE BLOWN BACK TO THE FARTHEST WALL OF THE APARTMENT IN AN ATTEMPT TO EVADE HIM.
HEY, I LIVE UPSTAIRS. I HEARD YOUR TV. LET'S MEET; OKAY?
HE WAITED, LISTENING. NO SOUND AND NO MOTION; HIS WORDS HAD NOT PRIED THE PERSON LOOSE.
I BROUGHT YOU A CUBE OF MARGARINE,
HE SAID, STANDING CLOSE TO THE DOOR IN AN EFFORT TO SPEAK THROUGH ITS THICKNESS.
MY NAME'S J.R.ISIDORE AND I WORK FOR THE WELL-KNOWN ANIMAL VET MR. HANNIBAL SLOAT; YOU'VE HEARD OF HIM.
I'M REPUTABLE; I HAVE A JOB. I DRIVE MR. SLOAT'S TRUCK.
THE DOOR, MEAGERLY, OPENED AND HE SAW WITHIN THE APARTMENT A FRAGMENTED AND MISALIGNED SHRINKING FIGURE, A GIRL WHO CRINGED AND SLUNK AWAY AND YET HELD ONTO THE DOOR, AS IF FOR PHYSICAL SUPPORT.
FEAR MADE HER SEEM ILL; IT DISTORTED HER BODY LINES, MADE HER APPEAR AS IF SOMEONE HAD BROKEN HER AND THEN, WITH MALICE, PATCHED HER TOGETHER BADLY.
HER EYES, ENORMOUS, GLAZED OVER FIXEDLY AS SHE ATTEMPTED TO SMILE. HE SAID, WITH SUDDEN UNDERSTANDING,
YOU THOUGHT NO ONE LIVED IN THIS BUILDING. YOU THOUGHT IT WAS ABANDONED.
NODDING, THE GIRL WHISPERED,
YES.
BUT IT'S GOOD TO HAVE NEIGHBORS. HECK, UNTIL YOU CAME ALONG I DIDN'T HAVE ANY.
AND THAT WAS NO FUN, GOD KNEW.
YOU'RE THE ONLY ONE? IN THIS BUILDING BESIDES ME?

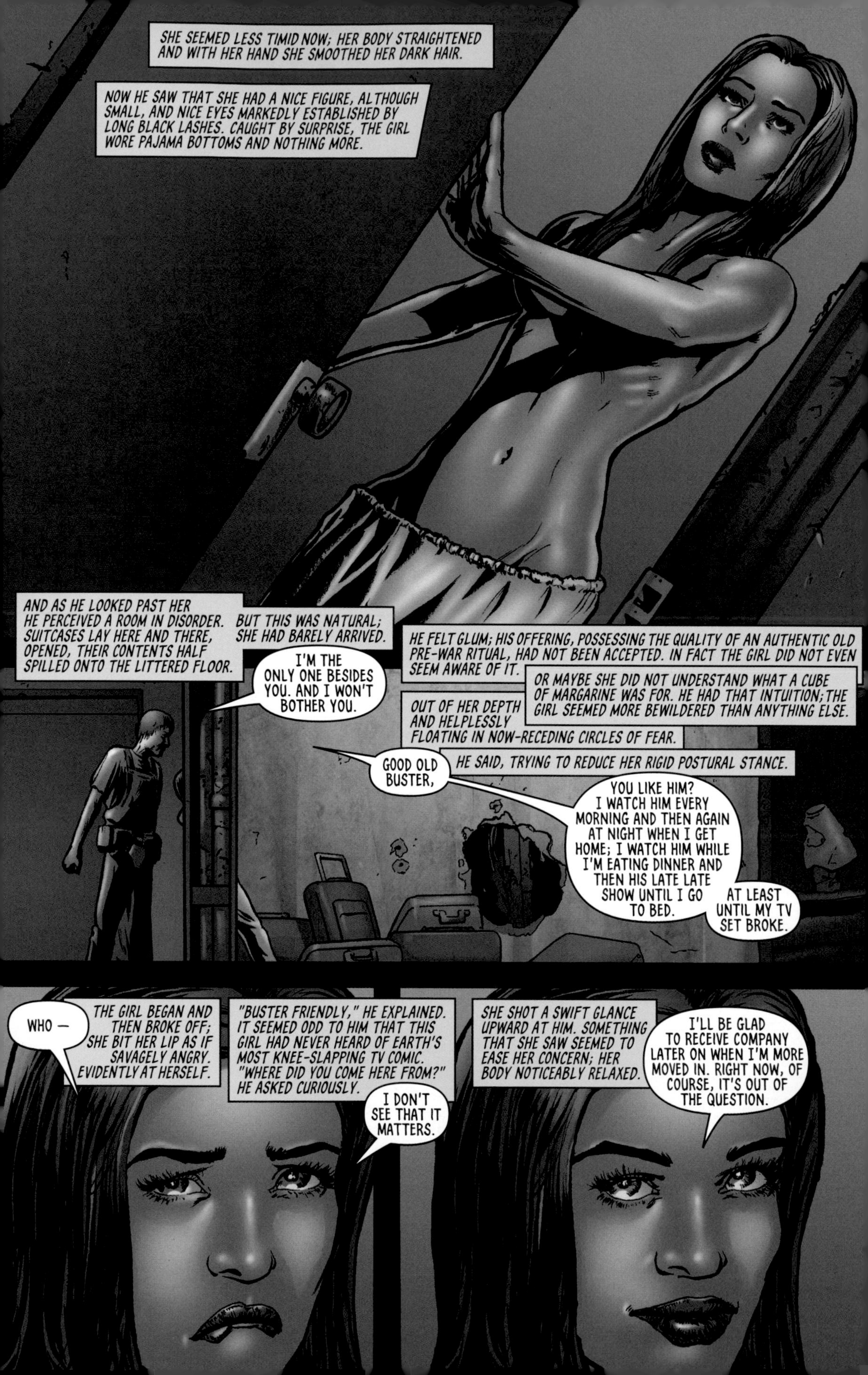
SHE SEEMED LESS TIMID NOW; HER BODY STRAIGHTENED AND WITH HER HAND SHE SMOOTHED HER DARK HAIR.
NOW HE SAW THAT SHE HAD A NICE FIGURE, ALTHOUGH SMALL, AND NICE EYES MARKEDLY ESTABLISHED BY LONG BLACK LASHES. CAUGHT BY SURPRISE, THE GIRL WORE PAJAMA BOTTOMS AND NOTHING MORE.
AND AS HE LOOKED PAST HER HE PERCEIVED A ROOM IN DISORDER. SUITCASES LAY HERE AND THERE, OPENED, THEIR CONTENTS HALF SPILLED ONTO THE LITTERED FLOOR.
BUT THIS WAS NATURAL; SHE HAD BARELY ARRIVED.
I'M THE ONLY ONE BESIDES YOU. AND I WON'T BOTHER YOU.
HE FELT GLUM; HIS OFFERING, POSSESSING THE QUALITY OF AN AUTHENTIC OLD PRE-WAR RITUAL, HAD NOT BEEN ACCEPTED. IN FACT THE GIRL DID NOT EVEN SEEM AWARE OF IT.
OR MAYBE SHE DID NOT UNDERSTAND WHAT A CUBE OF MARGARINE WAS FOR. HE HAD THAT INTUITION; THE GIRL SEEMED MORE BEWILDERED THAN ANYTHING ELSE.
OUT OF HER DEPTH AND HELPLESSLY FLOATING IN NOW-RECEDING CIRCLES OF FEAR.
GOOD OLD BUSTER,
HE SAID, TRYING TO REDUCE HER RIGID POSTURAL STANCE.
YOU LIKE HIM? I WATCH HIM EVERY MORNING AND THEN AGAIN AT NIGHT WHEN I GET HOME; I WATCH HIM WHILE I'M EATING DINNER AND THEN HIS LATE LATE SHOW UNTIL I GO TO BED.
AT LEAST UNTIL MY TV SET BROKE.
WHO —
THE GIRL BEGAN AND THEN BROKE OFF; SHE BIT HER LIP AS IF SAVAGELY ANGRY. EVIDENTLY AT HERSELF.
"BUSTER FRIENDLY," HE EXPLAINED. IT SEEMED ODD TO HIM THAT THIS GIRL HAD NEVER HEARD OF EARTH'S MOST KNEE-SLAPPING TV COMIC. "WHERE DID YOU COME HERE FROM?" HE ASKED CURIOUSLY.
I DON'T SEE THAT IT MATTERS.
SHE SHOT A SWIFT GLANCE UPWARD AT HIM. SOMETHING THAT SHE SAW SEEMED TO EASE HER CONCERN; HER BODY NOTICEABLY RELAXED.
I'LL BE GLAD TO RECEIVE COMPANY LATER ON WHEN I'M MORE MOVED IN. RIGHT NOW, OF COURSE, IT'S OUT OF THE QUESTION.

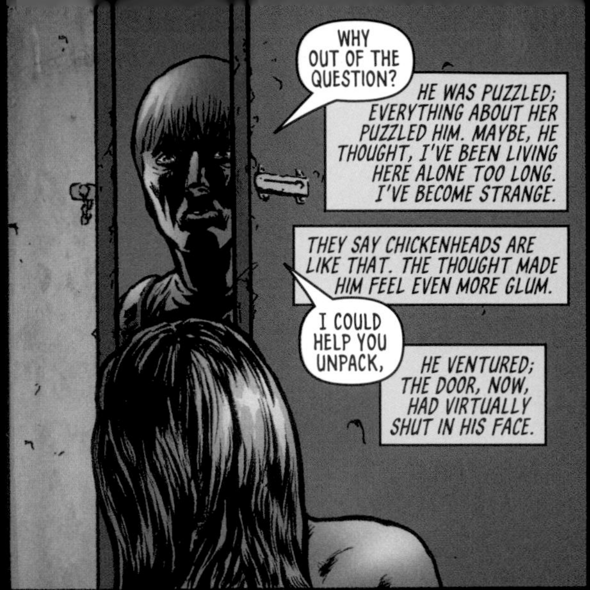
WHY OUT OF THE QUESTION?
HE WAS PUZZLED; EVERYTHING ABOUT HER PUZZLED HIM. MAYBE, HE THOUGHT, I'VE BEEN LIVING HERE ALONE TOO LONG. I'VE BECOME STRANGE.
THEY SAY CHICKENHEADS ARE LIKE THAT. THE THOUGHT MADE HIM FEEL EVEN MORE GLUM.
I COULD HELP YOU UNPACK,
HE VENTURED; THE DOOR, NOW, HAD VIRTUALLY SHUT IN HIS FACE.

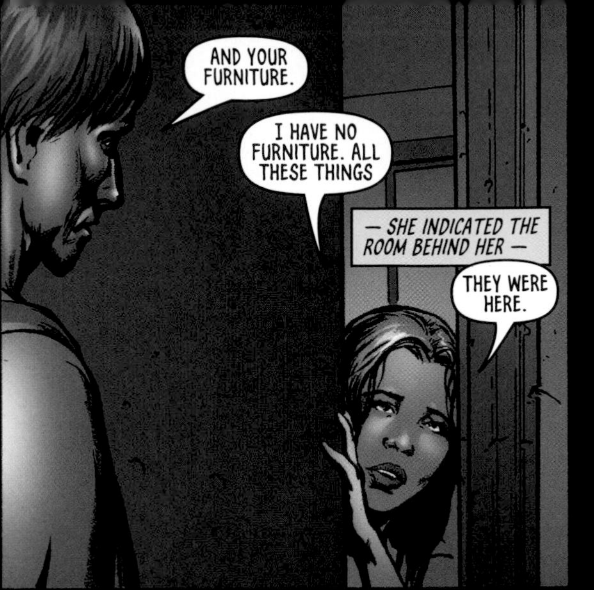
AND YOUR FURNITURE.
I HAVE NO FURNITURE. ALL THESE THINGS
— SHE INDICATED THE ROOM BEHIND HER —
THEY WERE HERE.

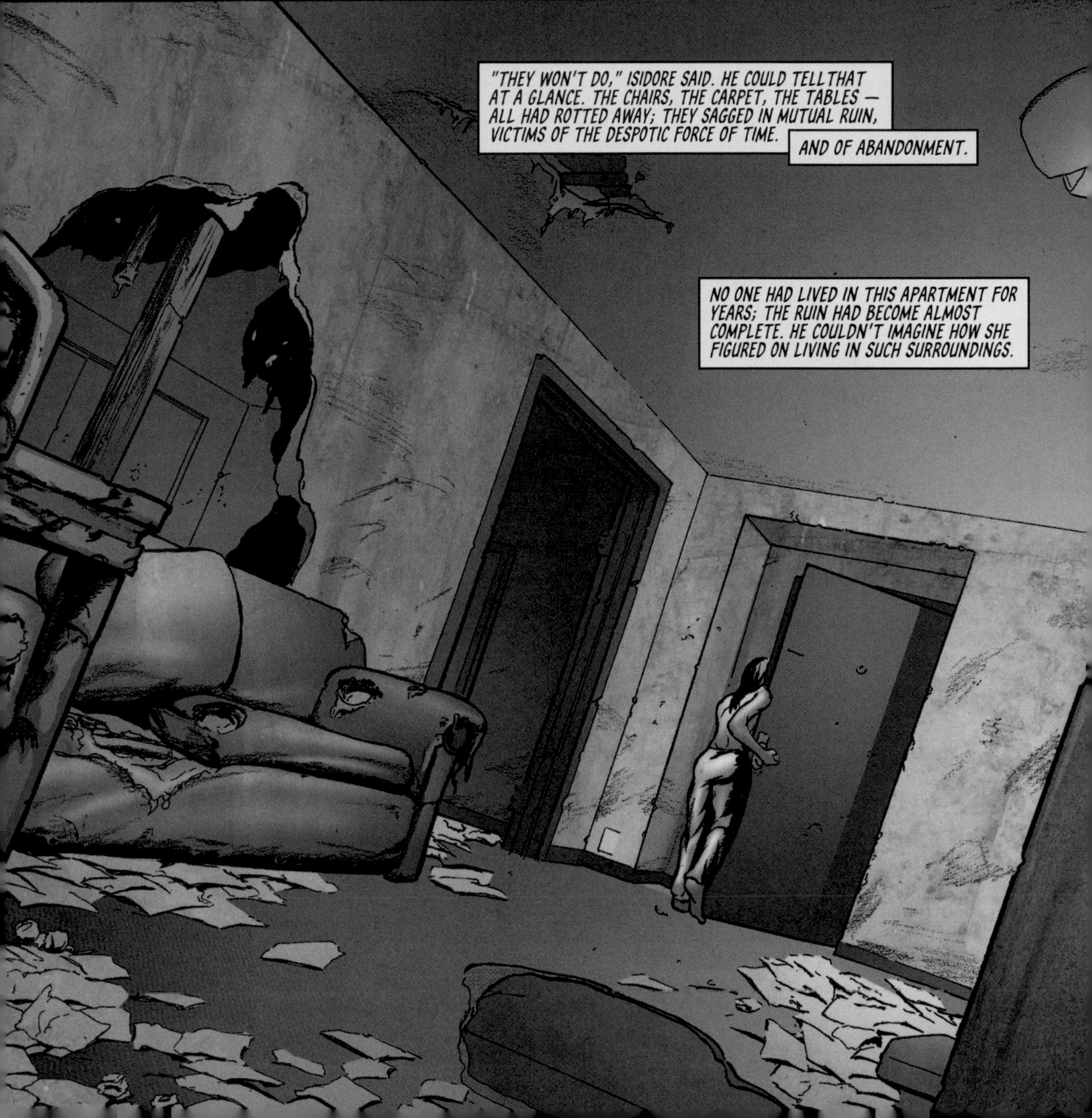
"THEY WON'T DO," ISIDORE SAID. HE COULD TELL THAT AT A GLANCE. THE CHAIRS, THE CARPET, THE TABLES — ALL HAD ROTTED AWAY; THEY SAGGED IN MUTUAL RUIN, VICTIMS OF THE DESPOTIC FORCE OF TIME.
AND OF ABANDONMENT.
NO ONE HAD LIVED IN THIS APARTMENT FOR YEARS; THE RUIN HAD BECOME ALMOST COMPLETE. HE COULDN'T IMAGINE HOW SHE FIGURED ON LIVING IN SUCH SURROUNDINGS.

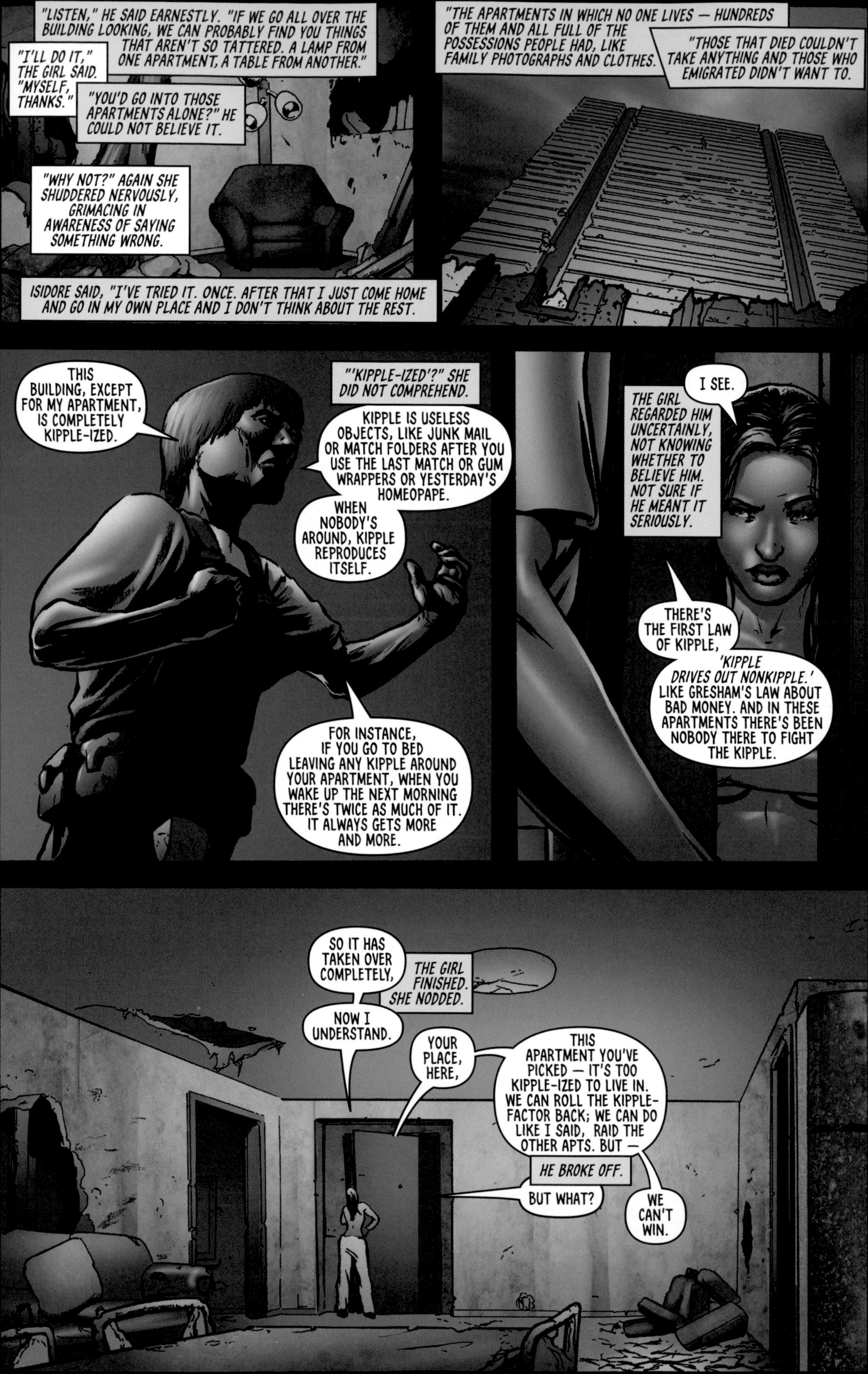
"LISTEN," HE SAID EARNESTLY. "IF WE GO ALL OVER THE BUILDING LOOKING, WE CAN PROBABLY FIND YOU THINGS THAT AREN'T SO TATTERED. A LAMP FROM ONE APARTMENT, A TABLE FROM ANOTHER."
"I'LL DO IT," THE GIRL SAID. "MYSELF, THANKS."
"YOU'D GO INTO THOSE APARTMENTS ALONE?" HE COULD NOT BELIEVE IT.
"WHY NOT?" AGAIN SHE SHUDDERED NERVOUSLY, GRIMACING IN AWARENESS OF SAYING SOMETHING WRONG.
ISIDORE SAID, "I'VE TRIED IT. ONCE. AFTER THAT I JUST COME HOME AND GO IN MY OWN PLACE AND I DON'T THINK ABOUT THE REST.
"THE APARTMENTS IN WHICH NO ONE LIVES — HUNDREDS OF THEM AND ALL FULL OF THE POSSESSIONS PEOPLE HAD, LIKE FAMILY PHOTOGRAPHS AND CLOTHES.
"THOSE THAT DIED COULDN'T TAKE ANYTHING AND THOSE WHO EMIGRATED DIDN'T WANT TO.
THIS BUILDING, EXCEPT FOR MY APARTMENT, IS COMPLETELY KIPPLE-IZED.
"'KIPPLE-IZED'?" SHE DID NOT COMPREHEND.
KIPPLE IS USELESS OBJECTS, LIKE JUNK MAIL OR MATCH FOLDERS AFTER YOU USE THE LAST MATCH OR GUM WRAPPERS OR YESTERDAY'S HOMEOPAPE.
WHEN NOBODY'S AROUND, KIPPLE REPRODUCES ITSELF.
FOR INSTANCE, IF YOU GO TO BED LEAVING ANY KIPPLE AROUND YOUR APARTMENT, WHEN YOU WAKE UP THE NEXT MORNING THERE'S TWICE AS MUCH OF IT. IT ALWAYS GETS MORE AND MORE.
I SEE.
THE GIRL REGARDED HIM UNCERTAINLY, NOT KNOWING WHETHER TO BELIEVE HIM. NOT SURE IF HE MEANT IT SERIOUSLY.
THERE'S THE FIRST LAW OF KIPPLE, 'KIPPLE DRIVES OUT NONKIPPLE.' LIKE GRESHAM'S LAW ABOUT BAD MONEY. AND IN THESE APARTMENTS THERE'S BEEN NOBODY THERE TO FIGHT THE KIPPLE.
SO IT HAS TAKEN OVER COMPLETELY,
THE GIRL FINISHED. SHE NODDED.
NOW I UNDERSTAND.
YOUR PLACE, HERE,
THIS APARTMENT YOU'VE PICKED — IT'S TOO KIPPLE-IZED TO LIVE IN. WE CAN ROLL THE KIPPLE-FACTOR BACK; WE CAN DO LIKE I SAID, RAID THE OTHER APTS. BUT —
HE BROKE OFF.
BUT WHAT?
WE CAN'T WIN.

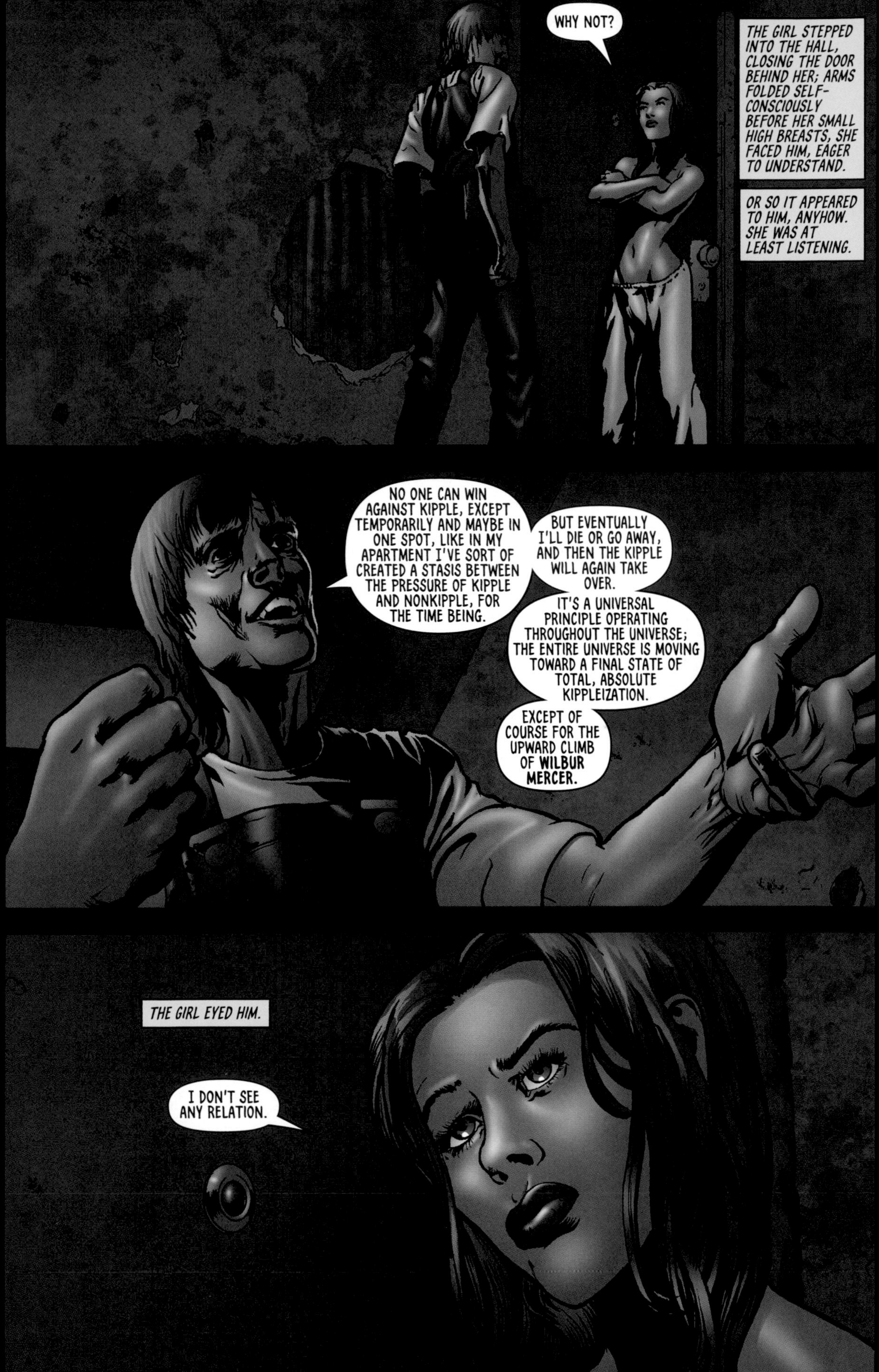
WHY NOT?
THE GIRL STEPPED INTO THE HALL, CLOSING THE DOOR BEHIND HER; ARMS FOLDED SELF-CONSCIOUSLY BEFORE HER SMALL HIGH BREASTS, SHE FACED HIM, EAGER TO UNDERSTAND.
OR SO IT APPEARED TO HIM, ANYHOW. SHE WAS AT LEAST LISTENING.
NO ONE CAN WIN AGAINST KIPPLE, EXCEPT TEMPORARILY AND MAYBE IN ONE SPOT, LIKE IN MY APARTMENT I'VE SORT OF CREATED A STASIS BETWEEN THE PRESSURE OF KIPPLE AND NONKIPPLE, FOR THE TIME BEING.
BUT EVENTUALLY I'LL DIE OR GO AWAY, AND THEN THE KIPPLE WILL AGAIN TAKE OVER.
IT'S A UNIVERSAL PRINCIPLE OPERATING THROUGHOUT THE UNIVERSE; THE ENTIRE UNIVERSE IS MOVING TOWARD A FINAL STATE OF TOTAL, ABSOLUTE KIPPLEIZATION.
EXCEPT OF COURSE FOR THE UPWARD CLIMB OF **WILBUR MERCER.**
THE GIRL EYED HIM.
I DON'T SEE ANY RELATION.

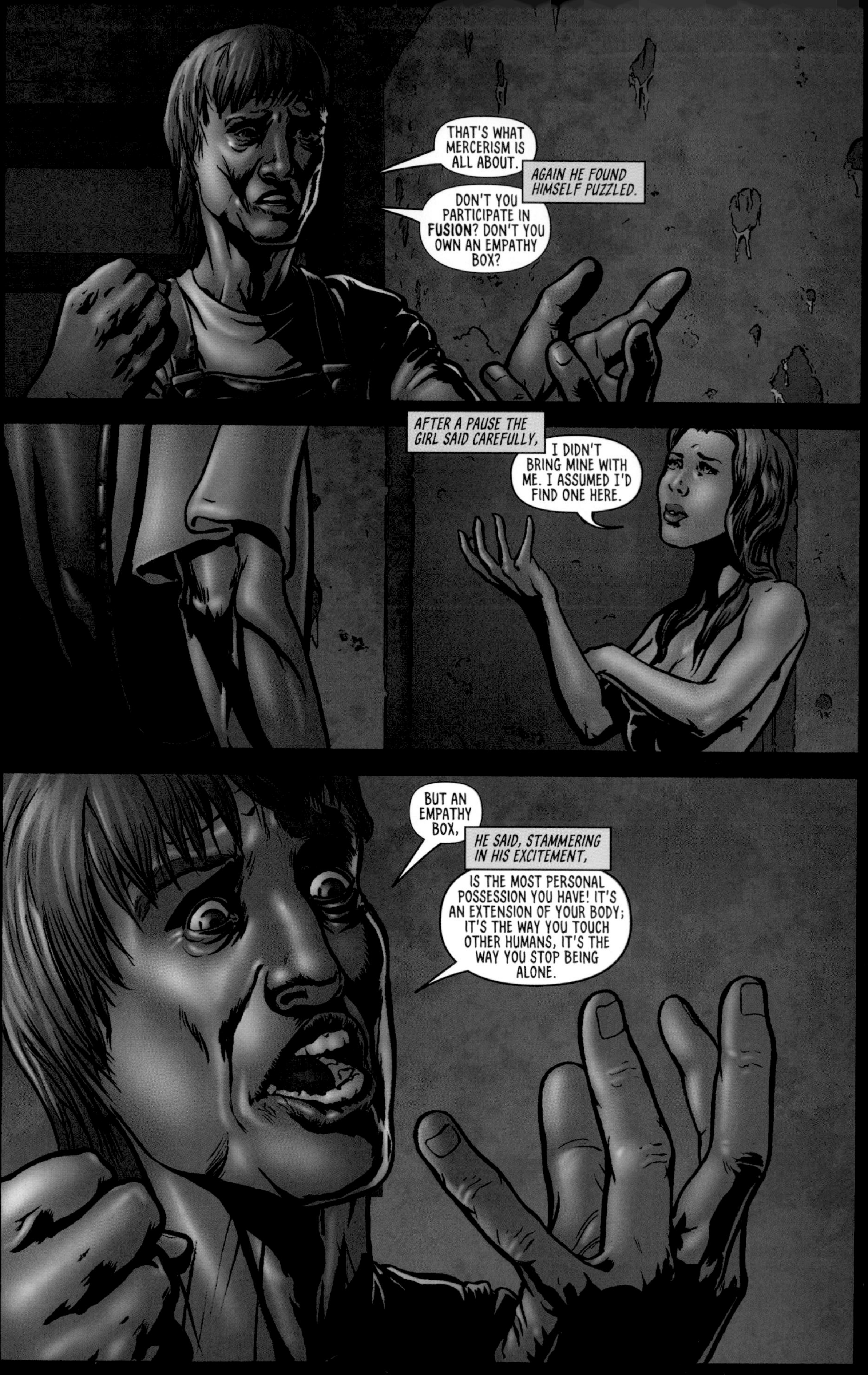
THAT'S WHAT MERCERISM IS ALL ABOUT.
AGAIN HE FOUND HIMSELF PUZZLED.
DON'T YOU PARTICIPATE IN FUSION? DON'T YOU OWN AN EMPATHY BOX?
AFTER A PAUSE THE GIRL SAID CAREFULLY,
I DIDN'T BRING MINE WITH ME. I ASSUMED I'D FIND ONE HERE.
BUT AN EMPATHY BOX,
HE SAID, STAMMERING IN HIS EXCITEMENT,
IS THE MOST PERSONAL POSSESSION YOU HAVE! IT'S AN EXTENSION OF YOUR BODY; IT'S THE WAY YOU TOUCH OTHER HUMANS, IT'S THE WAY YOU STOP BEING ALONE.

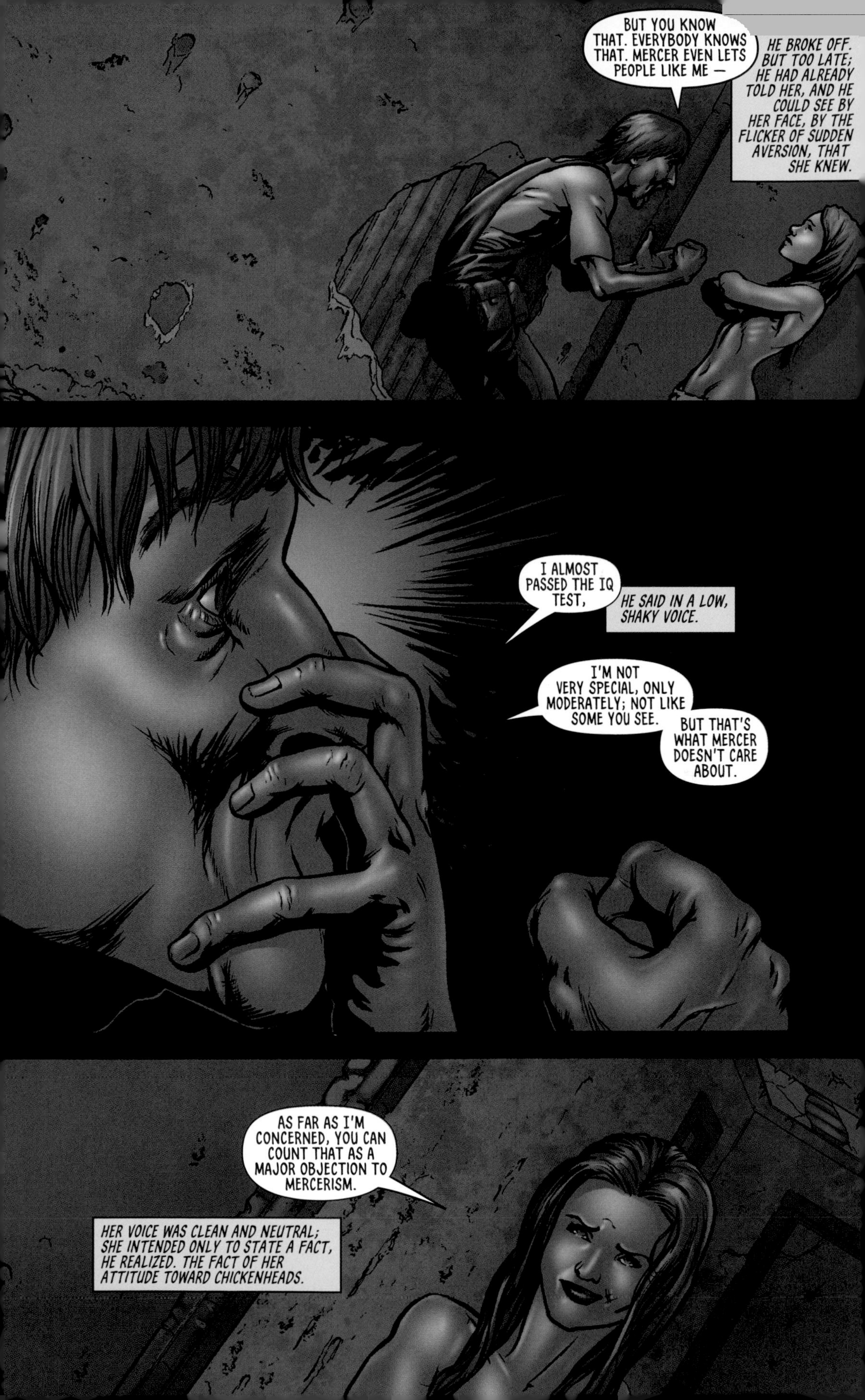
BUT YOU KNOW THAT. EVERYBODY KNOWS THAT. MERCER EVEN LETS PEOPLE LIKE ME —
HE BROKE OFF. BUT TOO LATE; HE HAD ALREADY TOLD HER, AND HE COULD SEE BY HER FACE, BY THE FLICKER OF SUDDEN AVERSION, THAT SHE KNEW.
I ALMOST PASSED THE IQ TEST,
HE SAID IN A LOW, SHAKY VOICE.
I'M NOT VERY SPECIAL, ONLY MODERATELY; NOT LIKE SOME YOU SEE.
BUT THAT'S WHAT MERCER DOESN'T CARE ABOUT.
AS FAR AS I'M CONCERNED, YOU CAN COUNT THAT AS A MAJOR OBJECTION TO MERCERISM.
HER VOICE WAS CLEAN AND NEUTRAL; SHE INTENDED ONLY TO STATE A FACT, HE REALIZED. THE FACT OF HER ATTITUDE TOWARD CHICKENHEADS.

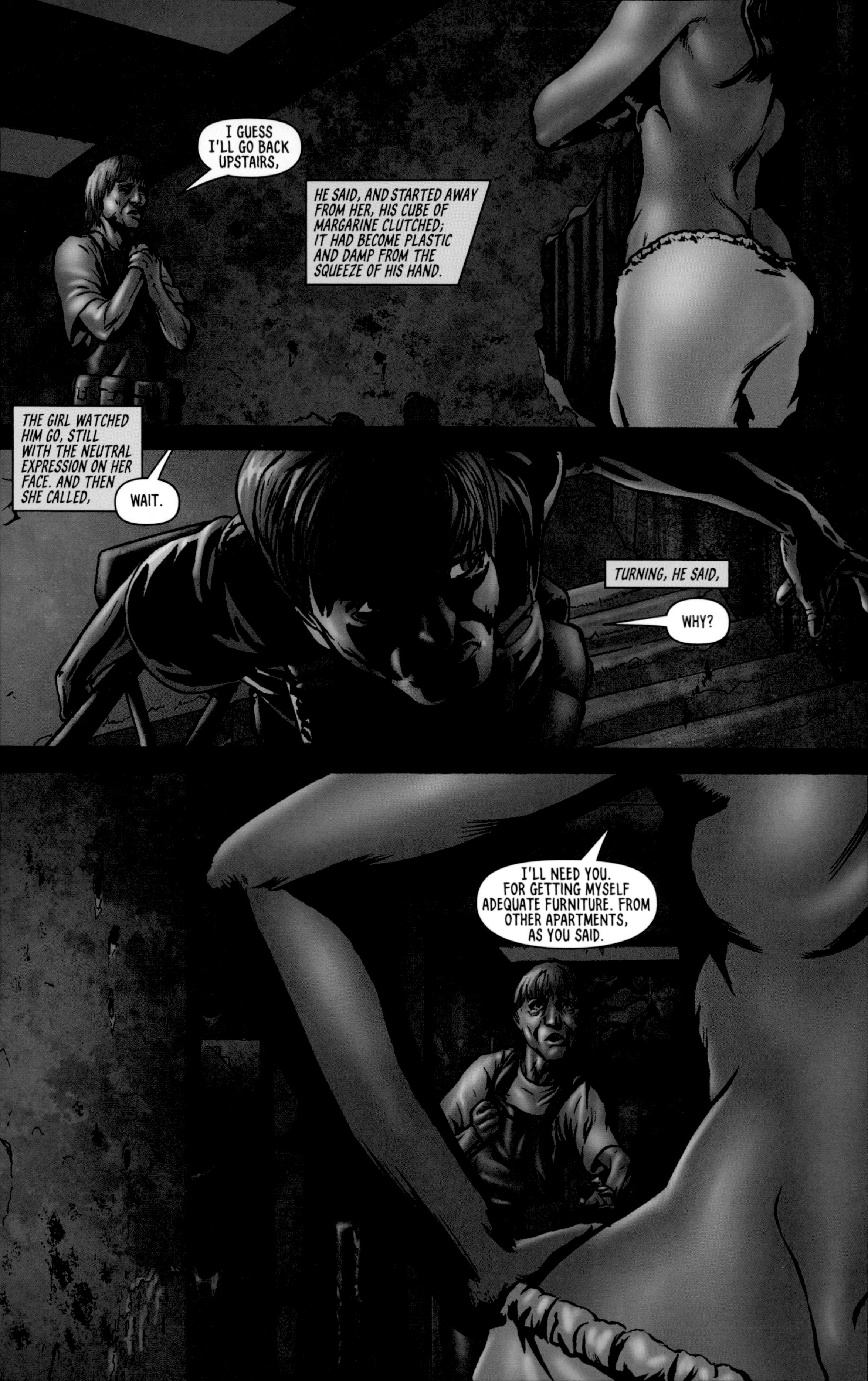
I GUESS I'LL GO BACK UPSTAIRS,
HE SAID, AND STARTED AWAY FROM HER, HIS CUBE OF MARGARINE CLUTCHED; IT HAD BECOME PLASTIC AND DAMP FROM THE SQUEEZE OF HIS HAND.
THE GIRL WATCHED HIM GO, STILL WITH THE NEUTRAL EXPRESSION ON HER FACE. AND THEN SHE CALLED,
WAIT.
TURNING, HE SAID,
WHY?
I'LL NEED YOU. FOR GETTING MYSELF ADEQUATE FURNITURE. FROM OTHER APARTMENTS, AS YOU SAID.

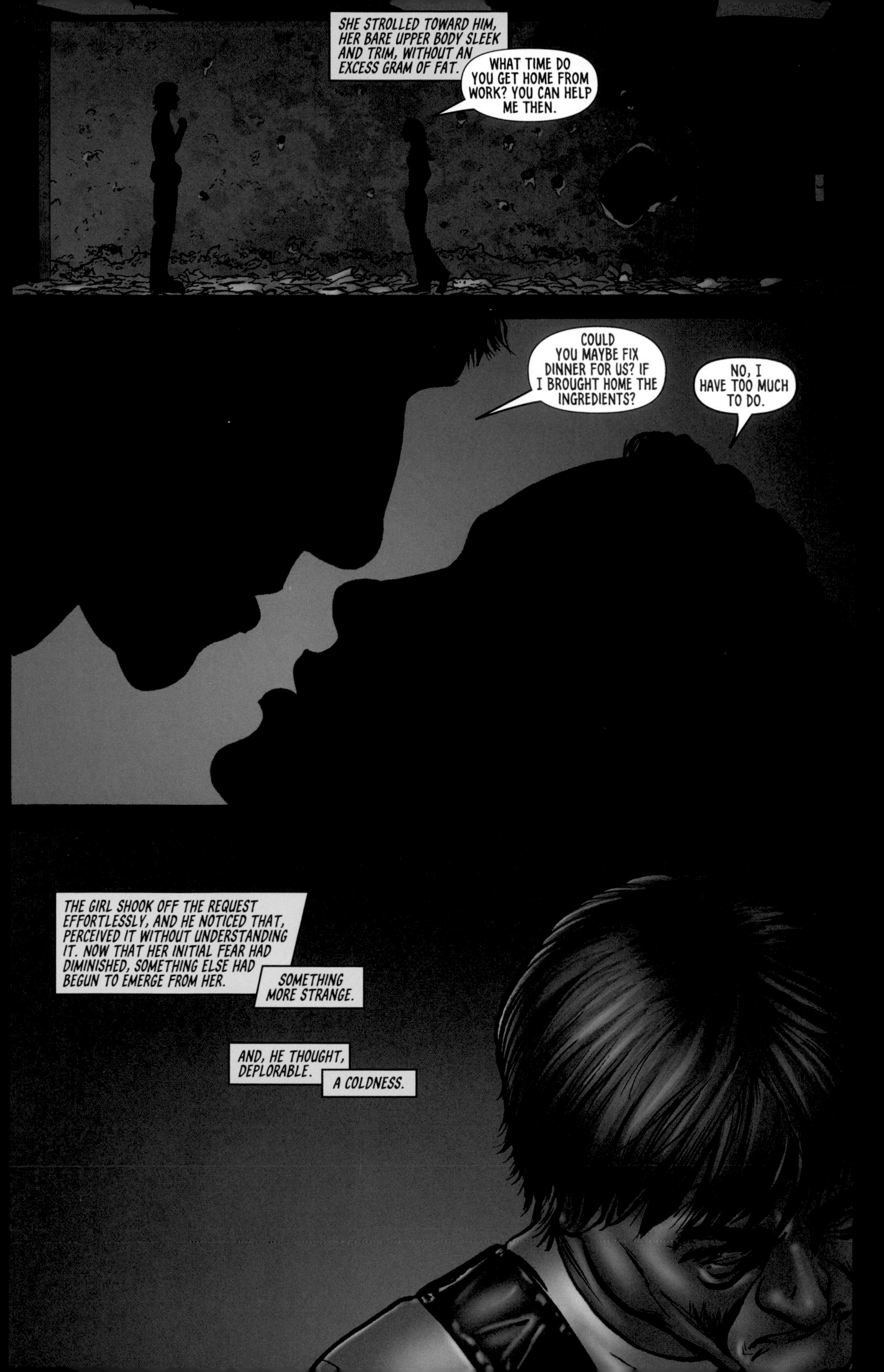
SHE STROLLED TOWARD HIM, HER BARE UPPER BODY SLEEK AND TRIM, WITHOUT AN EXCESS GRAM OF FAT.
WHAT TIME DO YOU GET HOME FROM WORK? YOU CAN HELP ME THEN.
COULD YOU MAYBE FIX DINNER FOR US? IF I BROUGHT HOME THE INGREDIENTS?
NO, I HAVE TOO MUCH TO DO.
THE GIRL SHOOK OFF THE REQUEST EFFORTLESSLY, AND HE NOTICED THAT, PERCEIVED IT WITHOUT UNDERSTANDING IT. NOW THAT HER INITIAL FEAR HAD DIMINISHED, SOMETHING ELSE HAD BEGUN TO EMERGE FROM HER.
SOMETHING MORE STRANGE.
AND, HE THOUGHT, DEPLORABLE.
A COLDNESS.

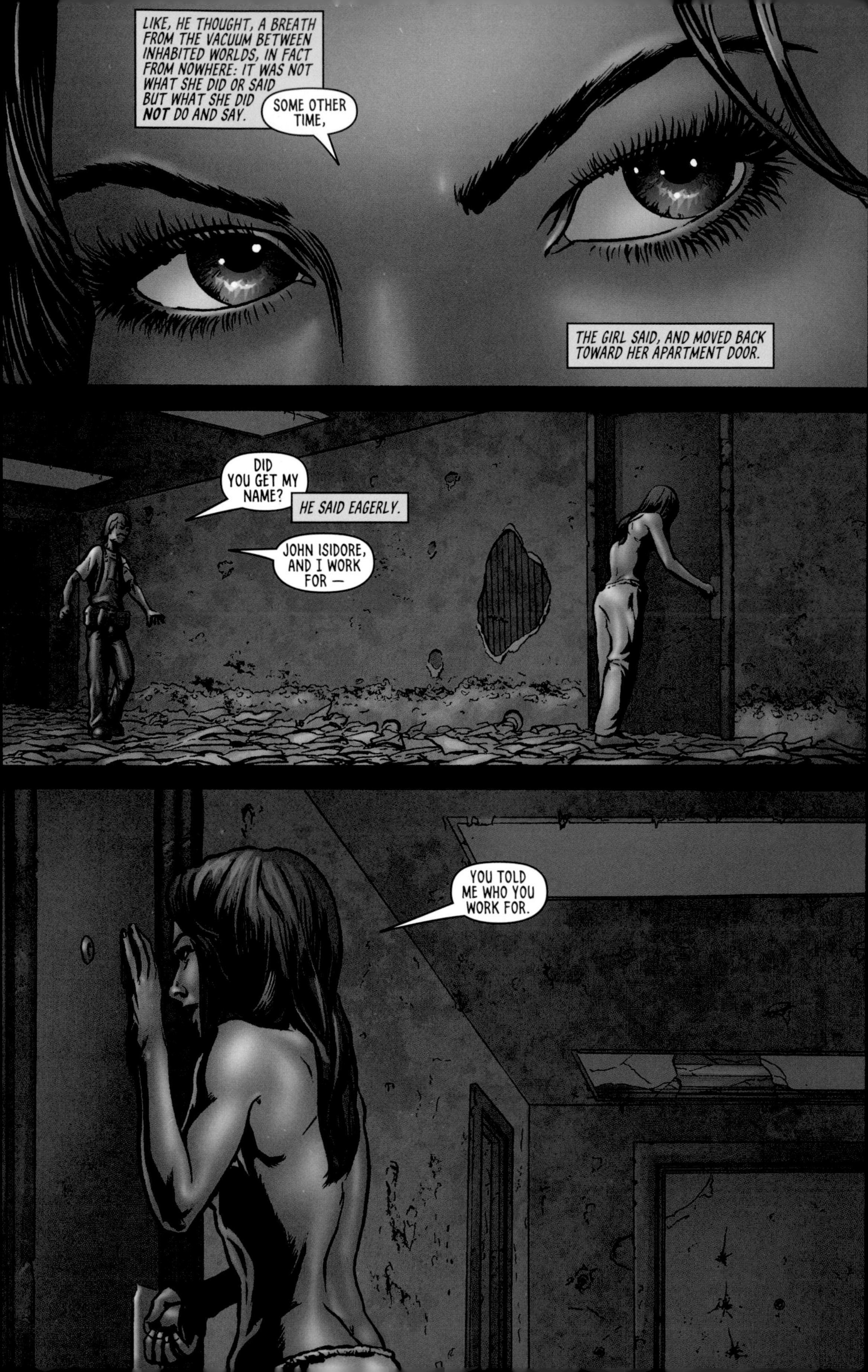
LIKE, HE THOUGHT, A BREATH FROM THE VACUUM BETWEEN INHABITED WORLDS, IN FACT FROM NOWHERE: IT WAS NOT WHAT SHE DID OR SAID BUT WHAT SHE DID **NOT** DO AND SAY.
SOME OTHER TIME,
THE GIRL SAID, AND MOVED BACK TOWARD HER APARTMENT DOOR.
DID YOU GET MY NAME?
HE SAID EAGERLY.
JOHN ISIDORE, AND I WORK FOR —
YOU TOLD ME WHO YOU WORK FOR.

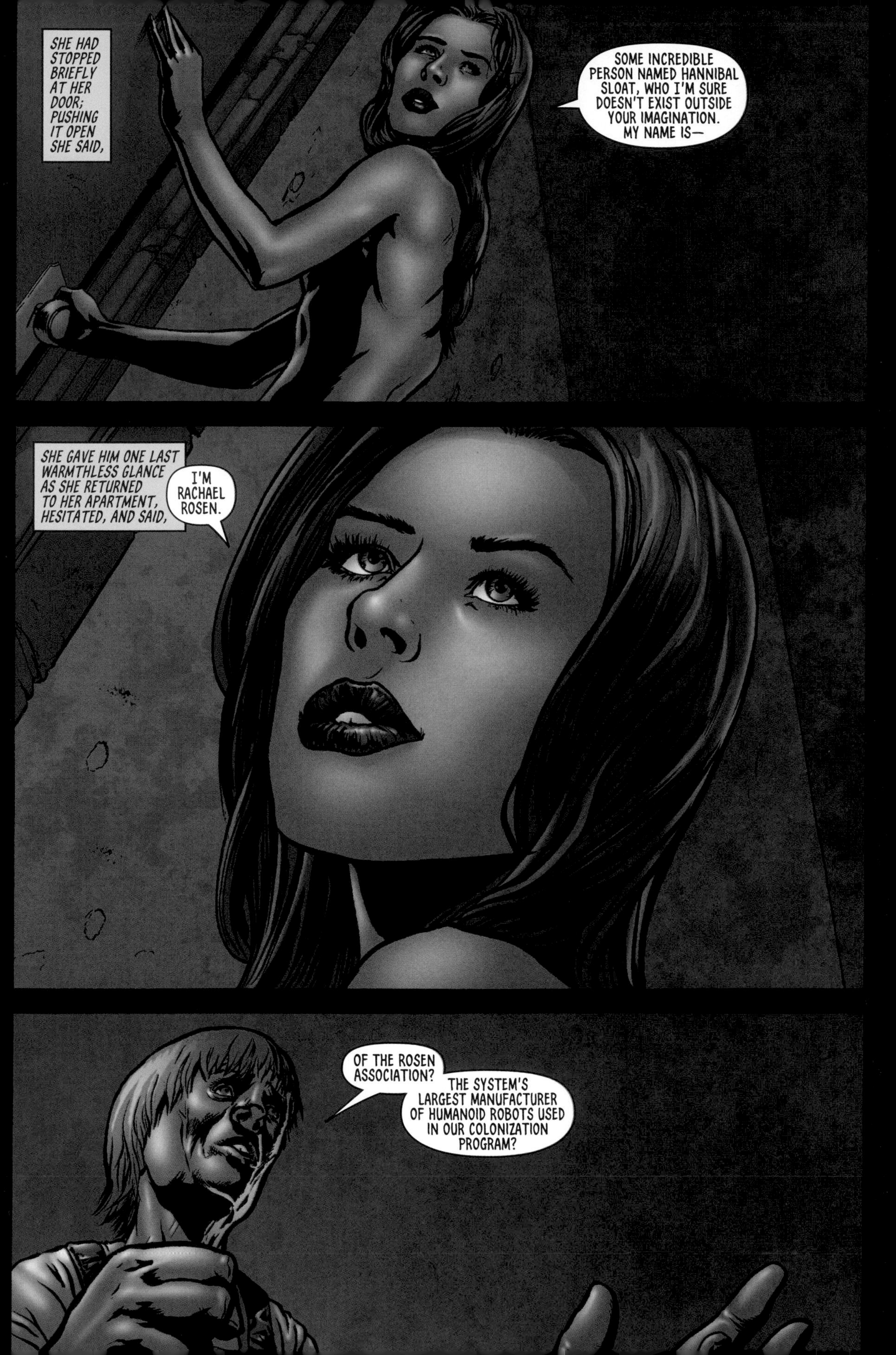
SHE HAD STOPPED BRIEFLY AT HER DOOR; PUSHING IT OPEN SHE SAID,
SOME INCREDIBLE PERSON NAMED HANNIBAL SLOAT, WHO I'M SURE DOESN'T EXIST OUTSIDE YOUR IMAGINATION. MY NAME IS—
SHE GAVE HIM ONE LAST WARMTHLESS GLANCE AS SHE RETURNED TO HER APARTMENT, HESITATED, AND SAID,
I'M RACHAEL ROSEN.
OF THE ROSEN ASSOCIATION?
THE SYSTEM'S LARGEST MANUFACTURER OF HUMANOID ROBOTS USED IN OUR COLONIZATION PROGRAM?

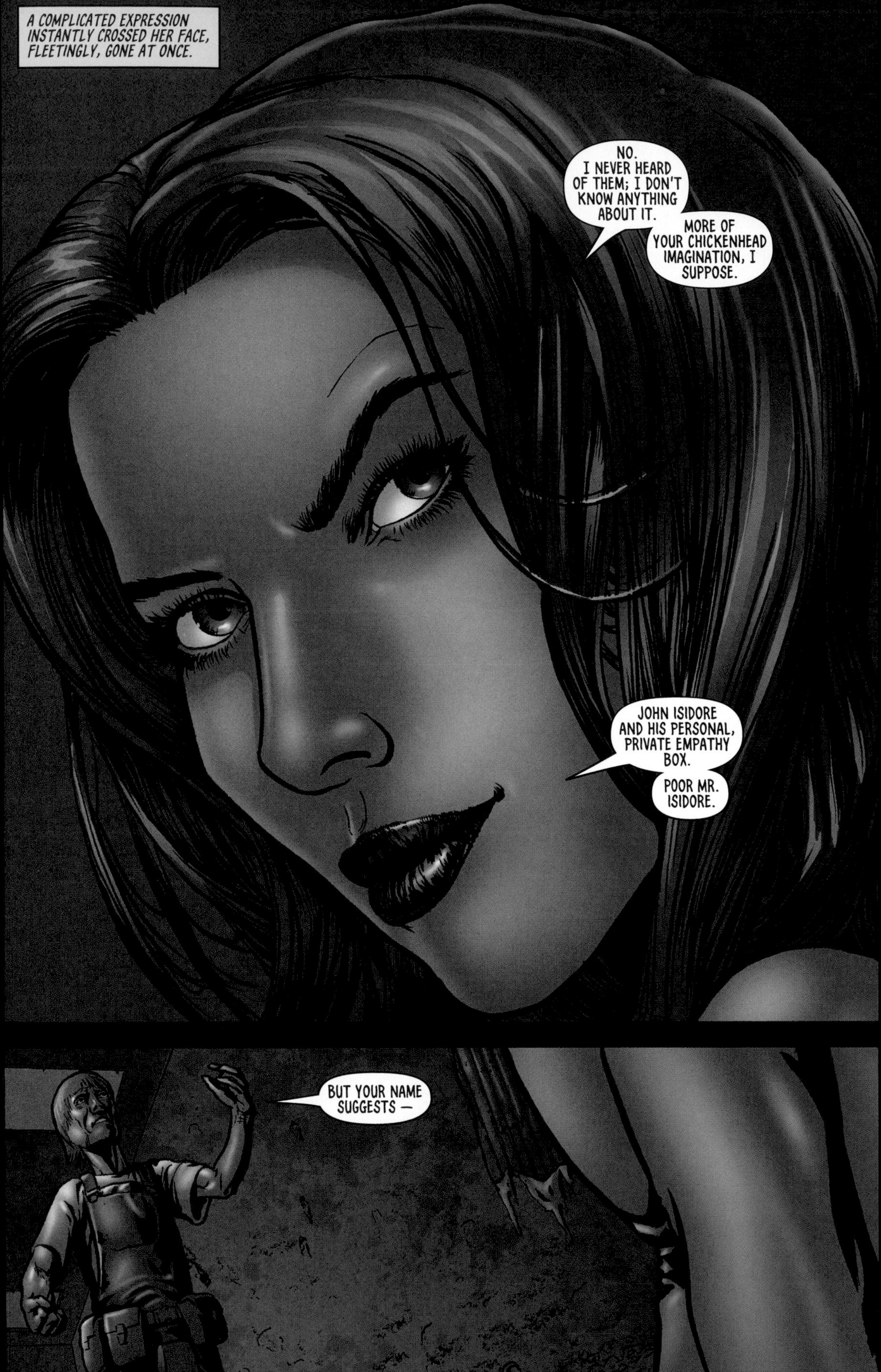
A COMPLICATED EXPRESSION INSTANTLY CROSSED HER FACE, FLEETINGLY, GONE AT ONCE.
NO. I NEVER HEARD OF THEM; I DON'T KNOW ANYTHING ABOUT IT.
MORE OF YOUR CHICKENHEAD IMAGINATION, I SUPPOSE.
JOHN ISIDORE AND HIS PERSONAL, PRIVATE EMPATHY BOX.
POOR MR. ISIDORE.
BUT YOUR NAME SUGGESTS —

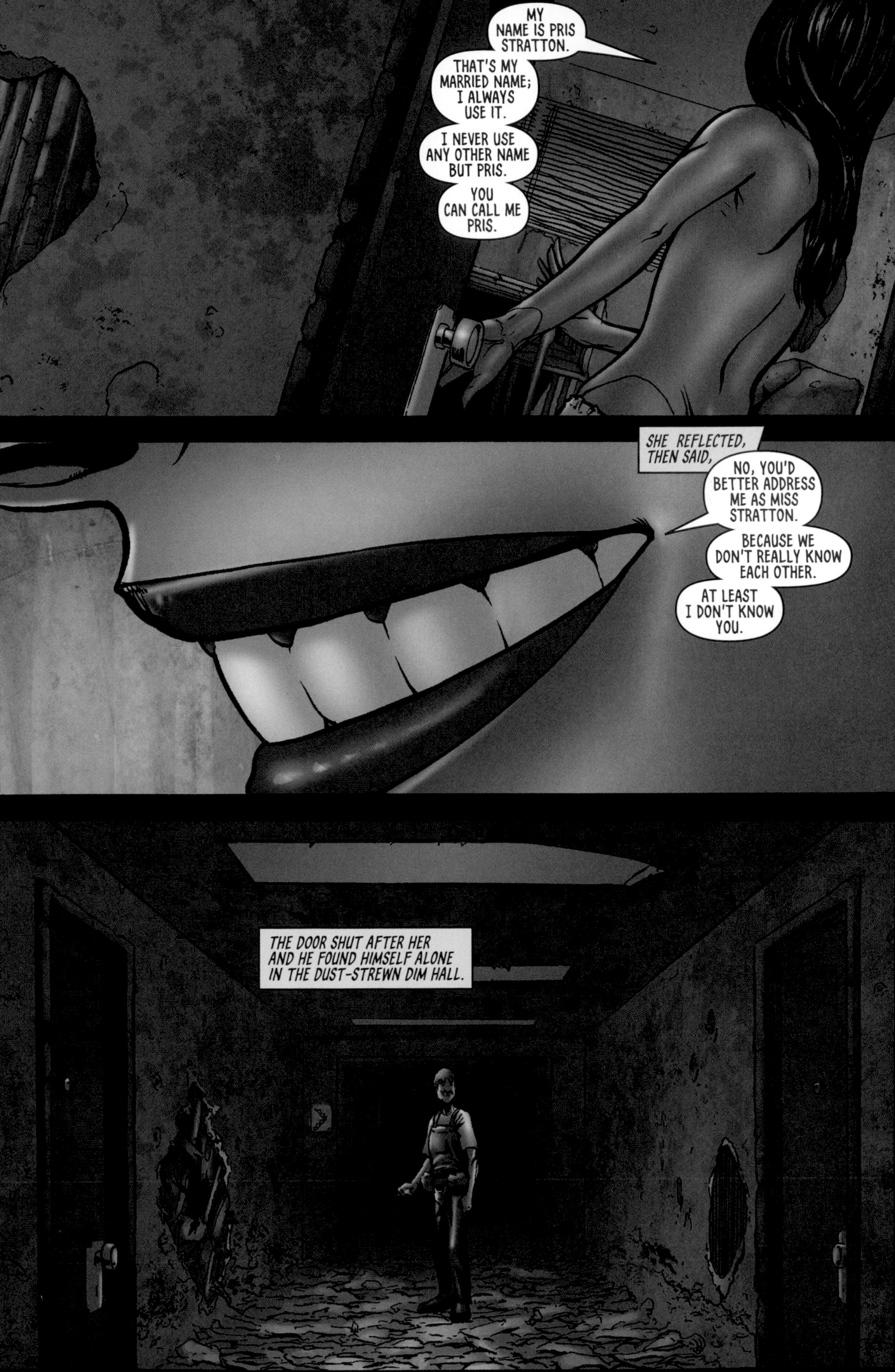
MY NAME IS PRIS STRATTON.
THAT'S MY MARRIED NAME; I ALWAYS USE IT.
I NEVER USE ANY OTHER NAME BUT PRIS.
YOU CAN CALL ME PRIS.
SHE REFLECTED, THEN SAID,
NO, YOU'D BETTER ADDRESS ME AS MISS STRATTON.
BECAUSE WE DON'T REALLY KNOW EACH OTHER.
AT LEAST I DON'T KNOW YOU.
THE DOOR SHUT AFTER HER AND HE FOUND HIMSELF ALONE IN THE DUST-STREWN DIM HALL.

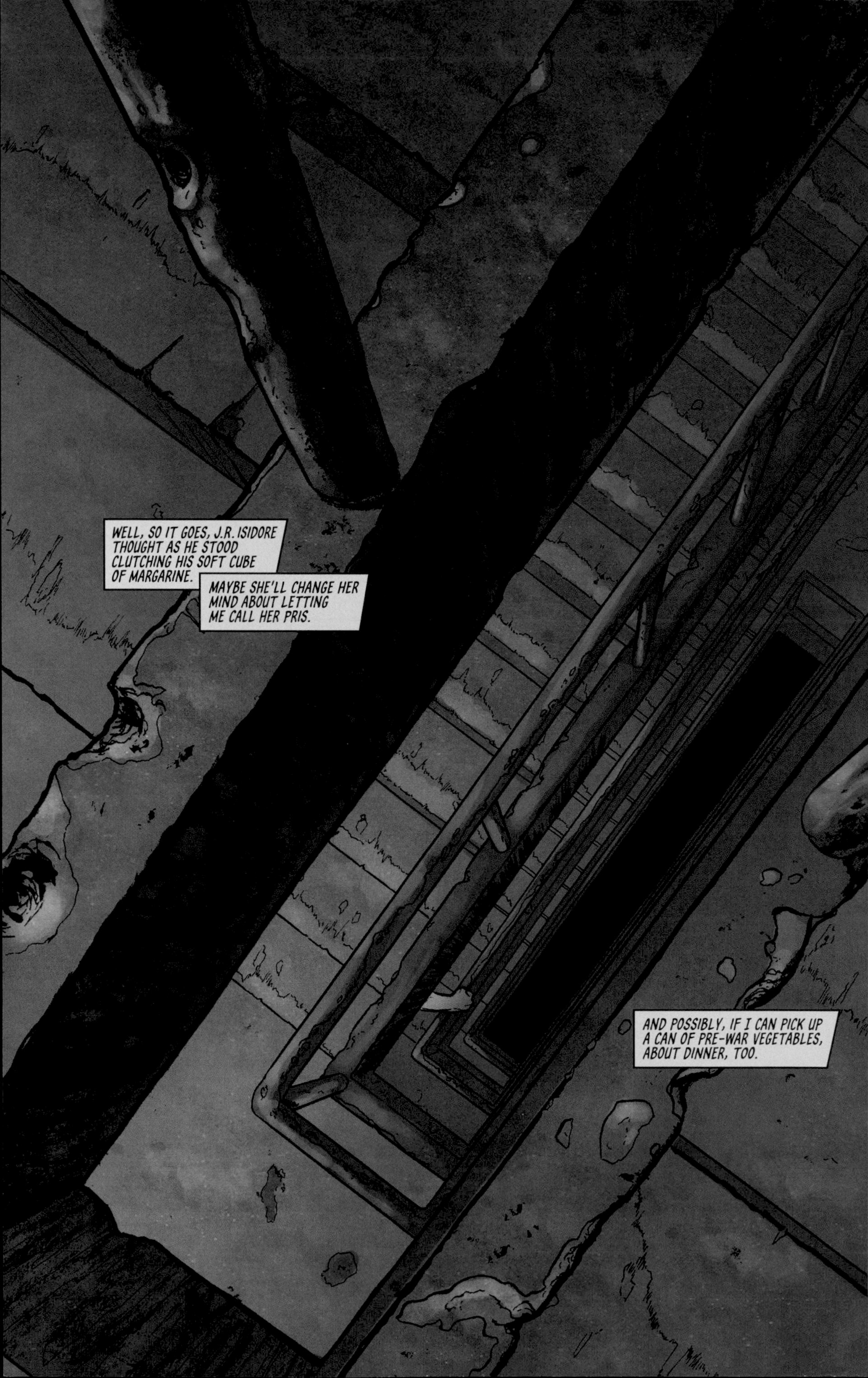
WELL, SO IT GOES, J.R. ISIDORE THOUGHT AS HE STOOD CLUTCHING HIS SOFT CUBE OF MARGARINE.
MAYBE SHE'LL CHANGE HER MIND ABOUT LETTING ME CALL HER PRIS.
AND POSSIBLY, IF I CAN PICK UP A CAN OF PRE-WAR VEGETABLES, ABOUT DINNER, TOO.

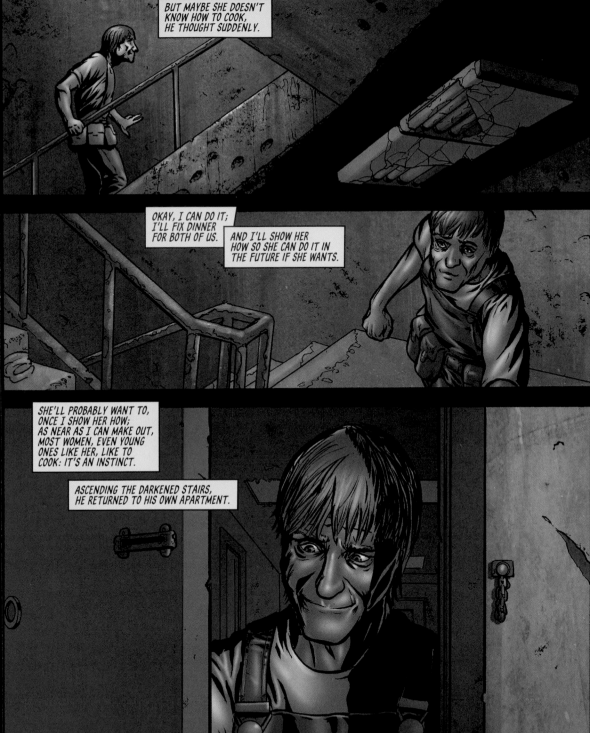

BUT MAYBE SHE DOESN'T KNOW HOW TO COOK, HE THOUGHT SUDDENLY.

OKAY, I CAN DO IT; I'LL FIX DINNER FOR BOTH OF US.

AND I'LL SHOW HER HOW SO SHE CAN DO IT IN THE FUTURE IF SHE WANTS.

SHE'LL PROBABLY WANT TO, ONCE I SHOW HER HOW; AS NEAR AS I CAN MAKE OUT, MOST WOMEN, EVEN YOUNG ONES LIKE HER, LIKE TO COOK: IT'S AN INSTINCT.

ASCENDING THE DARKENED STAIRS, HE RETURNED TO HIS OWN APARTMENT.

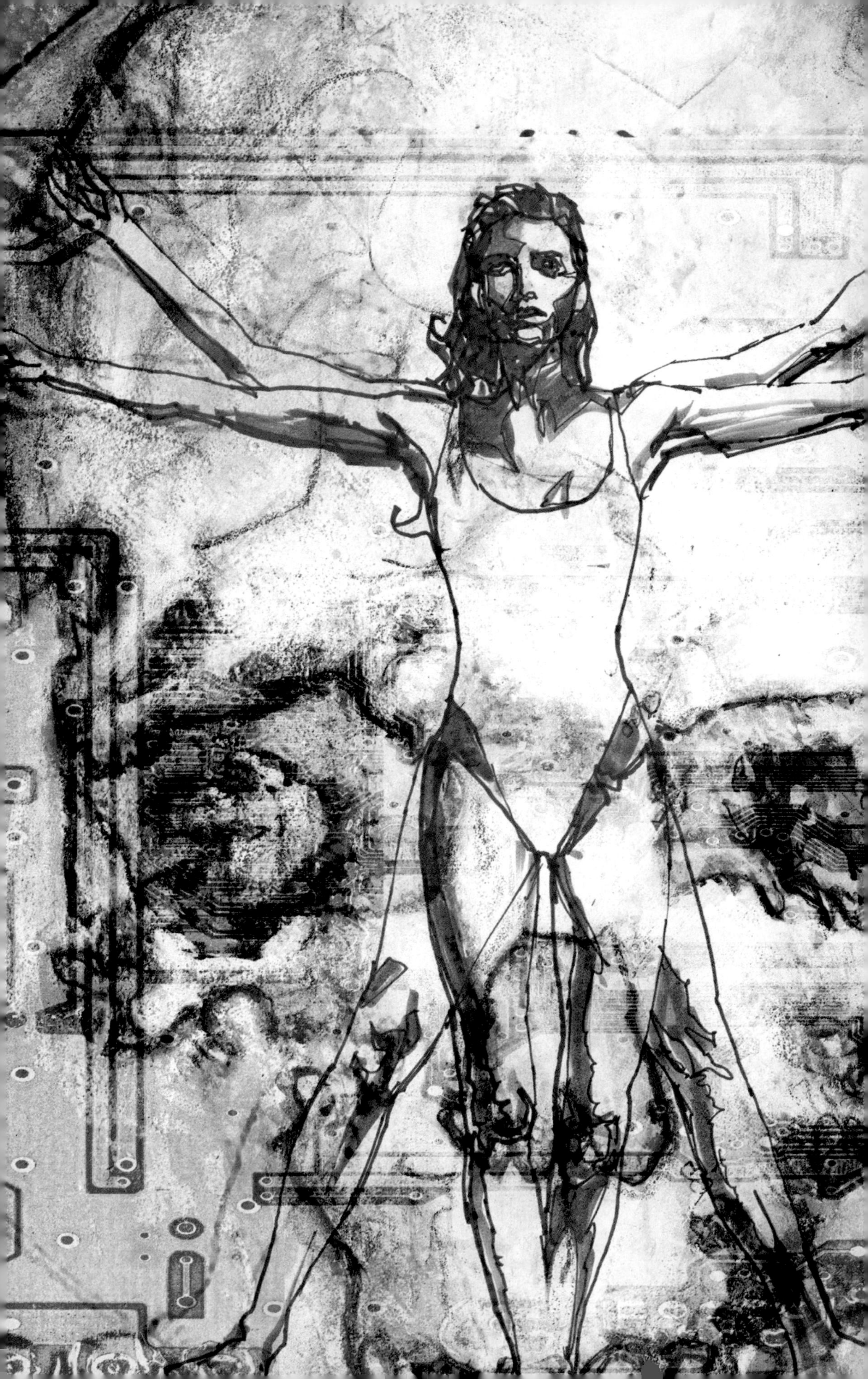

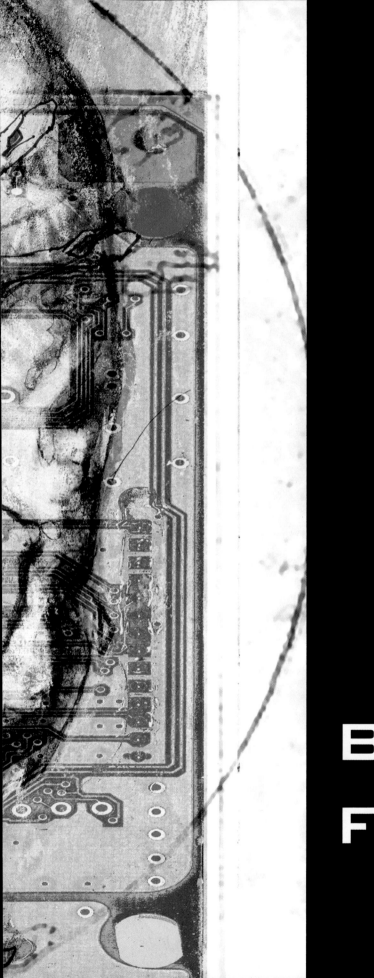

BOOK
FOUR

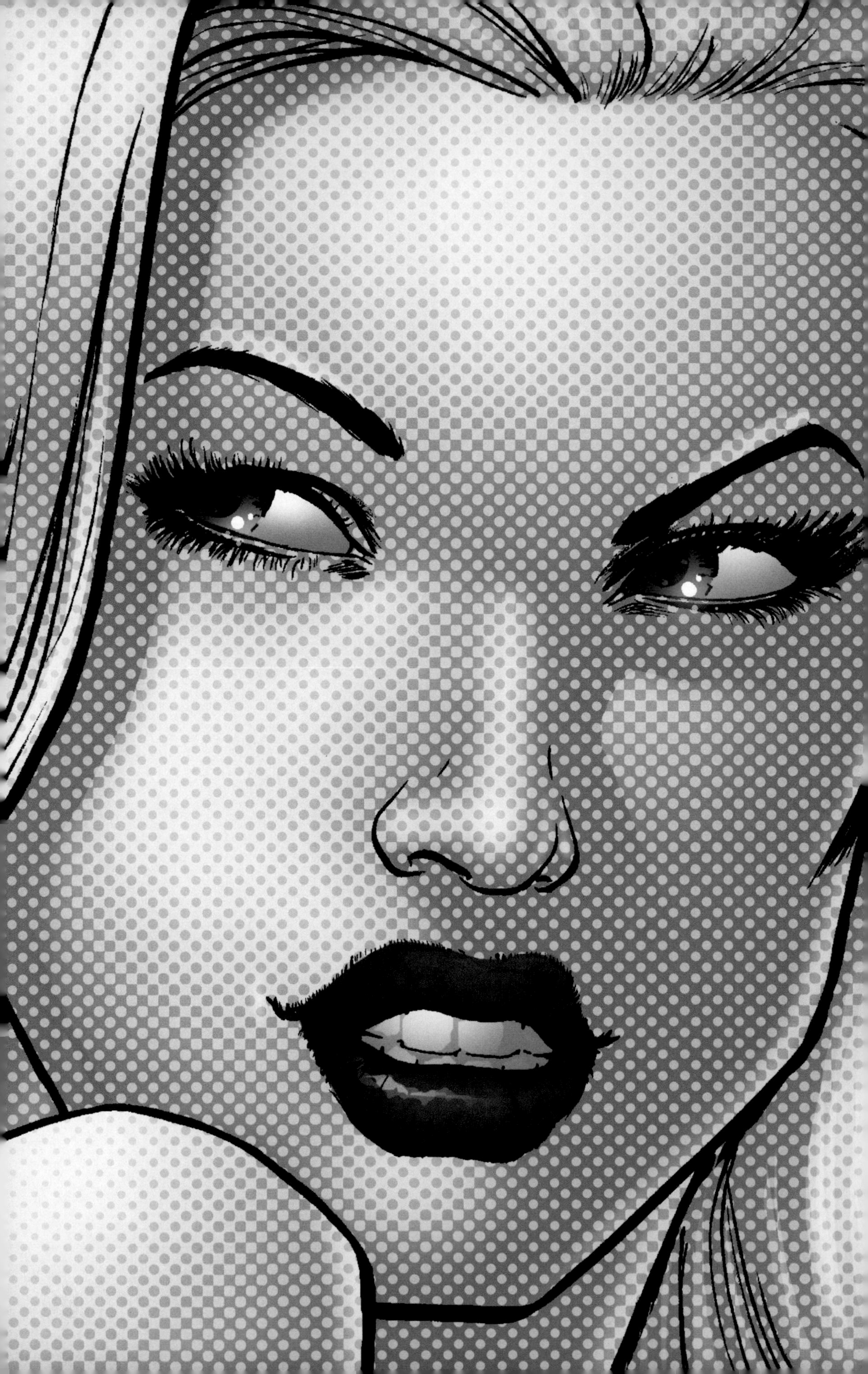

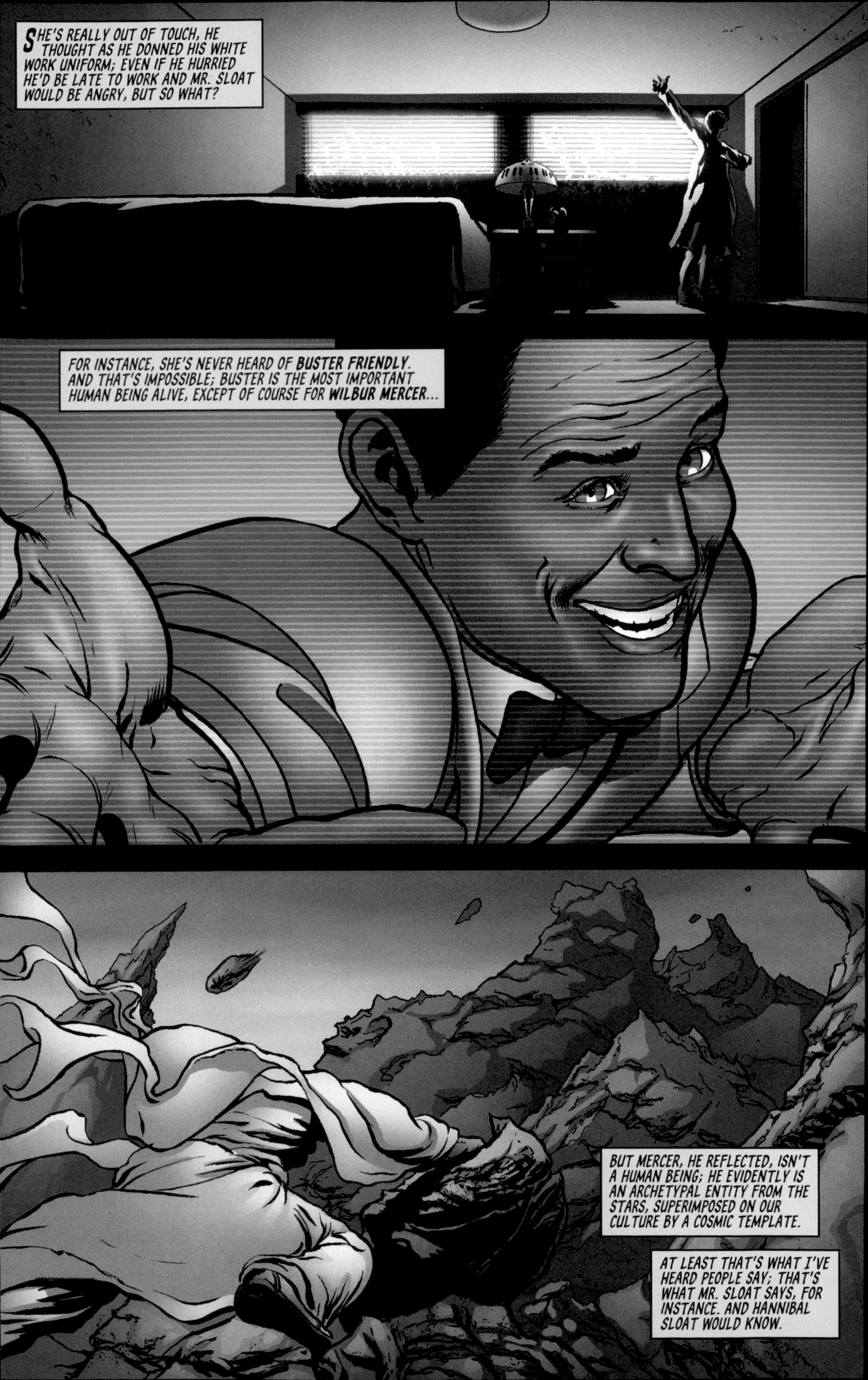
SHE'S REALLY OUT OF TOUCH, HE THOUGHT AS HE DONNED HIS WHITE WORK UNIFORM; EVEN IF HE HURRIED HE'D BE LATE TO WORK AND MR. SLOAT WOULD BE ANGRY, BUT SO WHAT?
FOR INSTANCE, SHE'S NEVER HEARD OF **BUSTER FRIENDLY**. AND THAT'S IMPOSSIBLE; BUSTER IS THE MOST IMPORTANT HUMAN BEING ALIVE, EXCEPT OF COURSE FOR **WILBUR MERCER**...
BUT MERCER, HE REFLECTED, ISN'T A HUMAN BEING; HE EVIDENTLY IS AN ARCHETYPAL ENTITY FROM THE STARS, SUPERIMPOSED ON OUR CULTURE BY A COSMIC TEMPLATE.
AT LEAST THAT'S WHAT I'VE HEARD PEOPLE SAY; THAT'S WHAT MR. SLOAT SAYS, FOR INSTANCE. AND HANNIBAL SLOAT WOULD KNOW.

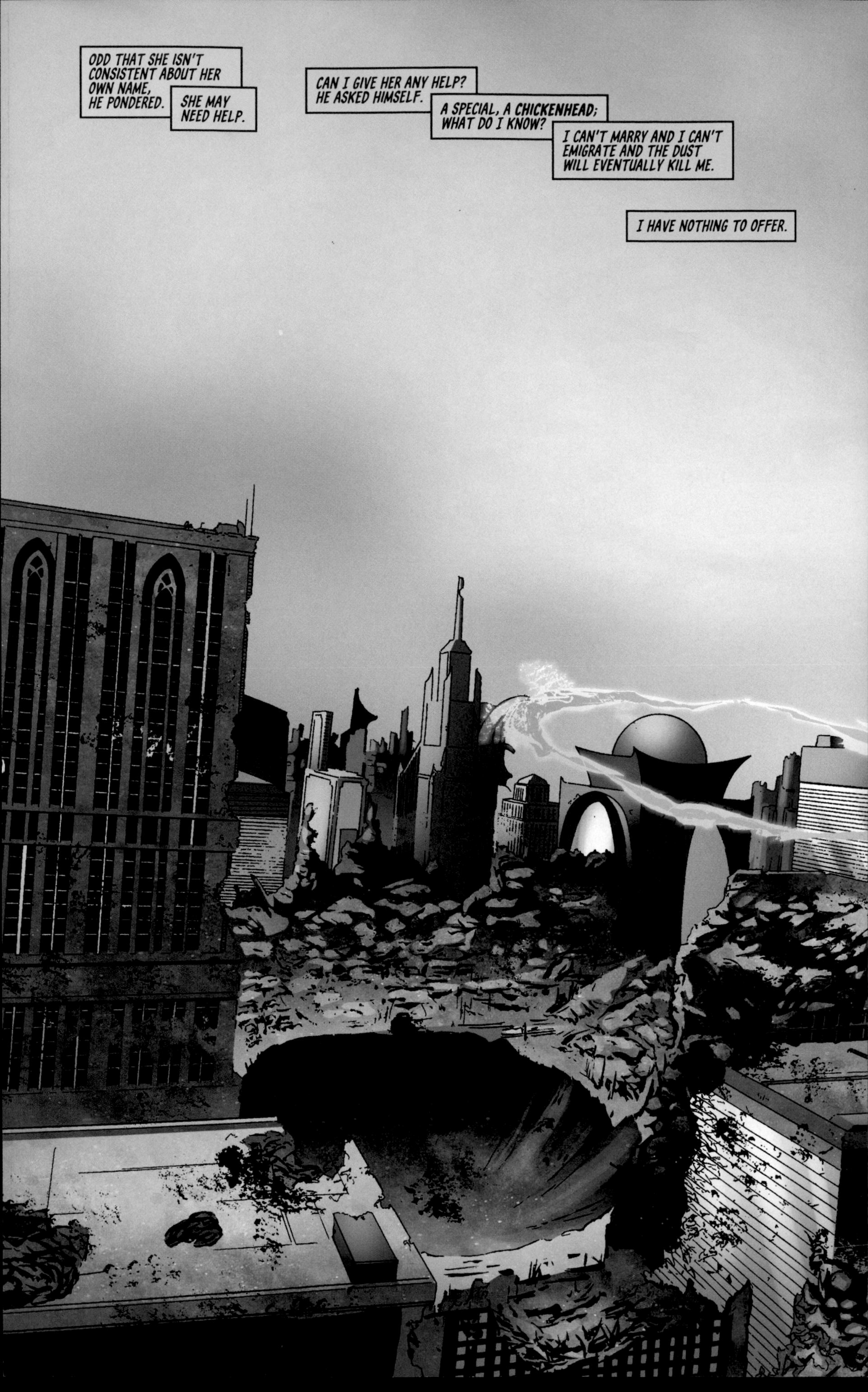
ODD THAT SHE ISN'T CONSISTENT ABOUT HER OWN NAME, HE PONDERED.
SHE MAY NEED HELP.
CAN I GIVE HER ANY HELP? HE ASKED HIMSELF.
A SPECIAL, A CHICKENHEAD; WHAT DO I KNOW?
I CAN'T MARRY AND I CAN'T EMIGRATE AND THE DUST WILL EVENTUALLY KILL ME.
I HAVE NOTHING TO OFFER.

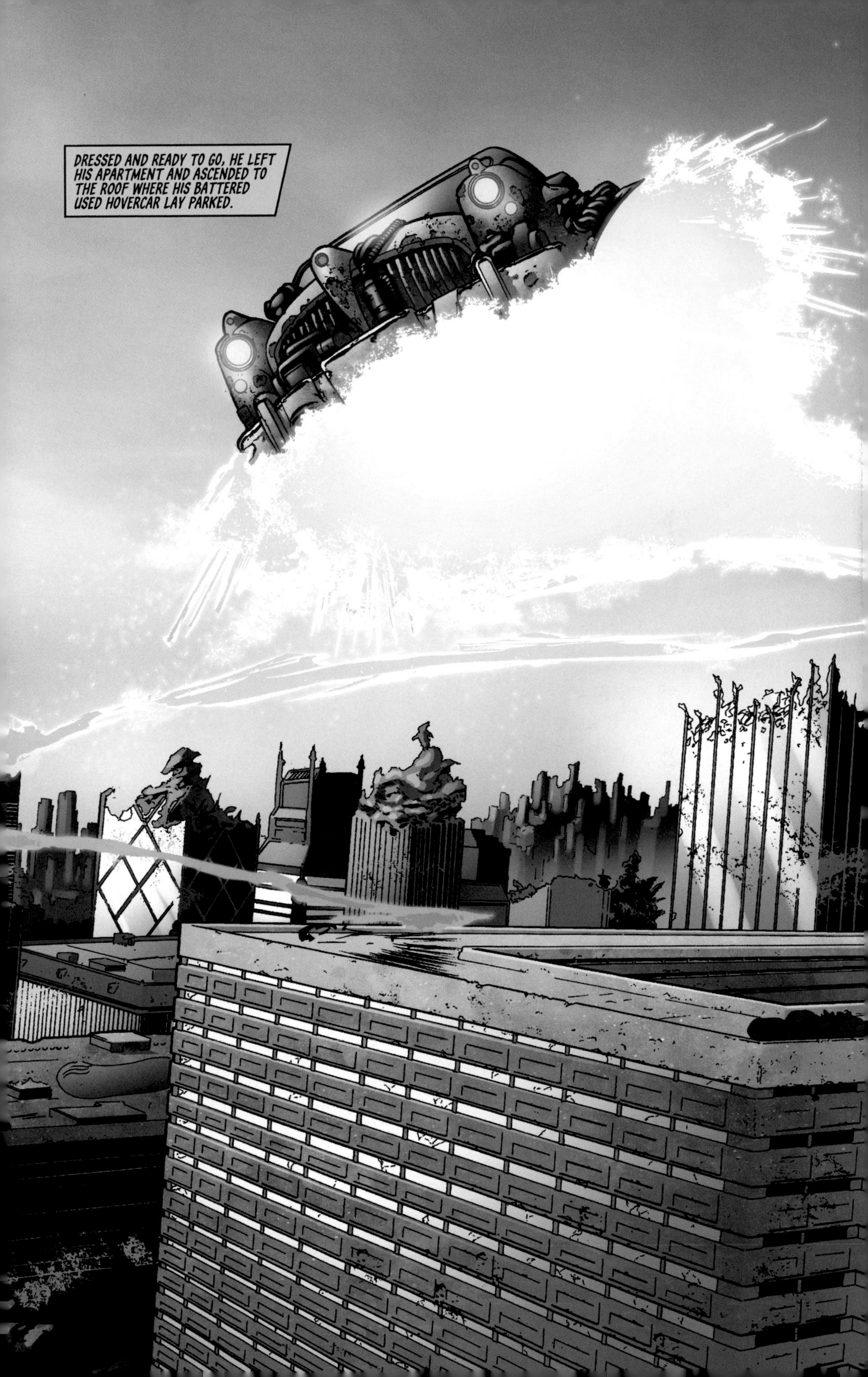
DRESSED AND READY TO GO, HE LEFT HIS APARTMENT AND ASCENDED TO THE ROOF WHERE HIS BATTERED USED HOVERCAR LAY PARKED.

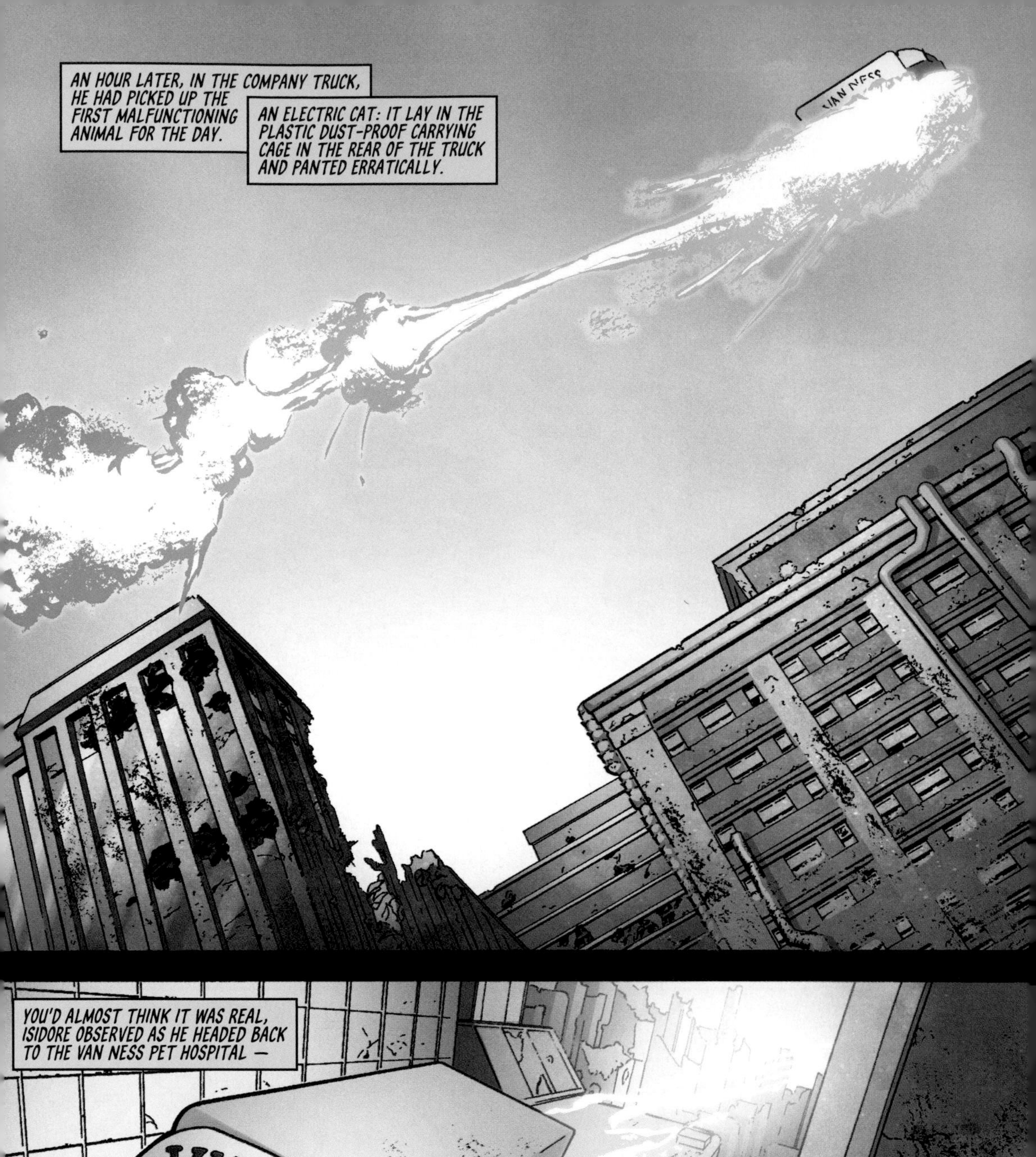
AN HOUR LATER, IN THE COMPANY TRUCK, HE HAD PICKED UP THE FIRST MALFUNCTIONING ANIMAL FOR THE DAY.
AN ELECTRIC CAT: IT LAY IN THE PLASTIC DUST-PROOF CARRYING CAGE IN THE REAR OF THE TRUCK AND PANTED ERRATICALLY.
VAN NESS

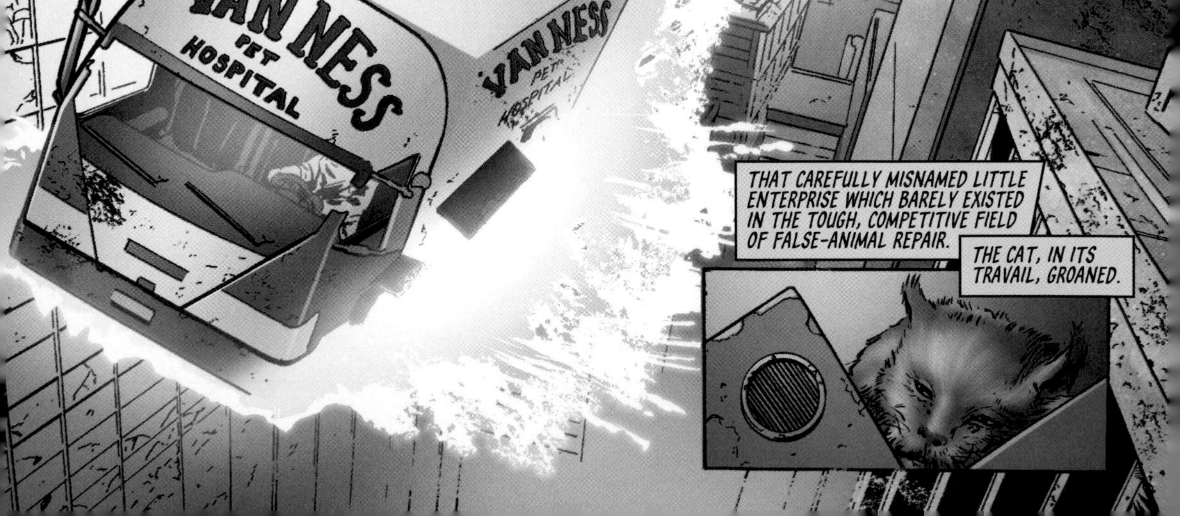
YOU'D ALMOST THINK IT WAS REAL, ISIDORE OBSERVED AS HE HEADED BACK TO THE VAN NESS PET HOSPITAL —
VAN NESS PET HOSPITAL
VAN NESS PET HOSPITAL
THAT CAREFULLY MISNAMED LITTLE ENTERPRISE WHICH BARELY EXISTED IN THE TOUGH, COMPETITIVE FIELD OF FALSE-ANIMAL REPAIR.
THE CAT, IN ITS TRAVAIL, GROANED.

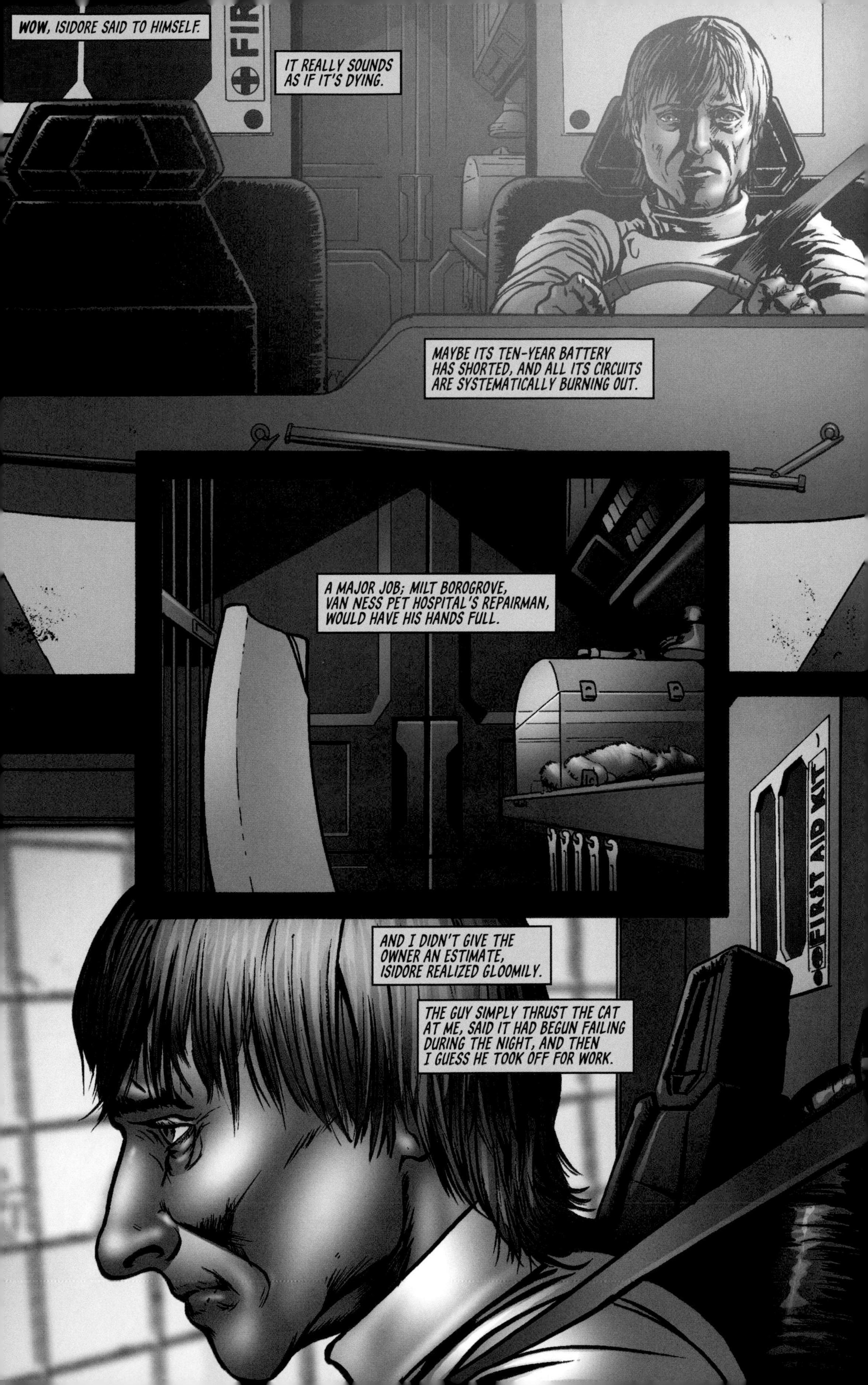
WOW, ISIDORE SAID TO HIMSELF.
IT REALLY SOUNDS AS IF IT'S DYING.
FIR
MAYBE ITS TEN-YEAR BATTERY HAS SHORTED, AND ALL ITS CIRCUITS ARE SYSTEMATICALLY BURNING OUT.
A MAJOR JOB; MILT BOROGROVE, VAN NESS PET HOSPITAL'S REPAIRMAN, WOULD HAVE HIS HANDS FULL.
FIRST AID KIT
AND I DIDN'T GIVE THE OWNER AN ESTIMATE, ISIDORE REALIZED GLOOMILY.
THE GUY SIMPLY THRUST THE CAT AT ME, SAID IT HAD BEGUN FAILING DURING THE NIGHT, AND THEN I GUESS HE TOOK OFF FOR WORK.

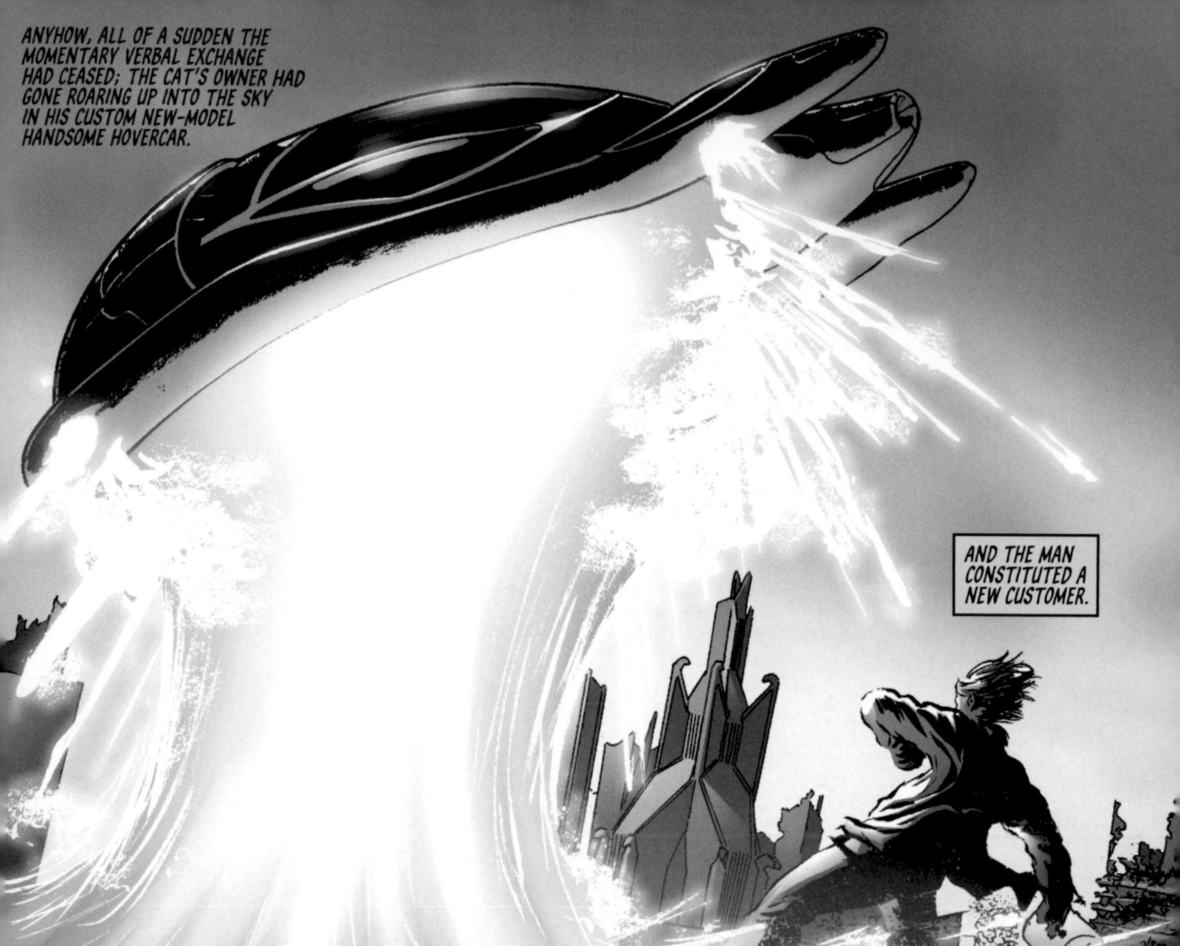
ANYHOW, ALL OF A SUDDEN THE MOMENTARY VERBAL EXCHANGE HAD CEASED; THE CAT'S OWNER HAD GONE ROARING UP INTO THE SKY IN HIS CUSTOM NEW-MODEL HANDSOME HOVERCAR.
AND THE MAN CONSTITUTED A NEW CUSTOMER.

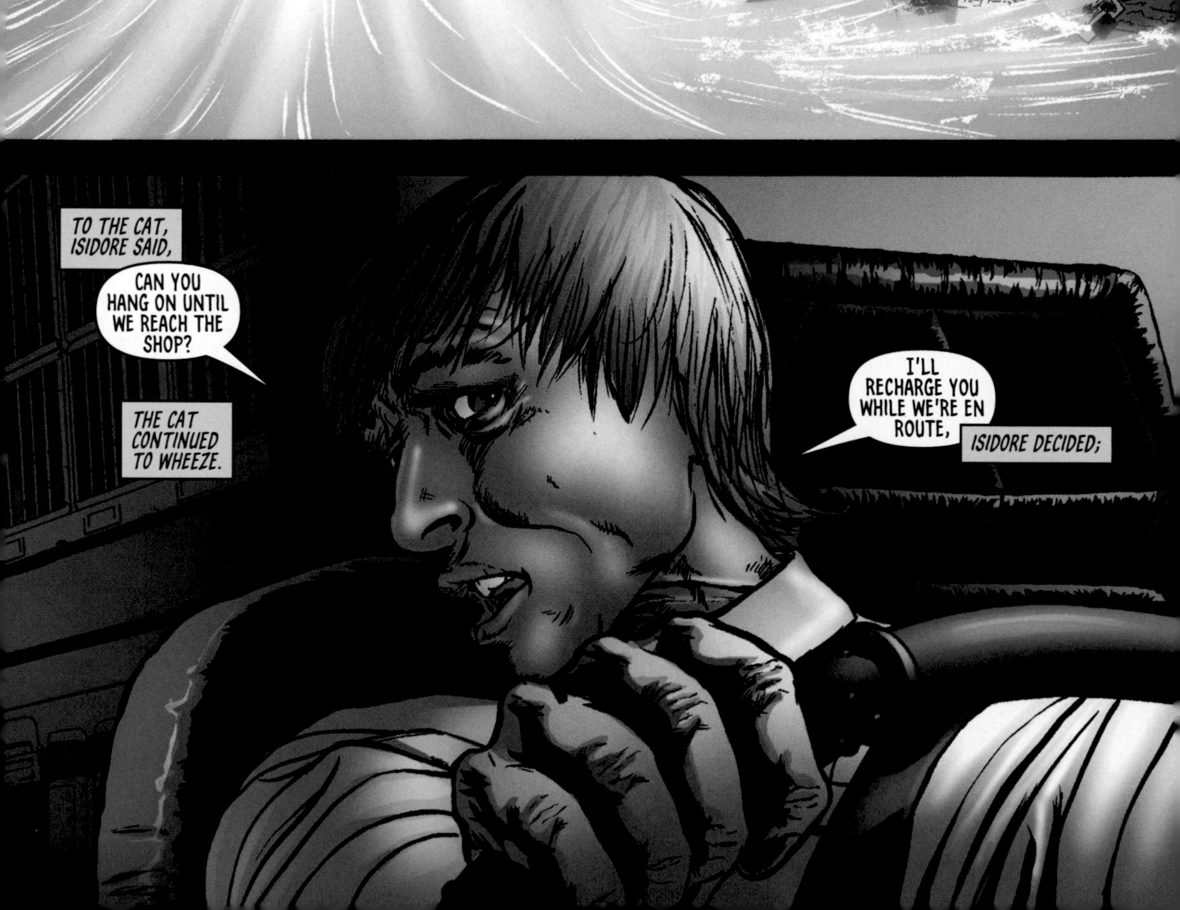
TO THE CAT, ISIDORE SAID,
CAN YOU HANG ON UNTIL WE REACH THE SHOP?
THE CAT CONTINUED TO WHEEZE.
I'LL RECHARGE YOU WHILE WE'RE EN ROUTE,
ISIDORE DECIDED;

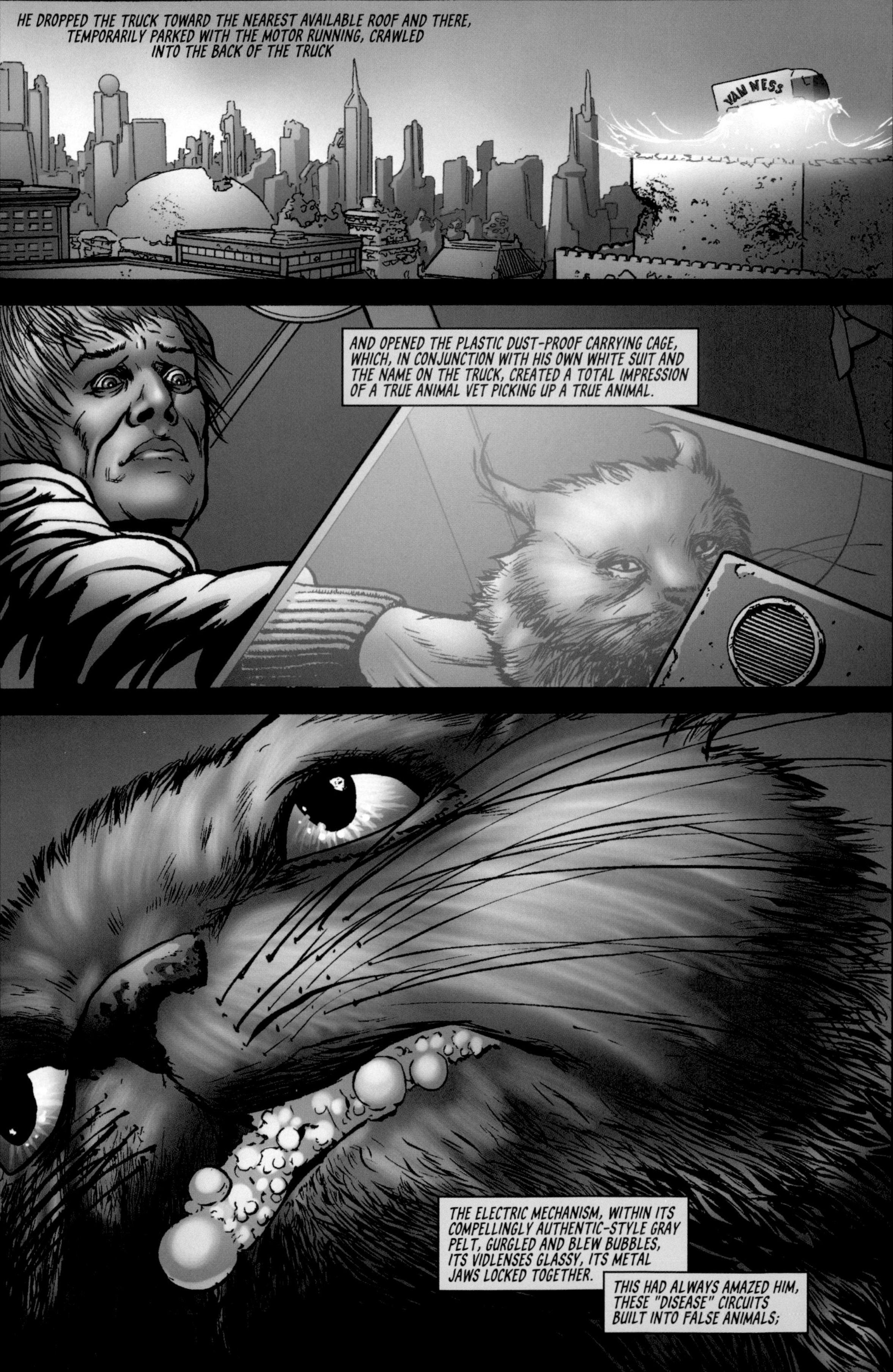

HE DROPPED THE TRUCK TOWARD THE NEAREST AVAILABLE ROOF AND THERE, TEMPORARILY PARKED WITH THE MOTOR RUNNING, CRAWLED INTO THE BACK OF THE TRUCK
VAN NESS
AND OPENED THE PLASTIC DUST-PROOF CARRYING CAGE, WHICH, IN CONJUNCTION WITH HIS OWN WHITE SUIT AND THE NAME ON THE TRUCK, CREATED A TOTAL IMPRESSION OF A TRUE ANIMAL VET PICKING UP A TRUE ANIMAL.
THE ELECTRIC MECHANISM, WITHIN ITS COMPELLINGLY AUTHENTIC-STYLE GRAY PELT, GURGLED AND BLEW BUBBLES, ITS VIDLENSES GLASSY, ITS METAL JAWS LOCKED TOGETHER.
THIS HAD ALWAYS AMAZED HIM, THESE "DISEASE" CIRCUITS BUILT INTO FALSE ANIMALS;

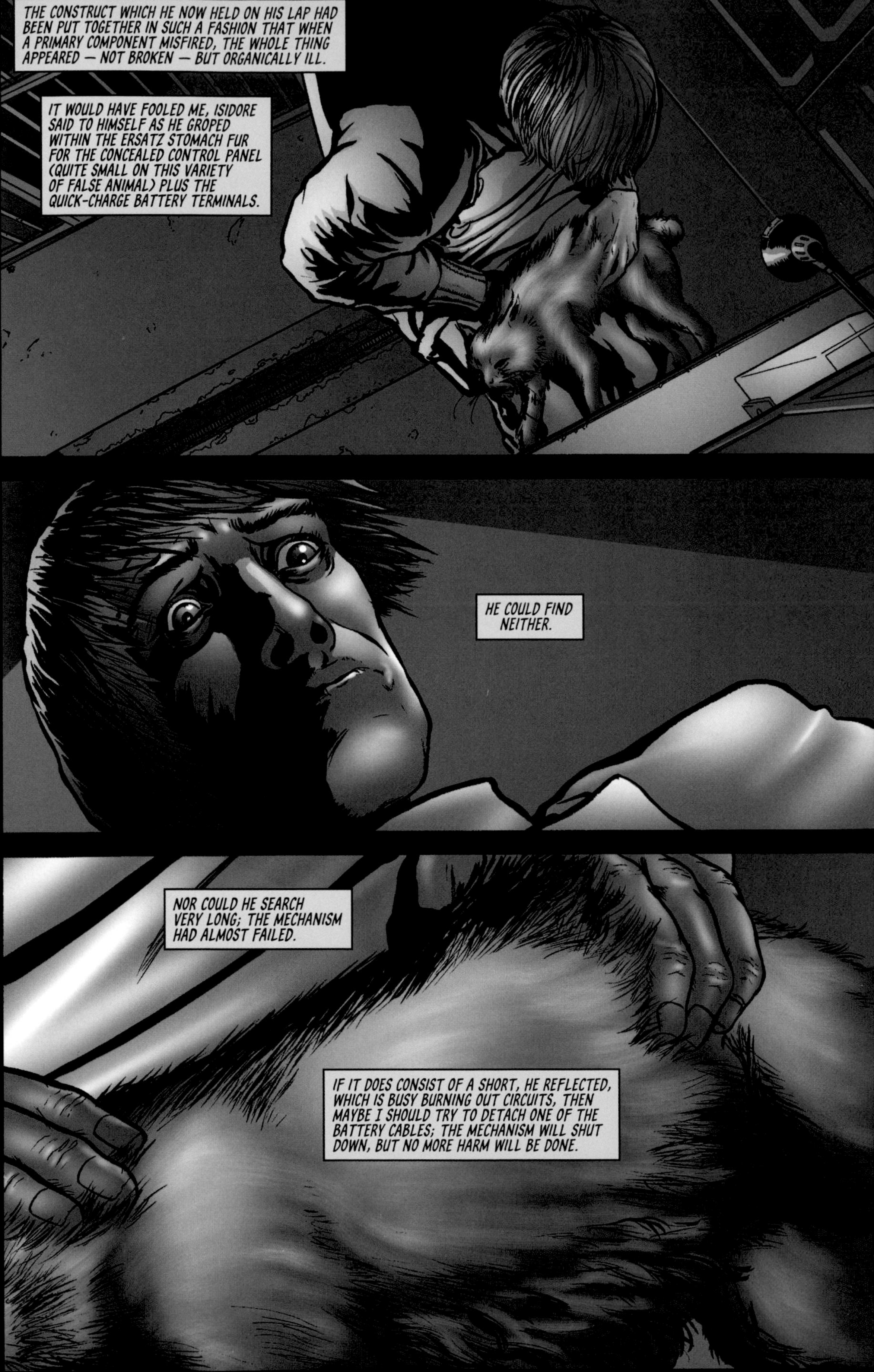
THE CONSTRUCT WHICH HE NOW HELD ON HIS LAP HAD BEEN PUT TOGETHER IN SUCH A FASHION THAT WHEN A PRIMARY COMPONENT MISFIRED, THE WHOLE THING APPEARED — NOT BROKEN — BUT ORGANICALLY ILL.
IT WOULD HAVE FOOLED ME, ISIDORE SAID TO HIMSELF AS HE GROPED WITHIN THE ERSATZ STOMACH FUR FOR THE CONCEALED CONTROL PANEL (QUITE SMALL ON THIS VARIETY OF FALSE ANIMAL) PLUS THE QUICK-CHARGE BATTERY TERMINALS.
HE COULD FIND NEITHER.
NOR COULD HE SEARCH VERY LONG; THE MECHANISM HAD ALMOST FAILED.
IF IT DOES CONSIST OF A SHORT, HE REFLECTED, WHICH IS BUSY BURNING OUT CIRCUITS, THEN MAYBE I SHOULD TRY TO DETACH ONE OF THE BATTERY CABLES; THE MECHANISM WILL SHUT DOWN, BUT NO MORE HARM WILL BE DONE.

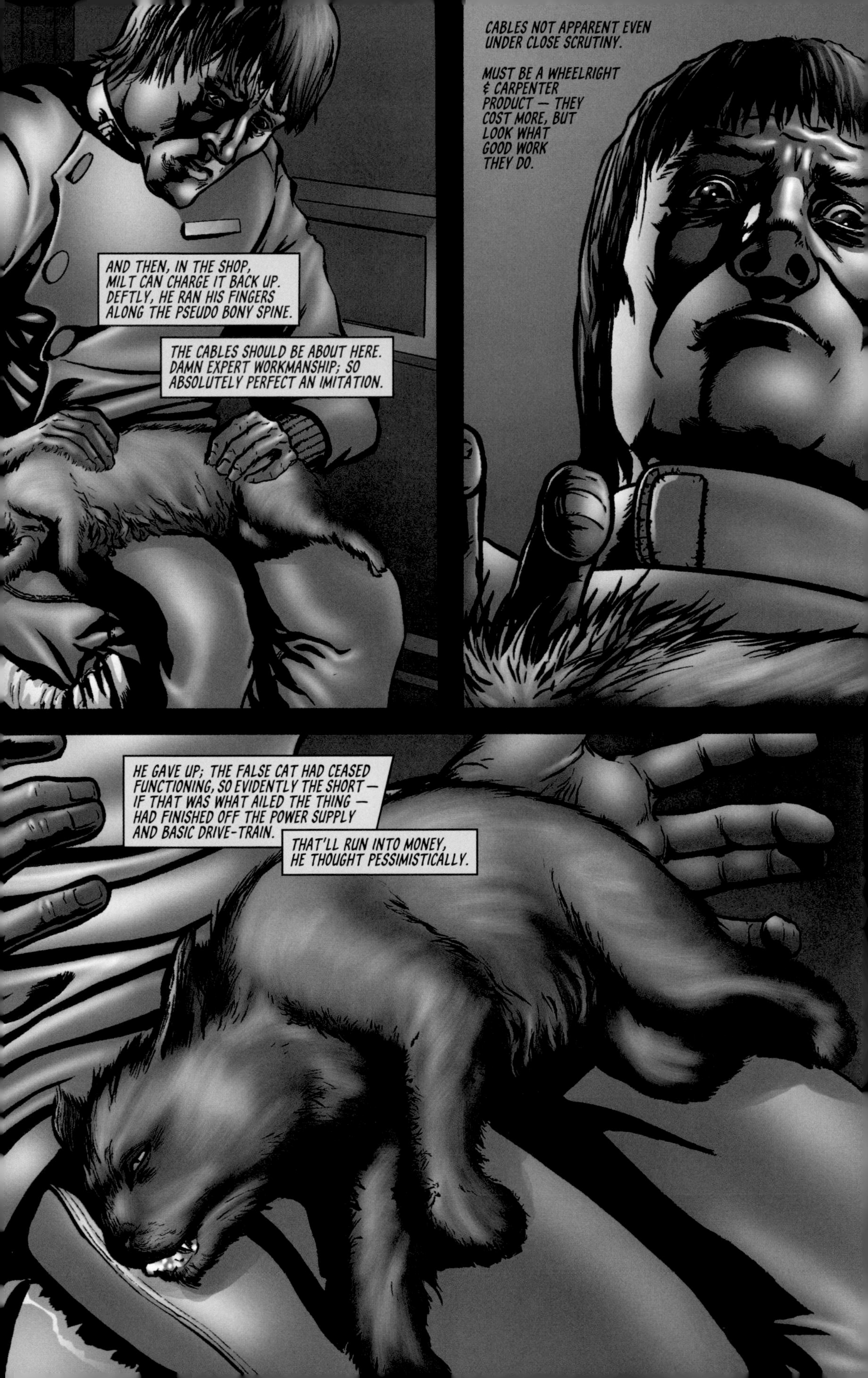
AND THEN, IN THE SHOP, MILT CAN CHARGE IT BACK UP. DEFTLY, HE RAN HIS FINGERS ALONG THE PSEUDO BONY SPINE.
THE CABLES SHOULD BE ABOUT HERE. DAMN EXPERT WORKMANSHIP; SO ABSOLUTELY PERFECT AN IMITATION.
CABLES NOT APPARENT EVEN UNDER CLOSE SCRUTINY.
MUST BE A WHEELRIGHT & CARPENTER PRODUCT — THEY COST MORE, BUT LOOK WHAT GOOD WORK THEY DO.
HE GAVE UP; THE FALSE CAT HAD CEASED FUNCTIONING, SO EVIDENTLY THE SHORT — IF THAT WAS WHAT AILED THE THING — HAD FINISHED OFF THE POWER SUPPLY AND BASIC DRIVE-TRAIN.
THAT'LL RUN INTO MONEY, HE THOUGHT PESSIMISTICALLY.

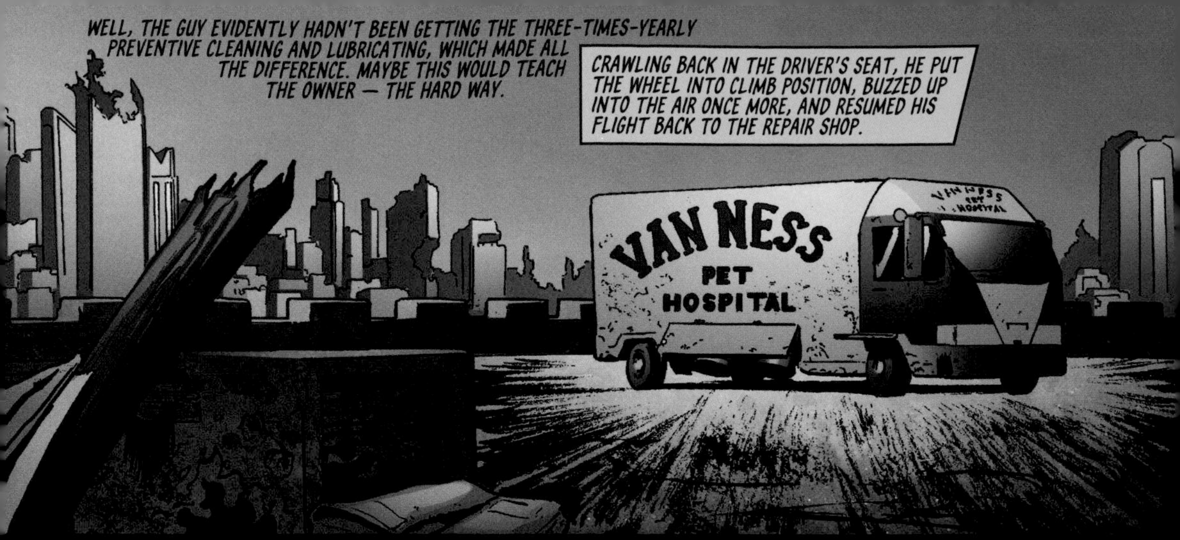
WELL, THE GUY EVIDENTLY HADN'T BEEN GETTING THE THREE-TIMES-YEARLY PREVENTIVE CLEANING AND LUBRICATING, WHICH MADE ALL THE DIFFERENCE. MAYBE THIS WOULD TEACH THE OWNER — THE HARD WAY.
CRAWLING BACK IN THE DRIVER'S SEAT, HE PUT THE WHEEL INTO CLIMB POSITION, BUZZED UP INTO THE AIR ONCE MORE, AND RESUMED HIS FLIGHT BACK TO THE REPAIR SHOP.
VAN NESS PET HOSPITAL

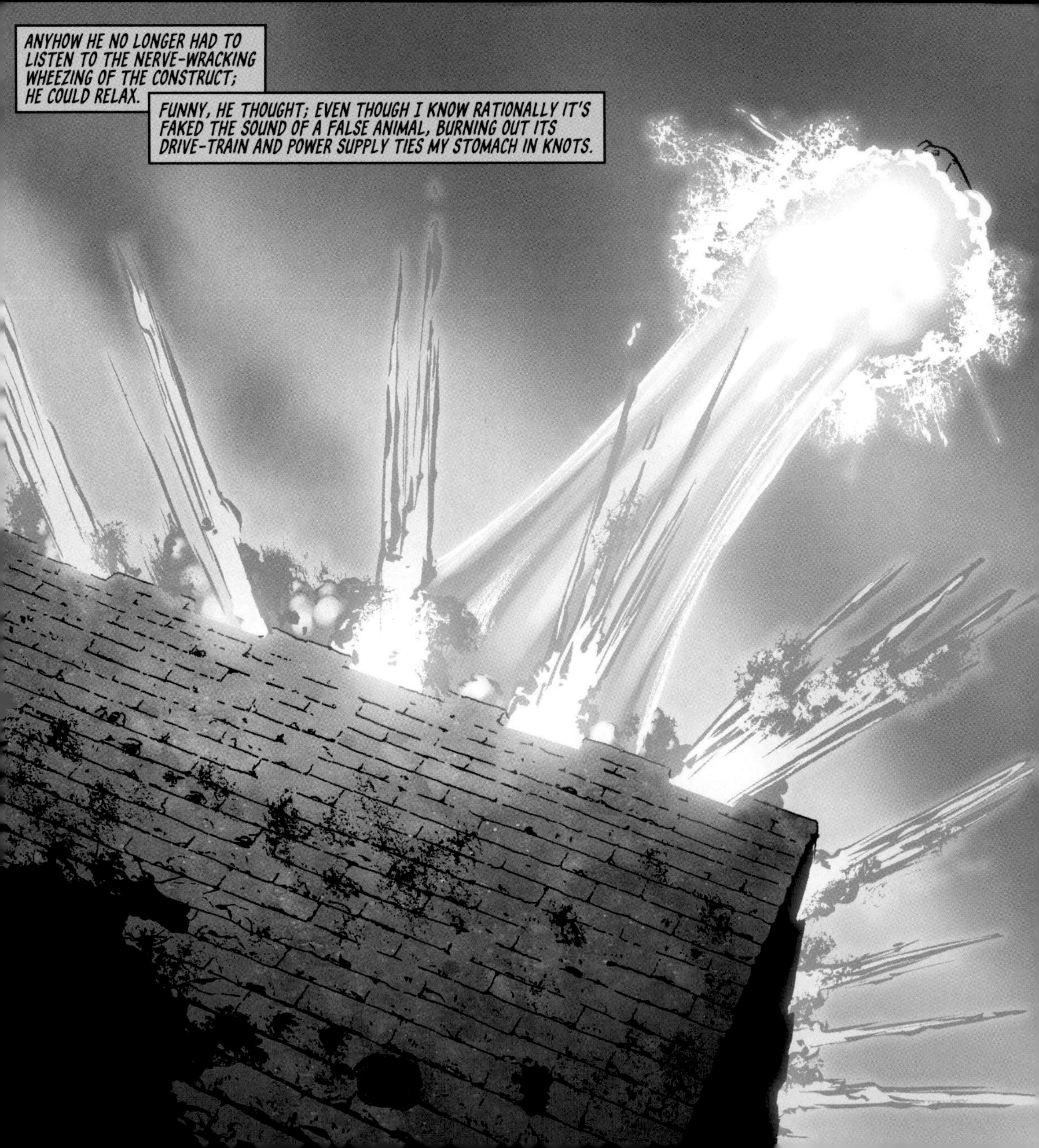
ANYHOW HE NO LONGER HAD TO LISTEN TO THE NERVE-WRACKING WHEEZING OF THE CONSTRUCT; HE COULD RELAX.
FUNNY, HE THOUGHT; EVEN THOUGH I KNOW RATIONALLY IT'S FAKED THE SOUND OF A FALSE ANIMAL, BURNING OUT ITS DRIVE-TRAIN AND POWER SUPPLY TIES MY STOMACH IN KNOTS.

I WISH, HE THOUGHT PAINFULLY, THAT I COULD GET ANOTHER JOB.

IF I HADN'T FAILED THAT IQ TEST I WOULDN'T BE REDUCED TO THIS IGNOMINIOUS TASK WITH ITS ATTENDANT EMOTIONAL BY-PRODUCTS.

ON THE OTHER HAND, THE SYNTHETIC SUFFERINGS OF FALSE ANIMALS DIDN'T BOTHER MILT BOROGROVE OR THEIR BOSS HANNIBAL SLOAT.

SO MAYBE IT'S I, JOHN ISIDORE SAID TO HIMSELF.

MAYBE WHEN YOU DETERIORATE BACK DOWN THE LADDER OF EVOLUTION AS I HAVE, WHEN YOU SINK INTO THE TOMB WORLD SLOUGH OF BEING A SPECIAL —

WELL, BEST TO ABANDON THAT LINE OF INQUIRY.

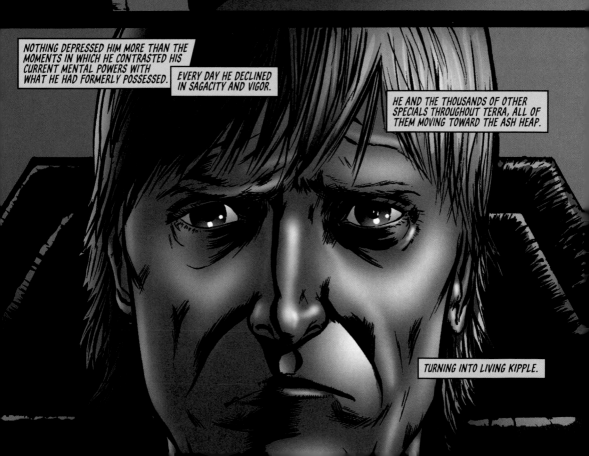

NOTHING DEPRESSED HIM MORE THAN THE MOMENTS IN WHICH HE CONTRASTED HIS CURRENT MENTAL POWERS WITH WHAT HE HAD FORMERLY POSSESSED.

EVERY DAY HE DECLINED IN SAGACITY AND VIGOR.

HE AND THE THOUSANDS OF OTHER SPECIALS THROUGHOUT TERRA, ALL OF THEM MOVING TOWARD THE ASH HEAP.

TURNING INTO LIVING KIPPLE.

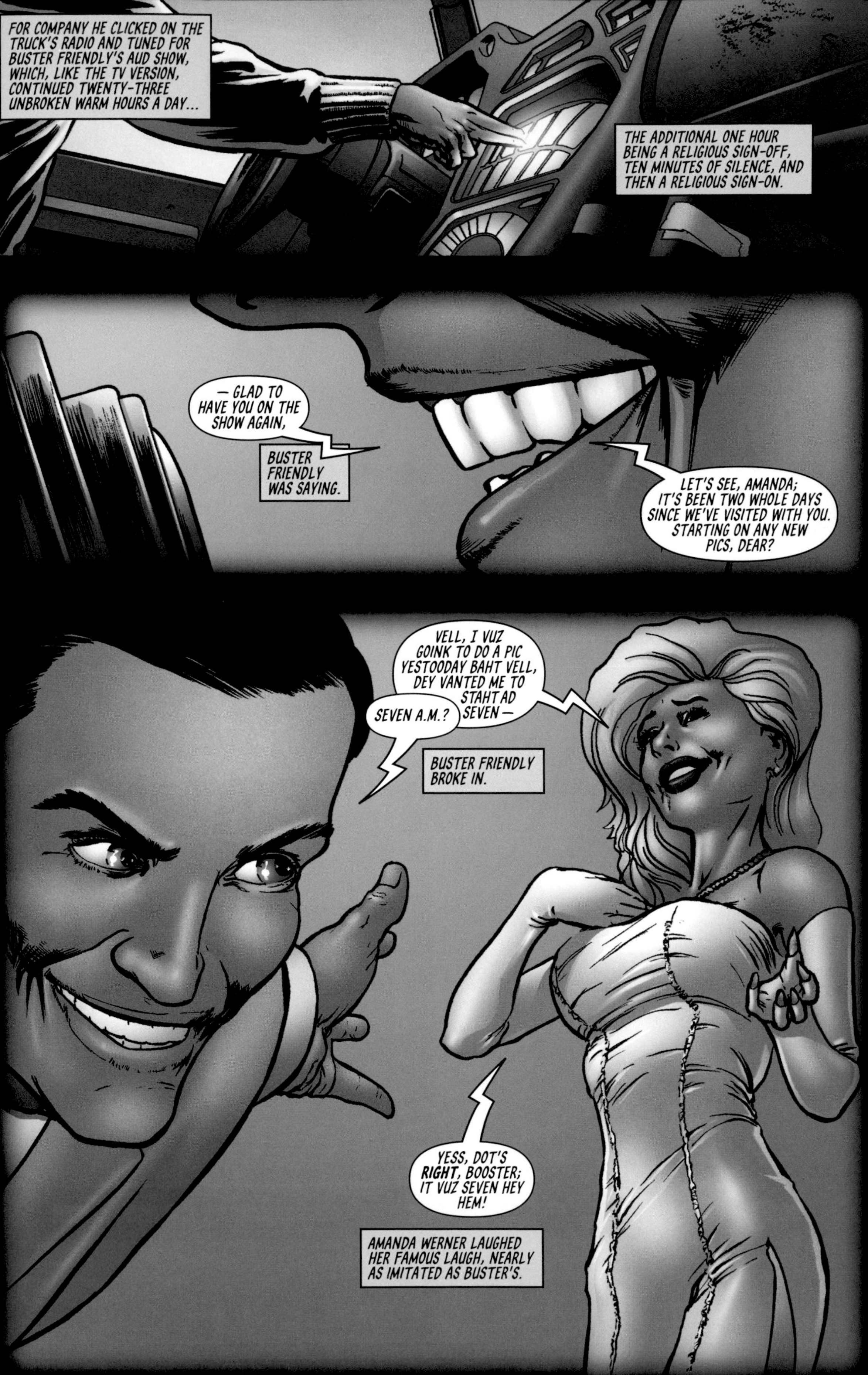
FOR COMPANY HE CLICKED ON THE TRUCK'S RADIO AND TUNED FOR BUSTER FRIENDLY'S AUD SHOW, WHICH, LIKE THE TV VERSION, CONTINUED TWENTY-THREE UNBROKEN WARM HOURS A DAY...
THE ADDITIONAL ONE HOUR BEING A RELIGIOUS SIGN-OFF, TEN MINUTES OF SILENCE, AND THEN A RELIGIOUS SIGN-ON.
— GLAD TO HAVE YOU ON THE SHOW AGAIN,
BUSTER FRIENDLY WAS SAYING.
LET'S SEE, AMANDA; IT'S BEEN TWO WHOLE DAYS SINCE WE'VE VISITED WITH YOU. STARTING ON ANY NEW PICS, DEAR?
VELL, I VUZ GOINK TO DO A PIC YESTOODAY BAHT VELL, DEY VANTED ME TO STAHT AD SEVEN —
SEVEN A.M.?
BUSTER FRIENDLY BROKE IN.
YESS, DOT'S **RIGHT**, BOOSTER; IT VUZ SEVEN HEY HEM!
AMANDA WERNER LAUGHED HER FAMOUS LAUGH, NEARLY AS IMITATED AS BUSTER'S.

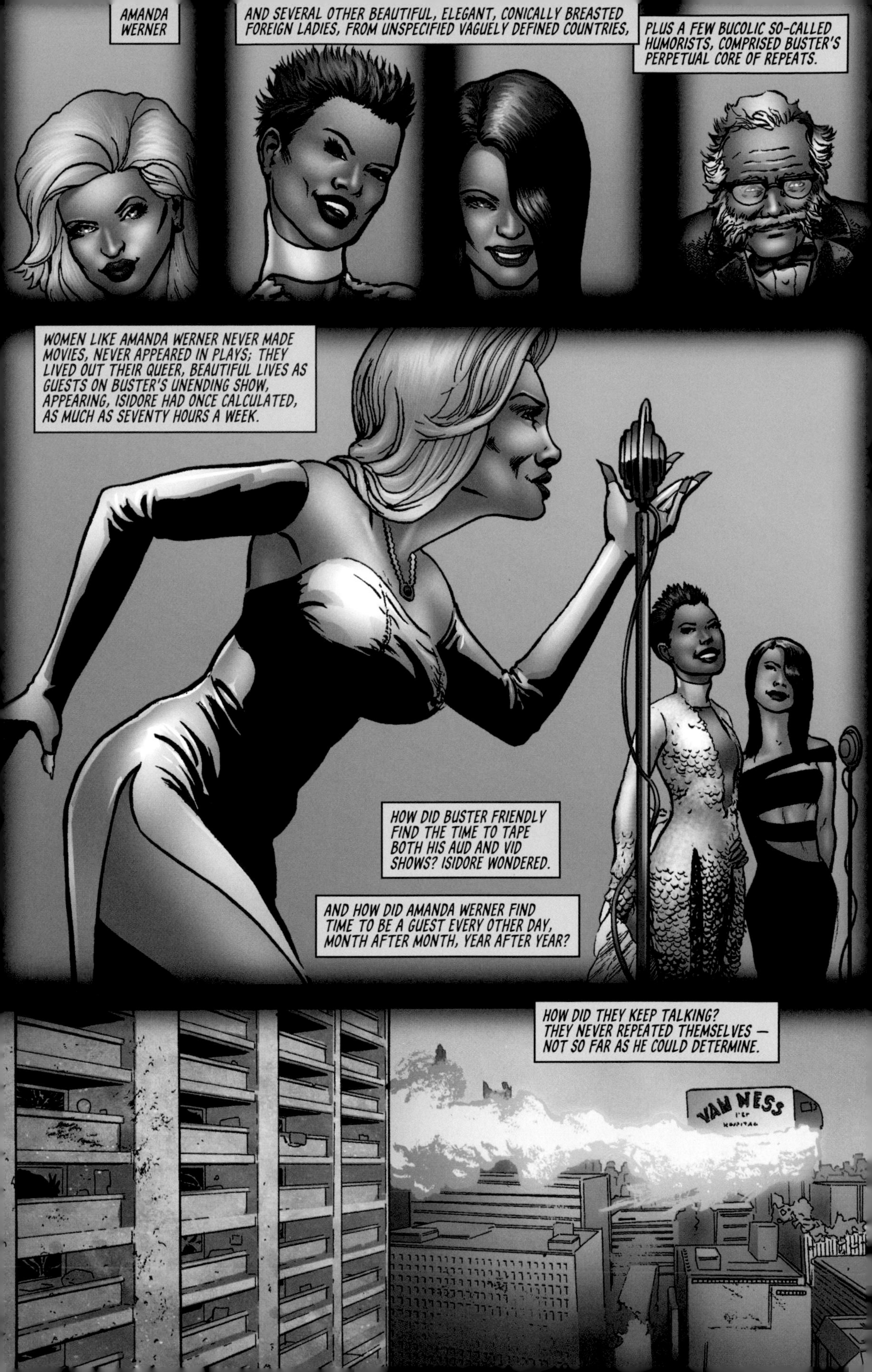
AMANDA WERNER
AND SEVERAL OTHER BEAUTIFUL, ELEGANT, CONICALLY BREASTED FOREIGN LADIES, FROM UNSPECIFIED VAGUELY DEFINED COUNTRIES,
PLUS A FEW BUCOLIC SO-CALLED HUMORISTS, COMPRISED BUSTER'S PERPETUAL CORE OF REPEATS.
WOMEN LIKE AMANDA WERNER NEVER MADE MOVIES, NEVER APPEARED IN PLAYS; THEY LIVED OUT THEIR QUEER, BEAUTIFUL LIVES AS GUESTS ON BUSTER'S UNENDING SHOW, APPEARING, ISIDORE HAD ONCE CALCULATED, AS MUCH AS SEVENTY HOURS A WEEK.
HOW DID BUSTER FRIENDLY FIND THE TIME TO TAPE BOTH HIS AUD AND VID SHOWS? ISIDORE WONDERED.
AND HOW DID AMANDA WERNER FIND TIME TO BE A GUEST EVERY OTHER DAY, MONTH AFTER MONTH, YEAR AFTER YEAR?
HOW DID THEY KEEP TALKING? THEY NEVER REPEATED THEMSELVES — NOT SO FAR AS HE COULD DETERMINE.
VAN NESS

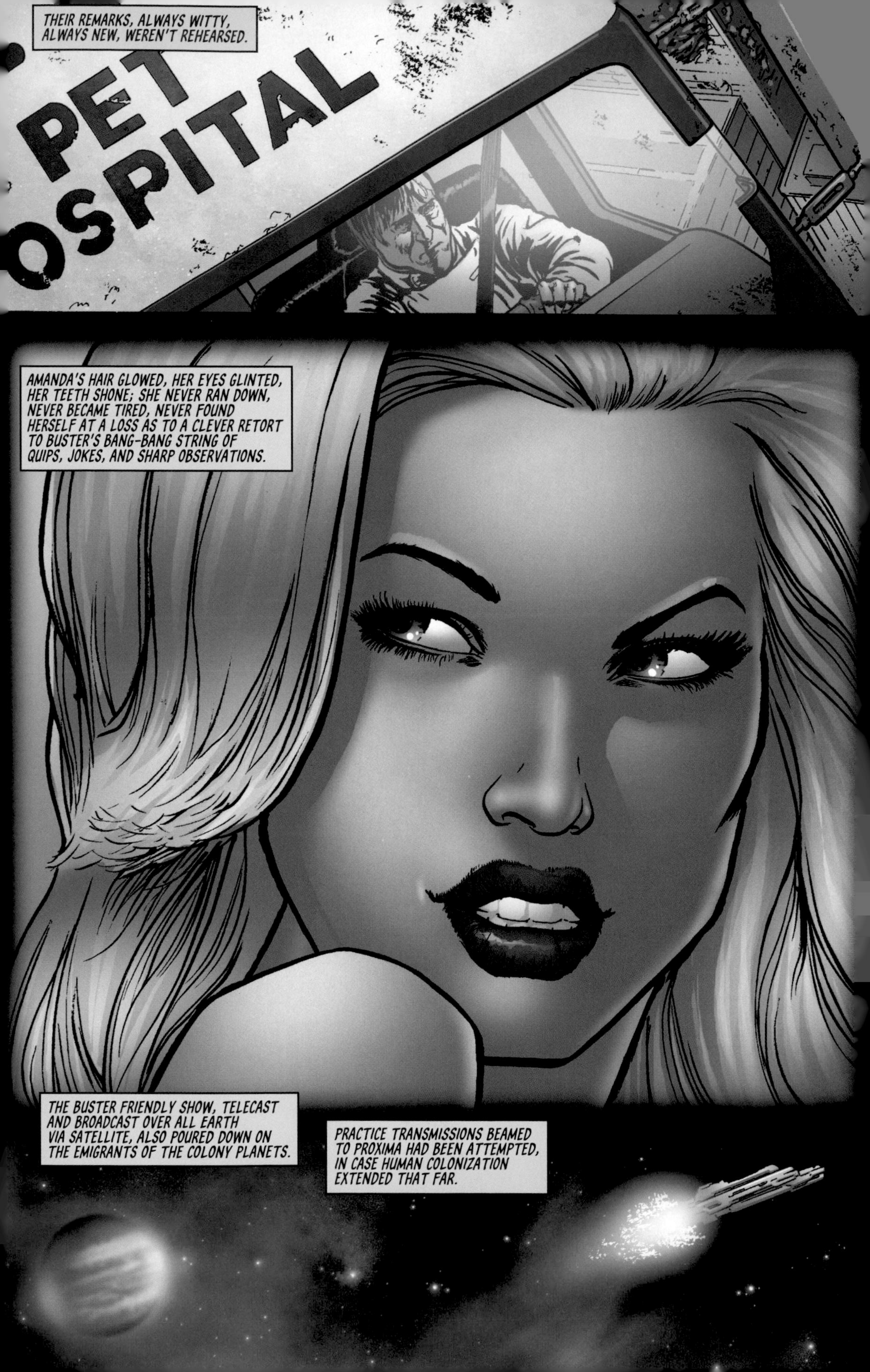
THEIR REMARKS, ALWAYS WITTY, ALWAYS NEW, WEREN'T REHEARSED.
PET
OSPITAL
AMANDA'S HAIR GLOWED, HER EYES GLINTED, HER TEETH SHONE; SHE NEVER RAN DOWN, NEVER BECAME TIRED, NEVER FOUND HERSELF AT A LOSS AS TO A CLEVER RETORT TO BUSTER'S BANG-BANG STRING OF QUIPS, JOKES, AND SHARP OBSERVATIONS.
THE BUSTER FRIENDLY SHOW, TELECAST AND BROADCAST OVER ALL EARTH VIA SATELLITE, ALSO POURED DOWN ON THE EMIGRANTS OF THE COLONY PLANETS.
PRACTICE TRANSMISSIONS BEAMED TO PROXIMA HAD BEEN ATTEMPTED, IN CASE HUMAN COLONIZATION EXTENDED THAT FAR.

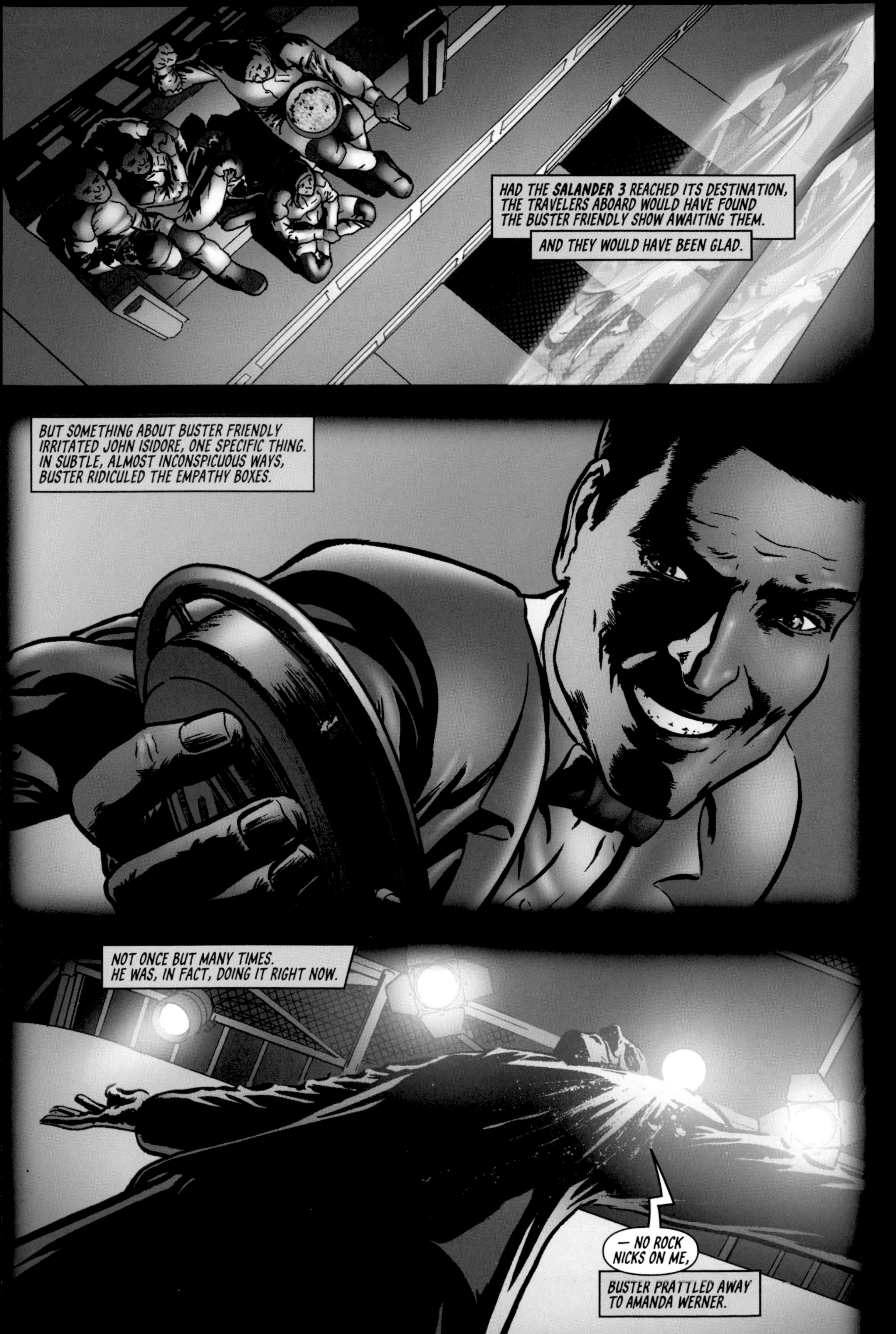
HAD THE **SALANDER 3** REACHED ITS DESTINATION, THE TRAVELERS ABOARD WOULD HAVE FOUND THE BUSTER FRIENDLY SHOW AWAITING THEM.
AND THEY WOULD HAVE BEEN GLAD.
BUT SOMETHING ABOUT BUSTER FRIENDLY IRRITATED JOHN ISIDORE, ONE SPECIFIC THING. IN SUBTLE, ALMOST INCONSPICUOUS WAYS, BUSTER RIDICULED THE EMPATHY BOXES.
NOT ONCE BUT MANY TIMES. HE WAS, IN FACT, DOING IT RIGHT NOW.
— NO ROCK NICKS ON ME,
BUSTER PRATTLED AWAY TO AMANDA WERNER.

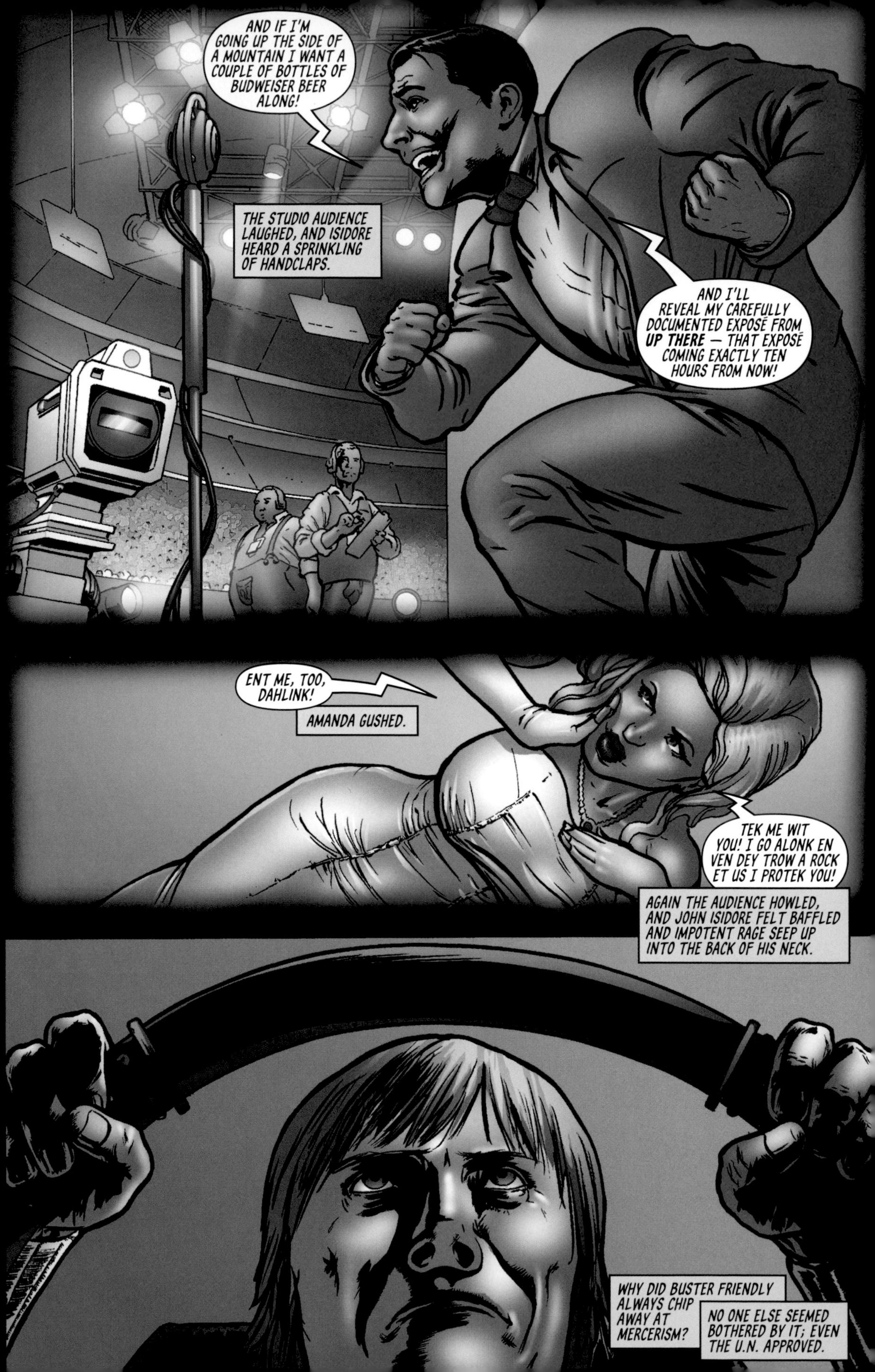
AND IF I'M GOING UP THE SIDE OF A MOUNTAIN I WANT A COUPLE OF BOTTLES OF BUDWEISER BEER ALONG!
THE STUDIO AUDIENCE LAUGHED, AND ISIDORE HEARD A SPRINKLING OF HANDCLAPS.
AND I'LL REVEAL MY CAREFULLY DOCUMENTED EXPOSÉ FROM UP THERE — THAT EXPOSÉ COMING EXACTLY TEN HOURS FROM NOW!
ENT ME, TOO, DAHLINK!
AMANDA GUSHED.
TEK ME WIT YOU! I GO ALONK EN VEN DEY TROW A ROCK ET US I PROTEK YOU!
AGAIN THE AUDIENCE HOWLED, AND JOHN ISIDORE FELT BAFFLED AND IMPOTENT RAGE SEEP UP INTO THE BACK OF HIS NECK.
WHY DID BUSTER FRIENDLY ALWAYS CHIP AWAY AT MERCERISM?
NO ONE ELSE SEEMED BOTHERED BY IT; EVEN THE U.N. APPROVED.

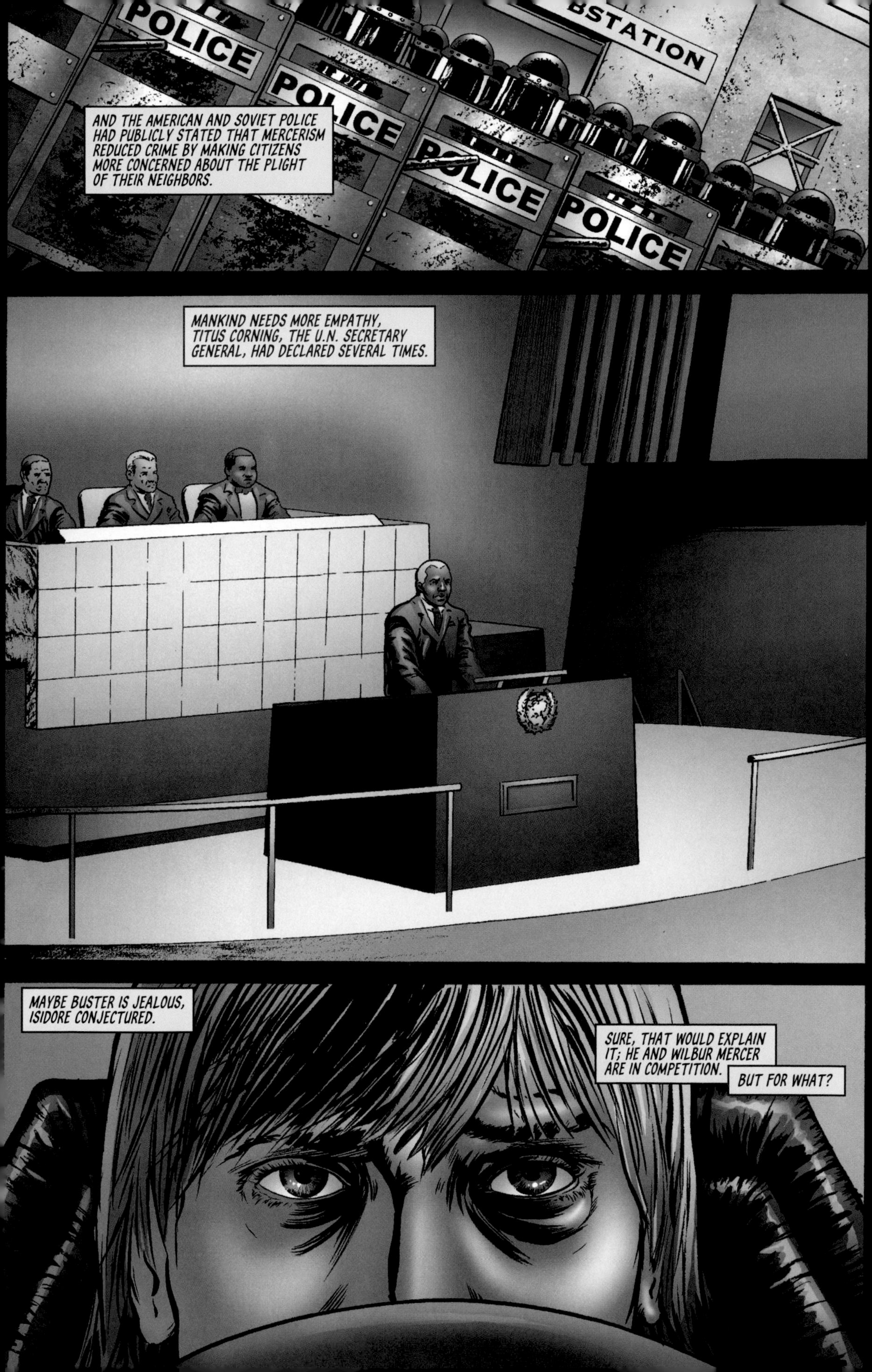
POLICE
BSTATION
AND THE AMERICAN AND SOVIET POLICE HAD PUBLICLY STATED THAT MERCERISM REDUCED CRIME BY MAKING CITIZENS MORE CONCERNED ABOUT THE PLIGHT OF THEIR NEIGHBORS.
MANKIND NEEDS MORE EMPATHY, TITUS CORNING, THE U.N. SECRETARY GENERAL, HAD DECLARED SEVERAL TIMES.
MAYBE BUSTER IS JEALOUS, ISIDORE CONJECTURED.
SURE, THAT WOULD EXPLAIN IT; HE AND WILBUR MERCER ARE IN COMPETITION.
BUT FOR WHAT?

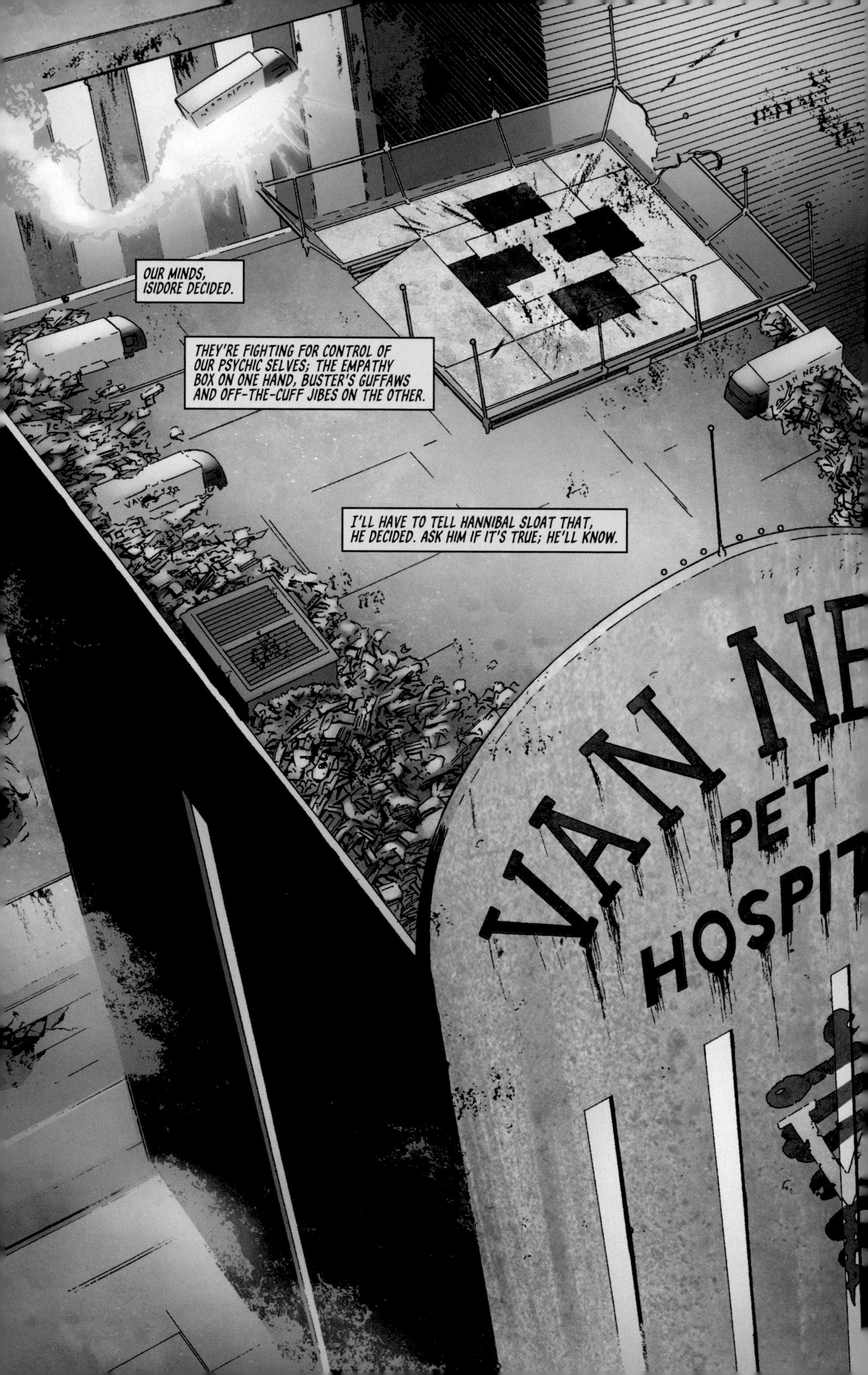
OUR MINDS, ISIDORE DECIDED.
THEY'RE FIGHTING FOR CONTROL OF OUR PSYCHIC SELVES; THE EMPATHY BOX ON ONE HAND, BUSTER'S GUFFAWS AND OFF-THE-CUFF JIBES ON THE OTHER.
I'LL HAVE TO TELL HANNIBAL SLOAT THAT, HE DECIDED. ASK HIM IF IT'S TRUE; HE'LL KNOW.

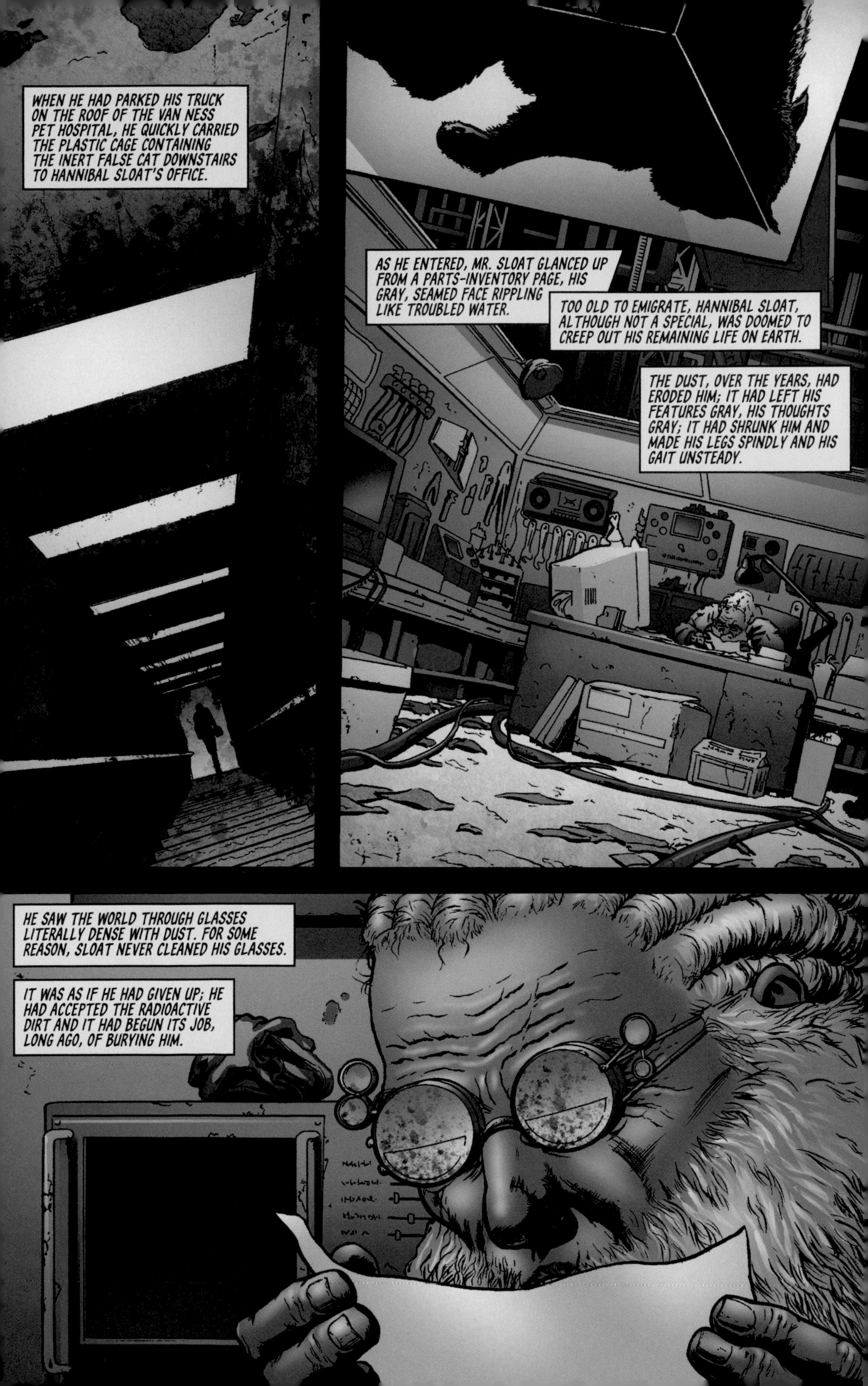
WHEN HE HAD PARKED HIS TRUCK ON THE ROOF OF THE VAN NESS PET HOSPITAL, HE QUICKLY CARRIED THE PLASTIC CAGE CONTAINING THE INERT FALSE CAT DOWNSTAIRS TO HANNIBAL SLOAT'S OFFICE.
AS HE ENTERED, MR. SLOAT GLANCED UP FROM A PARTS-INVENTORY PAGE, HIS GRAY, SEAMED FACE RIPPLING LIKE TROUBLED WATER.
TOO OLD TO EMIGRATE, HANNIBAL SLOAT, ALTHOUGH NOT A SPECIAL, WAS DOOMED TO CREEP OUT HIS REMAINING LIFE ON EARTH.
THE DUST, OVER THE YEARS, HAD ERODED HIM; IT HAD LEFT HIS FEATURES GRAY, HIS THOUGHTS GRAY; IT HAD SHRUNK HIM AND MADE HIS LEGS SPINDLY AND HIS GAIT UNSTEADY.
HE SAW THE WORLD THROUGH GLASSES LITERALLY DENSE WITH DUST. FOR SOME REASON, SLOAT NEVER CLEANED HIS GLASSES.
IT WAS AS IF HE HAD GIVEN UP; HE HAD ACCEPTED THE RADIOACTIVE DIRT AND IT HAD BEGUN ITS JOB, LONG AGO, OF BURYING HIM.

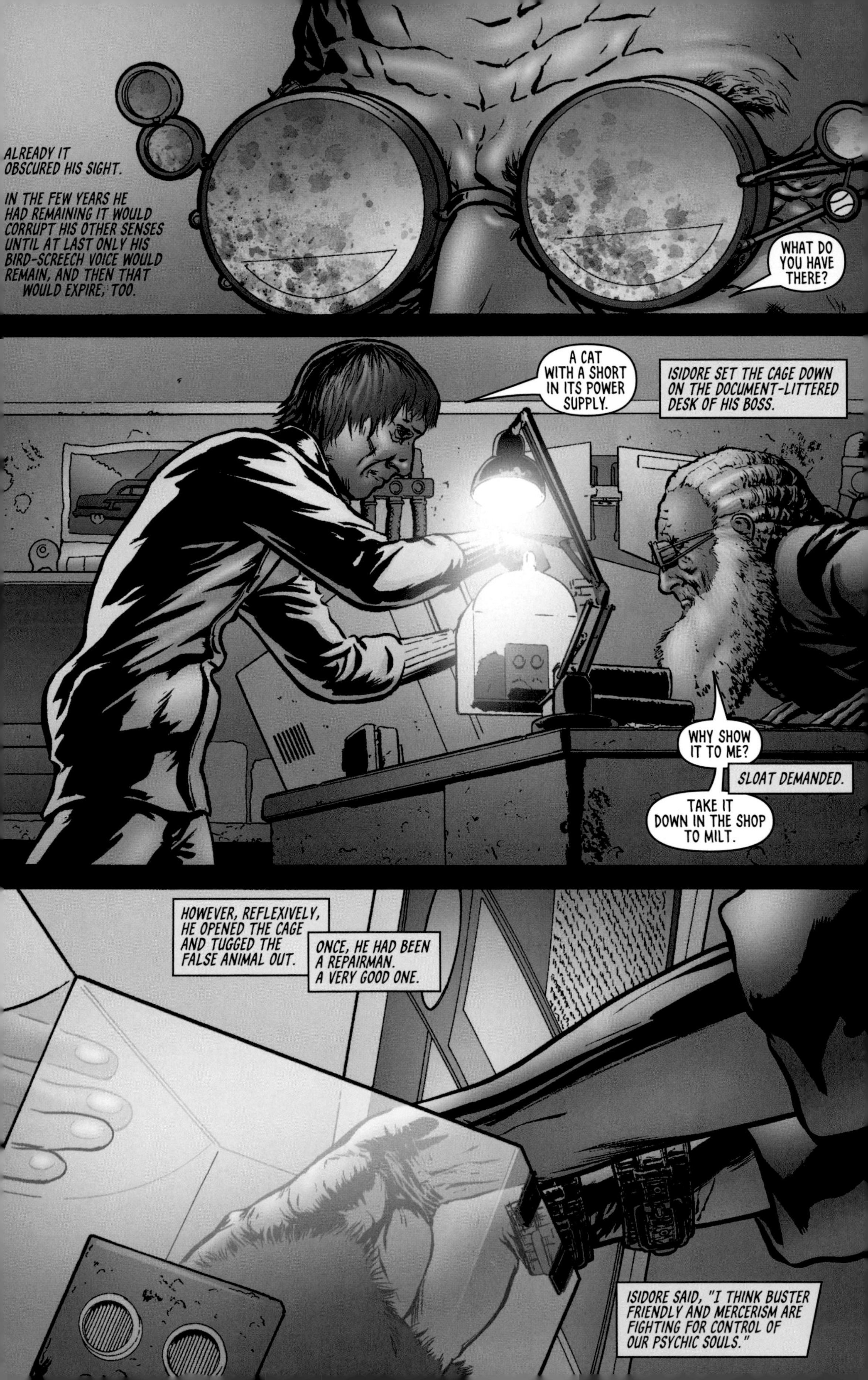
ALREADY IT OBSCURED HIS SIGHT.
IN THE FEW YEARS HE HAD REMAINING IT WOULD CORRUPT HIS OTHER SENSES UNTIL AT LAST ONLY HIS BIRD-SCREECH VOICE WOULD REMAIN, AND THEN THAT WOULD EXPIRE, TOO.
WHAT DO YOU HAVE THERE?
A CAT WITH A SHORT IN ITS POWER SUPPLY.
ISIDORE SET THE CAGE DOWN ON THE DOCUMENT-LITTERED DESK OF HIS BOSS.
WHY SHOW IT TO ME?
SLOAT DEMANDED.
TAKE IT DOWN IN THE SHOP TO MILT.
HOWEVER, REFLEXIVELY, HE OPENED THE CAGE AND TUGGED THE FALSE ANIMAL OUT.
ONCE, HE HAD BEEN A REPAIRMAN. A VERY GOOD ONE.
ISIDORE SAID, "I THINK BUSTER FRIENDLY AND MERCERISM ARE FIGHTING FOR CONTROL OF OUR PSYCHIC SOULS."

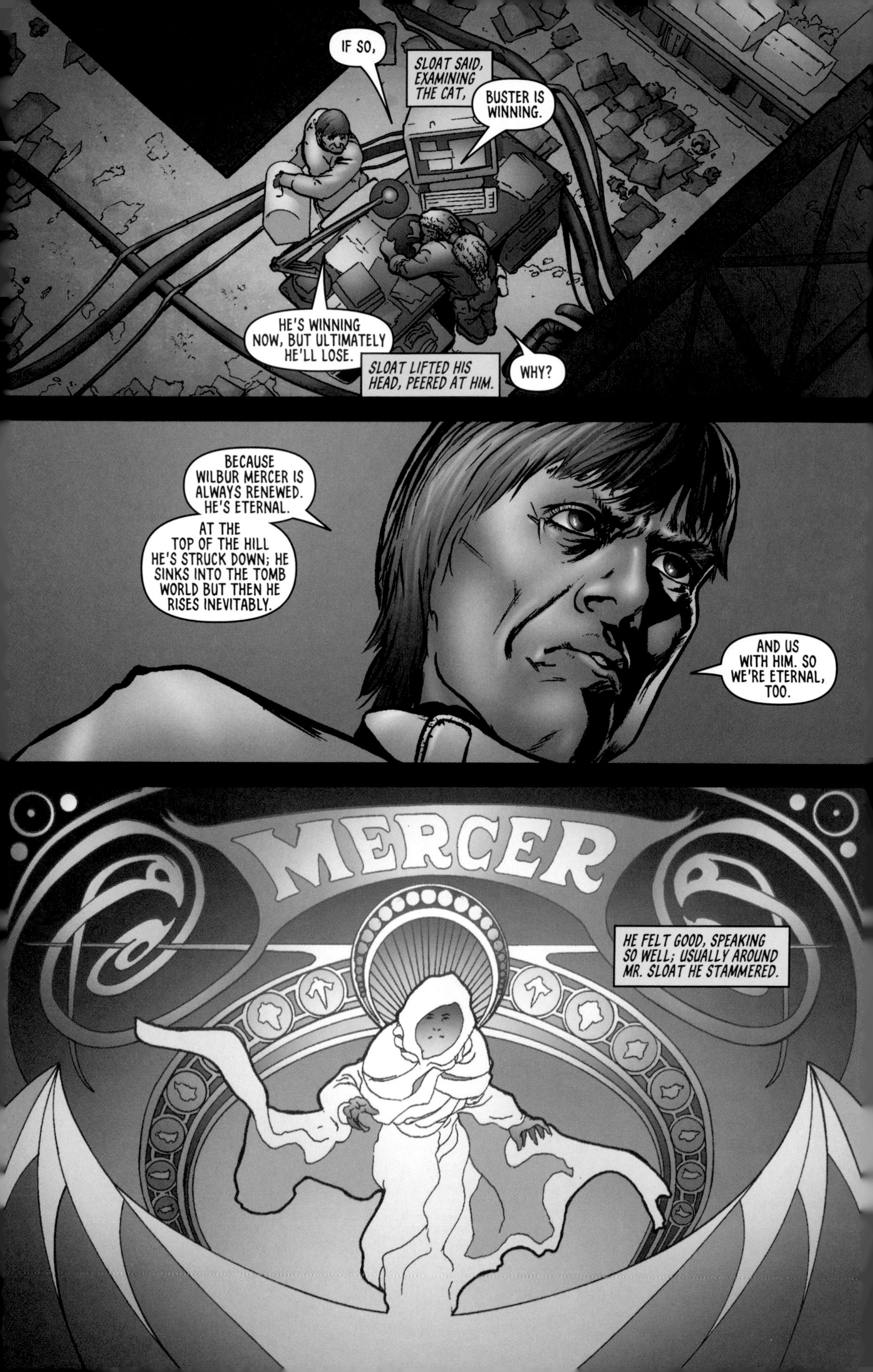
IF SO,
SLOAT SAID, EXAMINING THE CAT,
BUSTER IS WINNING.
HE'S WINNING NOW, BUT ULTIMATELY HE'LL LOSE.
SLOAT LIFTED HIS HEAD, PEERED AT HIM.
WHY?
BECAUSE WILBUR MERCER IS ALWAYS RENEWED. HE'S ETERNAL.
AT THE TOP OF THE HILL HE'S STRUCK DOWN; HE SINKS INTO THE TOMB WORLD BUT THEN HE RISES INEVITABLY.
AND US WITH HIM. SO WE'RE ETERNAL, TOO.
MERCER
HE FELT GOOD, SPEAKING SO WELL; USUALLY AROUND MR. SLOAT HE STAMMERED.

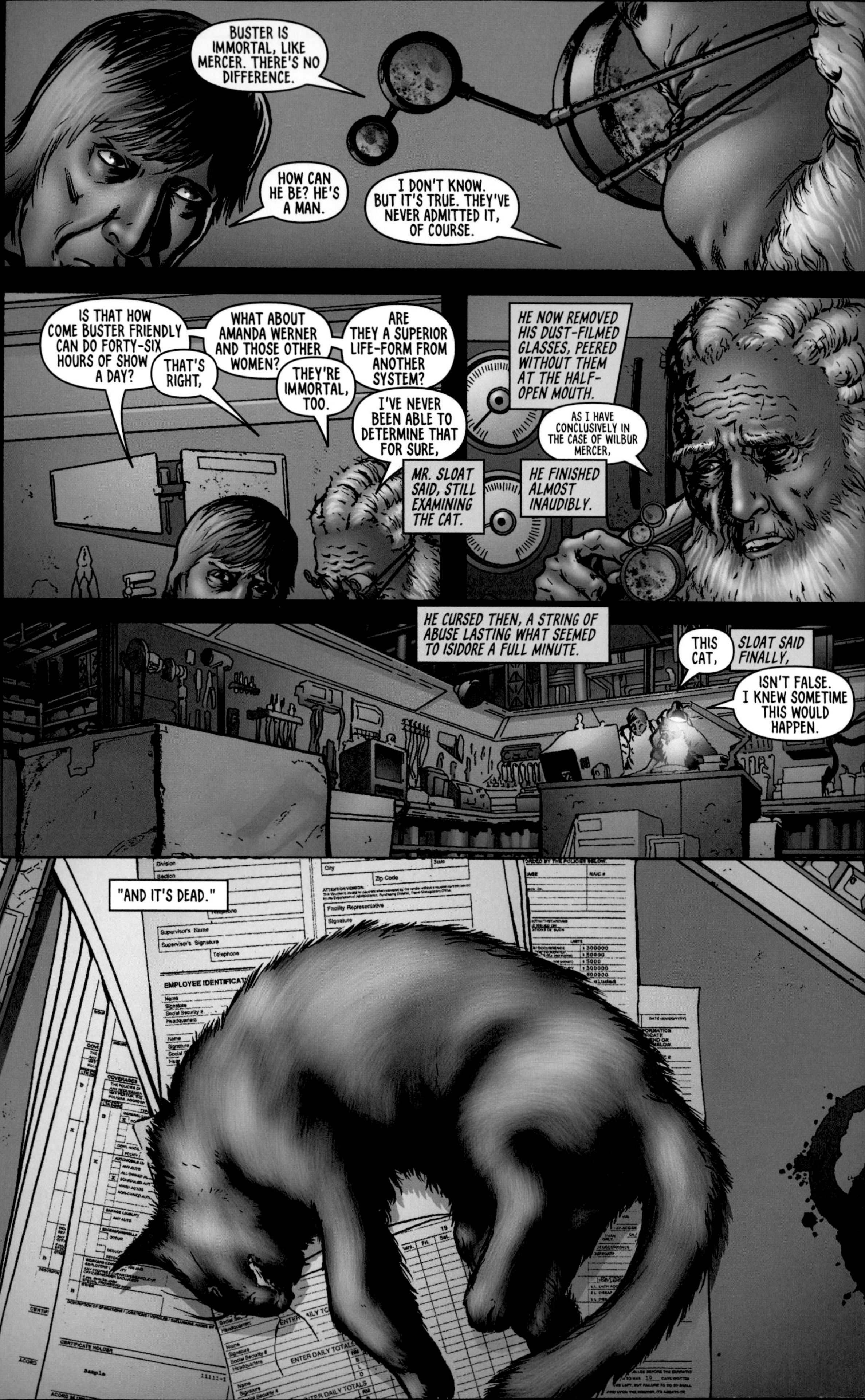

BUSTER IS IMMORTAL, LIKE MERCER. THERE'S NO DIFFERENCE.
HOW CAN HE BE? HE'S A MAN.
I DON'T KNOW. BUT IT'S TRUE. THEY'VE NEVER ADMITTED IT, OF COURSE.
IS THAT HOW COME BUSTER FRIENDLY CAN DO FORTY-SIX HOURS OF SHOW A DAY?
THAT'S RIGHT,
WHAT ABOUT AMANDA WERNER AND THOSE OTHER WOMEN?
THEY'RE IMMORTAL, TOO.
ARE THEY A SUPERIOR LIFE-FORM FROM ANOTHER SYSTEM?
I'VE NEVER BEEN ABLE TO DETERMINE THAT FOR SURE,
MR. SLOAT SAID, STILL EXAMINING THE CAT.
HE NOW REMOVED HIS DUST-FILMED GLASSES, PEERED WITHOUT THEM AT THE HALF-OPEN MOUTH.
AS I HAVE CONCLUSIVELY IN THE CASE OF WILBUR MERCER,
HE FINISHED ALMOST INAUDIBLY.
HE CURSED THEN, A STRING OF ABUSE LASTING WHAT SEEMED TO ISIDORE A FULL MINUTE.
THIS CAT,
SLOAT SAID FINALLY,
ISN'T FALSE. I KNEW SOMETIME THIS WOULD HAPPEN.
"AND IT'S DEAD."

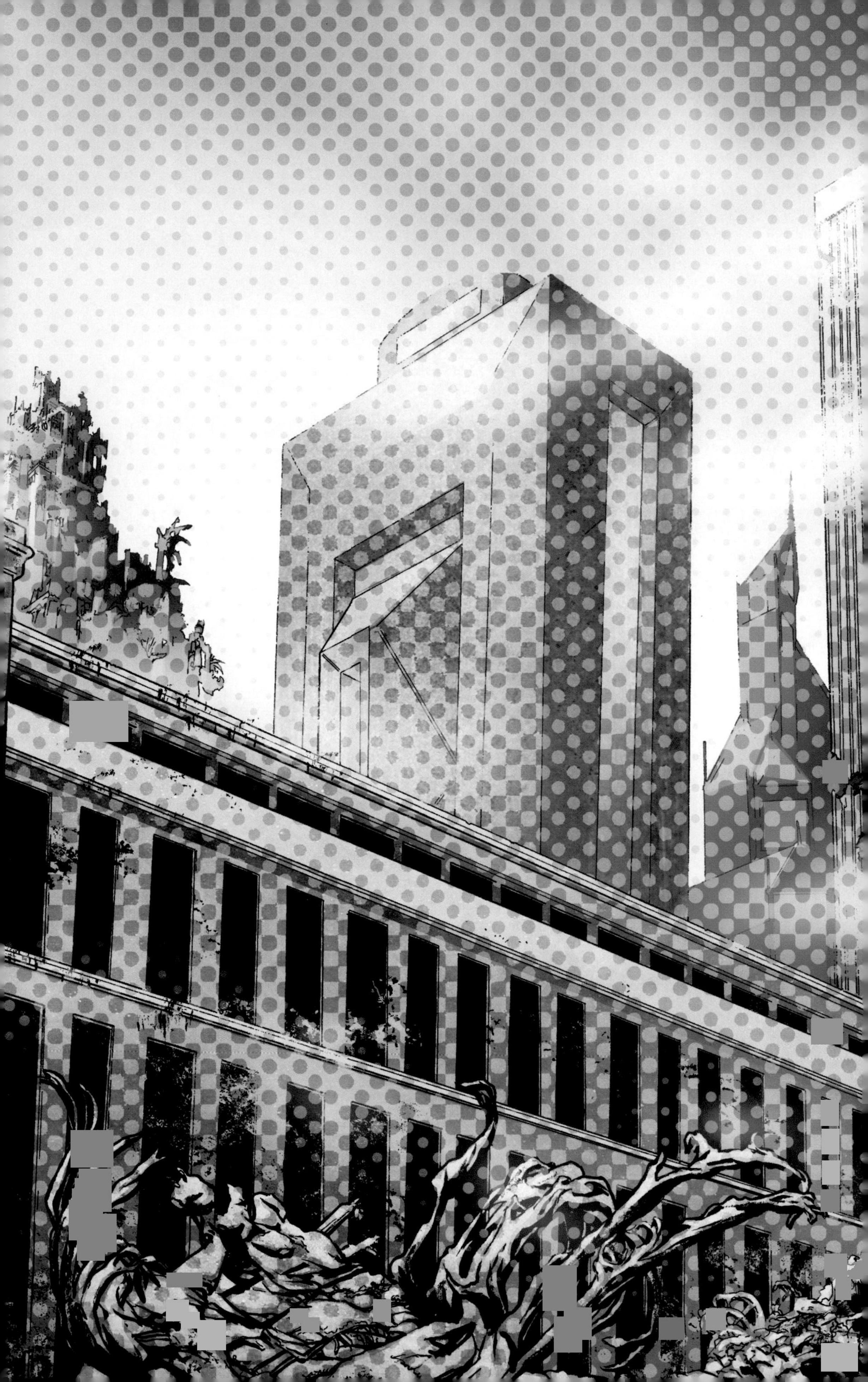

ON PHILIP K. DICK

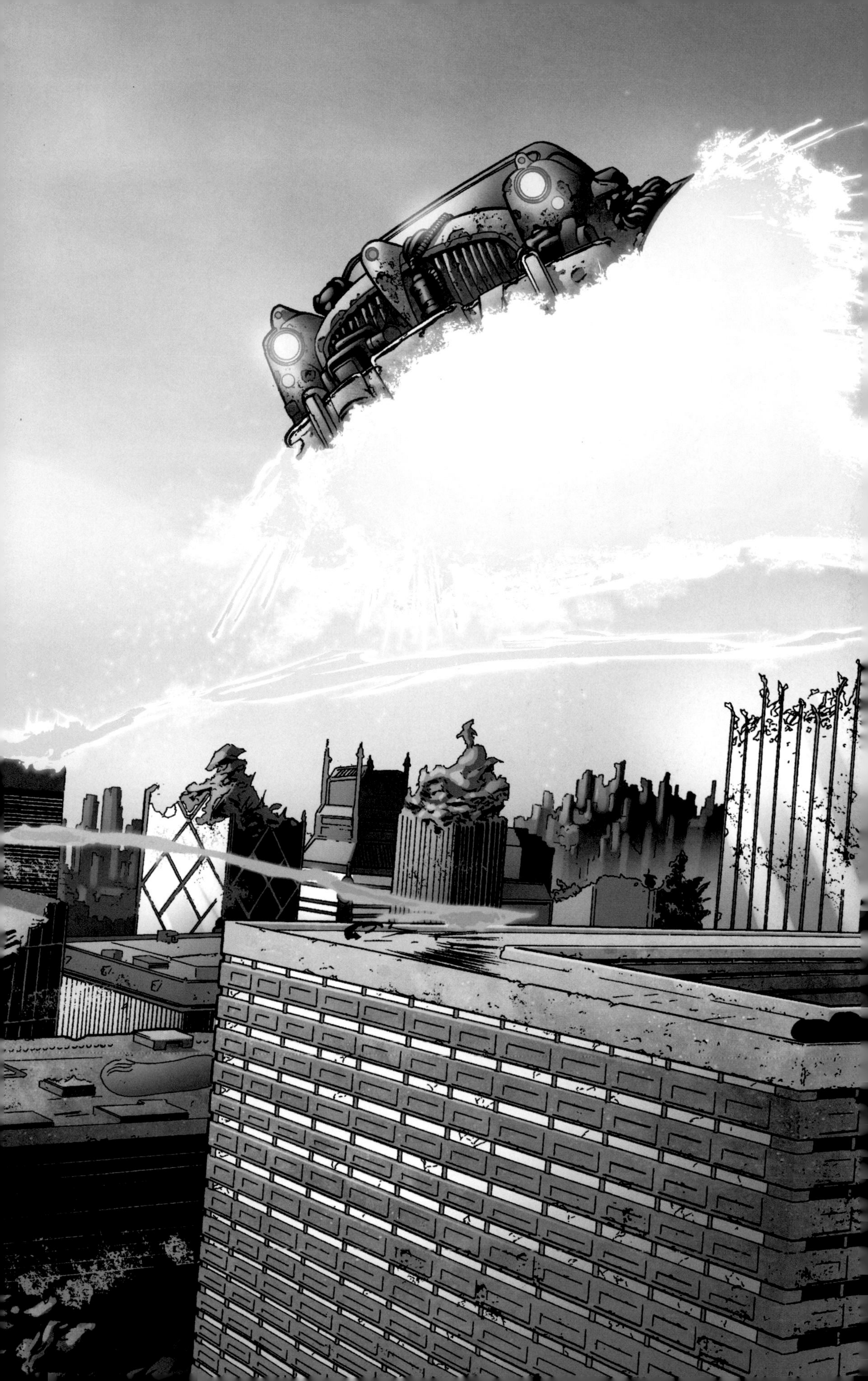

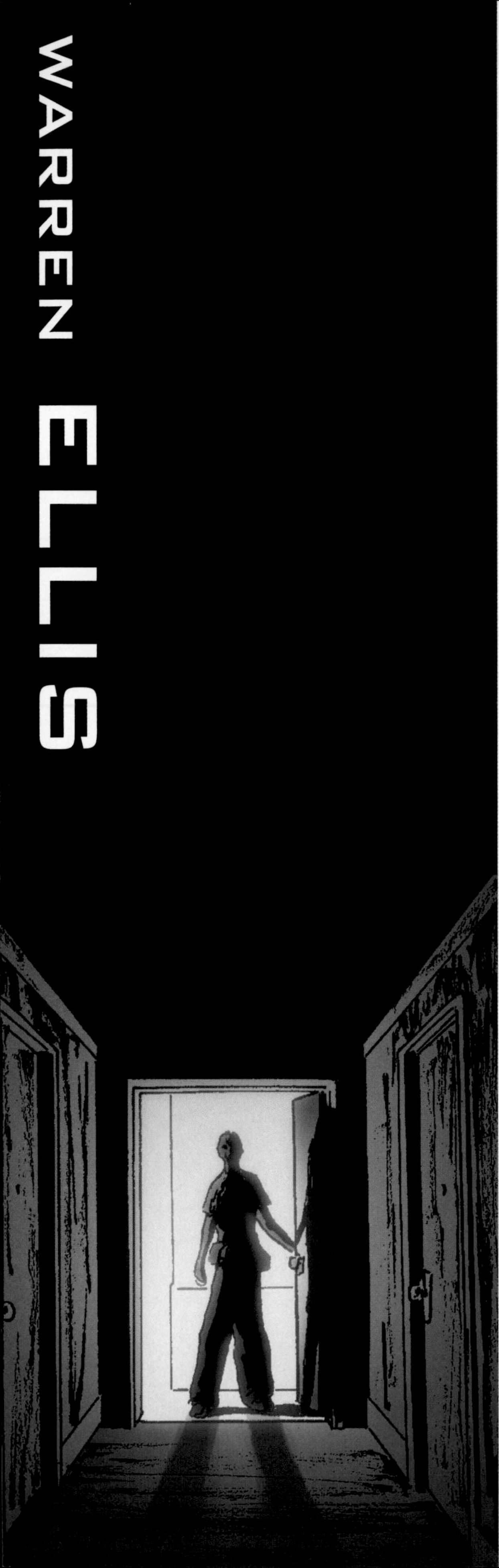
WARREN ELLIS

1929: Joseph Edgar Dick, variously reported as either a fraud investigator or a livestock inspector at the time, has just taken out a large life insurance policy on his family. The insurance company sends a nurse over to the family home to check them out. The twin Dick children, just five weeks old and born six weeks prematurely, are not in a good way. Philip and Jane have malnutrition. In later years, Philip repeatedly claimed that Jane was at that time dying of burns sustained from her mother Dorothy's misuse of an electric blanket. Philip's family members state that the Dicks were aware that the twins were not thriving, and had heard of a program whereby purchase of life insurance led to a visiting doctor being sent to their home to evaluate the babies. The nurse has the babies whisked to hospital, but Jane dies en route.

In a denatured world run on lies and incompetence, where the lucky few are rocketing to colonies in the heavens, Rick Deckard has replaced his dead sheep with an electric one and hoping no-one will notice.

DO ANDROIDS DREAM OF ELECTRIC SHEEP? has long been one of my favourite novels by an author I've been fascinated by for decades. I think Philip K. Dick is the great pulp visionary of the 20th Century. JG Ballard was never a pulp writer, even when he was being published in (the last of the British) pulp magazines, and Lovecraft was too disengaged from society and the 20th Century condition. ANDROIDS is a handbook for the postmodern condition. Forget everything you know about the film -- I've seen it stated that Ridley Scott never finished reading ANDROIDS, and even the title comes from the William Burroughs novella-length treatment of an Alan E. Nourse novel (about smugglers of medical supplies in a future where only sterilised eugenically-clean people get healthcare). If you picked up this comic because you understood BLADE RUNNER to be based upon ANDROIDS and wished to investigate, then, I've got to tell you, you're in for a hell of a ride.

1940: Dorothy is raising Philip alone. Philip is starting to experience episodes of extreme vertigo. He reads his first science fiction magazine, STIRRING SCIENCE STORIES. "I came across the magazine quite by accident; I was actually looking for POPULAR SCIENCE."

Philip K. Dick wrote like a madman. Forty-seven novels and more than a hundred and twenty short stories from a man who died at age fifty-three and also found time to get married five times and by his own admission suffered serious mental problems for much of his life.

When you write at that pace, with no time for editing, just trying to get it all out of your fingers and on to the page, parts of you leak out with it. There's no escaping it. All writers return to themes, but prolific writers recourse to obsessions, attacking them from different angles, letting bits of their own histories and personalities out into the wild as they look for new ways to study the things they can't let go of. ANDROIDS is one of those books. A book where science gets vertigo, and where Philip Dick again studies the two great questions of his life. What is real? What does it mean to be human?

And it goes on, in Dick's novels. The novel, it must be said, is not always the writer. But the parallels and connections in his work are hard to avoid. His women are often forces of nature, bringers of death, figures of fear, and ANDROIDS has many. A woman hurting a small life to see if it can keep moving. A woman killing the thing a man needed the most.

1968: I am born. Philip K. Dick publishes DO ANDROIDS DREAM OF ELECTRIC SHEEP? It is written in the period where he's banging out novels while his system is drenched in amphetamines. He says of this phase of his life that it wasn't unusual for him to type for seventy-two hours straight, stand up from the typewriter and pass clean out. He later claims to have been told by a doctor that his liver is so super-efficient that it actually processed out all the speed before it could light up his central nervous system. But the later period of his life is marked by increasing discomfort at being seen as "a drug writer," and complains when Harlan Ellison prefaces his story in a DANGEROUS VISIONS anthology with the statement that, by Ellison's request, Philip wrote the story while on acid.

Rick Deckard is a bounty hunter, working for the police, specialising in the destruction of rogue androids. The androids are slave machines who escape to Earth looking for a new life. "A new life awaits you in the Off-World Colonies!" Androids can be uncovered via the Voight-Kampff Test, which measures empathy, a quality androids do not possess.

That much, you recall from the film. But what Philip K. Dick is talking about in this book is people. You never get a sense, in the film, of what Rick Deckard really wants, aside maybe from not having to waste skinjobs anymore. That is in part why the alternate reading of the film as all-androids-together enriches it. In the book, Rick Deckard's wants are small and cheap and perhaps unworthy of him. But they make he and his world -- his denuded world, scattered with radioactive dust and sprinkled with people too tainted or lumpen to qualify for a place on the Martian colony -- much more real. More human. I can remember a time when people judged their self-worth on the quality of their goods in comparison to their neighbours'. God knows 50s America would still have been very present in Dick's mind. In the context of ANDROIDS, it makes perfect sense that Deckard's selfhood pivots on the possession of an animal.

1972: Philip K. Dick is informing on fellow sf writers to the FBI. There's a copy of one of the letters at website The Smoking Gun, wherein Philip tries to connect Thomas Disch to neo-Nazis.

He had a strange relationship with authority. He spoke of feeling the sudden urge to give himself up to parked police cars. Any encounter with anything he perceived as Authority, as when called out by a pet shop clerk for buying horsemeat petfood to eat himself -- tended to seize him up. When he writes authority figures, they tend to be twisted up: as brutal and impervious to reason as Dick feared they were, as human and broken as he dared to wish them be. The apotheosis of that might be Felix

Buckman in the magisterial concluding parts of FLOW MY TEARS, THE POLICEMAN SAID. Rick Deckard is more blue-collar, ameliorated as a bounty hunter, something Dick could conceive of as a drudge gig. The fear of authority comes later in the book, and it comes with mirroring, and it comes with a twin of sorts for Deckard.

He wants policemen to be empathetic, I think. He wants Deckard to be empathetic. Deckard cannot do his job if he is empathetic. Does that make him not human? Are the andys (androids) real? They look real, as real as he does.

1974: Philip K. Dick is repeatedly struck by something he first perceives as an information-rich pink laser from space, triggering a series of visions culminating in extended reveries involving his living a timeshifted second life as a Christian in 1st Century Rome. He spends the rest of his life trying to understand these and related experiences, writing an 8000-page document termed the Exegesis where he repeatedly generates and tests new explanations and hypotheses for the information-rich pink laser and subsequent visions and wonders. Slivers of it are on the web today, and more significant excerpts are contained in a book called IN PURSUIT OF VALIS.

Possibly the most stunning part of DO ANDROIDS DREAM, for me, was the creation of the religion of Mercerism. Take the handles of the "empathy box" -- industrialised caring, sudden connection with those Oprah scare-stories of kids raised by the Box being placed into special therapeutic sessions to teach them social cues and human empathy -- and you are transported into the awful Sisyphean experience of Wilbur Mercer, walking up a hill forever while people throw rocks at you. Of all the fake religions spawned in and by science fiction, Mercerism remains the most affecting for me. It speaks of television, the yearning for immersion in other's emotions or sensoria, of the way all world pain is eventually condensed into phospordots for our remote consideration, of religion as consumer product.

Philip Dick once commented, "if God manifested Himself to us here He would do so in the form of a spraycan advertised on TV."

Mercer's "enemy" in the real world is Buster Friendly, a constantly-broadcasting talk show host who spends a great deal of time attacking and attempting to debunk Mercerism.

Joseph Edgar Dick reportedly did a radio show in LA at some point entitled "This Is Your Government."

1975: Philip K. Dick decides that sf novelist Stanislaw Lem is a Communist supervillain and works to have him removed from his honorary membership of the Science Fiction Writers of America. "The honorary voting of Stanislaw Lem to membership is the sheep voting the wolf a place at the communal hearth. They certainly must be licking their chops back in Krakow right now."
Lem, coincidentally, has previously praised Philip as the only great sf writer in America. Philip writes letters to the FBI about Lem. He also, according to many reports, leaves letters to the FBI under a garbage can outside his house, on the understanding that he's under constant surveillance and the letters will therefore be found and forwarded to the appropriate offices.

The monsters in Philip K. Dick novels are almost always the people without feeling. I don't want to give away anything, as this ramble is being implanted in the first issue, but the monstrousness of Roy Baty (note spelling) and his crew is revealed in their inability to empathise. They are the children of the future: they don't understand other people's experience of pain. Like babies.

1977: John Brunner writes an essay on Philip K. Dick that concludes with: "This I tell you straight up: I do not want to live in the sort of world Dick is so good at describing. I wish—I desperately wish—that

I dared believe we don't. Maybe if a lot of people read Dick's work I'll stand a better chance of not living in that world..."

Too late, of course. We are all living in the Philip K. Dick condition. You can write your own list. The only things we're missing are hovercars and offworld colonies. We've had the radioactive dust, we've done the extinct animals, we've got freaks in Japan designing robot "pleasure models"...I know of at least one podcast entitled "The Buster Friendly Show," too.

1982: Philip K. Dick dies following a stroke. Joseph Edgar Dick, still alive, transports Philip's body to Colorado. Fifty-three years ago, he had caused to have hewn a tombstone with the names of both Philip and Jane upon it, leaving a space for Philip's death date. Today, the date is carved into the stone, and Philip K. Dick is laid down next to the other he'd spent his life looking and writing for.

A little under four months later, BLADE RUNNER is released.

2005: A robot simulacrum of Philip K. Dick, running software filled with his writings, is revealed at NextFest. A year later, someone steals the head. It has never been seen again.

I once told a fellow writer the story of Raymond Chandler being interviewed at home by an eager young man who eventually blurted, "and how do you feel about Hollywood destroying your novels?" Chandler pointed to a nearby shelf stacked with hardback copies of his books, and said, "Nope. Still there." But ANDROIDS seemed close to being retired from memory. For years, reissues of the book bore the title BLADE RUNNER. I'm delighted that BOOM! is making this attempt to introduce the original novel to a new audience.

2009: I finish this and go outside to look at what stars I can see.

Warren Ellis
Southend
April 2009

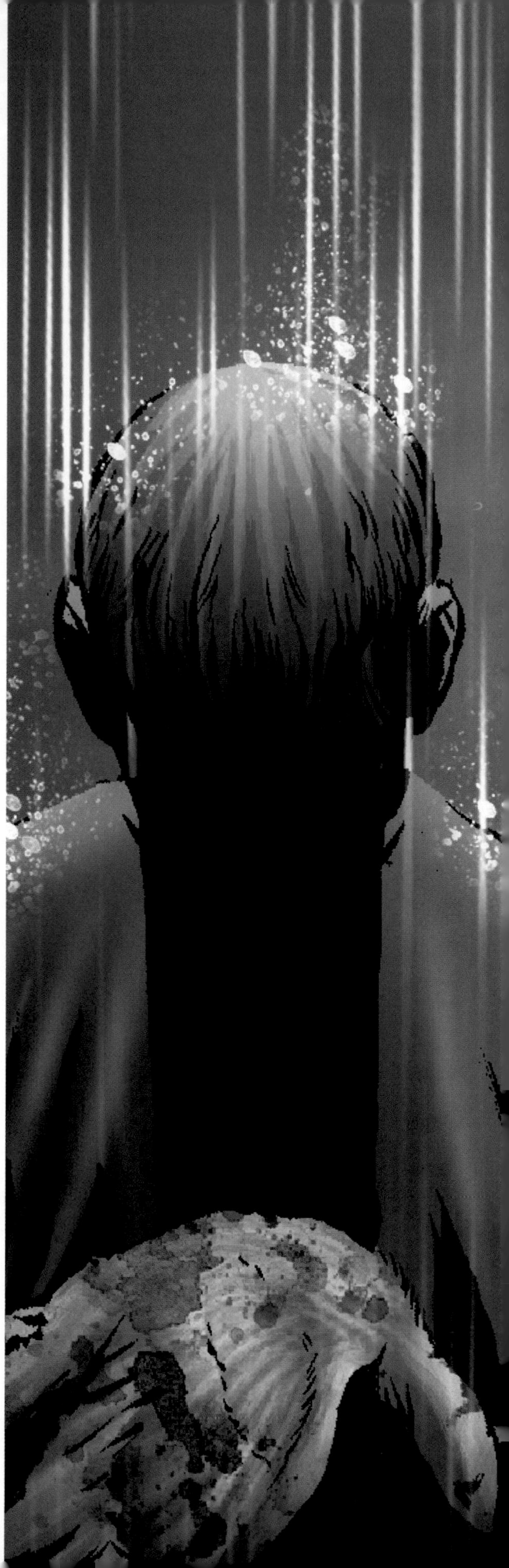

MATT FRACTION

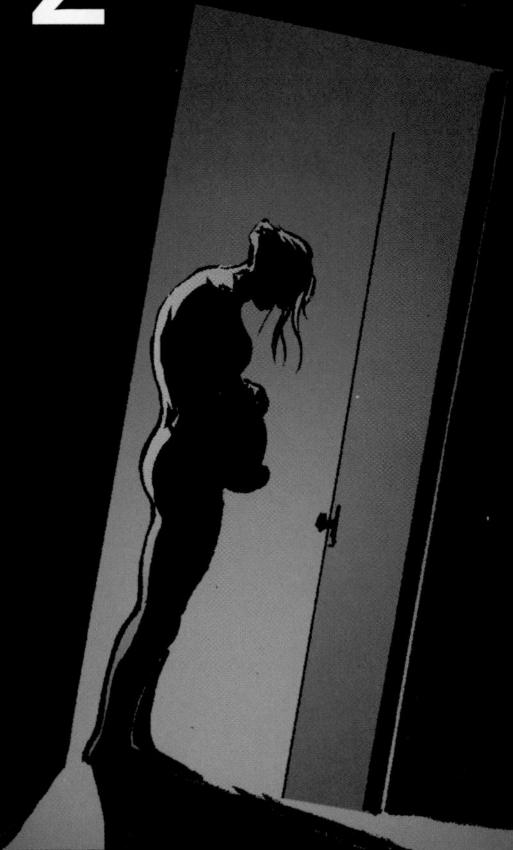

Dear Phil,

I think I've written this before. I had things to say; some things would've been about you, but honestly, I'm not you, and I'm nowhere near a suitable scholar of your work to say intelligent things about your work, to say things that've never been said before or thought of before, and to pretend otherwise would be moronic. *Hey remember when you wrote A SCANNER DARKLY? That book was good.*

Instead I asked if I could write about BLADE RUNNER. And they said OK and I said OK and then I... then I became convinced somehow I'd already written it. I have searched every conceivable phrase and keyword to no avail. I can remember it, though. All I have to do is close my eyes.

Here: the meridian, drawn in the minds of everyone of my generation, divides science fiction films between those that came before STAR WARS and those that were never quite as good as STAR WARS. Because you're, what, three, two, five, whatever, and it's the greatest thing ever. Seeing it is one of my earliest memories. Holding dad's hand. A room full of people staring at a rectangle of light-- is this church? The sound of the projector motor. Trapezoid of light cutting the darkness overhead. And then the movie. And then a crease permanently made into the brain. Persistence of inner-vision.

Because it works, for what it is, and that's a shamelessly wondrous adventure story, a cliffhanger, all sizzle with just the slightest hint of Campbell-ian underpinning as steak. A mythic stage in a new set dressing. Special effects. Robots. That it happens in space is completely irrelevant, but it made a generation of kids dream of blasters and lightsabers and wheezing, asthmatic evil.

It was my first movie. It was my first-- and give me this, Phil, and let's not argue, but rather for the sake of space and time, give me this semantic win-- my first encounter with science fiction.

You can't be expected to know Orwell, or Lem, or, hell, even Wells when you're three or four. So action figures and bedsheets defined the territories of the genre then. For some people, it was the AMAZING STORIES of Aug '28; for others it was the kid from CORVETTE SUMMER.

Time is getting out of order in my head.

I'm in California right now, Phil. The northern part. My first time in the southern part, as an adult, I stayed in an amazing hotel right there on the edge of the water. Los Angeles, Santa Monica, I don't know the difference. It's a town made for you these days, you and Ballard maybe. Digging around before the trip, I discovered the hotel I was to be interred in was somewhere you'd stayed, wracked with your demons and searching for a way out. Or a way down in, I don't know. A big old building haunted by the long road back to sane; my whole time I was haunted by thoughts of you, haunted by your work as I understood it. Hotels are ghost generators and I felt lucky to have yours there-- protect me from all this madness. My spirit guide. If you survived it I surely could. Out of my element, out of my league. I wanted to tear out my hair and walk into the ocean. The Long Goodbye.

Ballard died, Phil.

I am wearing a ROZZ TOX t-shirt Gary Panter's daughter sold me. I have a picture of you wearing another one, a different one. Space Grandpa. Uncle Weirdo. Nodal points colliding. I'm not the only one, too, who freaked out when you, your generation, and Panter's, collided. It made sense. Makes sense. Where was I? When was I? Right: Blade Runner. Err-- BLADE RUNNER. Do Androids Dream of Infinite Director's Cuts?

I saw it because the guy from STAR WARS was in it. All I knew was it was another sci-fi movie and back then I was obsessed. They're spelling it SYFY now which kind of sounds like the kind of things people in your book would take to get high on, like, linguistics and agoraphobia.

Back then, with me and movies, if there were stars in it, and robots, and lasers, I was there. BATTLE BEYOND THE STARS? Sure. THE BLACK HOLE? Okay. ICE PIRATES? You got it. The guy from STAR WARS and RAIDERS was in BLADE RUNNER but it was rated R. But I'd already read and read and reread the Marvel Comics adaptation-- a comic, based on a movie, based on a book you wrote-- and was able to make the case to my mother that it was Rated R for violence only and I could handle that-- see mom, look, mom, read the comic, mom, it's okay, and I guess she thought okay because one day she brought it home on VHS from the rental store.

The book was by Archie Goodwin, and the best bits of art were by Al Williamson. Al, who drew like photographs. Was he using photo reference? Lightboxing photos? Or just that good and recreating with his brush what he saw? A drawing of a photograph of a still frame of a film of a script of a book? Where is Al Williamson's artist cut of the BLADE RUNNER graphic novel? Is it true that Noel Sickles adapted William S. Burrough's BLADE RUNNER in a limited edition chapbook for an ultra high-end cabal of fabulist collectors? Because I'm pretty sure I just made it up but it wouldn't surprise me if it was out there somewhere. *Somewhere in space this could all be happening right now...*

So Mom hands me the BLADE RUNNER tape. I shouted out HOLY S---! Got scolded. Didn't care.

The VCR had wood paneling. Or a wood patterned bit of aluminum wrapped around it. Shells and wrappers. So it would look like a piece of furniture instead of technology. A robot made to look like a coffee table. Top loading. A big spring hid inside-- you'd eject the tape and it made a noise like a catapult firing. You could push a magic button and dub in your own audio track. You could rewrite films, in real time, forever! I did. A lot. I reworked movies. I wrote my own scripts, timed to flow out of the mouths of movie stars. Dubbed in music. A guy, playing a guy, playing a copy of a copy, thinking the words of another guy, but saying totally different words with my voice. It's like a machine you'd have invented.

And so anyway kerchunk went the robot furniture and in went the copy of the tape of the film of the script of the book and I watched BLADE RUNNER and another fold was inflicted, another definition given violent, messy birth. I was granted a new sense: I became suspicious.

As much as STAR WARS warped and affected me, so too did BLADE RUNNER.

I read the comics until they fell apart; I bought the paperback reprints and did the same. That one fell apart because I spilled water on it but still-- it fell apart all the same.

Hey, Phil, I think I finally found my point: I'd argue that for a generation of kids like me, it was BLADE RUNNER that first suggested that science fiction wasn't the latest set dressing on that Campbellian myth cycle but rather something so much more, and it was BLADE RUNNER, in spite of its fidelity, or lack of fidelity, to the source material, that taught us how to raise our eyebrows. Maybe it's not all polite robots and gentle old shamen. Maybe it's identity and corrosion and paranoia and worry. If nothing else maybe we should at least ASK why the old man wants to lead us out into the desert...

I had never wondered if I was who I thought I was before BLADE RUNNER. That was that movie, Phil; that was YOU, Phil.

I'm in film school, obsessing over BLADE RUNNER. One of Ridley Scott's many extant cuts had been released in some form or fashion somehwere. Played forever at midnight on Fridays. And Scott said something like: Why isn't there a John Ford of Science Fiction? And that line gave me, however momentarily, the answer to *What do you want to be when you grow up?*

This was, I believe, the first Final Cut of BLADE RUNNER. I now own four. A set came out. The original lesser film-- which, still, come on, is pretty amazing, bad dubbing and screw ups and all; the Director's Cut, with the unicorn, the lack of narration; now there's the Ultimate Final Director's Vision, complete with disingenuous CGI massaging and 20/20 digital hindsight and a weird Rough Cut version that's full of alternate takes and other cinematic aberrations that is truly scraping the edges of the BLADE RUNNER vat. The same film refracted and remixed time and time again. Copies of copies. More filmic than film.

I'm in Chicago and I'm sick. Sick in my head, sick in my heart. I need to go stay in a ghost battery on the California shore and learn how to live a life that's got menus and bills to pay and expectations. I'm clinging to two books. One is a book about a writer who can't write a book and is falling apart; the other was A SCANNER DARKLY. I am sick and I am in agony and I read and reread these two things. Not just because I saw myself inside of them but because I saw what I wanted to DO inside of them. That their topics offered ironic, or at least emblematic, commentary on my particular lowly station at the time was coincidental at best and a hand-of-god bitchslap at best. I could beat the devil. I could get off of this sinking ship of a life and sail up on the California shore, wiggle up on dry land.

November 6th, 1975; you tell ROLLING STONE you wrote A SCANNER DARKLY *sans amphetamines*. You were born fifteen days after that, forty-seven years prior to that. I'm born forty-seven years and twenty-five days later. Twenty-five years later I read that issue of ROLLING STONE. My heart both breaks and melts for you.

Because that was you, Phil. That was me, finding hope and faith in you. In all of your dark corners, in all of the devils we both knew and love. You, who showed me, seven or eight or whatever years old and filled with wookies, that the world is more than puppets and matte paintings. That science fiction wasn't solely defined as greasy kid stuff. That tomorrow wasn't necessarily better just because it wasn't today. That none of us were defined as who we said we were but rather we are forever defined by our actions alone. That addiction is an illness and not a crime. That identity is transitory, that faith is fleeting, authority is anathema. To dream about magic-- to wish for some great and mystical force that surrounds us, penetrates us, and binds the universe together is to wish for a Space Jesus that does not exist to come Save Us because we are chronically incapable of saving ourselves... and that's bulls---. That the surface can never be trusted. That paranoia is a gift. And that all that matters-- be we master, slave, clone or copy-- is how we live and take care of one another no matter how much the ground shudders beneath our feet.

Oh, and Eddie Olmos is up to no good.

Dear Phil, dear dear Phil, I hope you found rest.

Your friend,

Matt

PS: They made an android of you and someone stole its head.

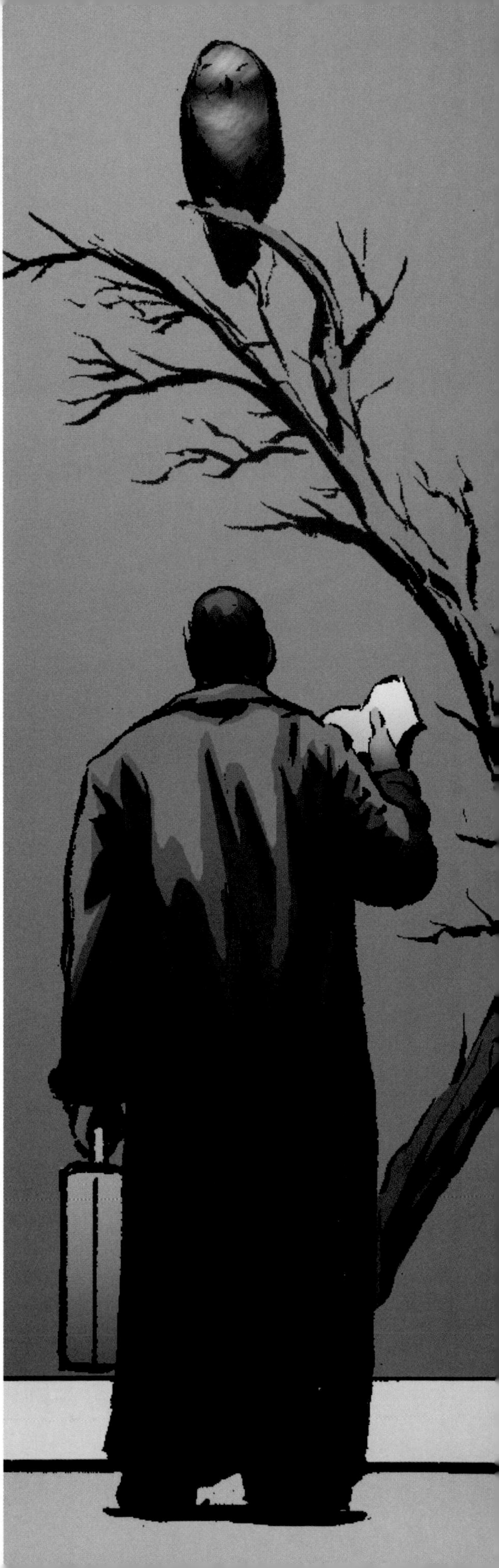

ROCKNE S. O'BANNON

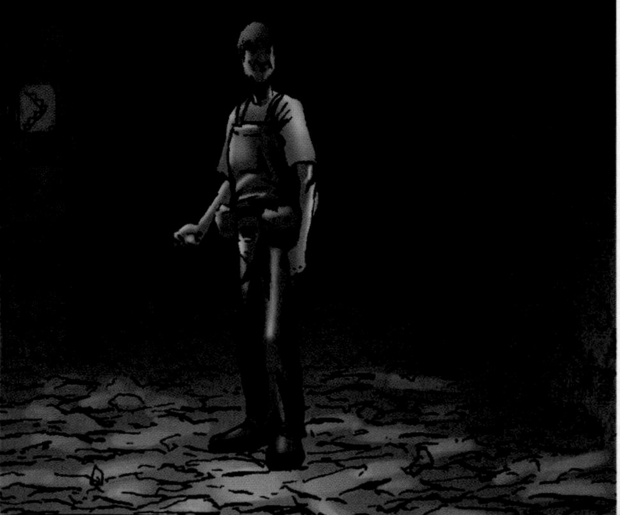

28 May 09

Funny thing.

Just yesterday I was in the offices of a network discussing a new series I'm developing for them (I should probably say **with** them, but c'mon, "with" suggests the other party is actually contributing something). Anyway, I was in there, and this particular series idea has a couple of different science fiction tangents in play, and one of those tangents is the notion that the world that 99.99999% of humanity is currently experiencing simply isn't real. The **real** reality is something else entirely.

And two things struck me in this meeting. One was how everyone in the meeting suddenly perked up and leaned forward when this part of the idea came under discussion (and this meeting had studio execs **and** network execs, so there were a lot of people there). That notion, the untrustworthy perception of what is "real", was just instantly fascinating to everybody in the room. The other thing that struck me was that by exploring this particular science fiction construct, I'd soon be playing in the same sandbox where Philip K. Dick once played, and played so brilliantly. And how very cool, and more than a little humbling, was that going to be?

Turning the prism of our common everyday perceptions and suggesting that suddenly **all you know is wrong** is at the heart of the PKD stories that I relished most. After all, our only window onto reality is through our five senses. But what if the messages those senses are sending us are flat out wrong? How fascinating -- how horrifying -- a revelation is that? And PKD not only explored the uncertainty of external reality, he evened dare stir distrust of our inner reality, as well. What if the essence of my world, my**self**, isn't what I always believed it to be? What then?

I've heard that PKD preferred to refer to himself as a fictionalizing philosopher rather than a novelist. Certainly the singular ideas and unique explorations within his stories support this self-description. But if the foremost mission of a novelist is to evoke an emotional response in a reader, a visceral, very personal reaction, then PKD succeeded magnificently as a novelist, as well. He did so in the way he took his ideas and explorations and personalized them, so that the reader isn't only left thinking about them, but also **experiencing** them through story. PKD not only challenged the reality of the character on the page, but in his talent as a novelist, he succeeded in temporarily challenging the reality of the reader herself.

There's a phrase I keep taped to the top of my computer screen: The Uncommon Idea. I keep that in view when I'm writing as a constant reminder to steer clear of concepts, characters, actions, and reactions that audiences are familiar with, comfortable with. And I realize as I sit here at this same computer right now, it is a phrase that perhaps best describes the essential reason I picked up Philip K. Dick in the earliest days of my sf reading. Because I learned very young that in reading his work, I would be guaranteed to come in contact with The Uncommon Idea. It may be unsettling, certainly provocative, always entertaining -- but most significantly, it was writing that would linger. My thanks always to Philip K. Dick for sharing with the world, with **me**, his oeuvre so uniquely rich with The Uncommon Idea.

ED BRUBAKER

My first exposure to Dick was BLADE RUNNER, although I didn't know what I was being exposed to at the time, being 12 or 13. In the final analysis, of course, I was being exposed to more Ridley Scott than Philip K. Dick there, but the themes of Dick's work are in the movie, just polished up and darkened and lit with neon. I recall wanting to like the movie a lot more than I did... Harrison Ford's listless VO track echoing in my head for days. I'm not sure who was less interested in that voice-over, Ford or the audience.

And while I did buy the Marvel comic tie-in adaptation, I didn't rush out to hunt down any of Dick's novels. I can only imagine what I would have thought of them at that virgin age, wrapped in my tight cocoon of superhero comics and reruns of LEAVE IT TO BEAVER. But luckily, I didn't get seriously into Dick until after I'd discovered drugs. Yeah, I know that Dick hated being thought of as the druggie sci-fi writer, but being as he supposedly wrote some of his books on fourteen day drug binges and being as his novels are among the most mind-expanding substances I've encountered outside of LSD, I'm afraid he's just going to be stuck with that one.

But then again, Dick was well-known for being uncomfortable with the things he was known best for. I've read in interviews with friends of his, and in various biographies, that he wanted to write both mainstream fiction and fantasy, instead of science fiction. Thank god he failed and instead became the most important and influential voice of sci-fi in the 20th Century.

I've read theories by other writers that it was this "failure" to get his mainstream work published that helped push his sci-fi work into what it became – the strange small obsessions of his main characters feels much more modern and real than most sci-fi of his era did. And in the end, of course, Dick won out, because the mainstream came to him, instead. The guy who was at best a hard-working cult figure in his lifetime is now a high dollar Intellectual

Property factory that Hollywood still can't figure out how to get right.

And I know why -- and as much as I love Ridley Scott's Final Cut of BLADE RUNNER, it fails at this, too -- because Hollywood can't make movies where the stars are flawed and strange and well... losers. Because Dick is the king of the losers. Much as I love the feel and look and beauty of BLADE RUNNER, the heart of the story circles around a very simple and mean humanity... pettiness, jealousy and bitterness. His stars are almost always the little guy. They aren't the handsome Tom Cruises who know everything, or the Ben Afflecks who are really the good guys after all. They're not trying to save the world. They're often just pissed at their neighbor for some tiny wound unintentionally inflicted. At their most heroic, they're trying against all good advice to prove that something big is a lie, because they can't help themselves. But it always starts out small and petty and human and real.

But the ones I love the most aren't trying to do anything more heroic than to survive and figure out what the hell is going on in the world around them. They're Bob Arctor who loses himself in his undercover drug addict role so much that he can't remember who he's spying on, and so spies on himself. And Horselover Fat, a Dick stand-in who is getting signals from the stars, or maybe from god, but he has to find a David Bowie stand-in to find out for sure. Or in his posthumously published mainstream book THE MAN WHOSE TEETH WERE ALL EXACTLY ALIKE they're Leo Runcible, who gets in a feud with his neighbor that unravels their whole Marin County community in the end.

VALIS is actually my favorite Dick novel, probably because it's the first one I read. I was living with a friend who had actually corresponded with Dick when he was 14 or 15. He'd met him thru a fanzine interview, and Dick had been interested because even at that young age, my friend was a Sufi. So Dick would write letters and discuss religion with him in that last year before he died. Around this same time, R. Crumb published THE RELIGIOUS EXPERIENCE OF PHILIP K. DICK in *Weirdo*, and so my roommate said if I found that stuff fascinating, I should check out VALIS, as that's where Dick was processing a lot of the weirdness that happened to him in fiction. Ten pages in, young druggie that I was, I knew I'd found a kindred soul (no pun intended).

A few years later, I was living in Berkeley, CA, and reading DIVINE INVASIONS, Lawrence Sutin's fantastic bio of Dick. I would walk down Telegraph past the location of the store where Dick worked, and where Dr. Bloodmoney's apocalypse is shown from. (Who besides Dick would have a nuclear strike be described from the POV of a TV Shop?) I would walk past his old house on Dwight and wonder if that was the place he claimed the FBI had invaded and blown open his safe one night (it wasn't, that place was on the other side of the Bay) and wonder how much of the inspiration for A SCANNER DARKLY took place there, back in those dark days. And back then, I felt even smaller than I do now, and I couldn't help but see Dick's world all around me, see his future approaching fast.

His writing was a big influence on me, and still is. Even in my superhero writing, my bad guys are often corporations, for the same reason Dick used them... their lack of empathy. It's against their bylaws to care, of course. He saw corporations much the same as he saw robots, except the difference being the people in the corporations had a choice, and the robots did not. That's the main thing that they got right in BLADE RUNNER. But Deckard himself is so much more real in the book. His arguments with his wife, his jealousy of his neighbor for having a real animal. Even in this big story of androids and bounty-hunting and death, it's the small details that make the story mean anything. And Hollywood has long forgotten about small details.

I'm not sure whether to be sad or not that we're so clearly living in Dick's future, but it can't really be argued. Look at this country trying yet again to fix health care, where the corporate-paid puppet politicians are the only gathering of people who seem okay with the current system while the vast majority of the populace wants major change. Look at the no-bid contracts in Iraq to Halliburton. Look at the private army of Blackwater. And the funniest and most fitting example, look at Halliburton bidding on mineral rights on Mars a few years back. How long until they're buying prisoners and exporting them there to build refineries? Probably not soon enough. But just like Philip K. Dick, corporations are immortal so we know it's only a matter of time. And how strange that the guy who wanted to write anything but sci-fi turned out to be the modern Cassandra, writing books that just seem more and more like a reflection of the modern world we live in everyday.

Personally, I was promised spaceship cities and flying cars when I was a kid, and as long as I have to live in Philip K. Dick's world, I would at least like a flying car.

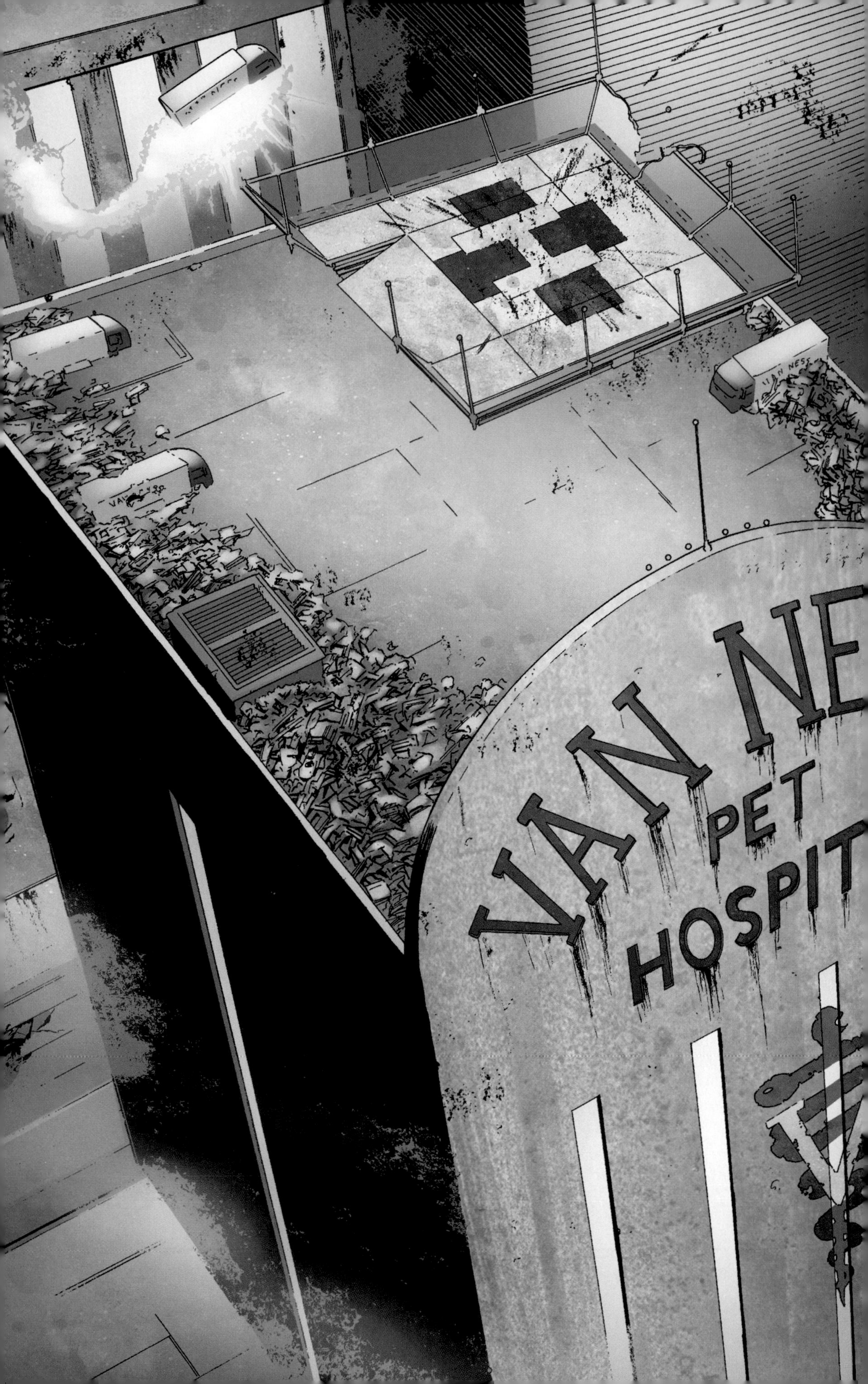

VAN NE
PET
HOSPIT

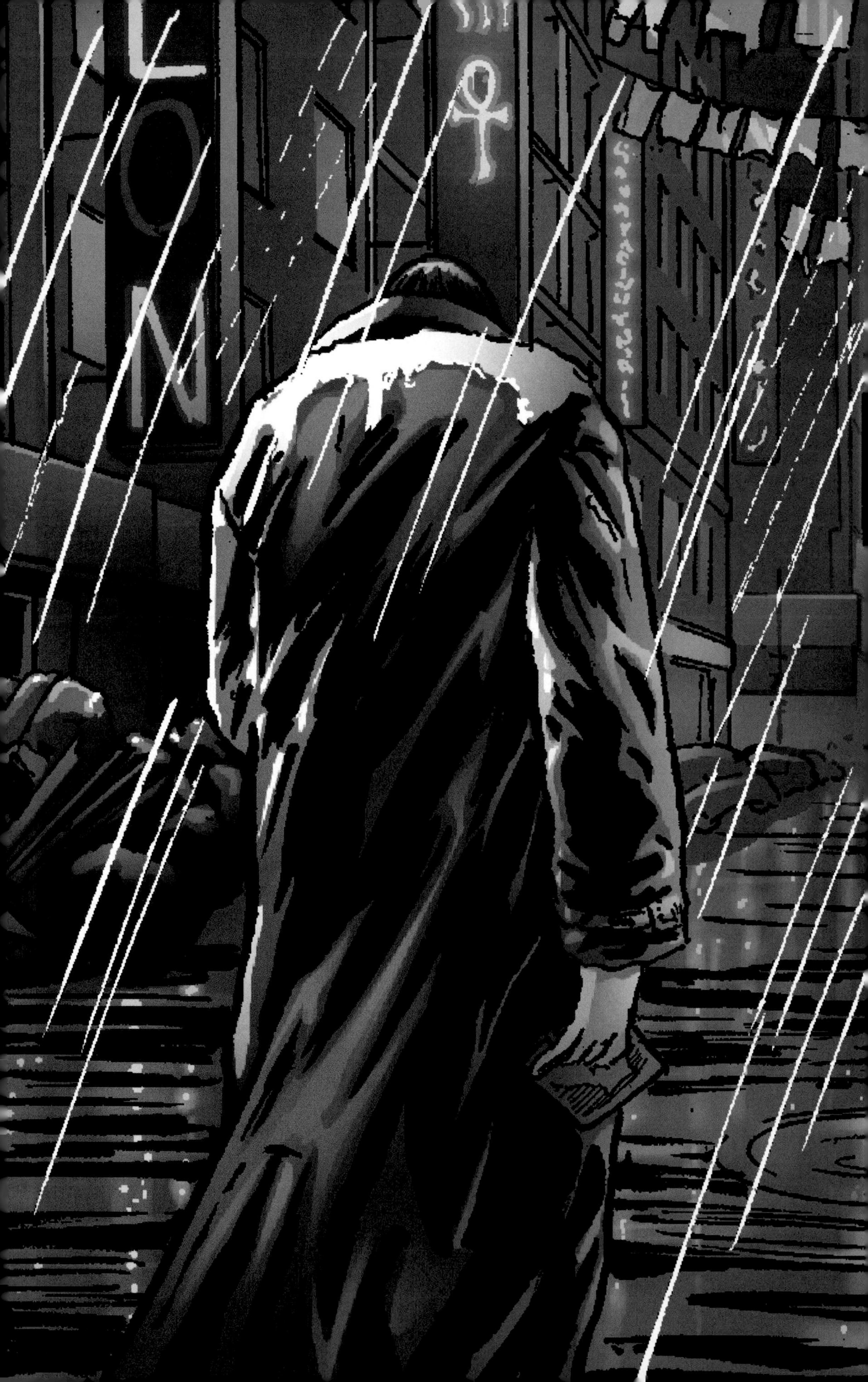

COVER **GALLERY**

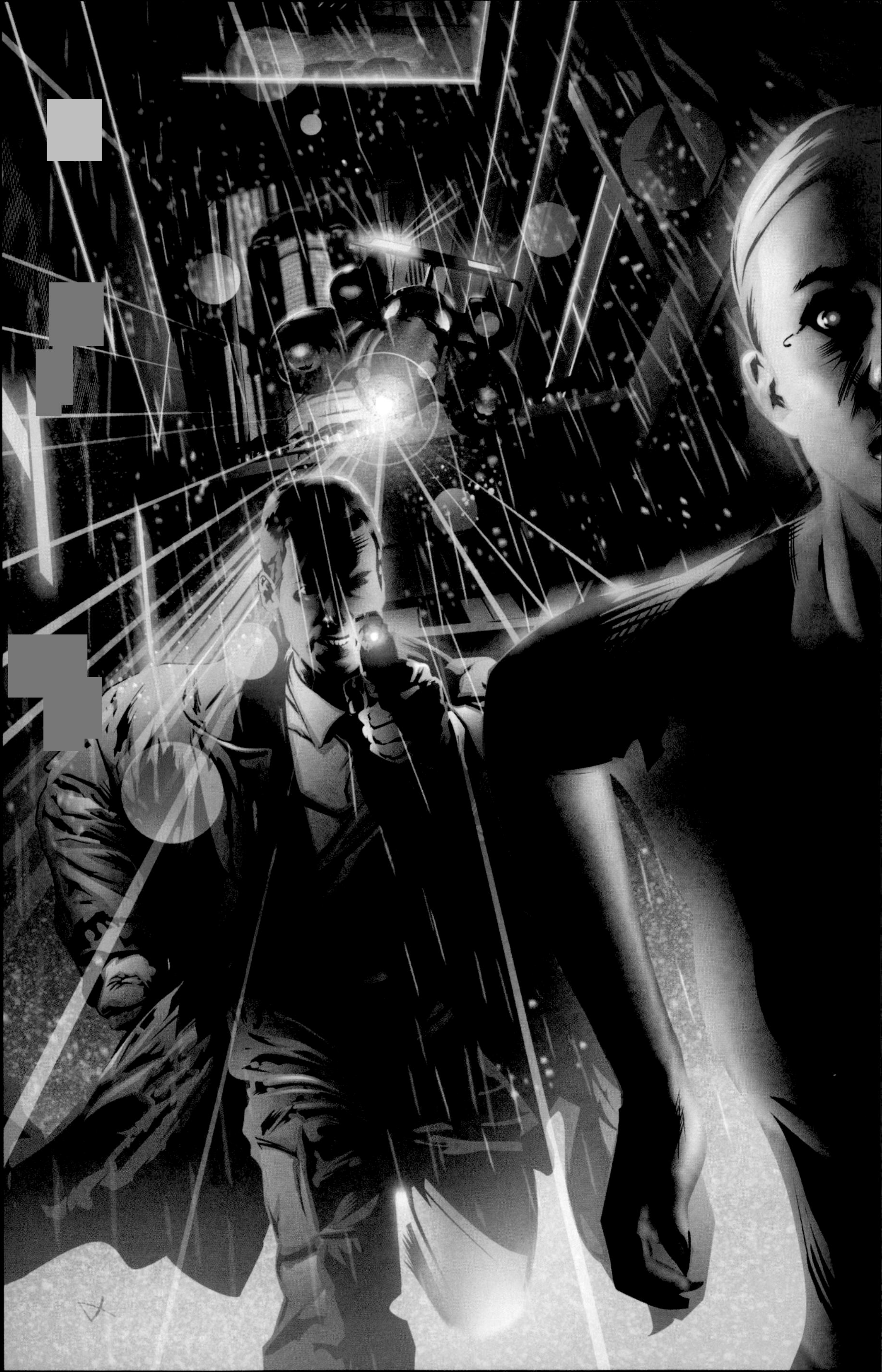

COVER 1A
DENNIS CALERO

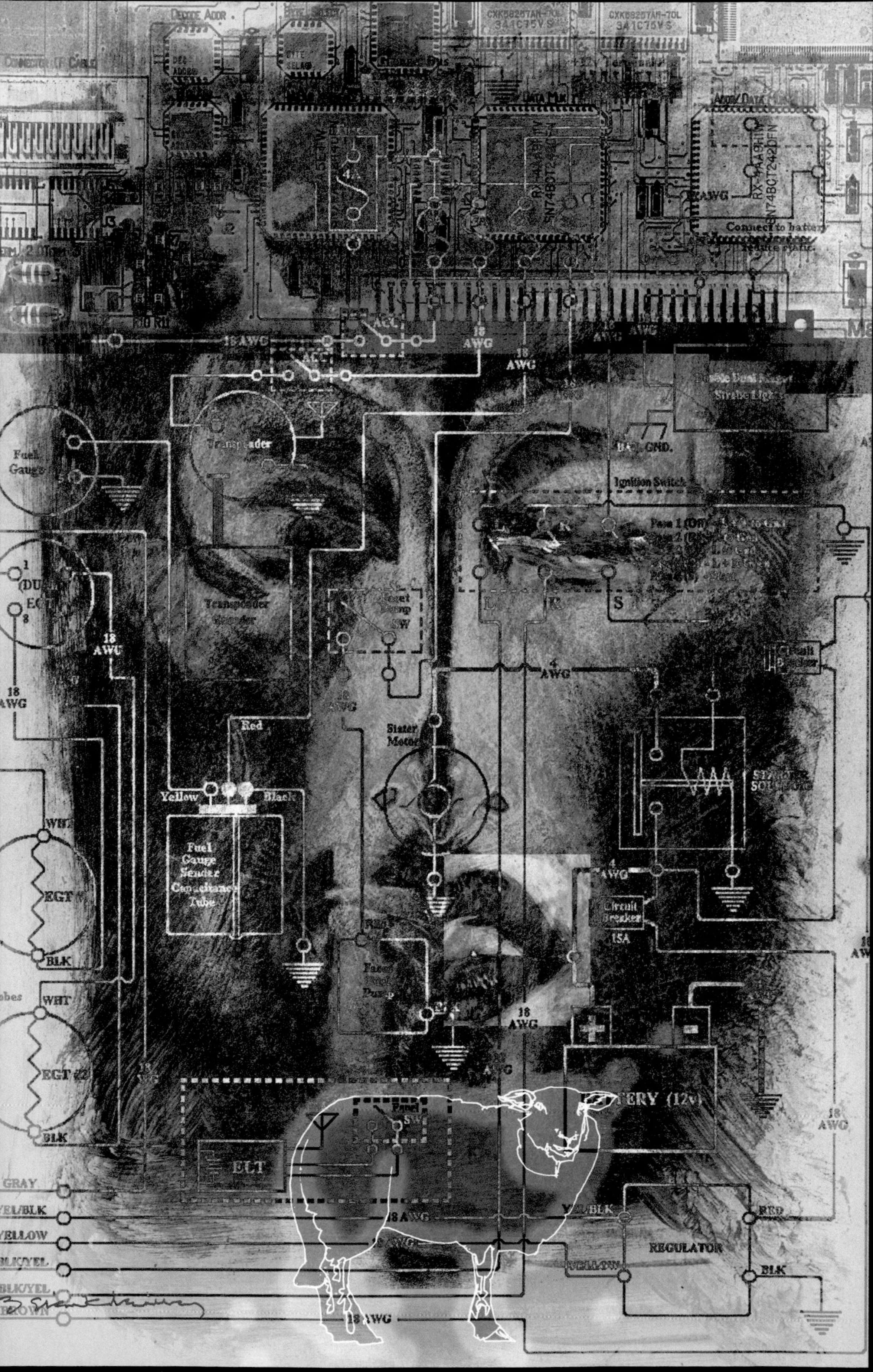
18 AWG
Fuel Gauge
Transponder
Ignition Switch
Starter Motor
Yellow
Red
Black
Fuel Gauge Sender Capacitance Tube
4 AWG
Circuit Breaker
WHT
EGT #2
BLK
ELT
GRAY
YEL/BLK
YELLOW
BLK/YEL
BROWN
REGULATOR
RED
18 AWG

COVER 1B
BILL SIENKIEWICZ

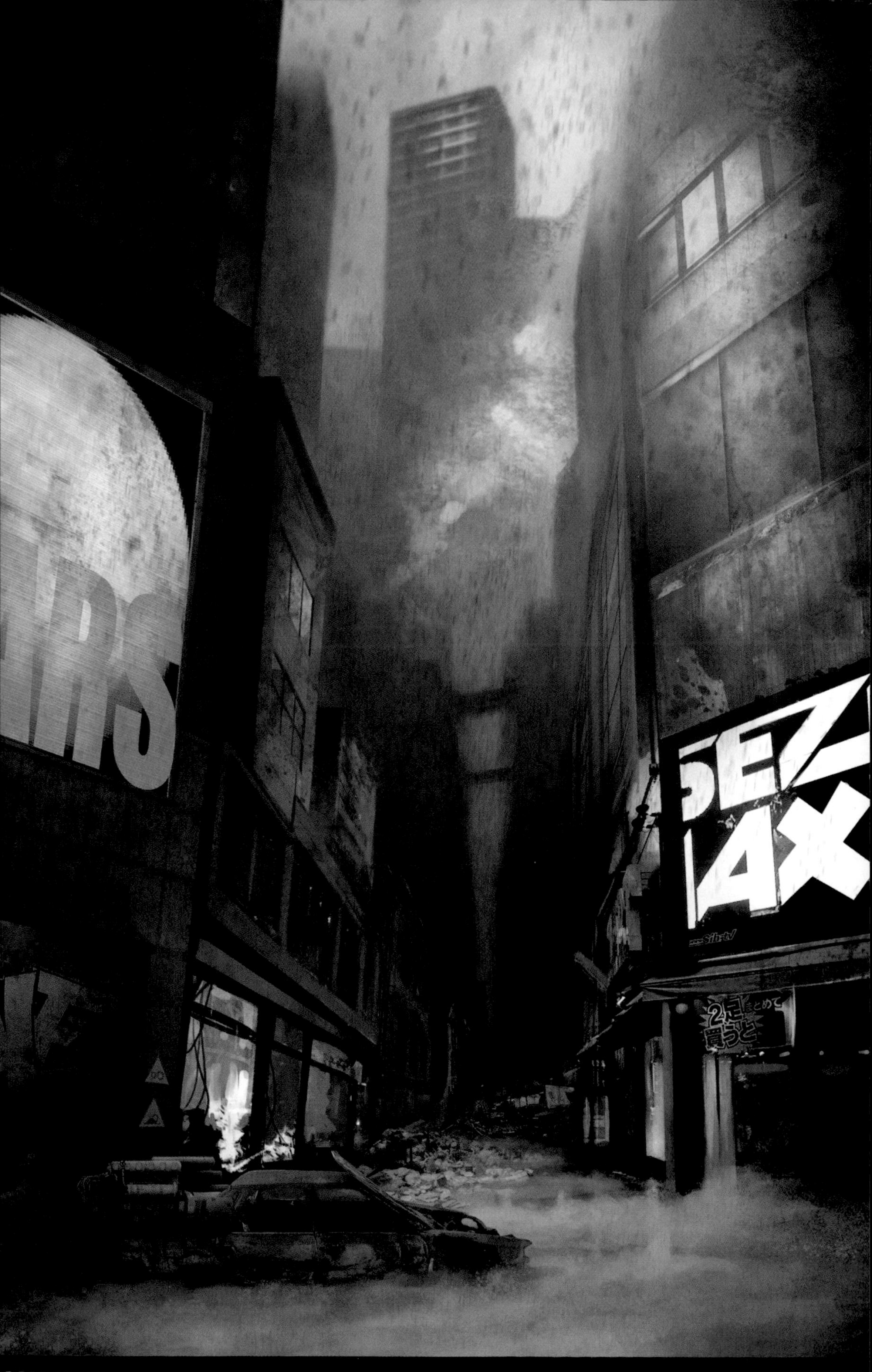
2足まとめて
買うと

COVER 1C
SCOTT KEATING

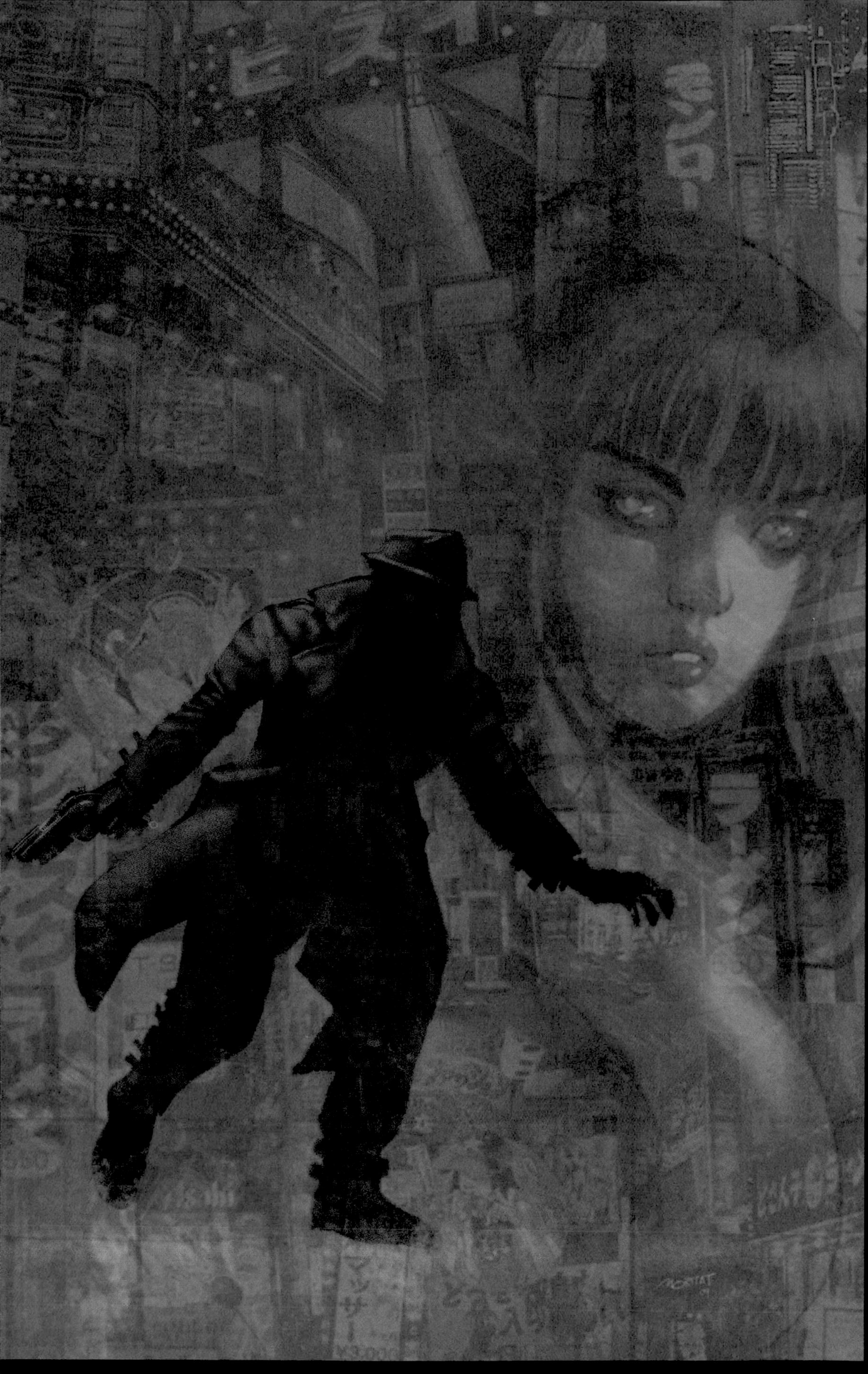

COVER 1D
MORITAT

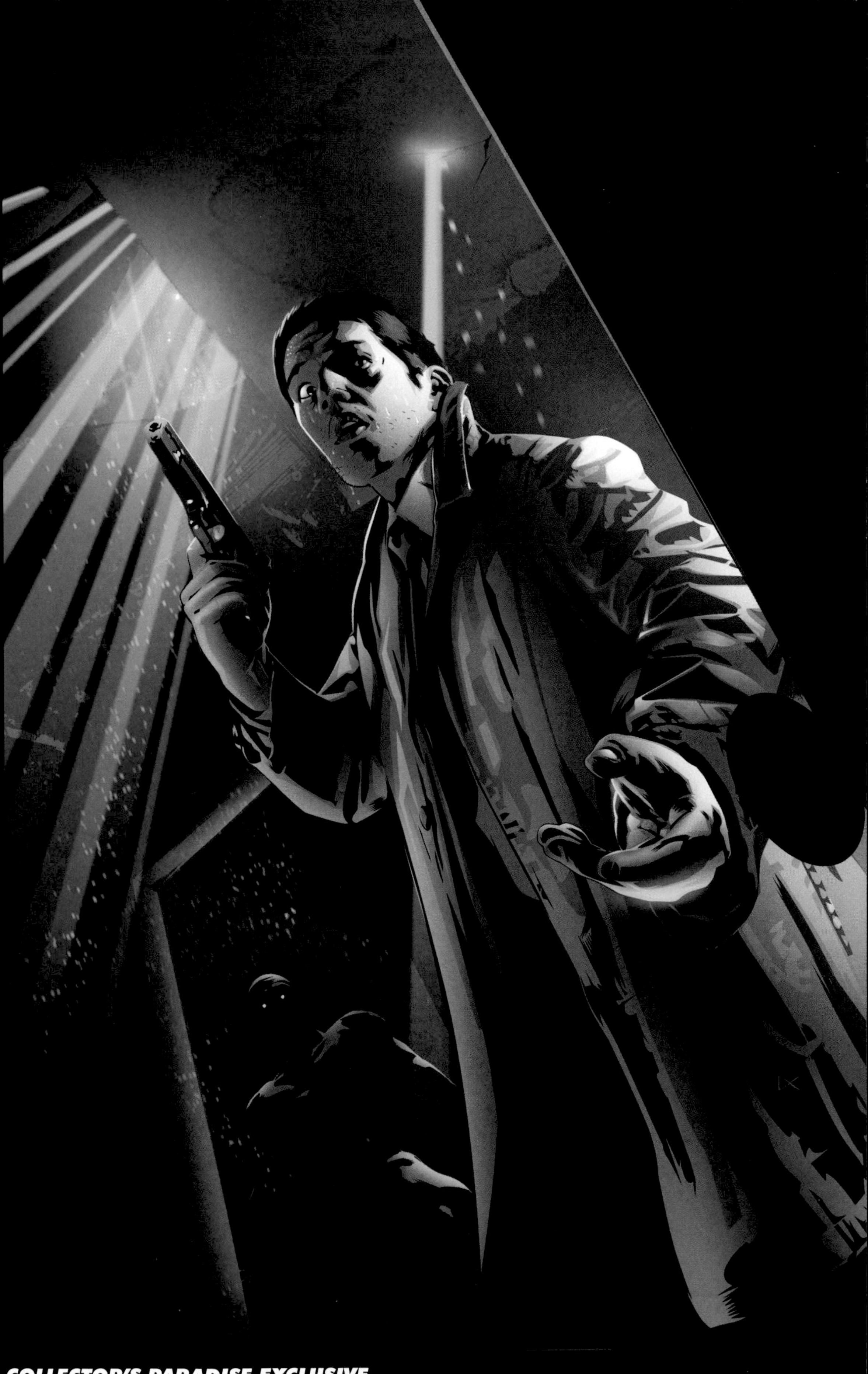

COLLECTOR'S PARADISE EXCLUSIVE
DENNIS CALERO

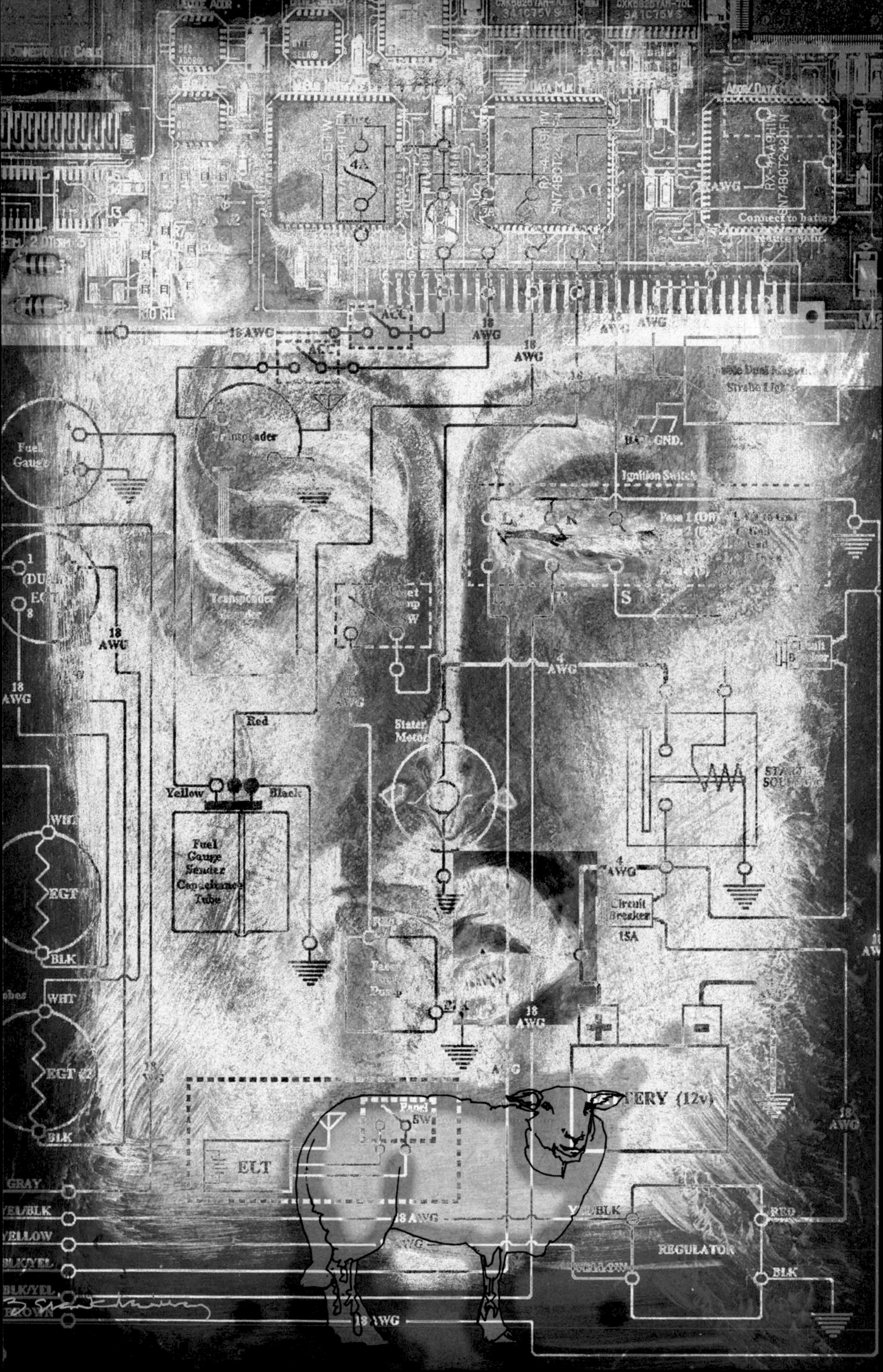
Fuel Gauge
Transponder
Ignition Switch
BAT GND.
18 AWG
4 AWG
Red
Yellow
Black
Fuel Gauge Sender Capacitance Tube
Circuit Breaker
15A
ELT
GRAY
YEL/BLK
YELLOW
BLK/YEL
WHT
BLK
REGULATOR
RED

ISSUE 1 2ND PRINT REVERSE NEGATIVE COVER
BILL SIENKIEWICZ

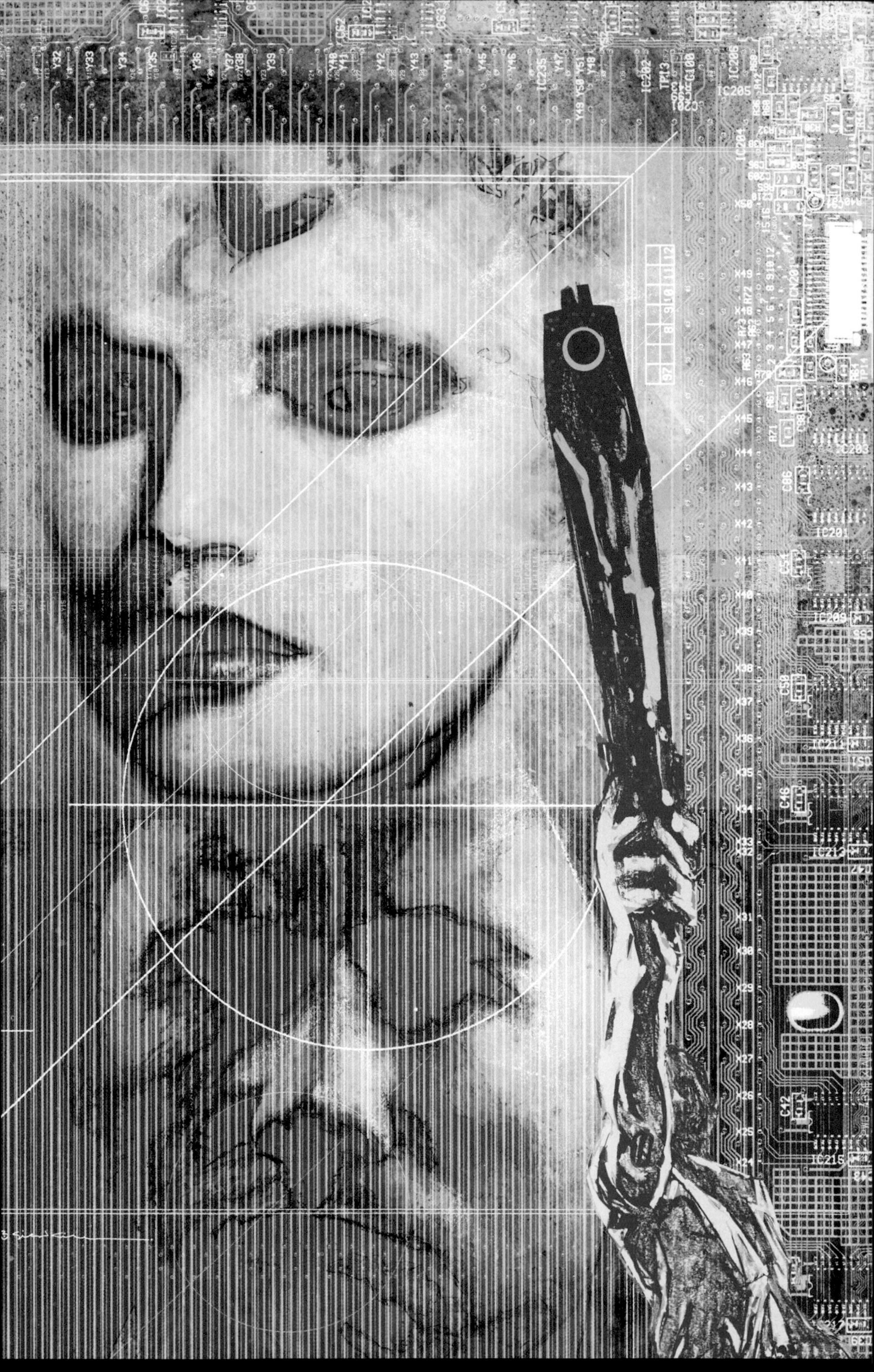

COVER 2A
BILL SIENKIEWICZ

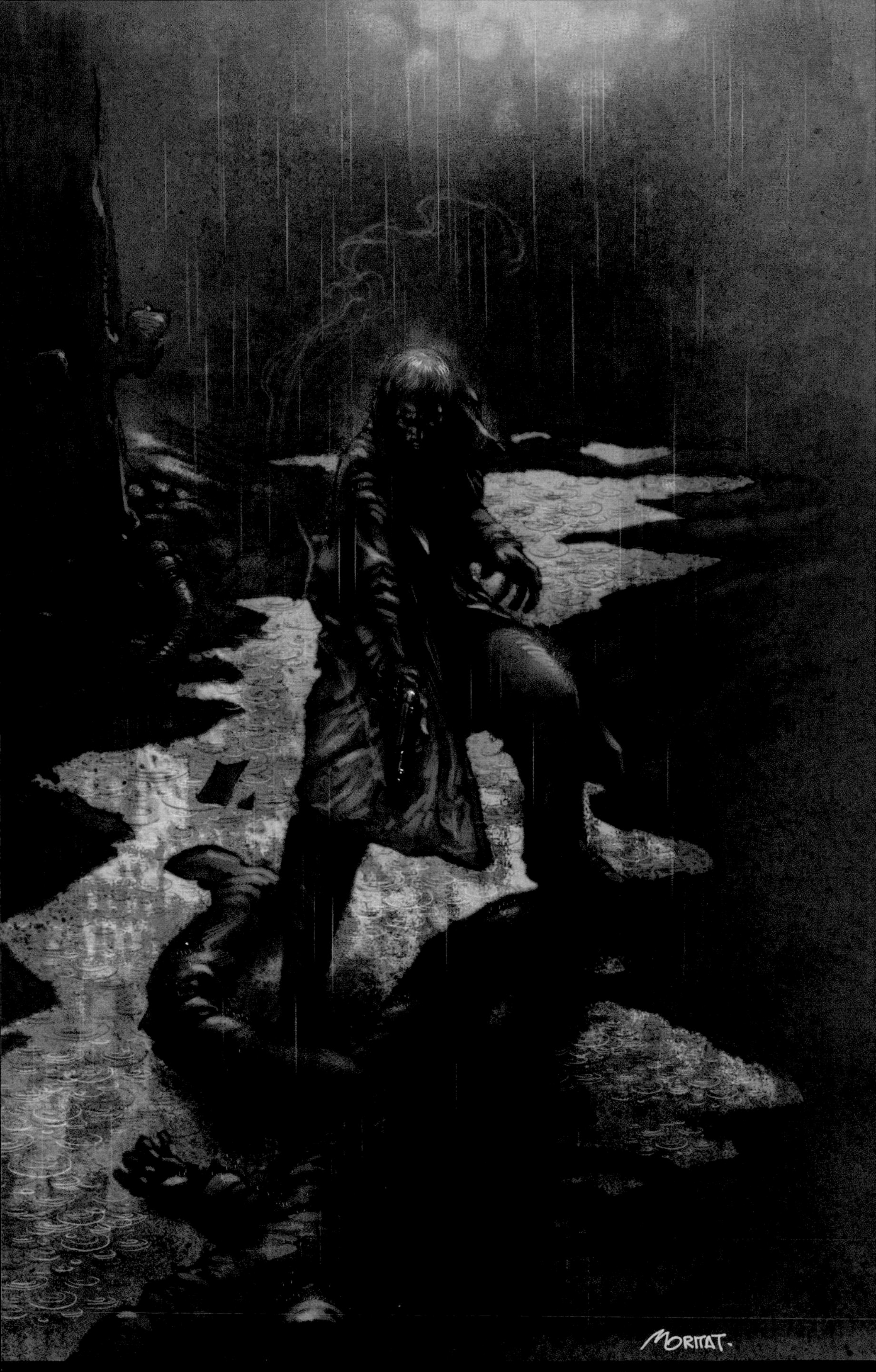
MORITAT.

COVER 2B
MORITAT

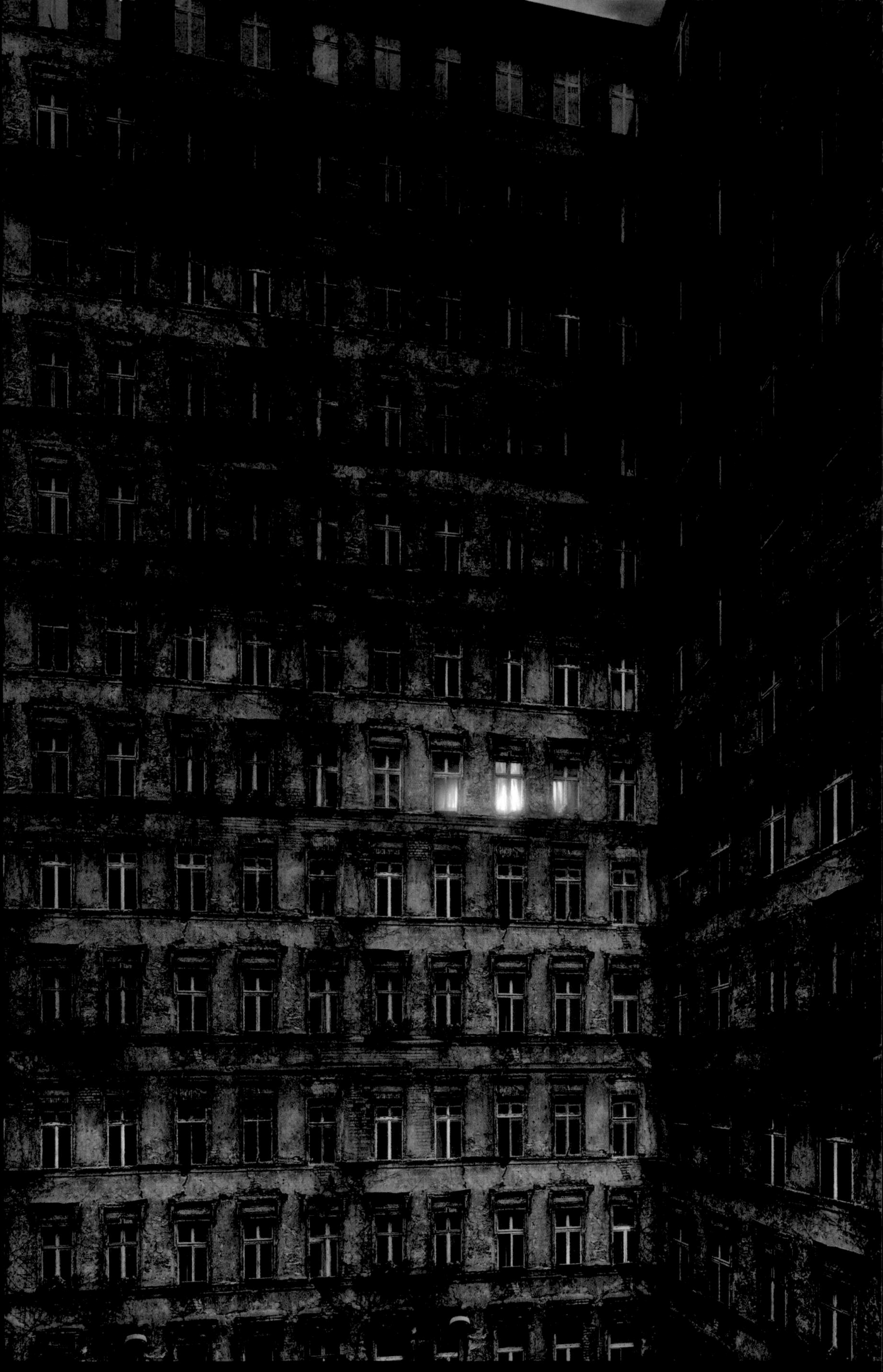

COLLECTOR'S PARADISE EXCLUSIVE
SCOTT KEATING

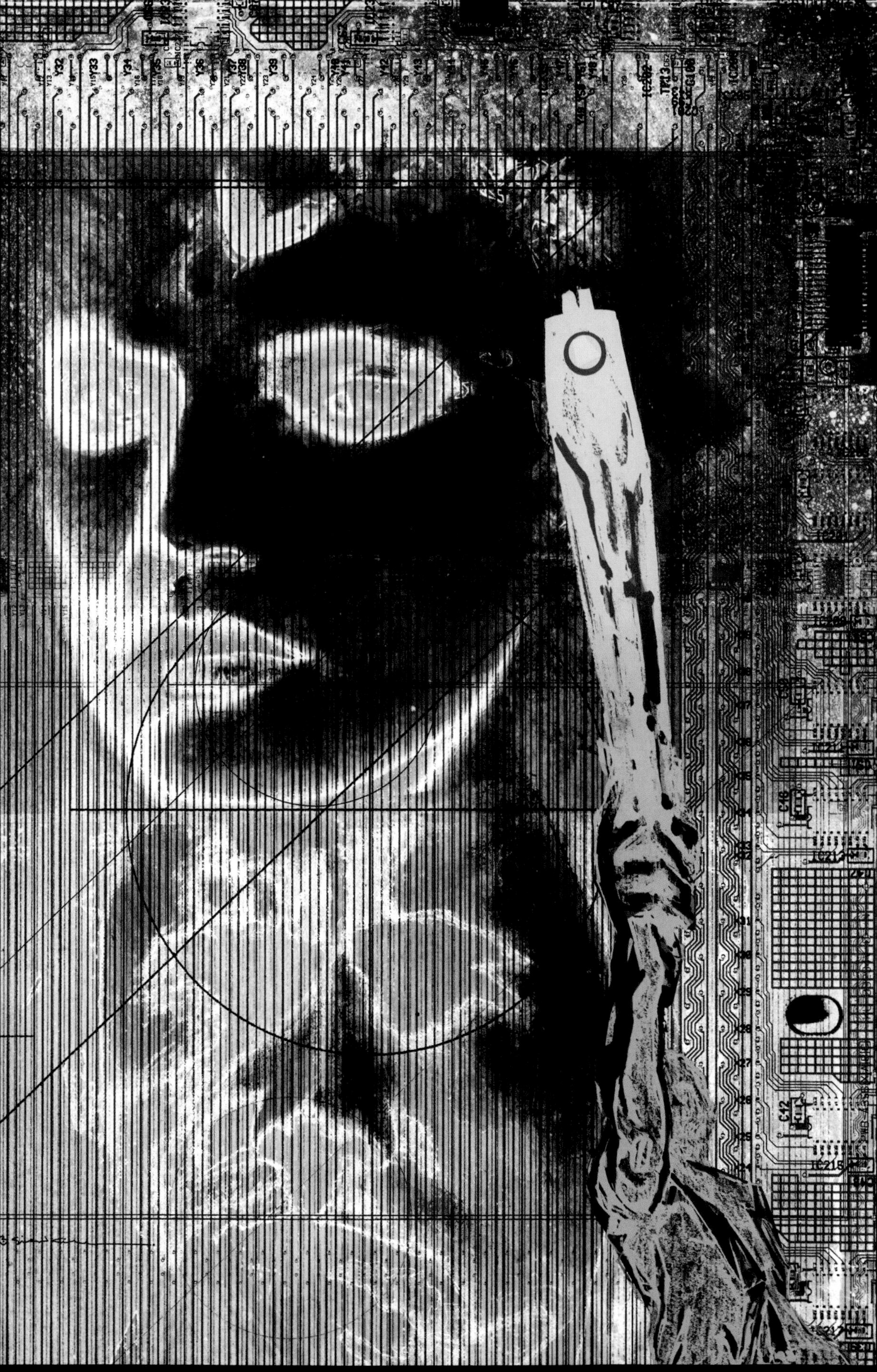

ISSUE 2 2ND PRINT REVERSE NEGATIVE COVER
BILL SIENKIEWICZ

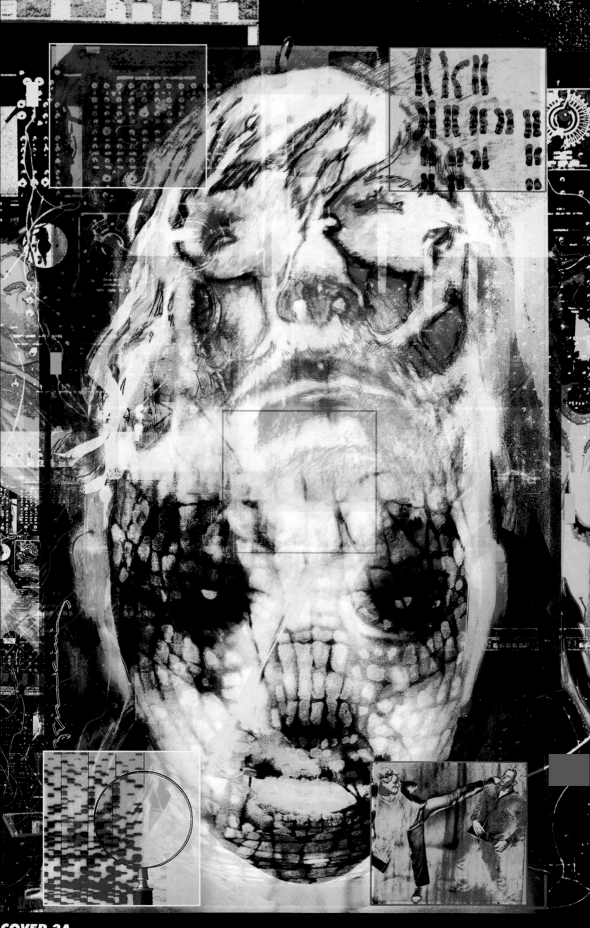

COVER 3A
BILL SIENKIEWICZ

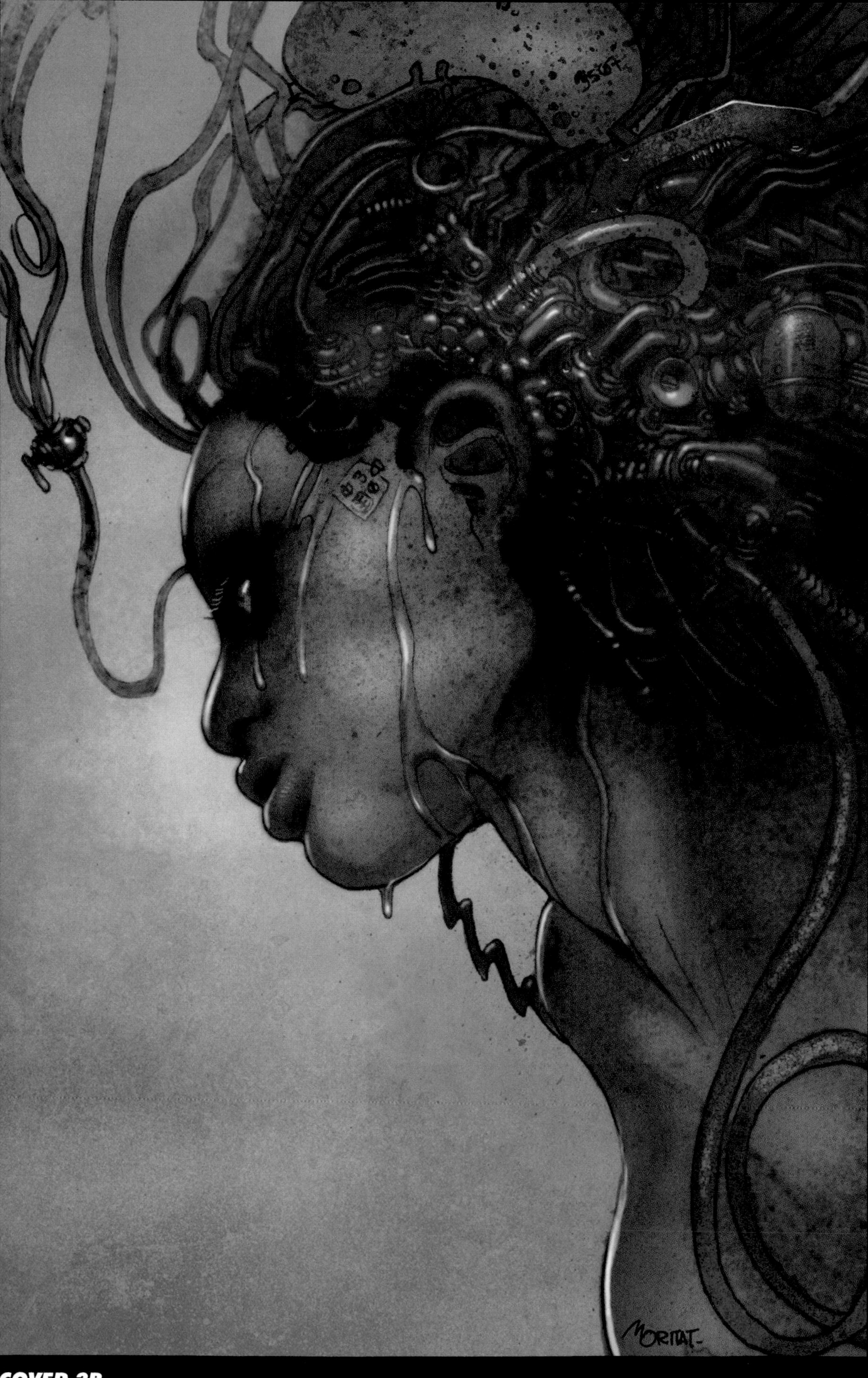
MORITAT

COVER 3B
MORITAT

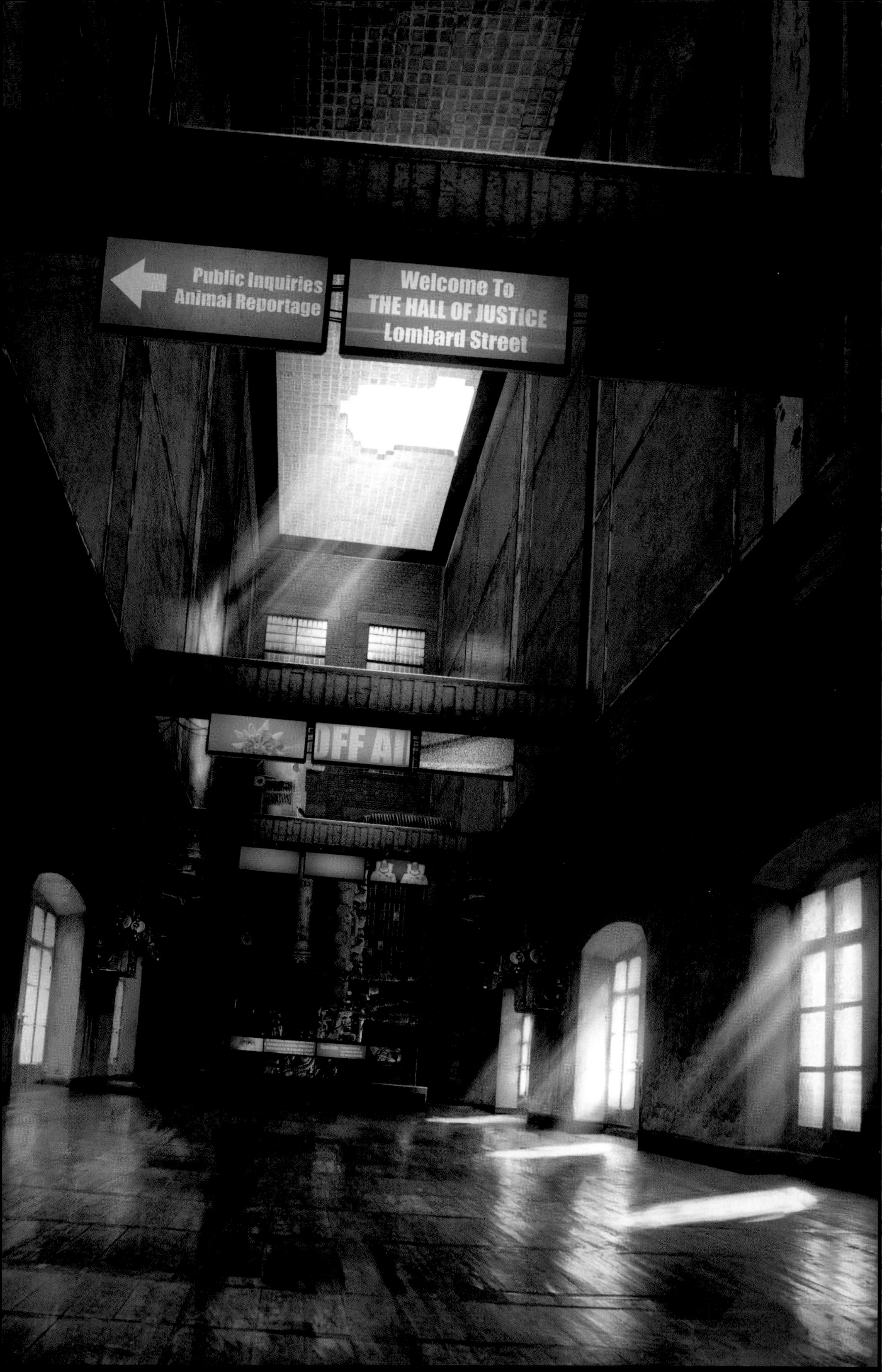
Public Inquiries
Animal Reportage
Welcome To
THE HALL OF JUSTICE
Lombard Street

COLLECTOR'S PARADISE EXCLUSIVE
SCOTT KEATING

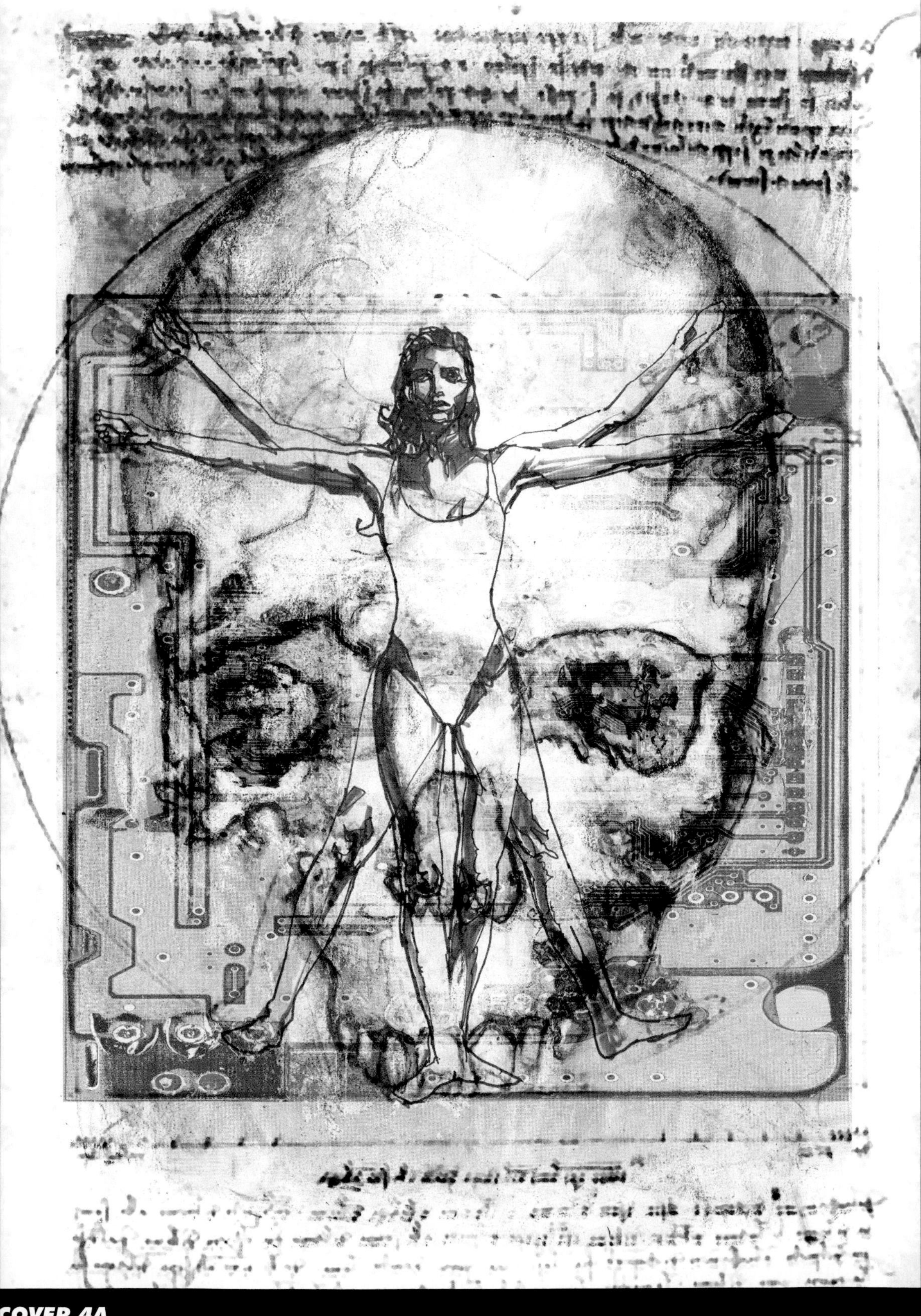

COVER 4A
BILL SIENKIEWICZ

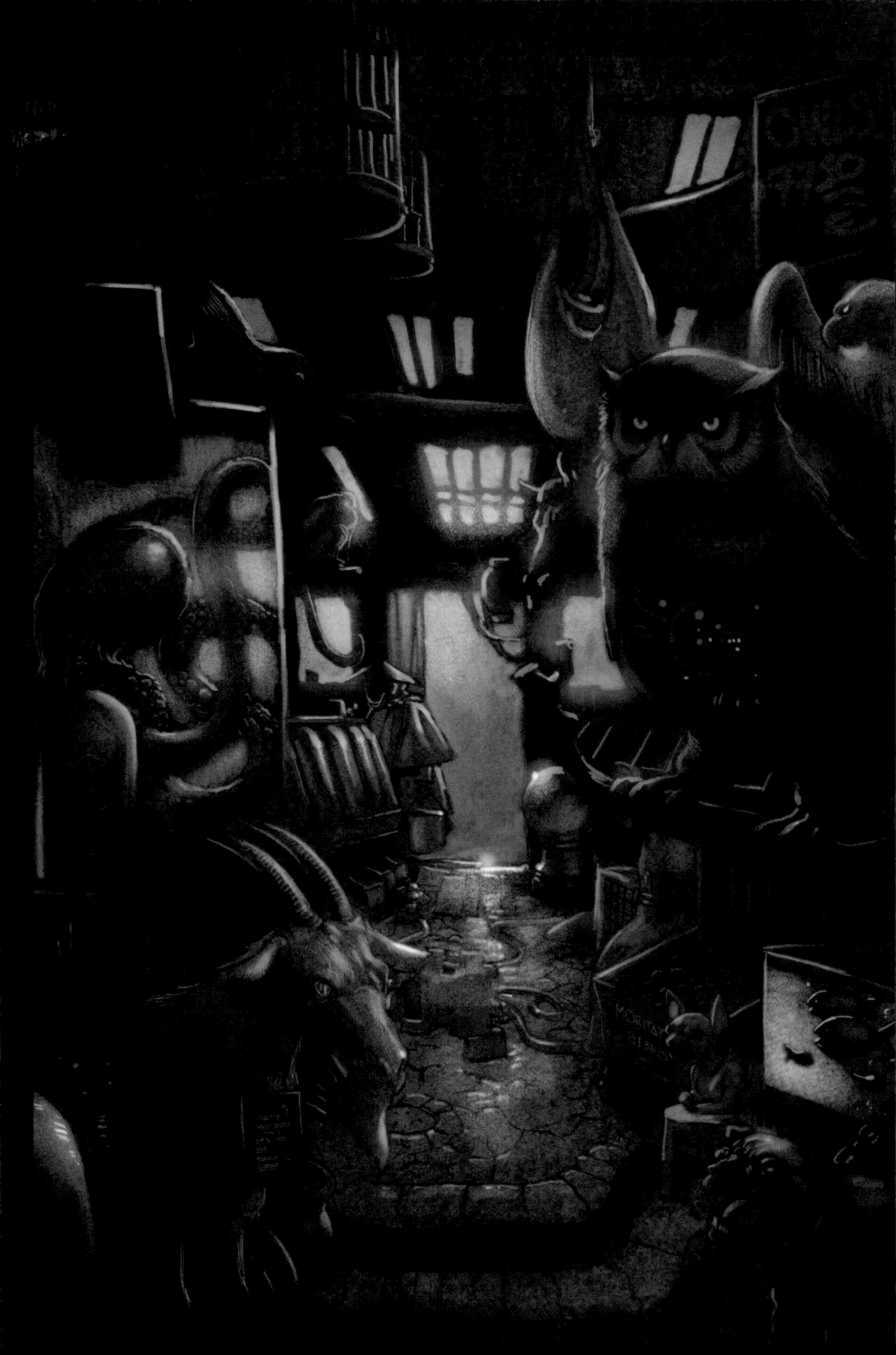

COVER 4B
MORITAT

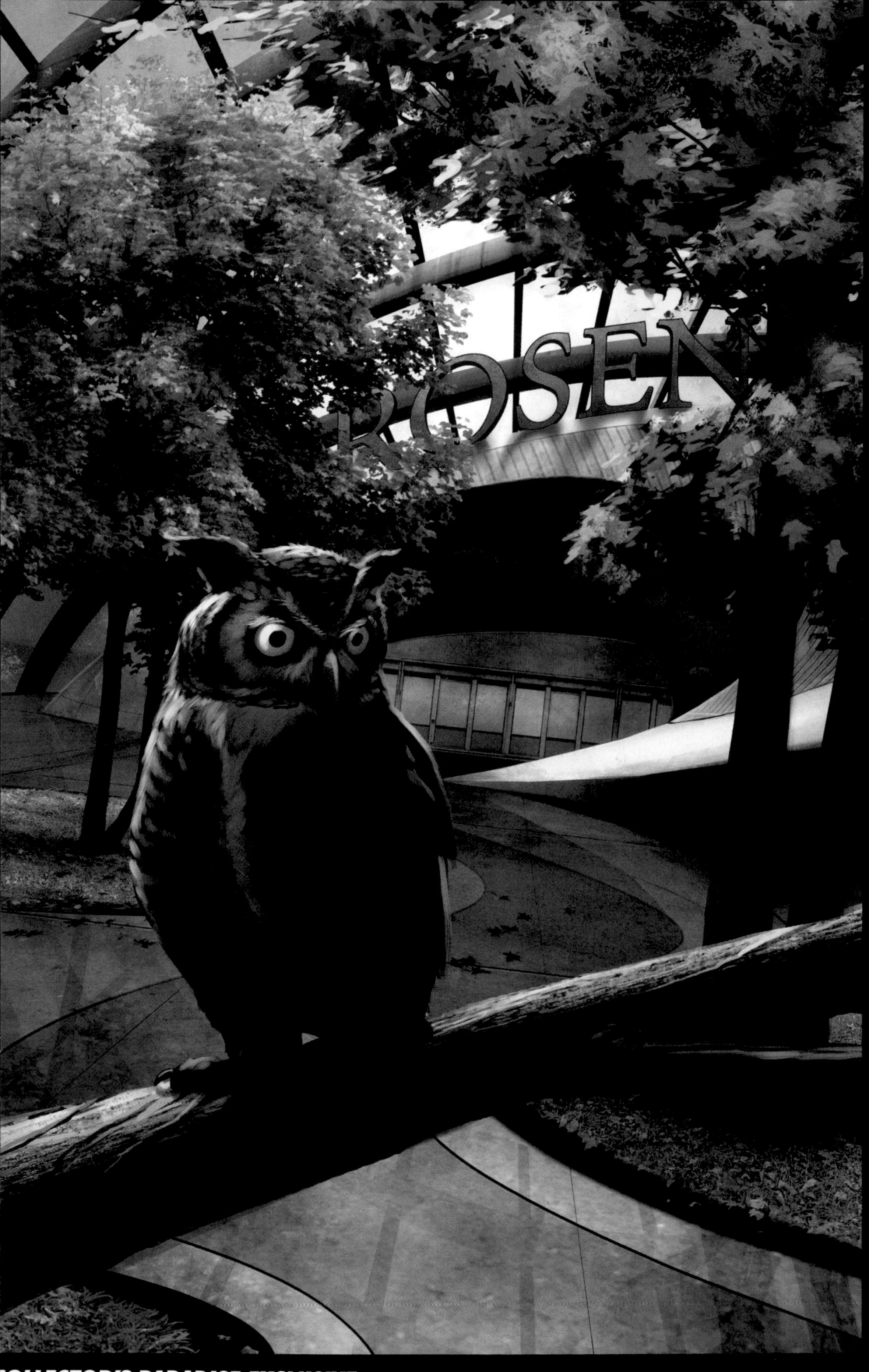
ROSEN

COLLECTOR'S PARADISE EXCLUSIVE
SCOTT KEATING

PHILIP K. DICK

Over his writing career, which spanned three decades, Philip K. Dick wrote and published 36 Science Fiction novels and 120 short stories. The themes that intrigued him in his writing still resonate with readers today, asking difficult philosophical questions such as "What makes us human?" and "What is reality?" Toward the end of his life, he explored deeply personal metaphysical questions about the essence of God.

DO **ANDROI**

OF **ELECTR**

Dick's greatest desire was to be recognized as a literary writer, not as a science fiction "hack." Unfortunately, this was not realized during his lifetime. Of twelve realist novels written by Dick, only one—*Confessions of A Crap Artist*—was published before his death.

Some of his most critically acclaimed and award-winning sci-fi titles include: *The Man in the High Castle* (1963 Hugo Award), *A Scanner Darkly* (Grand Prix du Festival at Metz, France 1979), *Ubik* (Time Magazine selection of 100 best English-language novels 1923 - 2006), *Flow My Tears, the Policeman Said* (John W. Campbell Award), *The Three Stigmata of Palmer Eldritch*, and *VALIS*. Dick's work is published in 27 countries and has been translated into 25 languages.

Dick was inducted into the SF Hall of Fame in 2005, and between 2007 and 2009 the Library of America published thirteen of his sci-fi novels, placing Philip K. Dick's name beside William Faulkner and Ernest Hemingway.

ine of Dick's novels and short stories have been adapted to film, most notably: *Blade Runner* (1982, based on the novel *Do Androids Dream of Electric Sheep?*), *Total Recall* (1990, based on the short story *We Can Remember it For You Wholesale*), *Minority Report* (2002), and *A Scanner Darkly* (2006).

Dick struggled his entire life with the loss of his twin sister shortly after birth, as well as with depression (for which he was prescribed amphetamines) and numerous other phobias. He later became addicted to amphetamines and used them to fuel his drive to write quickly and sell his work to support his family. He incorporated much of his personal struggles, including depression and drug addiction, into his writing. Seeking female companionship was a constant throughout his adult life; he married five times and had three children.

On March 2, 1982, Philip K. Dick died of heart failure following a stroke in Santa Ana, California.

TONY PARKER has lent his art beyond the worl(of Philip K. Dick. In addition to the BOOM! Studios titles *Warhamme 40,000: Fire and Honour*, *Warhammer 40,000: Defenders of Ultramar* and the exclusive Warhammer Online graphic novel *Warhamme Online: Prelude to War*, Parker has worked on over 125 pen and pape RPG books (including several painted covers). Parker has also offere(his artistic hand to Upper Deck for their Marvel Masterpiece cards *Conan*, and *The Ultimate Spider-man 100 Project* and *The Hulk 10(Project* for the HERO Initiative.

DO ANDROI

OF ELECTR

BLOND is one of the most prolific and talented colorists i the comic book industry today. In addition to *Do Androids Dream o Electric Sheep?*, he has colored Top Cow's *Hunter-Killer*, *Witchblade*, *Th Darkness*, Marvel and IDW's *New Avengers/Transformers*, *Marvel'. Ultimate Fantastic Four*, and DC's *Superman*, *Superman: World of Nev Krypton*, *Superman: Last Stand of New Krypton*, *Superman: War of th Supermen*, and *Adventure Comics*.

RICHARD STARKINGS is the creator of Image Comics' hit series *Elephantmen* and the Eisner Award-winning series *Hip Flask*. Although he lettered *Batman: The Killing Joke* with a pen, Starkings is perhaps best known for his work with the Comicraft Design and Lettering Studio, which he co-founded in 1992.

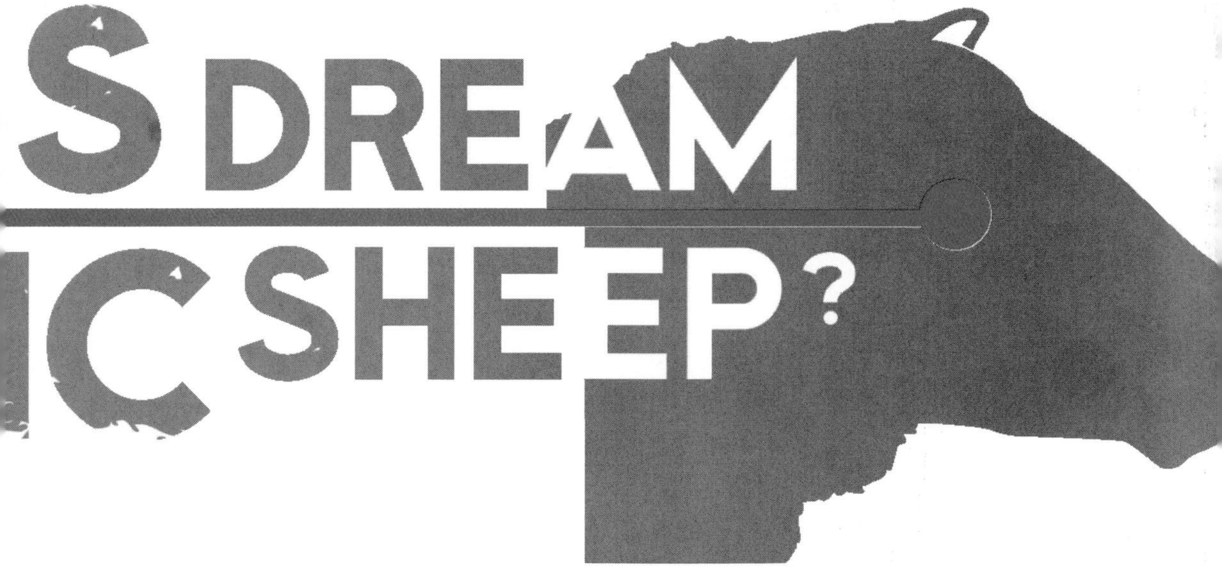
S DREAM
IC SHEEP?

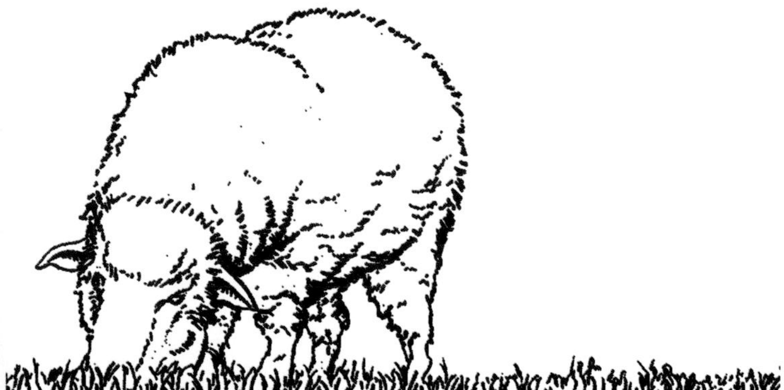

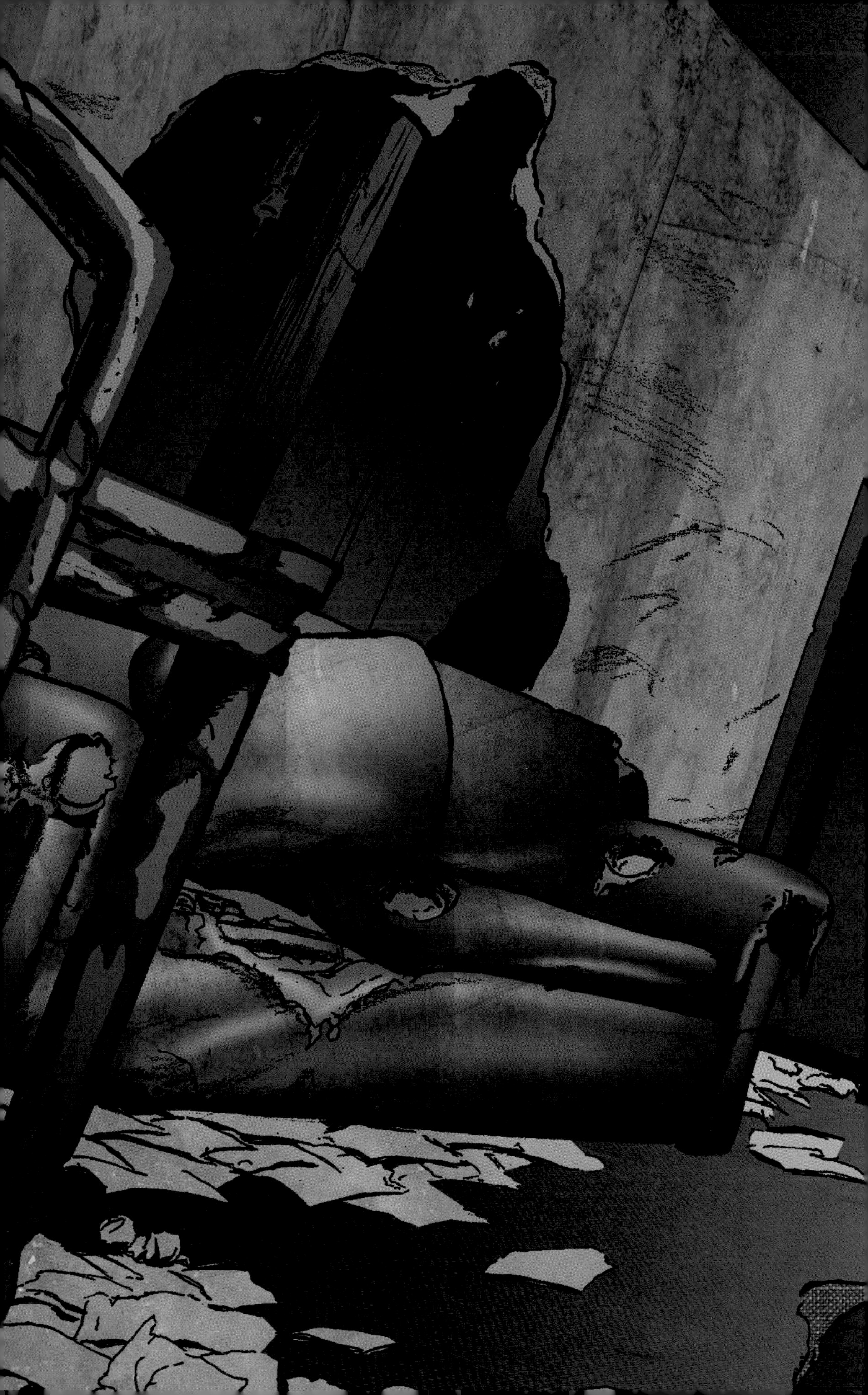

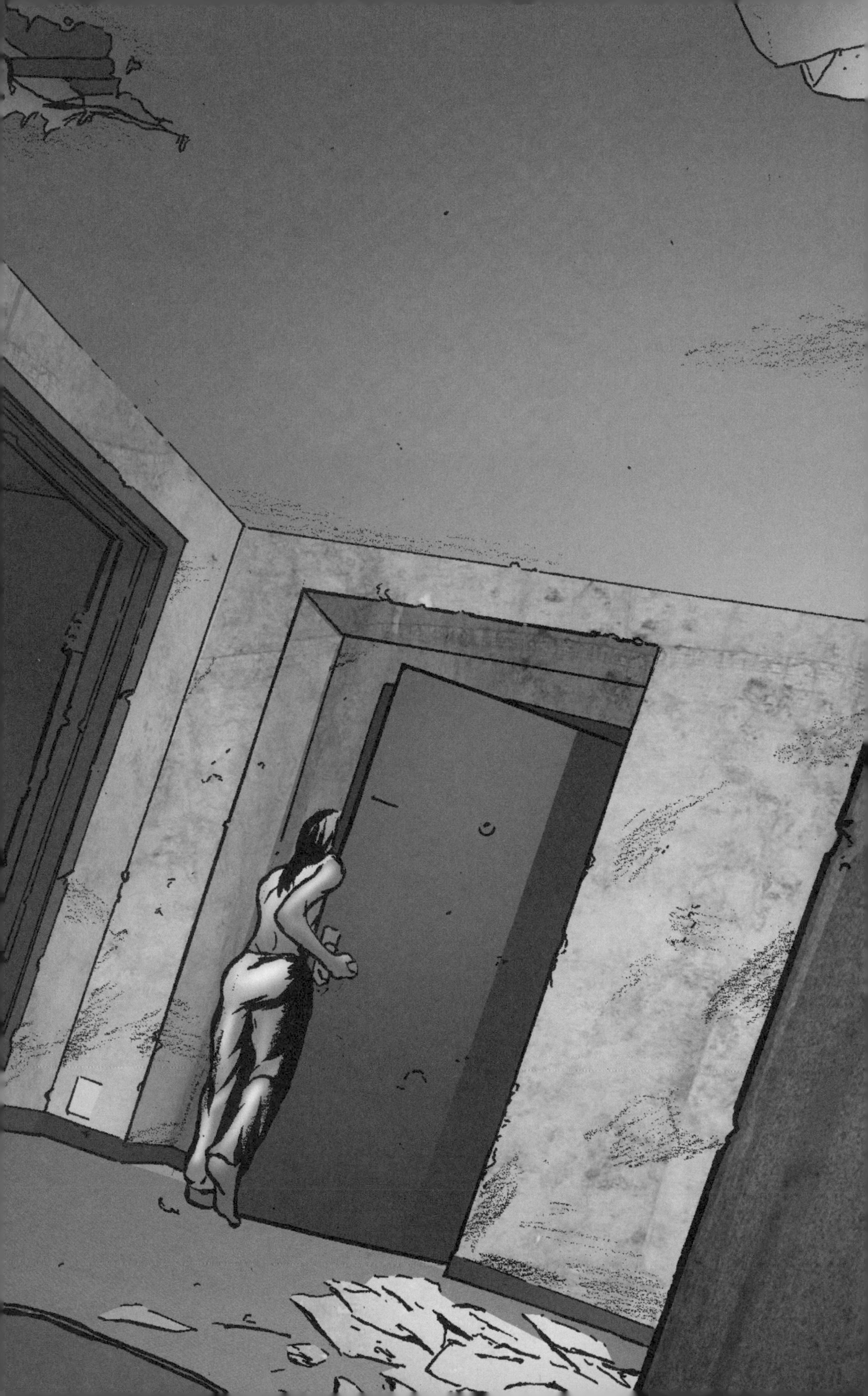